BLACK
HANDS
OF
BEIJING

BLACK HANDS OF BEIJING

Lives of Defiance in China's Democracy Movement

GEORGE BLACK
ROBIN MUNRO

A ROBERT L. BERNSTEIN BOOK

John Wiley & Sons, Inc.
New York • Chichester • Brisbane • Toronto • Singapore

In recognition of the importance of preserving what
has been written, it is a policy of John Wiley & Sons,
Inc., to have books of enduring value published in
the United States printed on acid-free paper,
and we exert our best efforts to that end.

951. 05
B
C. 1

Library of Congress Cataloging-in-Publication Data

Black, George
    Black hands of Beijing : lives of defiance in China's democracy
movement / George Black, Robin Munro.
        p.   cm.
    Includes index.
    ISBN 0-471-57977-7
    1. China—Politics and government—1976– 2. Democracy—China.
3. China—History—Tiananmen Square Incident, 1989. 4. Political
prisoners—China. I. Munro, Robin. II. Title.
DS779.26.B57   1993
951.05—dc20   92-45120

Printed in the United States of America
10 9 8 7 6 5 4 3 2 1

PREFACE

Of all the hundreds of conversations that went into the making of this book, one exchange in particular sticks in our minds. It took place in a taxi in Manhattan at the end of a long interview with an exiled Chinese student leader. In the course of our research in Hong Kong, we had recently come across some previously unknown documents that shed new light on the events in Tiananmen Square in the spring of 1989. With each new discovery, we told him, our understanding of the events not only deepened but also, at times, was radically challenged. When could one ever be sure of having the whole story? Never, he answered without a second's hesitation. There is no such thing as the whole story. There is only the official history or myth that passes into public consciousness, and then the morass of loose ends, broken threads, and conflicting accounts, all subject to endless reinterpretation. There are always more documents to find. Memory is selective; time and ego distort its powers. His comments reminded us of a remark once made by the dean of American China scholars, John King Fairbank: "After all, history is in our minds. It is what we think happened."

One should be cautious therefore when one speaks of writing "revisionist" history, for it suggests a desire to erect a new truth in place of the official versions that already exist. That is hubris. What we have tried to do here is to enlarge and expand upon what is known in the West about the Chinese democracy movement, and we are aware that much of our story fundamentally challenges previous accounts. But we do not claim it is the whole story; as the student said, there is no such thing.

Our point of departure was an enigma. There are, as it were, two official histories of the 1989 Tiananmen Square movement, and they have very few points of convergence. The first was constructed by the Chinese Communist Party, and was written largely in the form of trials and jail sentences. In this history, rebellious students are of only marginal importance when compared to the true "black hands," the behind-the-scenes conspirators who threatened one-party rule. The second, for which the machinery of state propaganda cannot be held responsible, is the story of Tiananmen Square as it is generally understood in the West. In this, the students are everything; Tiananmen was their story. The "black hands" are not mentioned in any of the press dispatches from Beijing. And in the slew of books that were published in the wake of the June 4 massacre, the reader will search in vain for their names. Only in the rare footnote may one find a passing reference to Chen Ziming, Wang Juntao, and Han Dongfang—the three central figures in our story.

To the Communist Party, figures like these incarnated the threat posed by Tiananmen. In one sense, at least, the Party was correct: The events of 1989 were only an episode, albeit a bloody and tragic one, in an epic story that stretches back to the twilight of the Maoist era. The reporters who converged on Beijing in the spring of 1989 brought many qualities to their work; but a sense of history is not usually thought of as one of their strong points. Without it, the larger meaning of Tiananmen is impossible to grasp, and the importance of figures like Chen Ziming, Wang Juntao, and Han Dongfang remains obscure. For the Communist Party, on the other hand, their importance was very clear. Chen and Wang were the threatening survivors of a movement that had challenged the Party since 1976. Han, as leader of China's first independent labor union since Liberation, embodied the threat of what Tiananmen might have led to if left unchecked.

The Chinese democracy movement has been poorly served in print. There are some signal exceptions, of course. Andrew Nathan's *Chinese Democracy* brilliantly illuminates the years between 1978 and 1980. Orville Schell's reports on the 1980s provide many keys to understanding the process of reform under Deng Xiaoping. Merle Goldman's work helps us understand the singular problems of the Chinese intelligentsia. Geremie Barmé's stirring collections have given voice to many of China's leading dissident intellectuals. The autobiographical accounts of Nien Cheng, Liang Heng, and others have won wide audiences, teaching us that not the least of the attributes of China's democrats is their chronic obstinacy—a quality shared by the central figures in this book.

Naturally we hope that our work will add to the existing body of scholarship on China. But scholarship is not our primary aim. With the exception of the evanescent heroes of the 1989 student movement, the Chinese democracy movement has been faceless for too long. Our goal has been to bring the drama of modern China alive to the broadest possible audience, and as our vehicle we have chosen the lives of three people. Chen Ziming, Wang Juntao, and Han Dongfang are, in a phrase that has been cheapened through overuse, inspiring figures, and their story belongs to the world.

GEORGE BLACK
ROBIN MUNRO

New York/Hong Kong
January 1993

Contents

1

Growing Up in the Big Storm

By February it seemed that the Beijing winter would never end. The vast city hunkered down against the cold. The bleak gray of its public buildings and apartment blocks was at its most oppressive. The air was filled with gritty dust, borne on the bone-chilling winds that sweep across the North China plain.

Inside the spartan courtroom, the spectators removed their heavy overcoats and cheap fur hats and stamped their feet to restore circulation. They were few in number. No public notice of the trial had been posted; the public was not invited until that morning. Those in attendance were Justice Ministry officials, members of the security services, or scribes from the official media. The only exceptions were the prisoner's mother and younger sister. Even his wife had been barred. The room fell silent as the clerk stood to read the charges. "The People's Republic of China versus Chen Ziming, male, thirty-nine, born in Haiyang County, Zhejiang Province, former head of the Beijing Social and Economic Sciences Research Institute. The prisoner stands charged with counterrevolutionary propaganda and incitement, and with conspiracy to overthrow the government and the People's Democratic Dictatorship."

The two women at first did not recognize the man who had risen to receive the charges. Standing only five foot six, Chen Ziming had never cut an imposing figure, and his round shoulders and thick spectacles only served to heighten the impression of the unworldly scholar. Nevertheless, from childhood he had always been barrel-chested and physically powerful. Now, standing before the court, he looked frighteningly pale, he had lost some of his hair, and his clothes hung loosely on him. Fifteen months in two of China's top-security prisons had taken their toll on his health. So had the four-day hunger strike he had undertaken in a vain effort to have the trial postponed so that his lawyers would have time to prepare an effective defense.

How will they judge me? Chen wondered. Had the rule of law really taken root in Deng Xiaoping's China? Or would he be judged by the standards that had prevailed during the Cultural Revolution, when the law was no more than the whim of the Party clique that held power? Fifteen years had passed since the death of Mao and under the leadership of Deng, China had charted a new path toward becoming a modern society.

The question was almost academic, Chen realized. Chinese courts did not make a habit of handing down not-guilty verdicts, especially in sensitive political cases. To find a prisoner innocent meant an unacceptable loss of face for the Party, and Chen was well aware that he was no ordinary prisoner. The long months of interrogation he was subjected to made it clear that the Party regarded him as a "black hand," a conspirator, one of the behind-the-scenes orchestrators of the tumultuous protests in Tiananmen Square in the spring of 1989.

"Black," in the lexicon of the Chinese Communist Party, means the antithesis of "Red." The term originated in Mao Zedong's radical land-reform program, which targeted the Black Five Elements: landlords, rich peasants, reactionaries, rightists, and the catchall category of "bad elements." During the Cultural Revolution the list was expanded, notably to include "capitalist roaders." In recent years, usage has grown wider still: "Black elements" attend "black meetings" in which they concoct "black materials." If they rise high enough to manipulate others, they become "black hands."

Chen found the charges against him incomprehensible. He had been labeled a bad element many times over the past twenty years, often enough to know that the Communist Party's conservative old guard certainly had no affection for him. He was also an acute enough student of the Party's inner workings to know that scapegoats would have to be found for the events in Tiananmen Square. Master conspirators would need to be found, those whose plots had presented Communist rule with its greatest challenge since Liberation in 1949. But he, Chen Ziming, a "black hand"? He lamented the tragic folly of the students in Tiananmen Square almost as much as he admired their courage and idealism. The notion that he had controlled their actions seemed preposterous to him; even now, a year and a half later, he was not sure he fully understood their motives. In his own student days, he had wished for nothing more than to be a loyal servant of the Party.

He was born into the intelligentsia.[1] Four relatives in his grand-father's generation had headed famous academic institutions, including China's most distinguished center of higher learning, Beijing University, known more familiarly as Beida. Chen's father, who had joined the Communist underground as a student in the 1940s, was an engineer at a government design institute; his mother had a managerial job in a Beijing film production studio; both parents were middle-ranking party officials, the kind of solid cadres who were the bone and sinew of the Party.

Chen's parents named him "Ziming"—bright seed, or bright son. At fourteen, as a freshman at Beijing's renowned Number 8 Middle School, Chen expected to embark on a glittering academic career. Instead, his world turned upside down.

That year, 1966, Mao Zedong became convinced that his revolution was in grave danger. The Great Helmsman saw a new ruling class emerging in the Communist Party, bureaucrats who might pervert China's march to socialism. To forestall a repeat of what he saw happening in the Soviet Union—"revisionism," the slow restoration of capitalism—Mao launched his Great Proletarian Cultural Revolution. It brought sweeping purges of the Party hierarchy and ushered in an era of what he called "extensive democracy," the mobilization of the masses to confront the bureaucracy. But extensive democracy quickly took on all the appearances of fascism. The agents of change chosen by Mao to root out "feudal-capitalist values" were fanatical, inexperienced teenagers—the Red Guards.

China's schools became the main vehicle for the inculcation of "proletarian" values. Beijing's middle schools in particular were the seedbed of the Red Guards. The higher a school's academic reputation, the more suspect the values of its teachers and the more fearsome its Red Guards. Number 8 Middle School became a Red Guard stronghold.

The first Red Guard units appeared in May of 1966. By August of that year, Mao, at the zenith of his power, stood on the rostrum of the ancient gate of Tiananmen—the Gate of Heavenly Peace—and received the adulation of a million young zealots.

The Party dispatched Red Guard "workteams" to the city's schools, closing them down altogether for a while that summer. They derided the intelligentsia as the lowest of the low, the "stinking ninth category." The workteams scrutinized the lessons and publications of the teaching staff to find "bad thoughts"; they replaced regular classes with open meetings to discuss the latest pronouncements from Party headquarters; they organized "criticism meetings" to pillory teachers and administrators suspected of harboring "bourgeois sentiments"; they demanded the abolition of the examination system as a "feudal" remnant; they threw out the school curriculum and announced that the sole purpose of education was to study Mao's writings on "class struggle."

For Chen, a typical school day now consisted of four sessions: the study of Mao's thoughts and central party directives; criticism and struggle meetings and the study of *dazibao*—"big-character" wall posters;[2] the learning of proletarian industrial skills and military training; and, finally, the study of texts on class struggle. For teachers searching for appropriate classroom materials, the only safe option was the writings of Mao. Soon eighty million copies of his *Selected Works* were in circulation, along with fifty-seven million copies of his *Poems* and thirty-five million of his *Quotations*.

Despite the veneration accorded to his every word, Mao recognized by the early months of 1968 that China's schools, like the country as a whole, were fast spinning off the rails. The classroom criticism meetings had rapidly degenerated into turbulent, faction-ridden shouting matches. The shouting matches turned into fist-fights, and before long the fists gave way to cudgels, knives, and guns. The children of cadres battled with the children of intellectuals, even if some students, like Chen Ziming, did not know with any certainty into which of these rigid and arbitrary categories their parents were to be slotted.

To quell the chaos, Mao ordered detachments of the People's Liberation Army (PLA) into the schools to disarm and demobilize the warring factions of Red Guards. But the army did not restore the old classes and curriculum; instead, the middle schools were divided along PLA lines into squads, platoons, and companies for the further study of Chairman Mao's thoughts. These were supplemented by limited readings from the works of Marx, Engels, Lenin, and Lin Biao, the brilliant, moody, taciturn military commander who was Mao's own chosen successor. Military training remained part of the school day, but combat skills were no longer taught; there had been enough bloodshed.[3] Instead, Chen and his fellow students learned the virtues of military discipline. Beijing in these days was full of chanting children marching in close formation, flanked by PLA soldiers, on their way to clean streets and railroad stations, or to help nearby communes bring in the harvest.

When the army restored control, Mao placed the administration of the schools in the hands of "proletarian propaganda teams" of factory workers, instructing them to "cleanse the class ranks" of the schools. A more useful outlet had to be found for the destructive energies of the rebellious young.

It was time, as one headline in the official *People's Daily* put it, to "Grow Up in the Big Storm" that was sweeping China. "Go where your country needs you most," the paper exhorted. To Mao, a child of the harsh Chinese countryside who never lost his mistrust of city ways, this could mean only one thing.

Over the next nine years, approximately sixteen million people became "sent-down youth," packed off to learn revolution the hard way from an often unwelcoming peasantry. The Red Guards were the first to be sent down; millions of other students—or "educated youth"—followed, as did disgraced Party officials. This was meant to be a cleansing experience, but it had effects Mao had not intended. The sent-down youth discovered that twenty years after Liberation, four out of five Chinese still lived in grinding poverty, subject to the arbitrary tyranny of local Party cadres. And later, when they returned home, they found an educational system in chaos and an absence of suitable employment—in short, a society that had little or no idea of what to do with them. When the Cultural Revolution finally ended, they took to calling themselves China's "Lost Generation."

Although Chen Ziming was one of the youngest of his group, the Party was impressed by his sharp intellect and his purposeful manner, and in 1968, at the age of sixteen, he was appointed leader of the brigade of educated youth from Number 8 Middle School. At Beijing station, he boarded a northbound train that was packed with eight hundred young people from the western part of the city, where his family lived. The neighborhoods to the west of Tiananmen Square were then and still are home to a number of the city's elite schools, such as Number 8. They also contain many of the organs of the Communist Party Central Committee, the State Council, and government ministries, as well as Zhongnanhai, the walled Party leadership compound that was originally built by the emperors as a pleasure park. The crowd on Chen's train was no ordinary cross section of young Beijing; it contained more than its share of the sons and daughters of high Party officials.

The train pulled away slowly from the drab sprawl of the Beijing suburbs and climbed through the mountains to the northwest of the city, leaving behind the Great Wall that Qin Shi Huang Di, first emperor of the Qin dynasty, built to keep out the barbarian hordes. Beyond the Wall, the mountains fell away sharply to where "the grasslands gleam golden for a thousand *li*"[4]—the vast open spaces of Inner Mongolia.

The trip promised many exotic experiences. The Inner Mongolia Autonomous Region was the showcase of the Communist Party's "minority nationalities" policy. Whereas the persecuted Buddhists of Tibet and the fractious Muslims of Xinjiang were screened off from prying eyes, official propaganda depicted Inner Mongolia's nomadic horsemen and herders as a happy warrior breed given to colorful ethnic costumes and festive displays of local sports.

Chen and his classmates in the Abag Banner[5] Production Brigade traveled far beyond the regional capital of Hohhot. Where the railroad ended, they struck out by road across the featureless northern expanses of semidesert. Their final destination was the

E'erdenggaobi Commune, some fifty miles south of the border with the Soviet-allied Mongolian People's Republic.

As soon as Chen arrived, he heard stories that contradicted the Party's carefully constructed ethnic idyll. He saw suffering written harshly in the faces of the Mongol herders, whose lives he was now to share. Two years of the Cultural Revolution had lacerated the region. Successive Chinese governments—warlord, Nationalist, and Communist—had colonized Inner Mongolia with Han Chinese, to the point where the Mongols were outnumbered by more than five to one. The Communists had at least appointed an ethnic Mongol, Ulanfu, to lead the local Party. But the radicals of the Cultural Revolution turned on him.

In 1966, the Red Guards accused Ulanfu of leading an "anti-Party treasonous clique," promoting "national splittism," and "inciting discord between the Han and Mongol peoples." Pitched battles ensued in Hohhot between rival Red Guard factions, and in February 1967 the PLA was sent in to quell the disorder. An unpublicized slaughter began. Then, the following summer, the radicals' attacks culminated in the charge that Ulanfu was plotting a "counterrevolutionary coup" that would unite the two Mongolias into an independent kingdom under his leadership. Tales of these two episodes were whispered to Chen Ziming and his fellow students when they arrived. The third and ugliest of the purges began shortly thereafter. This time, Lin Biao's troops and Red Guard thugs dragged tens of thousands of Mongolians from their homes, in the name of uprooting an underground group of insurrectionary Mongol nationalists—the New Inner Mongolian People's Revolutionary Party (NIMPRP).

In all, in the course of the three "major unjust and mishandled cases,"[6] 790,000 Mongolians were wrongfully persecuted; of these, 120,000 were left crippled and 22,900 died. Many put the number of dead higher, perhaps as many as 50,000. "In Inner Mongolia," wrote one scholar, "it was said that the Cultural Revolution claimed more lives among the Mongols than the massacres of the famed 'Slayer of the Mongols'—a notorious Han general of the Ming dynasty."[7] In 1981, the Party would admit that the case of the NIMPRP was a pure fabrication, and that "Left errors" had been committed.

For Chen Ziming the impact of the Mongol purges was visceral. The Red Guard battles at Number 8 Middle School could perhaps be written off as the excesses of youth. But the persecution of the Mongols taught him the indelible lesson that a ruling Party not accountable to the people can inflict terrible abuse.

Two or three hundred of the educated youth from western Beijing were assigned to one of several production brigades, each covering hundreds of square miles of prairie. Like the others, Chen made his home for the next six years in a herder's yurt, a single-room, circular hut of animal-hair felt or plastic sheeting stretched over a frame of thin wooden poles. The domed roof kept snow and rain from accumulating; a central stove, fueled by dried sheep dung, helped ward off the harsh winds. A narrow opening in the top of the yurt provided light and ventilation and let out the smoke from the stove. More prosperous families sometimes decorated the floor with a richly ornamented carpet. For the shrinking number of Mongols who were still nomadic, the whole affair was designed to be collapsible so that it could be transported easily to new grazing lands.

The physical labor in Inner Mongolia was as demanding as the harsh climate of winter, when frozen snow often covered the sand dunes. Plenty of sent-down youth threw themselves into splashy public works projects in order to catch the eye of Party higher-ups and earn a transfer back to the city. One of the most perplexing dilemmas needing attention was how to mitigate the effects of the drought that ravaged Inner Mongolia each year during the dry season. The sent-down youth came up with schemes to capture water during the winter rains, but the wells stayed dry and the irrigation channels were always empty. Chen distinguished himself by devising an ingenious solution to the problem: a man-made pond, hidden among the hills, that collected the rainwater runoff from the surrounding slopes. He organized a work gang to hack rocks out of the hillsides with pickaxes, using oxen to drag the rocks to the construction site. No machinery was used because none was available. The local people were delighted with the solution and with the young problem solver who had come up with it.

In 1969, a year after Chen was sent to Inner Mongolia, he became one of Chairman Mao's barefoot doctors, carrying out inoculation campaigns, learning to treat the herders' illnesses with a mix of Western, Chinese, and traditional Mongolian medicine, and steadily winning the Mongols' trust. Mongolian customs fascinated him, and he developed a passion for the local style of wrestling. Every year in late summer, each community organized its *Nadamu,* a festival of horseback riding, archery, and wrestling—the "Three Skills of Man." Chen competed with an almost childlike enthusiasm and carried off second prize in a regional wrestling contest.

In the herders' value system, nothing ranked higher than a fine steed. It was horses that knit the widely dispersed communities together, horses that allowed the brigade members to celebrate the wild freedom of the open spaces, and horses that were the staple of conversation when groups gathered to talk in their yurts in the evenings. In his novel *Heartstrings,* the writer Li Datong, who was also sent down to Abag Banner at this time, describes how an invitation sometimes came to visit a brigade on a neighboring commune. Selecting the swiftest horses, a large group would race across the grasslands for a two- or three-day stay.

The hospitality might have lacked something in refinement, but it was always generous. There were, as in the Chinese expression, "great bowls of wine to drink and great chunks of meat to eat." Hungry after their long ride, the students would sit down to devour whole roast lambs and heaping plates of noodles and fried millet, washing them down with steaming cups of milky Mongolian tea. Late into the night, they would down one glass after another of the potent local wine, which was distilled from grain or fermented mare's milk.

The conversation at these gatherings covered the spectrum from the merits of horses to the latest rumors of political intrigue in Beijing—what the Chinese call "small path" news. Through their families' Party connections, the brigades quickly got wind of each new round of power struggles behind the walls of Zhongnanhai, or of the alleged sexual scandals involving Mao's third wife, the former Shanghai movie starlet Jiang Qing. But Chen Ziming had little time for gossip; instead, when the talk turned to politics, he preferred to discuss the deeper injustices and inefficiencies of the system. There was no small risk involved in this, since many of the listeners were the children of high Party cadres.

Chen Ziming and his closest friend, Xu Yun, often hosted late-night get-togethers, and although Chen was not a naturally gregarious person, he made an affable and indulgent host. Some of the all-night talkers in Chen's yurt lost themselves in utopian imaginings of a sunlit Communist future; others were still starry-eyed at the memory of the mass reviews of the Red Guards in 1966. During this time Chen became absorbed in political theory and immersed himself in the Marxist classics. By lamplight, he worked his way through the Chinese translation of *Das Kapital* and the major works of Lenin and Engels, rereading each volume several times during his years in Mongolia. He was moved, he wrote later, by Marx's acute critical intelligence and by the "high-minded attitude" of the founding fathers of modern Marxism. Like the young Mao, Chen also studied the classics of Western philosophy, such as Montesquieu's *Spirit of the Laws,* the masterpiece of the eighteenth-century French Enlightenment. But political philosophy was not his only passion: With books scarce and his schooling disrupted, Chen delved into whatever textbooks he could find on subjects that ranged from industrial engineering and mathematics to economics and animal husbandry.

The Party looked with favor on the bright, serious-minded young man and did not appear to detect any signs of political unorthodoxy in him. In 1970, Chen was appointed chairman of the Abag Banner Brigade's Revolutionary Committee, one of the political organs set up during the Cultural Revolution to bypass the old bureaucracy and take direct action at the grass-roots level. The following year, he was accorded the greatest honor to which a nineteen-year-old could aspire: membership in the Communist Youth League, the vital first step toward full Party membership.

From the small path gossip, the educated youth learned of a heated debate that was under way within the Party over the future of higher education. Since the start of the Cultural Revolution in 1966, the radicals had been in control. They had suspended China's competitive university entrance system; political "redness" was touted as superior to technical skills and knowledge. Formerly elite campuses were now showplaces for a new generation of "worker-peasant-soldier students" selected by class background and the "recommendation of the masses" rather than by academic credentials. Beida itself, the most prestigious of the schools, was taken over by a "People's Liberation Army Mao Zedong Thought Propaganda Team."

The less radical Party leaders knew that eliminating the exam system had flooded the universities with semiliterate zealots who possessed none of the technical skills that China required. In April 1973, the moderates won a small victory when the State Council decreed that "while considerations of the candidate's political qualities should come first, there should also be a small examination to ascertain the candidate's educational level."

As someone from a cadre background like Chen Ziming's well knew, what really counted for college admission was *guanxi*—personal connections. On the strength of their *guanxi,* many members of the Inner Mongolian brigades waltzed into university after 1973. Chen, with fewer connections in high places, needed to rely on his own talents; to prepare for college admission, he flung himself into the high school curriculum that the Cultural Revolution had forced him to miss. Many of the brigade members began teaching themselves. They gave each other snap tests: to memorize and recite a passage, for example, from the classic Chinese novel *Dream of the Red Chamber.* The penalty for any mistake was to down a glass of mare's-milk wine. Bleary-eyed from their late-night studies, the prospective college entrants became clumsy and absentminded over their daytime tasks in the fields. They took to calling themselves the Scatterbrain Association.

Those who flunked the entrance exam became known as the Failures Club. But Chen Ziming sailed through it, and he was admitted to the Beijing Chemical Industry College. His friend Xu Yun stayed in Inner Mongolia to study at a local teachers college. But they promised to keep in touch by letter.

The Beijing to which Chen Ziming returned to attend college in the autumn of 1974 was not the city he had left behind in 1968.[8] There were rows of new concrete apartment buildings and a relatively efficient public transportation system. But all the new facilities were drab and strictly utilitarian. The city was bleak and gray. A harsh puritan ethic held sway: It was socially unacceptable to use cosmetics, have your hair curled, listen to love songs. Unmarried women who became pregnant could be banished to the countryside, or even sent to a labor camp. Physical beauty was viewed as a suspect "bourgeois" value. The lovely Beihai lake, a favorite picnic spot, had been closed for several years without explanation. The traditional Dragon Boat and Lantern festivals, two of China's most cherished holidays, had been suspended. Ancient temples had been converted into makeshift factories.

The sordid slums had been bulldozed, but so too had Beijing's ancient city walls, torn apart stone by stone to build flimsy air-raid shelters, all in the name of the campaign to destroy the "Four Olds"—old ideas, old customs, old culture, old habits. Contact with foreigners was frowned upon. Foreign art was considered degenerate; only Jiang Qing's "eight revolutionary classics" were officially approved.[9] In the name of cleansing China of ancient superstitions and bourgeois influences, the Red Guards had desecrated Buddhist temples, vandalized historic monuments, burned precious libraries of Western books, and seized priceless private collections of antique porcelain and classic pen-and-ink drawings, many of which quietly found their way into the homes of top Party leaders in Zhongnanhai.

During Chen's time in the grasslands of Inner Mongolia, the incessant mass campaigns of the Cultural Revolution had brought China to its knees. The economy was at a standstill; there had been no general wage increase for more than a decade. Every last sign of private enterprise—the tea seller, the newspaper vendor—had been eliminated as the "spontaneous shoots of capitalism." The Cultural Revolution had spoken of "liberating the masses," but years of unbridled "class struggle" had produced widespread alienation. At the Chemical Industry College, Chen found an atmosphere of intimidation and a general terror of expressing new or dangerous ideas.

He wrote regularly to his friend Xu Yun in Inner Mongolia. They reminisced about their happy days with the Abag Banner brigade and shared their fears about the direction in which they saw China heading. And, clearly, the future of the country was in serious question. Chairman Mao—the Great Helmsman, the Red Sun, the Great Saving Star—was increasingly infirm. He was ravaged by Parkinson's disease, able to communicate his wishes only in grunts and mutterings to the nurse who never left his side. Those whom he had chosen to lead his Great Proletarian Cultural Revolution interpreted his utterances as they wished and manipulated the old man without shame. They began their careers as Mao's acolytes; they ended up as his puppet-masters. Before long they would be universally known as the Gang of Four.

All of them originally rose to prominence in Shanghai, less than forty miles from Chen Ziming's birthplace in the coastal province of Zhejiang.[10] The senior figure in the Gang was Jiang Qing, Mao's ambitious and vindictive third wife. Zhang Chunqiao was the Gang's least extreme member, a former journalist in his sixties with a gaunt, bespectacled face. Wang Hongwen was a handsome and arrogant textile-mill worker with finely sculpted features and a reputation as a playboy. He first came to Mao's attention as a leader of the ultraradical Shanghai People's Commune in the early days of the Cultural Revolution and rose quickly from the factory floor to take political command of the PLA. The fourth member of the Gang was the man who had, arguably, launched the Cultural Revolution in the first place: Yao Wenyuan, a round-faced propagandist who acted as a hatchet man for the leftist radicals.[11]

A cohort of thugs attended the Gang of Four, men like Kang Sheng, the cruel, Machiavellian head of the secret police; Wang Dongxing, the commander of Army Unit 8341, Mao's personal palace guard; and Xie Fuzhi, the former Red Army commander and public security chief who was now head of the Beijing Revolutionary Committee. When Chen Ziming returned to the capital in 1974, he had only the dimmest notion of what these men, and this woman, had inflicted on their enemies.

Since 1966 Mao and the radicals had scourged the original leadership of the Chinese Revolution, rooting out heretics, traitors, and backsliders. Almost none of the old guard remained unscathed—those who had joined the Party in the 1920s, survived the Long March, accompanied Mao to Yan'an, and stood at his side on the Tiananmen rostrum in 1949 when he proclaimed to the world that China had "stood up."[12] The veteran revolutionaries were persecuted and vilified, their children shunned for the "black blood" that ran in their veins.

Marshal Zhu De, once Mao's most intimate collaborator, was hounded as the "black general"; Chen Yun, the former guerrilla leader who salvaged the Chinese economy from the disasters of Mao's Great Leap Forward,[13] was cast aside and placed under strict police surveillance; Bo Yibo, the guerrilla leader turned finance minister, was packed off to the countryside to learn from the peasants.

And these were the lucky ones; worse treatment was reserved for the diminutive first Vice-Premier Deng Xiaoping, who was beaten, spat upon by Red Guard mobs, and vilified as a "renegade, scab, and traitor" before being dispatched to remote Jiangxi Province to do manual labor in a tractor-repair shop. Deng's close associate Hu Yaobang, a fiery little man who had been head of the Communist Youth League, was paraded through the streets of Beijing in a heavy wooden collar and then sent to a prison camp for "reform through labor."

Beijing Party boss and mayor Peng Zhen was imprisoned and tortured as a member of an "anti-Party clique." Yang Shangkun, formerly a top political commissar in the PLA, was sentenced to thirteen years in jail as a Soviet spy and traitor. The leathery old Peng Dehuai, Mao's toughest general and China's current Vice-Premier, was arrested in 1966 and repeatedly tortured until his battered body finally gave out; he died in 1974. And Liu Shaoqi, the country's white-haired President and previously the number two man in the Party, was savagely beaten by his captors and left naked to die on the floor of a prison hospital in 1969.

In their correspondence, Chen Ziming and Xu Yun shared their thoughts about whatever hope they could find in all of this turmoil. Among the top leadership, they placed their greatest faith in Premier Zhou Enlai. Zhou was the antithesis of all that the Gang of Four stood for. Where the Gang was harsh and austere, Zhou was urbane and cosmopolitan; where the Gang was zealous and uncompromising, he was subtle and sagacious. Despite all the purges of the late 1960s, Zhou used his still considerable influence to shield his friends from greater suffering.

Before Chen Ziming left Inner Mongolia, he had read mixed signals in the outcome of the Party's Tenth Congress, which had convened secretly in Beijing in August 1973. The good news was the restoration of the reformer Deng Xiaoping, who was brought back from his Jiangxi exile and appointed to the Central Committee, with Zhou Enlai's help. Chen admired the energetic Deng enormously. The bad news was the continued meteoric ascent of the Shanghai textile worker Wang Hongwen, who became number three in the Party hierarchy, behind only Mao and Zhou. It was a sensational appointment. Mao was eighty, Zhou seventy-five. Wang Hongwen was just thirty-six.

By the spring of 1975 it was impossible to ignore the power struggle in the Party between the Gang of Four and the Zhou Enlai–Deng Xiaoping faction. Mao appeared to be siding with the Gang, even giving them the green light to attack the Premier, who was dying of cancer. Chen Ziming was dismayed at this new turn of events. "I don't think we can trust [Wang Hongwen]," he wrote in one letter to Xu Yun in May 1975. "I don't believe that he is capable of ruling the nation." In this same letter Chen expressed contempt for a newly published collection of the *Theoretical Writings* of two other members of the Gang of Four. He criticized most sharply Zhang Chunqiao's article, "On Exercising All-Round Dictatorship over the Bourgeoisie," and an essay by Yao Wenyuan, "On the Social Basis of the Lin Biao Anti-Party Clique."[14] Xu wrote back, agreeing with everything his friend had said.

Chen, always busy and sometimes absentminded, read Xu's letter hastily in the yard outside his dormitory at the Chemical Industry College and left it on the table where he was sitting as he ran off to an appointment. When he came back, the letter was no longer on the table. He checked for it in his pocket, but it was not there either. Chen got in touch with Xu Yun right away. Neither man had to be told how serious the situation was: To express sentiments like these, even in private correspondence, was a terrible risk in the China of the Gang of Four. Chen and Xu agreed to shield each other, and for two months, thanks to the surprising inefficiency of the Gang's security system, nothing happened. But then, one day in July 1975, came the expected knock at the door.

The Public Security Bureau (PSB) agent informed Chen that he was under arrest; his correspondence with Xu Yun had been intercepted. For more than two months, Chen languished in a jail cell with no official charges brought against him while the bureau evaluated his case. During long sessions of pretrial questioning he chose to disregard the first rule of the Chinese penal system, expressed in the motto that hangs in every police station and cell: "To those who confess, lenience; to those who resist, severity." Yes, he freely acknowledged to his interrogator, "I would be very worried if someone like Wang Hongwen were in charge of China."

Chen was brought to trial in September. The prosecutor told the court that Chen's offense had been "counterrevolutionary in nature"; the exchange of letters with Xu Yun was nothing less than the machination of a "small counterrevolutionary clique" that aimed to "subvert the dictatorship of the proletariat and the socialist system." The judge passed sentence: three years of "reform through labor, under the supervision of the masses."[15] Chen listened quietly to the verdict and answered calmly: "It will take less than three years for the present situation to change." The madness of the Gang of Four's rule, he meant, could not continue for long.

Chen's sentence was a new twist on a basic penal practice of the Communist Party. The goal of reform through labor was to transform the criminal into a "New Man" through arduous manual toil, backed up with beatings and endless psychological pressure. In principle, this method of punishment was preferable to jail, since the prisoner was not confined to a cell all day. But the "supervision of the masses," an innovation of the Cultural Revolution, could actually make the punishment worse, because the prisoner was at the mercy of the leader of his *danwei,* or work unit. In Chen's case, this meant being placed in the custody of the director of the Chemical Industry College, who, like the head of every other university in Beijing, was a political appointee of the Gang of Four. Ironically, the college's Communist Party committee had actively discussed elevating the promising twenty-three-year-old Chen to full Party membership. But all those plans were now abandoned. Instead, night after night, Chen Ziming was brought before a large crowd of students to be "struggled against"—screamed at, spat upon, insulted, vilified, and humiliated. The next morning, the college director could do what he liked with the exhausted Chen: confine him to a pigpen, chain him to a wall, force him to clean out the toilets.

Chen's reform through labor went on like this for four months. Then, one day in early January 1976, he awoke to the news that Zhou Enlai had died. Like the rest of China, he grieved. Although other Communist leaders were admired or respected, Zhou was the only one to inspire love. Zhou's death was not unexpected, since the Premier had been ill for several years, but the manner in which the Party reacted took everyone by surprise. The radio announcement of Zhou's death was accompanied at first by the customary solemnities: martial music and dirges, a fulsome listing of the Premier's titles, responsibilities, and achievements as a Party leader. But the next day, the programming returned to normal, as if nothing out of the ordinary had occurred. Obviously, for an old Communist of Zhou's stature, the Party was obliged to adhere to the rituals of official mourning. But at the same time, the circles around Mao could scarcely conceal the hypocrisy involved in publicly honoring a man they had bitterly opposed in life. The leftists went through the motions, but their mean-spiritedness was obvious. Many people noticed a calculated petty gesture by Jiang Qing. As she passed Premier Zhou's bier, with the television cameras rolling, she pointedly declined the common courtesy of removing her hat. Mao, himself sick, did not attend the official memorial ceremony for Zhou; indeed, the small path news said that he had not even deigned to send a message to his old comrade on his deathbed.

Although temperatures in Beijing were below freezing on the day of Zhou's funeral, neither the harsh weather nor the animosity of the Gang of Four deterred a spontaneous display of grief by the *laobaixing*—"old hundred names," the ordinary people of Beijing. They flooded into the streets, many wearing black arm bands, many in tears, to pay their last respects. People lined Chang'an Boulevard, the eight-lane thoroughfare that forms the northern perimeter of Tiananmen Square, to catch a glimpse of the black limousine carrying Zhou's body. Yet there was no feeling of closure for the people; the outpouring of sorrow provided no real catharsis.

In the weeks after Zhou's burial, Beijing seemed afflicted by drift and uncertainty. Those who mourned the Premier were bitter about his treatment in death. It was apparent that Mao himself would soon disappear from the scene, but no one was sure about what would follow. The dynamic Deng Xiaoping, only recently restored to high office, was once again sidelined. Yet Mao seemed reluctant to grant full power to Deng's mortal enemies, the Gang of Four. Instead, he perplexed everyone by appointing as Acting Premier a relative nonentity, an amiable fellow from Hunan Province named Hua Guofeng, whose views were known to shift with every twist and turn of Mao's moods. Hua was not known for his intellect; some people took to calling him "Pumpkin Head."

Chen Ziming was pondering these enigmas one Friday morning when he was called in to see the college Party authorities. It was

April 2, 1976. They told him that a number of important decisions had been made regarding his case. He was to be stripped of his membership in the Communist Youth League and expelled from the Chemical Industry College. In a few days, he would be transferred to serve the rest of his sentence at the Yongledian Reform Through Labor Farm on the eastern outskirts of the capital. But in a compassionate gesture, the Public Security Bureau granted Chen a weekend furlough to go home and collect his personal effects. It was a time, after all, when Chinese like to be with their families, for it was the holiday of Qing Ming, China's Festival of the Dead.

2

Festival of the Dead

Tiananmen Square is an immense concrete rectangle of close to a hundred acres. Even the assembly of a million Red Guards in the summer of 1966 did not quite fill the space. It is not beauty that is expressed here in the heart of modern Beijing, but naked power. The ancient Tiananmen Gate itself is lovely, in the ornate style of the Imperial City to the north, to which it leads. But the rest of the square is ugly and functional. Whereas the courtyards, chambers, bridges, avenues, and walls of the Imperial City were laid out according to an intricate geomantic design that symbolizes the organs, limbs, and tissue of the human body, Tiananmen Square was laid out as an arena in which the choreographed masses could parade and applaud. Yet the emperors would have understood the impulse that guided the builders of the square. Standing on the rostrum, looking down on the sea of fervent faces, Mao must have felt like a god.

At the center of the square is the Monument to the People's Heroes, a plain concrete cenotaph with a plinth consisting of three levels covered in bas reliefs of heroic scenes from the Chinese Revolution. The Monument dwarfs the twin columns, carved with imperial dragons, that stand in front of the great gate to the north. At the top of each of these columns is a mythical animal, the *hou*, half-dog and half-lion, perched on stone clouds to watch over the emperor's treatment of his people.

The buildings flanking the square are monumental. On the east side are the twin Museum of Chinese History and Museum of the Chinese Revolution; to the west stands the Great Hall of the People. The museums and the Great Hall are in late classic Stalinist style—all massive pillars and high windows, devoid of ornament except for the red and gold insignia of state and Party above the main doors. As a symbol of Mao's Great Leap Forward, all three buildings, and the square itself, were constructed in the space of ten fevered months during 1958–59.

Despite the vastness of these public monuments, no matter where on the square one stands, the eye is drawn to concrete paving stones and sky. There is no comfort in the space, nothing harmonious or integrated about it; being there feels a little like standing in the desert or on an airport runway. Chen Ziming had walked the flagstones of Tiananmen on innumerable occasions. But he had never seen the square as it appeared to him on the Sunday morning of his weekend furlough.

In the week leading up to that morning, Beijingers had seen signs that the Gang of Four did not have full control of the uneasy political situation that followed Zhou Enlai's death. The Gang's troubles began in Nanjing and were now spreading to the capital. Nanjing is a city with a powerful sense of history that remained more immune than most to the radical extremes of the Cultural Revolution, and Zhou Enlai had always been a popular figure there. The city was the Nationalists' capital in the 1940s, when Zhou went there to negotiate with them to avert a prolonged civil war. But on March 25, the Shanghai paper *Wenhui Bao*—a Party organ—indirectly attacked the beloved Zhou as a "capitalist roader." Nanjing erupted. Students and workers protested for days and painted pro-Zhou slogans on the sides of long-distance trains headed for Beijing. To be sure their messages would be read in the capital, they wrote in tar, not ink, which might wash off.

Events in Beijing, meanwhile, had a momentum of their own. The approaching festival of Qing Ming spurred a renewed burst of affection for the dead Premier. Qing Ming—"Clear and Bright"—is a time for honoring the dead and sweeping the graves of ancestors. Its precise date varies according to the lunar calendar; this year it fell on the first weekend of April.

The Communist Party had never been comfortable with Qing Ming, and since Liberation had turned it into a secular day for paying tribute to revolutionary martyrs. To the Gang of Four the very idea of the festival was an anathema, a hateful emblem of the ancient customs that the Cultural Revolution had attempted to wipe out with its campaign against the "Four Olds." Nevertheless, ordinary Chinese discreetly continued to pay homage to their ancestors each year.

The first sign that the contagion had reached the capital came with a single white wreath, the Chinese color of mourning, laid at the foot of the Monument to the People's Heroes. Soon, more appeared, as did poems and small-character posters—*xiaozibao*—with messages of praise for the dead Premier. Word of the wreaths spread, and people came to see. They, in turn, brought wreaths of their own, and their children carried white, hand-cut paper chrysanthemums. The visitors copied down the poems and the *xiaozibao,* and took them home to show family and friends. Paper flowers began to cover the shrubbery around the Monument, and the stack of wreaths climbed higher and higher on the pedestal.

On April 2, two days before the festival began, every work unit in the capital was informed by a sharply written Party directive that Qing Ming was a superstitious affair, a festival of "ghosts," and that all workers were forbidden to take part in the spontaneous mourning ceremonies in Tiananmen Square. The Party warned that anyone laying wreaths would "fall into the trap of the class enemy" and would be "severely punished." But the directive had little effect. Many *danwei* leaders simply defied the ban and, on April 4, led their workers to the square in the chilly rain in organized fashion, carrying wreaths and factory banners. This was emphatically a protest by ordinary Beijing citizens, most of them workers acting, ultimately, out of a sense of loyalty to the Party. University students, who would play a much more vigorous role in the protest movements of the 1980s, were all but invisible.

Chen Ziming had been sent home to collect his things on Saturday, April 3, and when he woke the next morning he knew that there was only one place for him to be—Tiananmen Square. From first light, Chang'an Boulevard and the square were swarming with hundreds of thousands of demonstrators. As their poems and chants grew more confrontational, the objects of their sympathy and scorn were identified more explicitly. "This woman really is crazy/She even wants to be an empress!" one poem began, in a transparent allusion to Jiang Qing. Some demonstrators called for China to exorcise its demons—its *yao,* a pun on the name of the Gang of Four's despised Yao Wenyuan. Others pledged allegiance to the proposal Zhou Enlai had made a few months before his death to rebuild China through the "Four Modernizations."[1] Some openly chanted support for the disgraced reformer Deng Xiaoping. Though no one dared to criticize Mao himself, there was an undeniable subtext in all this praise for Deng and Zhou. How could the crowds deplore the Cultural Revolution without also deploring Chairman Mao, whose idea it had been in the first place?

No one took any special notice of Chen Ziming as he elbowed his way through the sea of people. He seemed to be just another young Beijing worker, dressed in the standard blue suit of Mao's China, distinguished only by his prominent teeth and close-cropped hair. He moved through the crowds cautiously, wearing dark glasses, doing his best to remain inconspicuous, mindful of the consequences if he should be arrested again. Despite this risk, he spent the whole day at Tiananmen, mesmerized.

All day he watched the mountain of wreaths grow. One group of workers even managed to scale the sheer sides of the Monument to the People's Heroes and lay a wreath on the very top, where it sat like a halo. The crowds craned forward, or vaulted on each other's shoulders, to copy down the latest poems pasted to the Monument's base. Some were simple and sentimental, others florid and rhetorical. One in particular, although only four lines long, made the crowd gasp. It read:

In my grief I hear demons shriek;
I weep while wolves and jackals laugh.
Through tears I shed to mourn a hero,
With head raised high, I draw my sword.

At nightfall, Chen was still there. Just after eight o'clock he became aware of an unusual commotion in the darkness by the southwest corner of the Monument. Curious, Chen jostled his way through the crowd, but when he finally reached the balustrade, he saw that the cause of the excitement was only a *xiaozibao,* no more than a few lines really, drily entitled "A Record of the Major Events in the Eleventh Two-Line Struggle."[2] As he read it, however, he realized that this was no ordinary poster. It was a frontal attack on the Gang of Four, a direct challenge to Jiang Qing. The author had even taken the unheard-of step of signing his own name.

From several rows back in the crowd, a voice yelled, "Comrades at the front, please read the poster out loud!" Chen felt a gentle tap on his shoulder. "That hand on my shoulder," he told a group of friends several years later, "made a wave ten thousand feet high swell in my brain." To read such a text aloud would be a reckless act for anyone—but doubly so for a convicted counter-revolutionary awaiting transfer to a prison farm. For a long moment, Chen hesitated. Keep quiet, a voice told him; take a step back, you can still lead a quiet life, perhaps become an official one day. . . . But the gentle tapping on his shoulder spoke with a more insistent voice, and a four-character phrase from classical Chinese literature flashed through Chen's mind: *ting shen er chu*—show resolve, strike the posture of the hero, stand up and be counted.

Sentence by sentence, Chen and a young man next to him began to read the *xiaozibao* aloud. "Louder!" came the cries behind them. "We can't hear you back here." Why not turn the crowd into a human megaphone, Chen thought. He read each sentence out slowly; a chorus of ten voices around him repeated it in unison. "Well written!" exclaimed a voice from the darkness. "Jiang Qing has no shame!" cried someone else. Then one voice after another: "The people love Deng Xiaoping!" "Read it again!" And Chen did so, until he was hoarse.

The morning of April 5 was bathed in spring sunlight, unlike the rainy, overcast weather of the day before. Chen was in the square again by seven o'clock, with plans to make a poster of his own. In his pocket were pen, paper, and adhesive tape. But as the Monument to the People's Heroes came into sight, he stopped short. The Monument was bare; the tributes had vanished. Jiang Qing and her cohorts had watched the events of the previous day from a window in the Great Hall of the People, and the provocation had been too much for them to tolerate. Before dawn on Monday, scores of trucks, fire engines, and cranes had moved into Tiananmen Square and carted away the wreaths while security personnel ripped down the offending poems. Chen noticed that the crowd gathered in front of the Gate of Heavenly Peace was smaller this day, but like him, it was now seething with anger. The Monday crowd was made up mostly of young males around Chen's age. Many of them were former Red Guards, driven by Chairman Mao's declaration that "to rebel is justified"—though hardly, on this occasion, in the way that Mao had intended.

The mood soured further when officers of the Public Security Bureau used a police broadcast van to order the crowd to disperse or face the consequences. Chen was swept along in an angry mob that surged through the lines of police and militia guarding the Monument and succeeded in depositing the first wreath of the day. Several protesters were seized and arrested. Someone struck up the first lines of the *Internationale,* and the square was soon echoing to the solemn notes of the workers' anthem. Over by the Great Hall, a student supporter of the Gang of Four began to yell that the protests were wrong-headed: "Zhou Enlai was the biggest cap-italist roader in the Party." He was pursued by furious demonstra-tors, and Chen, his anger getting the better of him, led the chase. Fists flew. The police van continued to bark out the order for the protesters to disperse; the protesters responded by overturning the vehicle and forcing its occupants to flee. With Chen Ziming in the front line, the enraged crowd surged up the main staircase of the Great Hall, chanting "Give us back our wreaths! Give us back our arrested comrades!"

By midmorning, the security forces had lost control. Tens of thousands of demonstrators, their arms linked, made their way to a small building close to the Museum of Chinese History, which the PSB, the militia, and the Public Security Soldiers Corps (*Gong An Bing*) had requisitioned as their joint tactical command center. The demonstrators were blocked by a dense cordon of militia. In the melee, Chen snatched a megaphone from one of the guards.

"Come over and stand on the side of the people!" Chen yelled into the instrument, gesticulating to the guards. "Don't sell your souls to the careerists!"[3] He fell to his knees under a hail of kicks and punches from the guards. But the crowd surged forward again, and he managed to slip away, still clinging to the precious mega-phone. Smarting with pain and beside himself with anger, he put it to his lips again. "Punish the vicious thugs who destroyed our wreaths!" he screamed. "Whoever opposes Premier Zhou should be overthrown! I pledge to fight to the death against the careerists and conspirators in the Party!"

By lunchtime, the call had gone up for a team of delegates to be appointed to talk to the authorities. Chen was one of four men chosen to form an ad hoc negotiating group. Rather grandiosely, it called itself the Committee of the People of the Capital for Commemorating the Premier. "We have come to negotiate with your commanding officer," Chen snapped at the guards. "Let us pass." The militia refused, but they were simply shoved aside. The four negotiators strode up the stairs to the second floor of the tactical command center, where they were barred by a dozen soldiers and plainclothes police. Then an army officer, a nervous man of about forty, appeared and announced that he was in charge.

A surreal conversation ensued. "What do you want?" the officer asked.

"We have three demands," the committee replied. "Return the wreaths for Premier Zhou. Immediately release those you arrested this morning. And severely punish the evil criminals who are responsible."[4]

"You have committed terrible crimes," Chen added. "Go to the window and confess your crimes to the masses."

"I can't do that. It would have very bad international repercussions for China."

"But the only reason these protests are taking place is because you seized the wreaths and arrested our comrades this morning."

"I'm not responsible for that," the officer answered. "I'm not fully apprised of the situation."

The conversation went back and forth for another ten minutes, but the negotiators made no progress. "We shall report back to the masses that you are totally lacking in sincerity," Chen told the officer. "Your attitude is shocking and hateful." The four of them stormed out of the tactical command center.

When they gave their report to the waiting crowd, more violence erupted. A group of angry youths overturned an official car and set it ablaze. Then, more vehicles were set afire. The police and militia sent in reinforcements and encircled Tiananmen Square. But at 5:00 P.M. the protesters broke through their lines again and set fire to the security forces' command center.

At dusk, with smoke drifting across the square and the acrid smell of burning rubber in the air, the hard-line mayor of Beijing, Wu De, went on television and radio to deliver the Party's assessment of the situation. With his half-glasses and genial smile, Wu De looked like a Chinese version of Dickens's Mr. Pickwick.[5]

But what he had to say was harsh and uncompromising, and it was repeated throughout the evening as the militia went about its brutal job of clearing the square.[6]

> A handful of bad elements, out of ulterior motives, have made use of the Qing Ming festival to deliberately create a political incident, directing their spearhead at Chairman Mao and the Party Central Committee in a vain attempt to change the general orientation of the struggle to criticize the unrepentant capitalist roader Deng Xiaoping's revisionist line.

Many years later, Chen Ziming reflected on the symmetries between the April Fifth incident and the Tiananmen Square protests of 1989: the spontaneity of both events; the singing of the *Internationale* and the chants that "The People's Army should stand on the side of the people"; the authorities' mulish refusal to negotiate or acknowledge error; and the Party's judgment that such events could only be explained as the work of "a handful of bad elements."

The Gang of Four took only two days to identify and pronounce judgments on the principal conspirators. First, Deng Xiaoping was named as the black hand behind the protests and was stripped of all his official posts. His closest allies, including his principal protégé, Hu Yaobang, were given the same treatment. Hua Guofeng would become Vice-Chairman of the Central Committee and Premier of the State Council. The Gang did not, however, feel strong enough to purge the resilient little man altogether, and he was allowed to keep his Party membership "to see how he will behave himself in the future."

The second target was the "handful of class enemies" who were said to be guilty of "engineer[ing] an organized, premeditated and planned counterrevolutionary political incident." The Party singled out the four members of the Committee of the People of the Capital for Commemorating the Premier. It described them as "a few bad elements, sporting crewcuts, [who] took turns to incite the people, shouting themselves hoarse through a transistor megaphone."

The confrontation outside the tactical command center in Tiananmen Square had been recorded on film, and when Chinese viewers turned on the news that night, they saw Chen Ziming, in his dark glasses, in the act of delivering a fiery speech to the crowd.

The announcer declared that this *xiao pingtou,* or "crewcut shorty," had personally stormed the Great Hall of the People. But the report did not give Chen's name because the authorities had failed to identify him.[7] By the time the film was shown, Chen had already eluded the security net. On April 5, as darkness was falling, he had slipped away from the square on a bicycle, and although a police informer took down the license number, Chen was never found. In fact, he reported to the PSB as scheduled the following morning and was safely ensconced in the one place the authorities never dreamed of looking: under police guard at the Yongledian Reform Through Labor Farm. For Chen Ziming, a master-to-be of inconspicuous prodemocracy activism, this first appearance on China's political stage was thoroughly characteristic.

After the Gang of Four constructed the official version of the Tiananmen Incident, as the protests on April 5 came to be known, the only task that remained was the ritual repossession of the square in the name of the people. On the evening of April 7, and over the course of the next two days, the Party brought in as many as two million people to celebrate the correct line of the Central Committee. Peasants in blue Mao suits, workers with factory banners, students, contingents of the PLA, and the militia marched in close ranks through the square to the din of gongs and firecrackers, chanting "Long live the dictatorship of the proletariat!" and carrying banners that proclaimed "We'll defy death to defend Chairman Mao's proletarian revolutionary line."

The Gang of Four declared that they had crushed their enemies, but there was a general sense that they had done no more than paper over the cracks. Whatever the rhetoric about tiny handfuls of bad elements, the fact remained that hundreds of thousands of ordinary Chinese had taken to the streets to defy the Party leadership for the first time since 1949.

The Party faced a generational revolt. Chen Ziming was typical of those who took part in the events of April Fifth: young Chinese, sixteen to thirty years of age, who belonged to the first adult generation produced by the Cultural Revolution. They were disaffected and had no clear sense of the prospects for their future. Their formative political experiences had been of chaos, and they longed for stability and reform. What the young workers and intellectuals wanted was to place China's future in the hands of someone like Deng Xiaoping, a reformer who could get China back on a predictable path. In protesting the Gang of Four, they intended, for the most part, to save—and serve—the Party.

A description of the political temper of this Lost Generation calls for a subtle appreciation of the paradoxes of their lives. They can be described as pragmatists rather than ideologues, but these crude terms are hardly adequate. Calling them "democrats" is inappropriate, and "anti-Communists" is no better. In fact, with very few exceptions, Chen Ziming's generation emphatically rejected the label of "dissidents." As an intellectual, Chen saw himself as part of an ancient Chinese tradition, dating back to imperial times, of remonstrating with those in power, seeking peaceful change rather than the overthrow of the system.

But what particularly marked Chen and his generation was their visceral personal experiences of the Cultural Revolution. The fear of ever returning to the turmoil of that period gave Chen and his cohorts a sense of common cause with Deng Xiaoping and the other Party leaders whose careers and reputations had been torn down in Mao's later years. Both the reformers and the protesters of Chen's generation wanted to restore Party rule to an orderly path. Both spoke in praise of "the masses," but both were actually deeply ambivalent about what the masses might do. Under Mao, they had seen how setting the masses loose in the name of democracy could bring about chaos.

The greatest generational crisis of all, of course, is old age and death. The "veteran revolutionaries" who went through the Long March were the glue that held the Party together and the basic source of its legitimacy. But now they were beginning to die. Kang Sheng, the evil genius who headed the secret police, died in December 1975. Zhou Enlai was the first to leave the stage in 1976, that year of public deaths. The second, six months later on July 6, was Marshal Zhu De, the "black general," cofounder of the PLA. He was ninety. The only question that remained was how long Mao himself would hang on.

Because Communist China was founded on a cult of personality, political tensions could never truly be resolved while Mao lived. "With you in charge I am at ease," he was alleged to have mumbled to Hua Guofeng. But that solved nothing, for in the morass of contending factions, Hua had no discernible power base except his fidelity to Mao.

The Chinese have long believed that natural or supernatural auguries, something as small as a scrap of silk found in the belly of a fish or as large as a flood, signal the end of a dynasty. On this occasion the augury was an earthquake, one of the worst in China's history. It flattened the grimy coal-mining center of Tangshan, a little to the east of the capital, on July 28, 1976, killing three-quarters of a million people. Beijing itself was badly hit, as was the nearby port city of Tianjin. The vital road and rail network that served the industrial heartland of north China was disrupted for months.

Six weeks after the earthquake, Mao Zedong finally succumbed to his long degenerative illness. The Central Committee immediately issued a document purporting to be the Chairman's will, which directed venom against Deng Xiaoping for his alleged attempts to divide the Party. But with Mao gone, the entire panorama changed, and it changed in Deng's favor. Less than a month of undisputed control remained for the Gang of Four.

Chen Ziming awoke at the Yongledian farm on the morning of October 15, 1976, to the announcement that the Central Committee, under the wise leadership of First Party Vice-Chairman Hua Guofeng, had smashed the counterrevolutionary group known as the Gang of Four. The news was kept secret for more than a week until the Party was sure that it had mopped up the remnants of rebellion in Shanghai, the Gang's stronghold. On the night of October 6, Zhang Chunqiao, Yao Wenyuan, and Wang Hongwen were lured to a meeting in Zhongnanhai, supposedly to approve the text of a new volume of Mao's writings. As each man arrived, he was arrested for crimes against the people. Jiang Qing, at home in the new palace she had built herself, was detained separately.[8] The airbrushes of the Party's propaganda department quickly removed all signs of the Gang of Four from the photographs of Mao's funeral.

Chen Ziming could hardly contain his delight at the news. His long days in the fields at Yongledian seemed shorter. Even the struggle sessions seemed less arduous. Yet he realized that China's political drama was far from over. Official propaganda now explained the Cultural Revolution as an aberration, the responsibility for which was said to rest entirely with the Gang of Four, neatly sidestepping the question of Mao's own culpability. Chairman Hua, who had even taken to combing his hair back from his forehead in imitation of Mao, spoke only of continuity and a return to the status quo ante. But huge questions remained. What, for example, was to happen to Deng Xiaoping, the man whom Chairman Mao had once called "a needle wrapped in cotton"? Chen Ziming knew that Deng's reformers faced a hard political battle and resolved, even from his confinement, to play a part.

In January 1977, Chen was granted a weekend furlough from Yongledian, this time to petition the Beijing authorities for rehabilitation. Again he made his way to Tiananmen Square. The southern half of the great square was now disfigured by construction work for the new Mao Mausoleum. The Party had ignored the Chairman's own wish to be cremated, and Jiang Qing, before her downfall, insisted that he be embalmed and placed on public display.[9] The Gang of Four had argued for the body to be displayed in a tomb inside the Forbidden City, but on this point they were overruled. Instead, the Politburo settled on a site in Tiananmen Square itself for the squat new building.

In January, the work was still several months away from completion, and a tall wooden fence surrounded the site. This struck Chen as a perfect spot for what he had in mind. From his coat, he unfurled a big-character poster he had written and pasted it hurriedly to the fence. Later, he put up others along Wangfujing Street, Beijing's main shopping thoroughfare. He titled his *dazibao* "A Record of the April Fifth Movement." It called on the Party to reverse its verdict on the incident and rehabilitate Deng Xiaoping. The rumor was that Deng would return to power that very month, but Hua Guofeng stalled. Not until July was Deng fully restored to the Party's leadership ranks.

At about the same time, the warden of the Yongledian Reform Through Labor Farm informed Chen Ziming that he was free to leave. Having criticized the dreary theoretical writings of Zhang Chunqiao and Yao Wenyuan was no longer any reason to keep someone under lock and key. As he had predicted at his trial in 1975, the Gang of Four had been unable to keep China locked in their grip for even the three short years of his sentence.

3

The Thinking Generation

Everything about Beijing University delighted Wang Juntao. I was born to come here, thought the good-looking, ebullient nineteen-year-old as he strolled around the leafy campus in the late summer of 1978. He found Beida a place of curious contradictions. A tall, classically styled pagoda concealed a modern, utilitarian water tower. The students studied in classroom buildings built in the ornate style of the Ming dynasty but slept in grim, austere dormitories that more closely resembled cell blocks. The food was wretched. Arriving at the heart of the campus, Wang paused to read the leaflets posted on the long rusty notice board in an open space known as the Triangle.

The drive to root out the remnants of the Gang of Four had been played out in miniature at Beida over the preceding year. In November 1977, the Workers' Mao Zedong Thought Propaganda Team, which controlled campus affairs, was officially dismantled and given a noisy official send-off, with much banging of drums and clashing of cymbals. In its place came a new three-man Party committee, appointed by Deng Xiaoping, with express instructions to repudiate the Gang of Four and purge "all bad elements" from the university. Those willing to criticize the Gang and remold their worldview were allowed to continue in their jobs.

The issue that most concerned the new Party committee was the revival of the university entrance examination system. The question of exams touched a raw nerve, for it left in doubt the status of the thousands of "worker-peasant-soldier students" who had flocked to Beida since 1970. Many teachers, themselves former members of this now despised category, found that they were no match intellectually for the undergraduates in the entry classes of 1977 and 1978.[1]

The examinations could hardly have been more competitive. Across China some 5.7 million hopeful entrants took part, and less than one in twenty were admitted to college. In purely academic terms, the entry class of 1978 was the cream of Chinese youth— or rather more than youth. It included people who had been turned down for admission six, seven, and eight times during the Cultural Revolution because of their "bad class background"; the ages in this entry class ranged from sixteen to forty. The new students were full of critical questions about the defects of Chinese society. Many were experienced factory workers, some were peasants, some had seen service in the military. Others were Party members or the sons and daughters of cadres. Four out of five of the new students at Beida had spent a period in the countryside. Some, like Wang Juntao, had been imprisoned for counterrevolutionary offenses.

He was a child of privilege, one of those the Party thought of as its golden children. His father was a military officer, a colonel at the time Wang Juntao was born and a man loyal to the highest ideals of Chinese Communism. He eventually ascended to the rank of general, and at the time of his retirement had risen to become head of the Party history research and teaching section of the political academy of the PLA. The family lived luxuriously by Beijing standards. Their home had seven rooms, two separate street entrances, a television, and a tape recorder. His mother's four white, long-haired Persian cats lolled on the furniture. Each of the three Wang brothers had his own bedroom, and Juntao's was strewn with books on foreign affairs, many of them "internal circulation" (*neibu*) volumes on Eastern Europe that had found their way into the house as a result of General Wang's seniority in the Party.

Wang Juntao was born in July 1959. Construction of the new Tiananmen Square was nearing completion, and the Party had just begun its epic conference at Lushan mountain, where Mao gathered all the leading veterans of the Long March to chart the future course of the Chinese Revolution. The meeting reached its climax with the historic break between Mao and his tough defense minister, Peng Dehuai, the "lion of the Red Army."

Perhaps Colonel Wang intended some oblique commentary on the Peng Dehuai affair when he named his son Juntao—the name means "billowing wave of the army." Certainly he intended to pay homage to his own experience in the revolution in the 1930s as a soldier in the *Liu Deng Da Jun,* the Great Army of Liu and Deng, the Communists' Second Field Army. Liu was Liu Bocheng, the "one-eyed dragon" who was an early critic of Mao's "people's warfare" version of the Red Army guerrilla traditions. Deng was Deng Xiaoping, the "one-eyed dragon's" political commissar and intimate friend. Together they had swept Chiang Kai-shek's armies from China's central plains.[2] Colonel Wang bred a sense of loyalty to Deng Xiaoping into his son from the time Juntao was a small child.

A sickly boy, Juntao acquired a passion for reading *wuxia* novels, traditional Chinese tales of heroes battling against terrible odds. In the most famous of these tales, *The Water Margin,* a group of heroes is forced to climb Liangshan mountain, a rebel stronghold in the water marshes of the Wang family's Henan Province. The young Wang identified deeply with the romantic knight-errant characters of these tales and even modeled his behavior on theirs.

In high school, he commanded the respect of his peers. On April 5, 1976, three months shy of his seventeenth birthday, Wang marched at the head of his class to Tiananmen Square to deposit a memorial wreath in honor of Zhou Enlai. He pasted four poems of his own to the Monument to the People's Heroes.

In the crackdown that followed April Fifth, police visited every school and workplace in Beijing. The Party secretary attached to Wang's school demanded to know if any of the students had been involved. Wang, seeing nothing wrong in his actions, handed over copies of the four poems he had written. He gave no further thought to the matter until a Public Security Bureau jeep screeched to a halt outside his classroom a few days later and bundled him away.

Beyond the loss of his personal freedom and dignity, Wang carried one memory of jail for the rest of his life. Three months into his detention, he was awakened in his cell before dawn by a violent rumbling sound. It was July 28, 1976, and the shocks from the Tangshan earthquake were striking Beijing. The concrete ceiling shook; dust fell. In the darkness there was the noise of screams and running footsteps in the corridor. Wang hammered on the door, but the guards refused to open it. Terrified, Wang and his seven cellmates huddled against the wall. He was convinced he was going to die.

The PSB finally released him after 224 days. It was the end of November, seven weeks after the fall of the Gang of Four. Wang then served a year and a half as a sent-down youth on a collective farm in the Yanshan foothills to the east of Beijing, near the old summer palace of the Manchu emperors at Chengde. The authorities allowed him to return to the capital in order to take the Beida entrance exam.

Wang's parents hoped that university life would divert him from any further political escapades. He delighted them by performing well in the exams and was admitted on his first attempt to the department of physics at Beida. Although not a born scientist, Wang told his friends that he wanted "to receive training in the scientific way of rigorous thinking." When his father asked if he would like a career in government, Wang said he didn't see himself as "official material"; he preferred the role of an independent critic.

When Wang arrived at Beida as a freshman in 1978, the campus had quieted down after the bitter fights of the preceding year. An occasional argument erupted in the dormitory television room, with tempers flaring between the new arrivals and the old worker-peasant-soldier students, but in general the atmosphere was one of creative ferment. Political teaching loosened up; art students painted nudes; writers wrote love stories, which were previously taboo, or "scar literature" that depicted their sufferings under the Cultural Revolution.

Even so, a certain amount of caution still seemed necessary. The Lost Generation who had flocked to Tiananmen on April Fifth had seen during the Cultural Revolution how sharply and suddenly the Party's line could alter. Anyone approaching forty was likely to have bitter memories of how badly he or she had been deceived by Mao's promise of intellectual freedom. "Let a hundred flowers bloom and a hundred schools of thought contend," Mao had declared in 1956. But within a year, under pressure from Party conservatives, he reversed himself and launched an "Anti-Rightist

Campaign." Always adept at rationalizing policy reversals, Mao explained that the purpose of the Hundred Flowers campaign was "to let the demons and hobgoblins come out of their lairs in order to wipe them out better, and to let the seeds sprout to make it more convenient to hoe them." The independent thinkers who spoke out discovered that the freedoms they were granted were seen not as inherent human rights but as temporary privileges bestowed from above.

Optimists believed that Deng Xiaoping, however, was a genuine reformer. A month after his rehabilitation, in August 1977, a new Central Committee was convened, the Party's eleventh. More than half of its 201 members were "veteran cadres" who had been purged during the Cultural Revolution, and within six months China had a new constitution that granted "freedom of speech, correspondence, the press, demonstration and the freedom to strike." As Deputy Premier and Vice-Chairman of the Party, Deng had a number of specific responsibilities, overseeing the areas of science, education, and intellectual life. He announced a campaign for the "liberation of thought" and declared that his goal was to "shatter spiritual fetters."

There was as much pragmatism as idealism in this proclamation, since Deng badly needed skilled technicians for his program of economic modernization. His close ally, Hu Yaobang, whom Deng appointed as head of the Party's Organization Department, promised intellectuals they could take the new constitution at its word; China would never go back to the days of "seizing pigtails, wielding clubs, handing out [dunce's] caps, and building up dossiers." Hu was assigned to rewrite the historical record of the Party's actions since 1949 and rehabilitate those who had been unjustly persecuted. According to his calculations, as many as a hundred million Chinese had suffered at the hands of the Great Leap Forward, the Anti-Rightist Campaign, the Cultural Revolution, and the innumerable smaller upheavals of Mao's China. When Chen Ziming heard the news of Hu's appointment, he wrote to him, imploring him to reverse the Party's verdict on the April Fifth incident. That action waited another year, however, because Deng's position was not yet strong enough for him to move ahead on all fronts.

Chen Ziming discerned four factions in the Party's unfinished power struggle.[3] The immediate obstacle to Deng's reform proposals was the "Whateverist" faction, headed by the stopgap chairman, Hua Guofeng, who summed up his political position in his famous formulation, "We must resolutely uphold whatever policy decisions Chairman Mao made and unswervingly carry out whatever Chairman Mao instructed." Deng was the leader of a second faction that for now was in the ascendancy; these Chen thought of as the "Reformists."[4] Deng knew he could not hope to "shatter spiritual fetters" without discrediting the slavish devotion to Mao Zedong's infallibility. No one should be copied unquestioningly, he insisted—not Marx, not Lenin, not Chairman Mao himself. He even went as far as to say that Mao had been "70 percent good, 30 percent bad."[5]

Chen knew that the Reformists were determined to wrest power from the Whateverists by any means necessary. But he also believed Deng was sincere in offering a clean break from the bloody purges, secret killings, and strident public vilifications of the past. Deng's strength was that the other two factions in the Party also wanted Hua Guofeng out of the way. Chen Ziming identified these groups as the "Restorationists" and the "Radicals." The first comprised the traditional pillars of pre–Cultural Revolution Maoism who wanted to turn back the clock to the halcyon days of the 1950s. The second group, much smaller and on the margins of the Party, was uncomfortable with Deng's top-down style of reform; some of its adherents felt that the Cultural Revolution had been the logical outgrowth of the preceding seventeen years of Maoist rule. In the months before the crucial Third Plenum of the Eleventh Central Committee in December 1978, Deng assembled his coalition deftly and put the Whateverists on the defensive with a series of philosophical debates over his notion that "practice is the sole criterion for verifying truth."[6] A crucial ingredient in his campaign was to enlist the support of young Chinese of Chen Ziming's generation.

———

Chen admired Deng's shrewd skills, and he was gratified by the way the Reformists turned to his generation for support in their battles. Not until many years later would he come to understand the perils of accepting the Party's embrace.

One day that summer of 1978, Chen's eye was caught by the picture of a tall, lean young man in the *People's Daily*. He was fascinated by the story that accompanied it. The young man was Han Zhixiong, a worker at the Beijing Number 2 Municipal Housing Repair Company. On August 9, an audience of Party heavies had gathered to salute young heroes of the April Fifth struggle against the Gang of Four, and Han had been invited to tell them his story. He was a modest man and didn't like to dwell on his own accomplishments. Instead, according to the article, when he got the microphone, he praised the bravery of others who had been persecuted and were now being singled out for the Party's acclaim: men like the poet and student Zhou Weimin, who had defied the orthodoxy of Qinghua University, a bastion of hard-line Maoism, and laid a garland of white flowers for Premier Zhou at the Monument to the People's Heroes; men like Wang Juntao, a freshman physics student in the coming year's entry class at Beida, who had been the youngest of those arrested after April Fifth.

Han's own story was riveting. On April 3 he had posted a poem at the Monument: "With deepest sadness we mourn the premier/ With a roar of anger we behead the evil demons and ghosts." The Public Security Bureau followed him home and arrested him, two days before the main crackdown in the square. In prison, Han's torturers subjected him to savage beatings to force a confession that would incriminate "Deng Xiaoping's conspiratorial clique." Han resisted, and in March 1977 he was released for lack of evidence. Yet he had continued to live under strict surveillance by the Beijing security apparatus and was tyrannized by his superiors at the factory, until June 1978, when the harassment finally ended.

And there was the Dengists' point. Han Zhixiong's ordeal was a parable, chosen to illustrate how the leftists were still in positions of influence in Beijing. His appearance on the podium, in short, was part of Deng's attack on the hard-line mayor of the city, Wu De.

The story struck a deep chord in Chen Ziming, because it had striking parallels to his own. After his release from Yongledian, he had resumed his studies at the Chemical Industry College, but he was always under suspicion. The Beijing office of the Xinhua (New China) News Agency forwarded a "black report" on Chen to the Party's Central Committee, which reported that "Chen Ziming has continually failed to turn up at his college and his whereabouts are unknown." Chen *was* missing classes, but only because he was embroiled in a Kafkaesque legal battle with the Public Security Bureau. It started after he discovered that his release from reform through labor was only conditional, and that the bureau was reviewing his file to see if further action was required. The agent in charge of the case was the same Gang of Four sympathizer who had handled Chen's prosecution in 1975, and he was doing all he could to find a pretext for throwing the troublesome young student back in jail.

The worst irony of all was that Chen's role in the events of April Fifth, now his strongest defense, was still unknown to the authorities. "Crewcut shorty" had never been identified. But the *People's Daily* article about Han Zhixiong gave Chen an idea about what to do. He went to the paper's morgue and leafed through the back issues until he came to the one from April 6, 1976. On the front page was a photograph of the previous day's crowd of demonstrators striding across the square with linked arms. And there, in full view in the second row, was Chen Ziming. There could be no doubt about his identity. The picture alone was sufficient basis for him to be declared a Hero of Tiananmen.

The beauty of a Party line is that it does not have to proceed logically from point to point; rather, it consists of loops, detours, and zigzags. History has an infinite capacity to be rewritten by the victors. One day's reactionary aberration is the next day's revolutionary act. The aim of those responsible for the writing of history in Communist China, in any case, is to prove the continuity, wisdom, and correctness of the Party line.

During 1978 Deng prepared his revision of history with care. First came the release over the summer of hundreds of political prisoners jailed by the Gang of Four and the rehabilitation of two hundred thousand people persecuted in the Anti-Rightist Campaign of 1957. Then came the youth campaign in which Han Zhixiong played a starring role. Next, the Nanjing Incident of March 1976 received official praise. And finally the climax, which came when the Dengists, in their boldest display yet of political power, persuaded the Party to reverse its verdict on April Fifth.

On November 15, 1978, the Party resolved that the Tiananmen protests had been "a wholly revolutionary action of the masses" against the Gang of Four. For the first time since 1949 the Party had given its blessing to a spontaneous popular action free of official control. "Long live the people!" was the headline of the *People's Daily* editorial. The Tiananmen poems of 1976, which had been circulating in a samizdat edition put together by some of the staff at Beijing's Foreign Languages Institute, were now published officially. The April Fifth poets, wrote the editors, had prevented China from "being turned into a fascist state manipulated by a handful of ambitious leaders."

Yesterday's bad elements became today's heroes. And logically enough, the greatest accolades went to those who had been named by the Gang of Four as the leading villains. Han Zhixiong was made a full member of the Central Committee of the Communist Youth League, a high honor indeed. So was the poet Zhou Weimin, who had defied orthodoxy and placed a garland for Premier Zhou at the Monument. Wang Juntao became an alternate, nonvoting delegate and found himself an instant celebrity on campus.

Chen Ziming was a late addition to this pantheon, but the authorities now seemed intent on undoing the injustice he had suffered. He was fully rehabilitated and his membership in the Communist Youth League was restored. The Beijing Public Security Bureau even offered him a formal apology, and Chen was invited to address a special plenary meeting of the students and faculty at the Chemical Industry College, where he received a garland of red flowers. The Ministry of Education admitted Chen to the graduate school of the Chinese Academy of Sciences after only one year of undergraduate study instead of the usual three; his high marks on the entrance exam justified their faith that a brilliant scholarly career lay ahead for him. He was to start in September 1979, specializing in molecular biology.

———

Beijing in the early winter of 1978 was a ferment of parties, seminars, and family reunions. Sons and daughters returned home from the countryside, veterans of the Tiananmen Incident ran into each other on the street, ex-prisoners tried to pick up the pieces of their lives.

In the chilly days of November, Chen had taken to strolling over to Xidan, a busy commercial intersection that lies a little to the west of the Party leadership compound of Zhongnanhai. A small crowd usually gathered there, and Chen often ran across other veterans of the April Fifth movement, men like Han Zhixiong and Wang Juntao. They would chat animatedly in small groups under the sparse, leafless trees, brought together by their shared experiences. What drew them to the spot was an unprepossessing stretch of yellowish-gray brick wall that ran along the edge of a municipal bus depot. Each morning crowds assembled to find the wall covered with a fresh array of big- and small-character posters. People had begun to refer to the spot as Democracy Wall.

The major development at the Wall came on November 19, four days after the Party reversed its verdict on the Tiananmen Incident. A wall poster appearing at Xidan asserted that Mao had committed errors in his later years. The clear implication was that if no leader was infallible, then the entire system needed reform to make *all* leaders more accountable. Other posters followed in quick succession. Their subject matter could not have been more diverse: Calls for Sino-Soviet détente jostled for space with long theoretical essays about socialist democracy and calls for lifting the taboos against premarital sex. Some offered cutting street wisdom: "The nation used to be graced with slogans about the class struggle," one poster read, "but the people became fed up with it all. You do not suppress hunger by painting a picture of a cake." Similar posters soon sprang up on smaller Democracy Walls in other Chinese cities—Shanghai, Wuhan, Nanjing, and Guangzhou (Canton).

At the outset of the Democracy Wall movement, the citizens of Beijing watched astounded as a gigantic ninety-four-page wall poster, "God of Fire Symphonic Poems," was pasted up on a high fence along one side of Tiananmen Square, across from the new Mao Mausoleum. The sequence of poems spoke of a monstrous idol that suffocated the Chinese people and subjected them to a "war of spiritual enslavement."

> The war goes on in everyone's facial expression.
> The war is waged by numerous high-pitched loudspeakers.
> The war is waged in every pair of fearful, shifting eyes.

These lines, a tiny fragment from a work on an epic scale, described the China of the Gang of Four. This section of the poem was actually written in 1969 but for years had been kept hidden. Its author was a young man named Huang Xiang, a worker in a knitting mill in the southwestern city of Guiyang. He was the founder of a group called the Enlightenment Society, whose emblem was the flaming torch of learning. Huang had hidden his verses inside candles, laboriously wrapping each sheet in plastic, rolling them around a wax core, and then molding another layer of wax to seal them. On the day that he heard of the arrest of the Gang of Four, Huang melted his candles one by one and "liberated" his verses.

Huang Xiang became the unofficial poet laureate of Democracy Wall. Like so many of those who expressed their views there, he had been a Red Guard and then a sent-down youth—a witness to the dark side of China's political life. Young adults like Huang were no longer inclined to think of themselves as the Lost Generation. Instead, they called themselves the "Thinking Generation." Most still considered themselves Marxists—but Marxists who wanted to democratize Marxism.

From the outset, the Democracy Wall leaders drew a sharp distinction between themselves and dissidents in the Soviet Union. Wang Juntao and Chen Ziming often told friends that they had no desire to leave China, only to make it better. For the most part, the Democracy Wall activists saw themselves as the natural allies and street counterparts of the official Reformists, and, at least initially, Deng Xiaoping seemed to share that view. Through a visiting American reporter, Deng transmitted the message that he considered Democracy Wall "a good thing." All the same, when he gave his seal of approval to the principle of spontaneous action by the "masses," Deng had no idea how literally the masses would take him. Indeed, the poster writers seemed to have taken advantage of a curious momentary vacuum at the top. The Whateverists might be on the defensive, but they were not yet defeated; the Third Plenum was still a month away, and Deng's battles were not over. Thus, for a brief interlude, the Party had no line. On November 27, demonstrators spilled over into Tiananmen Square for a two-day free-for-all of speeches on everything from the need to support the Four Modernizations to the rising price of dumplings. The police kept a wary eye on the proceedings, but they did not have orders to intervene. As a precaution, however, the Ministry of Public Security did station several officers in a booth in the Xidan bus parking lot to keep Chen Ziming and his group under surveillance. The same unit continued its operations for the next ten years.

The project occupying most of Chen Ziming's time was the launch of a magazine. By early December, a number of publications were on sale at Democracy Wall. Most were crudely mimeographed and sold for a few cents. The first of the magazines was Huang Xiang's *Enlightenment*. Then came *April Fifth Forum,* which claimed in its first issue to be organized on the Leninist principle of democratic centralism. There were several dozen journals in all, a literary and theoretical output that dwarfed anything produced by the later democracy movement of 1989. The publications carried their editors' names and addresses to show the authorities that they had nothing to hide.

The close-knit group of April Fifth veterans called their magazine *Beijing Zhi Chun—Beijing Spring—*in homage, as they explained, to the Hundred Flowers Movement. The first issue was scheduled for January 8, 1979, the third anniversary of Zhou Enlai's death. It contained fulsome praise for China's beloved Premier, and the title was printed in red ink, symbolic of the "revolutionary cause initiated by the sacrifice of the blood of the martyrs of the Revolution."

Chen Ziming was discreet about his role on the editorial board of the new journal and preferred to avoid the public eye. But he helped assemble a strong team. The "White Flowers" poet Zhou Weimin became editor-in-chief, and the worker-hero Han Zhixiong was a key figure on the editorial board. What the magazine needed most, however, was a dynamic deputy editor, someone with good connections, who could act as the magazine's public face. The team settled on the precocious nineteen-year-old Wang Juntao.

Despite their difference in age—seven years separated them—Chen and Wang struck up an immediate friendship. They made an odd pair. Their personalities could not have been more different. Chen was the workaholic organizer, the entrepreneur, the maker of connections. Wang was outgoing and outspoken, given to sudden outbursts of song. Some people found Wang shallow and immature, Chen a little dry and humorless. Yet in the day-to-day running of *Beijing Spring,* they complemented each other well.

As the public spokesperson for the magazine, Wang Juntao seemed to be everywhere around the Beida campus—everywhere, that is, but in the classroom. His connections proved invaluable. *Beijing Spring* started modestly enough as a compilation of materials from the Xidan wall, but it soon became the most professionally edited and produced of the new magazines. After two mimeographed editions, it even produced a special typeset issue with a glossy cover, something unique in the annals of China's unofficial press. This feat was made possible by the friendship between the April Fifth poets—Wang Juntao, Han Zhixiong, and Zhou Weimin—and the print workers at the Beijing Foreign Languages Institute, the same people who had published the samizdat version of the *Tiananmen Poems*. The typeset issue of *Beijing Spring* sold an astonishing ten thousand copies, twenty times the magazine's normal print run.[7]

In addition to his organizing activities in Beijing, Wang kept in close touch with the prodemocracy groups in other cities. He played a prominent role, for example, in the campaign for the rehabilitation of "Li Yizhe," the collective pseudonym of a group of Guangzhou writers who had been jailed for publishing a critical wall poster in 1974 during one of the darkest periods of the Cultural Revolution. The Li Yizhe poster, with its warnings of an arbitrary despotism that condemned anyone who spoke out for human rights and democracy to "shackles, barred windows, leather whips, and bullets," or to detention in "scum-hole cowpens," was a direct inspiration for Democracy Wall.

When the group was officially rehabilitated on New Year's Day, 1979, Wang Juntao dashed off a telegram of congratulations on behalf of *Beijing Spring*. Soon afterward, news came that one of Li Yizhe's associates, a young woman named Gong Xiaoxia, had been released from house arrest and admitted to study history at Beida. Wang wrote her an enthusiastic letter of welcome. "Please contact us as soon as you get to Beijing," he wrote. "The address is Building 39, Room 109 at Beijing University."

———————————

The *Beijing Spring* group took full advantage of its various official connections. Some of the journal's articles were picked up and reprinted in the bulletin of the official Chinese Academy of Social Sciences, where Chen Ziming had several well-placed friends. Chen and Wang were rumored to have the tacit support of Deng Xiaoping himself; undeniably, they had ridden to prominence on his coattails. Of all the independent publication writers, they were the most measured in their criticisms, the most "insiderish" in their news and analysis. They openly declared their faith in Marxism. They believed in the Party's ability to reform itself under Deng and cited with approval his well-known pragmatic aphorism that, "White or black, any cat that catches mice is a good cat."

Yet while Chen Ziming and Wang Juntao were well informed about the battles under way at the Third Plenum, there was nothing especially controversial about the issues they chose to highlight. To call for the punishment of notorious leftists like the malevolent Wang Dongxing, commander of Mao's palace guard, or Wu De, who supervised the April Fifth crackdown and then hounded the Heroes of Tiananmen, was no more than an echo of the consensus that Deng was building. *Beijing Spring* had harsh words for the former secret police chief Kang Sheng ("special agent, traitor and Trotskyist") and his ally, public security boss Xie Fuzhi; but by then, no one in the Party would have considered defending such widely hated figures as these anyway.

Beijing Spring even lavished compliments on Deng Xiaoping as the spiritual forerunner of the endeavors of the independent press. "These magazines have pursued the same path as once did Deng Xiaoping, Doctor of Mimeography," the journal wrote. The reference is to the whimsical honorary title that had been bestowed on Deng in the 1920s, when, as a young student-worker in France, he edited the mimeographed Communist weekly *Chiguang* (*Red Light*). These young intellectuals knew their Party history.

Indeed, the Dengist faction may have deliberately used *Beijing Spring* as a conduit for its views. Perhaps the only time that *Beijing Spring* really risked a backlash from Party conservatives was when it praised Hu Yaobang, who had been newly elevated to the Politburo. Hu was the most liberal member of Deng's group and was seen as the chief sponsor and protector of the intellectuals. "Hu Yaobang is a man of action," issue number three gushed. "He is disgusted with phony politics and 'class struggle,' and dares to acknowledge that reality has a seamy side. He courageously appoints people on their merits and promotes 'top talents.' Today a dazzling new star is rising. The masses are pleased with him, watching with delight his glittering starlight."

The magazine was on safer ground when it came to the "old proletarian revolutionaries," Communist veterans now in their sixties and seventies who had run afoul of Mao at one time or another. The magazine painted a sentimental vignette of the return to Beijing of Peng Zhen, the city's former mayor. Peng was the first major casualty of the Cultural Revolution in 1966, arrested by Red Guards who broke into his house in the middle of the night, tortured in jail, and packed off to internal exile in Shaanxi Province.

When he returned to the capital, "a pale, white-haired old man" aged seventy-six, *Beijing Spring* declared breathlessly: "The eight million citizens of Beijing have been eagerly waiting, waiting, waiting for you to come back to us."

Similar praise was given to other members of the old guard: Yang Shangkun, the "Soviet spy" who would later become China's president; Bo Yibo, who had overseen the country's heavy industrial development; and Chen Yun, the seventy-three-year-old economic pragmatist who clashed with Mao over the wisdom of the Great Leap Forward.

There was a bitter irony to these tributes, for these "old proletarian revolutionaries" were the very authorities that Deng would rely upon ten years later to crush the democracy movement of 1989. Crucial differences in style and ideology distinguished them from such younger new leaders as the iconoclastic Hu Yaobang. According to Chen Ziming's later assessment of the Party's factions, Hu was a Reformist who bordered on being a Radical. Chen Yun and Peng Zhen were, by contrast, Restorationists. They were crusty old men who longed for the simpler days of the 1950s, when their power was unchallenged and the Russian-built limousines always arrived on time to take them to the Politburo. For the meantime, however, all that counted was that they were Deng's men, champions of stability and victims of the madness of the Gang of Four.

Wang Juntao and Chen Ziming were in a distinct minority within the Democracy Wall movement. The editors of most of the other journals were young workers, and they were less afraid to make direct criticisms of the government. The editor of *Voice of Democracy,* Fu Shenqi, was a repairman at the Shanghai Generator Factory; Xu Wenli, an electrician and army veteran, headed *April Fifth Forum;* Wei Jingsheng, another electrician, ran *Exploration.*[8] When the worker-editors proposed a meeting to coordinate the activities of all the journals, *Beijing Spring* declined the invitation.

The New Year, 1979, began in frigid cold. There was an almost comical quality to Deng Xiaoping's rapid opening to the West. The government announced that it would soon begin to import Coca-Cola. Deng flew off on a historic visit to the United States on January 28, and members of his entourage were soon being photographed dancing with Minnie Mouse at Disneyland. Bob Hope hosted an American television spectacular that showed the comedian swinging a golf club atop the Great Wall.

Yet with the Party's Third Plenum over and Deng's victory secured—almost at the same time the first issue of *Beijing Spring* hit the streets—Deng's attitude toward the Democracy Wall movement began to change. Up until then, the Dengists had found the voice of the streets useful. But at this point, Deng began to perceive the movement as a nuisance, even a threat.

Democracy Wall itself was containable: a few magazines, a handful of intellectuals. But Deng's greatest fear was that the masses would stir, and by January he sensed this happening. First, many of the sent-down youth poured back into the cities. They were incensed at having been cast aside, and to make matters worse, the Party no longer made any pretense that their marginal status was a matter of high-minded official policy. Thousands of them converged on Beijing and took part in mass demonstrations demanding work and residence permits. In Shanghai, the protests were worse. The city was the crucible of the Cultural Revolution, and as many as a million of its young people had been sent down to the countryside. Now, having returned, they were hungry for revenge.[9]

A second form of grass-roots protest was even more menacing to Deng. In response to an official promise of justice for those wrongfully persecuted, peasants from all over China flocked to the capital to demand reviews of their cases. They came by bus, or hitched rides, or simply walked. They saw their salvation in Deng *Qingtian*, "Deng Blue Skies," a phrase applied to an upright Confucian official of imperial times. They came in midwinter, and they lived on the streets in squalor, sleeping in doorways, cooking meager bowls of rice as they squatted in the gutters, surviving by begging or prostitution. Their petitions fell on deaf ears. The bureaucracy was overwhelmed.[10]

As the authorities refused to hear the petitioners, their despair grew. Some committed suicide; others starved to death.[11] On January 8, 1979, the third anniversary of Zhou Enlai's death, the petitioners converged, as if by historical necessity, on Tiananmen Square. They joined forces with thousands of factory workers who had come to lay memorial wreaths at the foot of the Monument. One angry contingent of peasants staged a sit-down strike. Ten days later, the police burst into the home of the petitioners' impromptu leader in the early hours of the morning and dragged her away. This was the first clear signal to the Democracy Wall movement that "the cold spring wind was succeeding the warm winter wind."[12]

On February 17, barely a week after his return from the United States, Deng sent eighty-five thousand troops storming across the border into Vietnam on what Beijing described as a "self-defense counterattack measure." His war was not successful. The PLA's tactic of fighting by "human wave" caused it to sustain heavy casualties. One wall poster at Xidan dared to ridicule China for bullying "little, childlike Vietnam." The Party's conservative elders, men like Chen Yun and Peng Zhen, warned Deng that he was doing too much too fast on too many fronts. Deng needed little prodding, for Democracy Wall had gone beyond what he regarded as acceptable criticism.

From the start, there was a palpable tension between the moderate and the radical wings of the movement, between those like *Beijing Spring,* who saw their role as supporting the official drive for reform, and those who took advantage of the new climate of intellectual freedom to make more sweeping criticisms of Communist Party rule. One freezing night in late December, a small poster was freshly pasted up on the Wall at Xidan.[13] Its content was stunningly bold. The poster demanded respect for human rights—an alien, Western notion—including the freedom to emigrate. It also gave a time and place for a meeting to discuss the future organization of the China Human Rights League.

The author was Ren Wanding, a short, self-effacing factory accountant with thick glasses. The meeting took place at his workplace, far from the center of Beijing. About twenty people showed up, most of them workers. They met at night, introduced themselves by false names, and lit candles to work by because they did not dare switch on the lights.

If Ren Wanding was outspoken, the electrician Wei Jingsheng, editor of *Exploration,* was a positive heretic. Wei had a magnetic effect on all who met him. He had the lean, ascetic features of a scholar-priest and a clear and dispassionate manner. In discussion, he emphasized his points with the cigarette that burned constantly between his fingers.

Wei came from a classic Communist "good family." His parents and siblings were revolutionary cadres from Anhui, an eastern province afflicted with the most bitter extremes of the Chinese countryside: the worst floods, the most severe famines. In the "three bad years"—the failed harvests of 1959, 1960, and 1961—Anhui's population was decimated. Wei's father, a high state official, was an ardent Maoist who forced his young son to commit a page of the Chairman's thoughts to memory every day; failure meant being sent to bed without dinner. Wei had gone to Tiananmen Square in 1966 for Mao's review of the massed Red Guards.

The following year he spent several months in jail after falling victim to one of the Red Guards' unending internecine struggles. On release, he was assigned to work as an electrician in the Beijing Zoo, but he soon quit to join the PLA. Four years of military service took him from one end of China to the other and left him with indelible memories. He saw homeless peasants forced to go naked, others who sold their children. He saw people selling dumplings—*baozi*—stuffed with human flesh. On April 5, 1976, he went to Tiananmen to mourn Zhou Enlai. Finally, he returned to his old job at the zoo.

Wei went so far in his criticisms of the government as to assert that Deng's ascent to power was meaningless. "We want no more gods and emperors, no more saviors of any kind," he wrote in a poster called *The Fifth Modernization*. "We want to be masters of our own country, not modernized tools for the expansionist ambitions of dictators. . . . Democracy, freedom and happiness are the only goals of modernization. Without this fifth modernization, the other four are nothing more than a new-fangled lie." When a friend recommended that Wei try to arrange an audience with Deng Xiaoping, Wei snapped back, "Why? He has no legal status to talk to me, he wasn't elected by the people."

As Chinese history had proved time and time again, such critical talk by an unprotected individual is suicidal. It was certainly too much for Deng Xiaoping to tolerate. In a speech on March 16, 1979, he laid down formal limits on the Democracy Wall movement. Deng insisted that Four Cardinal Principles must always be upheld: the socialist road, the people's democratic dictatorship, the leadership of the Communist Party, and "Marxism-Leninism–Mao

Zedong Thought"—an ideological hybrid that no one ever quite managed to define.

Nine days later, in an extraordinary display of defiance, Wei Jingsheng lambasted Deng as a "new dictator." This proved the final straw; within a few days Wei was arrested. When Ren Wanding tried to stage a protest at the Xidan Wall, the police picked him up as well.

These arrests briefly tempered the Democracy Wall movement. Wei was guilty, *People's Daily* proclaimed, of "ultrademocratization," precisely the crime of the Red Guards and the Gang of Four. And now that the Gang had been smashed, the official paper went on, what reason did anyone have for further agitation? Democracy was not to be confused with anarchy. *Beijing Spring* was in full agreement with this argument; as far as the magazine was concerned, Wei Jingsheng had gone too far. Wei might see Deng as a "new dictator," but the *Beijing Spring* group felt compelled to support Deng in his tactical maneuvers against a possible conservative backlash.

As Deng tacked to the left to reassure Party skeptics that the reform process would not get out of hand, *Beijing Spring* tacked with him. For several issues, the paper did not say a word about the arrests. Wang Juntao told Chen Ziming at the time that he longed for genuine "proletarian socialist democracy" and thought the best hope for this lay in backing the Central Committee; he had no time for the "phony democratic politics of capitalism." Chen was a little more circumspect. "Of course Democracy Wall has its shortcomings," he countered. "Some comrades still find the concept of democracy a strange and alien one. There are also a number of outright bad people who deliberately foment disorder and make trouble. Some of them have scrawled and scribbled all over other people's *dazibao*. Some have even ripped posters down. But where does one ever *not* find bad people? You always have bad people. There are bad people in the Central Committee. So what if some little clown pops up at Democracy Wall? Why is that anything to worry about? As long as the Party's line is correct, we don't need to worry about a few individuals making waves." The larger threat, Chen concluded, came from "those who try to strangle at birth the tender shoots of democracy, using as their pretext the presence of anarchism." In the end, these arguments led Wang and Chen to the same position regarding Deng: He must be supported at all costs against the holdover Maoists.[14]

While political realism such as this was no doubt an indispensable asset for activists like Wang and Chen, there was also sometimes a danger of straying too far in the direction of tactical accommodation with the authorities—or of engaging in too much second-guessing of the leadership's various moves and power-plays. Coming so soon after the arrests of Wei Jingsheng and Ren Wanding, in particular, Chen's reference to little clowns popping up at Democracy Wall had an almost ingratiating ring about it.

By the summer of 1979, Deng had again laid down the limits of dissent and temporarily shorn the democracy movement of its more radical wing. The Wall itself was closed down and an alternative venue provided in a park far from the city center where all posters had to be registered with the authorities and their contents approved in advance. At the same time, however, Deng had shunted aside more of his Maoist adversaries, and he soon began to outline important legal reforms, including China's first penal code, which appeared to promise greater protection for individual rights. In this altered climate, the fortunes of the democracy movement gradually revived, and even *Beijing Spring* threw a little of its innate caution to the winds. Throwing a person in jail because of his opinions, it now argued, was always a bad idea, an admission of one's weakness. The journal even ran a short story entitled "A Tragedy That Might Happen in the Year 2000." The plot was simple: Deng dies in 1998, at the age of ninety-four; a power struggle ensues, and the followers of the Gang of Four once more seize control. The story edged *Beijing Spring* a fraction closer to Wei Jingsheng's position: One could never rely on enlightened emperors, only on the rule of law.

Wei himself faded from people's minds over the summer of 1979. But then in October came the announcement that he had been found guilty of making counterrevolutionary propaganda and divulging state secrets.[15] The sentence was a brutal fifteen years, and no sooner was it announced than the party authorities at Beida called in Wang Juntao to offer a gentle warning. They thought it might be a good idea if Wang made a self-criticism, that most basic of China's ritual acts of penance. He said he would think about it. Next, the entire editorial committee of *Beijing Spring* was summoned to see the head of the Communist Youth League. The Party would prefer that the magazine cease publication forthwith. Although this was less a threat than a test of loyalty, the editors said no. But this was only a token gesture of defiance, and it allowed just enough time for one final issue of *Beijing Spring,* which carried an unexpected plea on behalf of the imprisoned Wei Jingsheng. What had Wei been guilty of opposing? the editors asked. "Certainly not public ownership, but privilege, injustice and dictatorship. Is this not in fact real socialism?" Wei would have been horrified, and perhaps a little amused, by the suggestion that he was unknowingly a true Marxist.

After this parting shot, Chen Ziming made the case for closing down operations. "We should trust the older Reformist generation," he told his colleagues at a meeting of the editorial board. "The most important contribution we can make to them is through doing research. We need to cultivate and enrich our scholarship." Chen was in his first semester of graduate study; Wang Juntao was embarking on his second year at Beida. Theirs were the brains that would be needed if Deng's reforms were to succeed, Chen reasoned.

In November 1979, after ten months and nine issues, the editors of *Beijing Spring* announced that they were halting publication. During the months that followed, Chen Ziming found additional grounds for optimism about reforms to the political system. In early 1980, the Party decided to revitalize China's district- and county-level People's Congresses (bodies that in the USSR would have been called *soviets*). Elections were promised for the following year, and they would be more open than any in China's history. The campuses would be a prime testing ground for Deng's reforms. "Why shouldn't we run as candidates?" Chen suggested.

4

The Frontiers of Gengshen

Twenty-year-old Wang Juntao, second-year Beida undergraduate, Hero of Tiananmen, and veteran of Democracy Wall, had a great deal on his mind in the spring of 1980. And when Wang had something on his mind, nothing seemed more natural than to talk about it.

Since Hu Yaobang was the Party leader most involved in overseeing the coming election process, Wang decided to knock on his door—literally. Hu was still some months away from his appointment to the position of General Secretary, when he would move to the official residence in Zhongnanhai that went with the post. At this time he lived in a modest courtyard house in the western part of Beijing. Even so, for someone to walk up to the front door of the house of a member of the Politburo was a bold move.

Hu Yaobang was the only member of the Party leadership to whom the word "populist" might reasonably be applied. He cultivated an image of being spontaneous and accessible, and he had a blunt, earthy manner and a peppery temper. After an early career in the Red Army, he headed the Communist Youth League. But Mao Zedong never entirely trusted his free-spirited young lieutenant, whom he thought lacked a firm ideological backbone. In their short stature and high energy level, Hu Yaobang and Deng Xiaoping were strikingly similar. Their careers had moved in tandem. When Deng was down, Hu was down. When Deng came back, so did Hu. Now China was in Deng's hands, and Hu Yaobang was his most trusted aide and chosen successor.

Just how far Hu intended to move in the direction of democratic reform is unclear. After his death in 1989, some of his former colleagues portrayed him as a Gorbachev *ante diem,* always straining at the leash of Deng's Four Cardinal Principles. Others were skeptical, citing Hu's criticism of Party officials who "think too highly of youths [involved in Democracy Wall], believing that they are already able to manage state affairs."[1] It was true that Hu made that criticism; but it was also true that he sent regular feelers to the Democracy Wall people, especially those from *Beijing Spring.*

Wang Juntao arrived at Hu Yaobang's house with a friend, a brilliant young editor from *April Fifth Forum* named Lu Pu, who was a mechanic by profession. They spent four hours with Hu Yaobang in a vigorous give-and-take about political reform and the democracy movement. Hu seemed to take Lu Pu, the older of the two young activists, more seriously, even reporting their discussion later in a speech to the Higher Party School. Hu told his comrades that he thought he "got the better" of Lu during their exchange; Lu reported to his friends that the conversation ended in an impasse. Hu was more avuncular toward Wang Juntao, perhaps even a little patronizing. "Little brother," he said, "I recognize that you have done correct things, but you need to do them at the correct time and in the correct place." He urged the impetuous young man to work within the official system. "When I was young, I too wanted to annihilate the reactionaries very quickly," he told Wang. "I too thought that everything within the ranks of the revolutionaries should be orderly. But later I came to realize how arduous and protracted a thing a revolution is. There are also things that are neither fine nor beautiful within the revolutionary ranks. Only then did I gradually learn how to wait and how to compromise."

Wang came away from the conversation impressed and a little awed. On a philosophical level, he agreed with what the older man said; his own most fervent wish was to help make the system work. The news of his meeting with Hu Yaobang spread quickly, further boosting his already considerable prestige on campus.

The only place where Wang's reputation was not enhanced was in the classroom. Whereas his friend Chen Ziming, across town at the Chinese Academy of Sciences, took his graduate studies very seriously (his master's thesis analyzed the structure of macro-molecules through their diffraction of X rays), Wang was a freer spirit. If an exam posed a question on dialectical materialism—an obligatory topic for all students, including science majors—Wang offered his forthright criticisms of Marxism as it had been practiced in China. This was not what his professors wanted to hear, and his marks suffered as a result.

Wang immersed himself in campus politics and his social life rather than his studies. Gong Xiaoxia, the young woman who had belonged to the Li Yizhe poster group in Guangzhou, became his constant friend and confidante. Gong's background made her something of a political celebrity. A couple of months after her arrival in the capital she was approached by the Xinhua News Agency. They were making a film about Lin Xiling, an older woman who was an outspoken student leader at People's University during the Hundred Flowers Movement of 1957 and a celebrated victim of the Anti-Rightist Campaign of 1958. Hu Yaobang was now rehabilitating Lin, but the case was bogged down by resistance from Party conservatives. Xinhua decided to try to advance her case by making a documentary about her life, and they wanted to include a staged encounter between the veteran Rightist and a group of Beida students. Could Gong suggest some suitable people? She proposed two female roommates and Wang Juntao. Wang, in turn, brought along his fellow Tiananmen heroes Chen Ziming and Han Zhixiong. They spent the day at Beihai, one of the three beautiful lakes inside the Forbidden City. As the cameras rolled, the two generations talked: an older woman who had tested the limits of the Party's tolerance more than twenty years earlier, and a group of youngsters who were now trying to do the same.

During this time, Gong Xiaoxia's dorm room often was turned into an impromptu debating chamber, with fierce arguments over literature and politics raging into the early hours. In spring and summer, the students continued their conversations under the willows beside the campus's Weiming (Nameless) Lake or made the ten-minute bicycle ride to the imperial ruins of Yuanmingyuan, which had been torched by the British and French in the nineteenth century. Wang usually showed up with a group of Gong Xiaoxia's roommates in tow. For decades China had been a sexually repressed society, but at Beida in 1980 the atmosphere was beginning to change—although by Western standards it was still innocent in the extreme. Wang spent much of his time fending off (or in some cases *not* fending off) the attentions of Gong Xiaoxia's adoring friends or crying on her shoulder in the wake of some broken romance.

As his twenty-first birthday approached, Wang's main concern was to find a forum for his political views. In the Communist Youth League, he began to voice increasingly radical opinions. Yet Wang saw no advantage in openly defying the government, as several of the independent magazines continued to do. He still felt that the way forward was to trust in Deng Xiaoping's promises of reform, even while probing their limits. The elections for the local People's Congresses, he thought, offered the best forum for the veterans of Democracy Wall—a possible parliamentary path to influence and a test case of Deng's sincerity.[2]

When Deng spoke of "modernization," however, what he intended was to raise living standards, not to introduce a multiparty system. His first reforms were directed to the countryside, where he granted sweeping powers to his new Premier, Zhao Ziyang. Together with Deng and Hu Yaobang, Zhao completed the troika that would dominate the politics of China in the 1980s. He was an unlikely candidate in many ways, a career technocrat with bland features, square glasses, and a distinct lack of charisma. He was also the first senior Communist leader not to have been with Mao on the Long March. For most of Mao's later years, Zhao had marched to a different drummer. Posted to Inner Mongolia, he tried to restore some sanity to the region after the "three unjust and mishandled cases," the infamous waves of Party persecution and slaughter of ethnic Mongolians in the late 1960s. He grew up in the countryside and spent most of his career there; rice and grain were his business. In Sichuan Province in the late 1970s, he turned famine into plenty by breaking up Mao's commune system and making peasants more responsible for their own food production. Deng saw Zhao's Sichuan as a model for all of China.

In 1980, Deng decided to make the political system more efficient. In the ancient Chinese calendar, the years have names that repeat in a sixty-year cycle, and 1980 was the year of Gengshen. In a speech announcing the "Gengshen reforms" in August, Deng listed five obstacles to China's emergence as a modern society: "bureaucratism, overcentralization of power, the patriarchal way of doing things, lifelong tenure of leading posts, and various kinds of privileges." But he offered little in the way of a democracy that would enshrine its citizens' rights in law.

The centerpiece of the Gengshen program was the 1980 election campaign. Deng explained that the newly elected Congresses were part of "a system of mass supervision so that the masses and ordinary Party members can supervise the cadres, especially the leading cadres." Like Mao, Deng saw "democracy" as a useful tool for mobilizing people in support of Party policies and perfecting one-Party rule. To the Western ear, "democratic dictatorship" is the perfect oxymoron. Yet to Deng Xiaoping there was no contradiction. A Shanghai newspaper explained that democracy was rather like basketball: a game to be played within a space confined by four lines—namely, Deng's Four Cardinal Principles. It was inevitable, however, that a freely contested election campaign would test those limits.

Beijing was among the last places to vote,[3] and the election made the Party conservatives nervous. The list of candidates read like a virtual Who's Who of the Democracy Wall leadership. Chen Ziming announced that he would contest the seat for the Chinese Academy of Sciences, where he was already chair of the graduate students' association. Wang Juntao was one of twenty-nine candidates declaring at Beida, where the student body was to elect two deputies to the People's Congress of the city's Haidian district. The Beida Party committee was a fairly open-minded body and took Deng's Gengshen speech as the green light for political liberalization. But from the beginning of a monthlong campaign starting on November 3, the conservatives were on edge and on guard.

Their greatest worry was that the students' heresies might spread to the broader population, and they saw disturbing signs that factory workers, supposedly the vanguard class of the Chinese Revolution, were beginning to link up with the defiant remnants of the Democracy Wall movement. Deng's clampdown the pre-vious spring had only a limited effect. It dampened the initial euphoria of the movement, but many of the Democracy Wall jour-nals continued to publish, and new ones were founded, despite the official media barrage against "ultra-democracy," "ultra-individ-ualism," and "anarchy." Xu Wenli, chief editor of *April Fifth Forum,* spoke for many when he argued that it was essential to keep up the pressure from below to complement the reform drive from above. Both the grass-roots and the Party leadership earnestly desired reform, Xu believed, but faced resistance from the im-mense tier of bureaucrats in between. Xu and others used the analogy of "an iron bar which is hot at both ends but cold in the middle." From the trenches of their independent journals and newsletters, the worker-editors fired a variety of theoretical shots. Zhu Jianbin, a young steelworker from the industrial tricity area of Wuhan and editor of a journal called *Sound of the Bell,* con-cluded that China was not a socialist society at all, but an "inter-mediate formation" that still contained elements of feudalism and capitalism. *Youth of Beijing,* edited by a group of chemical plant workers, carried extravagant praise for the quality of life in the Soviet Union, and two of its editors also ran as independents in the 1980 factory elections.[4]

The most celebrated of the worker-candidates was Fu Shenqi, a twenty-six-year-old mechanic at the Shanghai Generator Factory, who announced in April 1980 that he planned to contest his work-unit election. There was unusual significance in Fu's candidacy. As well as being the editor of the unofficial Shanghai periodical *Voice of Democracy,* Fu was deeply involved in the effort to give the Democracy Wall journals national reach. In August 1980, he began publishing *Responsibility,* the journal of the National Peo-ple's Periodicals Association—a body from which the more cau-tious editors, such as the former *Beijing Spring* group, kept their distance.[5] His candidacy met with fierce opposition; the Party com-mittee at the generator factory declared that he was mentally un-stable, and they threatened reprisals against anyone who voted for him. Barred from registering formally, Fu ran anyway as a write-in candidate. On the eve of the vote, he delivered an election address to five hundred of his coworkers. The evil motives of the Gang of Four were not enough to explain the catastrophe of the

Cultural Revolution, he argued; the deeper problem was that China had imported all the failings of the overcentralized Soviet model of government. When the votes were tallied the next day, Fu Shenqi came within seven points of a majority.

All this was especially worrisome for several reasons. First, the criticisms of Party rule were simply blunter and more radical than anything that *Beijing Spring* had attempted. Second, the workers' activities opened up the dreadful (to the Communist Party) possibility of dissent taking root in the industrial working class. And third, the workers were guilty of one of the most serious crimes in the Communist Party lexicon: embarking on *chuanlian,* or "link-ups," that tried to organize scattered critical voices in different parts of China.[6]

The idea of forming a nationwide network of unofficial journals came from a thirty-two-year-old Guangzhou shipyard worker, He Qiu, who edited *Road of the People.* He Qiu had gone "on the Red Guard bandwagon" in the early days of the Cultural Revolution, engaging in *chuanlian* across China. But he was soon sickened by the chaos and corruption he saw. Although he never abandoned his belief in Marxism, he did develop "a deep sense of anger towards the bureaucrats."

In January 1980, He Qiu joined the editors of two other South China journals in issuing a "Message to China's People-Run Pub-lications." They proposed starting a single national magazine, backed by a concerted campaign to have the unofficial journals legally registered under the Constitution. "We must unite to win the freedom to publish, to allow our publications to survive," He Qiu and his friends wrote. "The guerrilla tactics of those who act only on their own behalf will lead to the defeat of our publications one by one."

The old *Beijing Spring* group found these proposals much too controversial. Although activists from a dozen cities converged on the capital in August 1980 to convene the National People's Periodicals Association, the editors of the defunct *Beijing Spring* were conspicuous by their absence. Wang Juntao confided to his close friend Gong Xiaoxia that he thought it was "totally out of the question" for him to get involved in the conference. Its organizers were dangerously exposed, Wang thought; they seemed to be asking for reprisals.[7] Besides, the *Beijing Spring* group had always avoided any actions that might embarrass the Deng Xiaoping leadership of the Party.

All these initiatives, most of them worker-led, had the misfortune to coincide with the first of the great upheavals in the Communist world—the rise of Polish Solidarity. For historical reasons, the Chinese Communists have always had a soft spot for their fraternal party in Poland. Although China formally endorsed the Soviet invasion of Hungary in 1956, the Chinese leadership was privately sympathetic to the way the Polish government had handled its worker protests that same year. The Poles used their own troops to crack down on demonstrators in Poznan that June, killing more than one hundred; within a few months, a new friendship treaty with the Soviet Union gave Poland guarantees of noninvolvement in its internal affairs. This pleased Mao; after all, Soviet interference was precisely what he was trying to avoid in China.

In 1980, the Chinese party again faced a dilemma in deciding how to respond to the Gdansk shipyard strike and the emergence of Lech Walesa's independent union. Deng himself at first seemed ambivalent; ultimately he went on record in support of martial law in December 1981. But the early activities of the Polish union were given fair (or at least muted) coverage in the official Chinese media. All factions of the Chinese Party were happy to see Soviet "revisionism" cast in such an unflattering light. Yet Solidarity was a double-edged sword; reports of its successes produced the inevitable effect of inflaming domestic unrest, and the course of events in Poland clearly indicated that such unrest might quickly escalate into a crisis.

Even the most liberal of Deng's advisers, such as the Party historian Liao Gailong, were horrified by the prospect of working-class discontent, which they began to call "the Polish disease." The best argument for the Gengshen reforms, in Liao's mind, was precisely that they would avert a Polish-style crisis in China. Without deep reforms, he insisted, including increased independence for China's labor unions, "We could experience a similar situation—would the working class here not rise up and rebel also?" A similar line emerged in a report by the Party committee of Hunan Province, classified *neibu* (for internal circulation only). It warned that one of the root causes of the upheavals in Poland was the "serious bureaucratism" and corruption of the ruling Polish United Workers Party, which had "built a wall of mistrust between society and the Party." The message had obvious resonance in China.

Solidarity's direct influence in China was in fact quite limited, although the presence of even a couple of microbes in the air was enough to convince the conservatives that disease was rampant. They were infuriated by an open letter "to our dear brothers, the workers of Poland," which the editors of *April Fifth Forum* published in September 1980, in one of their final issues.[8] Two months later, editor Xu Wenli followed up with a personal letter to Lech Walesa, hailing him as "a shining example for working classes in socialist countries the world over."

These sentiments were bad enough when expressed in the form of open letters. They were even more dangerous when they led to real political action on the factory floor, which was what happened in the winter of 1980 in the modern industrial city of Taiyuan in Shanxi Province. In the first organized action by an independent workers' group since 1949, three thousand Taiyuan steelworkers united in protest against the poor conditions in which the Communists' heavy industrial "miracle" had left ordinary workers. A local unofficial journal, *Fengfan (Wind Against the Waves),* painted a stark picture of the lives of married workers forced to live apart from their families for years at a time. "They pay twice as much in the canteen as workers living with their families, and for worse food. They spend their lives in cramped single quarters that are seldom properly looked after. Some of these quarters are falling apart through neglect or are poorly lit and dirty, just like the capitalist slums they show us in the films. . . . They too create social wealth, just like the worker-cadres. But their families get no medical insurance."

Fengfan printed translations of the "Charter of Workers' Rights" from the Polish dissident journal *Robotnik* and the "21 Demands" put forth by Solidarity in August. *Fengfan* provoked the government still more brazenly when it drew an explicit connection between the upheavals in Poland, the Taiyuan protests, and the 1980 local election campaigns. The paper concluded that true reform could come only from working-class activity free of Party control. "The working class of our country has reawakened.

On the surface it would seem that they are merely out to protect their own legal rights. But in reality they have voted for democracy, whether they are aware of it or not. They know that if they want change, they must rely on their own power of organization and on their own elected representatives, for no messiah will achieve change for them."

Normal life on the Beida campus came to a halt for six weeks in November and December 1980. Twenty-nine candidates pasted up their speeches and manifestos at the Triangle and on dormitory and classroom notice boards and dashed from building to building in the evening darkness to canvass votes. Close to a dozen student-run newspapers sprang up overnight. "Everywhere," reported *Sixu* (*Train of Thought*), "there were wall posters, leaflets, opinion polls, investigations, advertisements for forums and candidates' opinion boxes. Everywhere people were arguing, discussing, asking naive questions and making stirring speeches."

Quiet messages of support filtered down from senior Party reformers. Wang Juntao received a message from Hu Yaobang himself: "Don't abandon your high ideals." The university was helpful and provided all the pens, paper, and duplicating materials needed to make posters. When classrooms and dining rooms could no longer hold the crowds that gathered to hear the candidates speak, they spilled over into the main auditoriums, with the approval of the Beida Party committee. On one occasion, Hu Ping, a graduate student in philosophy, reserved a large teaching room for a campaign meeting. He arrived to find that a Party committee congress in the same hall had run over into an extra day. But the election campaign took precedence, and the Party, not the independent candidate, relocated.

For all these encouraging signs of favor, the campaign took place under a bell jar of official surveillance. Anxious Party work-teams and investigative commissions descended on Beida to observe the election and to question the candidates on their views. There were reporters from *People's Daily;* delegations from the Beijing Municipal Party Committee and the Central Committee of the Communist Youth League; cadres from the Civil Administration Ministry, which had overall charge of the election campaign; and officials from the Education Ministry, who were especially hostile.

The cadres heard speeches of unprecedented audacity. Zhang Mangling, a thirty-two-year-old who was one of four female candidates, spoke out for a Chinese version of women's liberation. She ran on the slogan "Oriental Beauty" and demanded an end to the use of women's bodies as "dried-up units of labor power." Hu Ping declared that free speech did not exist in China and seemed to taunt the authorities when he remarked that the Beida election, though on the surface a humble and insignificant affair, nevertheless resembled "a young girl out on her first date, who arrives late and dressed in the most unflattering of clothes—perhaps to test the sincerity of her suitor."

The election meetings turned into free-for-all debates in which no topic, it seemed, was off-limits. One debate drifted into a lofty discussion about theories of proletarian democracy; the next lost itself in mundane local issues—the absence of shops and services near Beida, the noisy traffic on the roads around the campus. No one participated in the election more energetically than Wang Juntao. He cheerfully granted all requests for interviews and gave his opinions on the burning issues of the day. He was an anarchic campaigner—disorganized, invariably late for appointments, relying heavily on the patience of a committee of supporters headed by his friend Gong Xiaoxia. He held fully twice as many meetings as any competitor and allowed himself to be peppered with questions. The answers to these questions were then statistically tabulated in obsessive detail by the student newspapers. The campaign magazine *Election Storm* printed Wang's answers on a number of topics included in a questionnaire that it circulated to all the candidates in mid-November.

Q: What do you most appreciate in a woman?
A: Wide-ranging interests. A woman should be benign of speech and elegant, with an open, expansive character and a strong personality.
Q: In a man?
A: He should be upright, forthright, and broad-minded.
Q: What is your view of the present nature of Chinese society?
A: It is socialist in a broad sense.
Q: Your view of the Cultural Revolution?

A: A large-scale political reaction.

Q: What is your opinion of the case of Wei Jingsheng?

A: Wrongful conviction.

Q: What is the major question facing Chinese youth?

A: The search for a new lifestyle—political, economic, and cultural.

Q: Was Chairman Mao Zedong a great Marxist-Leninist?

A: He was a great Chinese revolutionary.

Q: What do you consider your own greatest strength?

A: My broad and extensive interests.

Q: Which subject have you studied in the greatest depth?

A: My interests are broad and extensive.

Q: What is the core problem facing China today?

A: To establish a system of democratic politics with separation of powers.

Q: What do you plan to do when you graduate?

A: Mainly to be a scholar, but also to engage in other activities.

Q: What is your greatest personal weakness?

A: I'm too stubborn.

Q: Your favorite novel?

A: The last thing I read. I love all sorts of novels.

Q: Whom did you worship as a child?

A: Mao Zedong.

Q: And now?

A: Nobody.

Q: What is your personal credo?

A: Scientific socialism.

Q: What are you most afraid of?

A: Doing bad things out of good intentions.

Q: What do you like most?

A: Creative thought.

Q: What do you hate most?

A: Those who cheat the weak and fear the strong.

Wang's answers gave the impression of an impetuous young man with plenty of high ideals but perhaps less of the patience required to work them through. Wang scored well when the voters were asked to evaluate each candidate's qualities as an orator, but less well when they were asked "Whose ideas are the most profound?"

He was no match for the sophistication of someone like Hu Ping. Hu was a native of Sichuan Province, China's granary, and he was Wang's elder by twelve years. A specialist in Locke, Hume, and the classics of Western political philosophy, Hu made the highest examination score of any Beida student in the entrance class of 1978.

As in the days of *Beijing Spring,* Wang's support for the Deng Xiaoping program could still come across as a little jejune. For example, Wang insisted that "those elected should replace, and provide a counterbalance against, our corrupt, muddleheaded, manipulative, untutored and apathetic 'emperorlike' bureaucrats and politicians." But in the next breath, he hailed the Communist Party as "the vanguard of reform" and concluded that it had "accepted and adopted the main ideas of the Democracy Wall movement"—despite the fact that the Party had jailed its most outspoken leaders.

Yet Wang delivered his speeches, which contained some dangerous ideas, with a passion and sincerity that moved his audiences. Although he hewed closely to Deng's line, Wang was the only candidate to offer a sustained critique of the entire thirty-year span of Party rule. The heroes he singled out for praise were the great victims of Mao's intolerance, men like Liu Shaoqi and Peng Dehuai. He condemned the follies of the Anti-Rightist Campaign, the Great Leap Forward, and the Cultural Revolution.

The one area in which Wang truly went out on a limb was in his assessment of Mao Zedong himself. The difference between calling the dead Chairman "a great Chinese revolutionary" rather than "a great Marxist-Leninist" may seem negligible, but in China in 1980 Wang's words were explosive. People had been jailed—even executed—for less in the past. Not until June 1981 did the Central Committee issue an official statement on Mao's mistakes. In the meantime, any public criticism of the dead leader was tantamount to a criticism of Party authority. In a debate on November 29, just four days before Beida voted, Wang and nine other candidates debated the thorny question of whether Mao had been a Marxist at all. Probably not, Wang concluded. Mao ran a private "oligarchy" in the Party; he was "a historical idealist who refused to learn from the experience of the advanced democracies"; he inflicted enormous harm on China's cultural heritage by writing it off as "feudal and bourgeois." According to Wang, a real Marxist would not have done such things.

Hu Ping, whatever he may have felt privately, thought that it was politically counterproductive to launch this kind of direct attack on Mao, and he told Wang so. "You're right, I know," Wang responded. "It's bound to involve me in a big battle and it'll probably lose me some votes. In fact, I assume the votes I lose will go to you. But it's been so long now since I spoke out publicly, and I have to use this opportunity to say what's on my mind. That's more important to me than getting elected."

But getting elected was extremely important to Hu Ping, and he thought it was senseless to provoke the Party into any kind of repressive backlash. He felt it was important to learn from the election experience and to build on it and to make the process of political change as gradual and nonconfrontational as possible. "If we do not lose," Hu commented, "then we win."

On December 3, six thousand Beida students filed into their spartan classrooms and dormitories to cast their ballots. Under the complicated election rules, this was only an elimination round. The students could vote for three candidates, but no one would be elected unless he or she received 50 percent of the total vote. The process was orderly, the ballot secret, and the count scrupulously fair. The next morning a crowd gathered at the Triangle to await the results. A cry went up: "Hu Ping first by a wide margin! Wang Juntao second." Hu and Wang moved to the runoff, along with a more middle-of-the-road student leader named Zhang Wei. From across town came the news that Chen Ziming was an easy winner at the Chinese Academy of Sciences, where he had just begun his graduate studies.

Hu Ping won the second ballot comfortably, but Wang fell just short of the percentage required. So did Zhang Wei. This made another runoff necessary, but the result was similar: Wang took 2,936 of the 5,976 votes cast—nine-tenths of a percentage point short of what he needed. The second Beida seat remained vacant. Wang's outspoken comments on Mao had cost him dearly, but he was stoic in defeat. As he had written in his election pledge, "My reason for running as a candidate is to try to promote the political democratization of China. Regardless of whether I am elected or not, I will continue to struggle toward this lofty goal for the rest of my life." Those were the words of a knight-errant, the sentimental hero of a *wuxia* novel.

For a brief time, the democracy movement seemed to be gathering fresh momentum and credibility. During a rally for all the city's election candidates, Chen Ziming told the crowd that he saw four lasting achievements coming out of the election campaign: It boosted the cause of the Party reformers; it allowed all sorts of new ideas to be aired; it strengthened the supervisory role of the National People's Congress; and it nurtured a new generation of political talent. Indeed, Chen predicted, the full impact of the 1980 elections would not be clear until the next century.

Although Chen had seen the Gengshen reforms as a genuine New Deal, even before the last of the Beida votes were counted the winds shifted again. In December, the Central Committee disappeared into a special "work meeting." Out of this emerged "Document No. 9," which began to circulate at the top levels of the Party during the first weeks of 1981. Document No. 9 called for the outlawing of "all illegal organizations and publications." For the first time, Chen Ziming realized that he had seriously misjudged Deng Xiaoping. "This concession [to the conservatives] was just too big," he wrote years later. "It went far beyond what we had expected." Deng was an unreliable ally, and the democracy movement could not afford to tie its fortunes to each new twist in the Party's unending factional battles.

What concerned the old guard most was the possible impact of the Polish situation,[9] and Deng now cracked down on the workers in the democracy movement with a severity that astonished everyone. On April 5, 1981, the fifth anniversary of the 1976 protests, police arrested the Shanghai worker-editor Fu Shenqi in Tiananmen Square. Within a matter of days, they seized dozens of other leaders and accused them of "anti-Party and anti-socialist activities." It was not until a year later that news leaked out of the appallingly severe sentences that were handed down. Xu Wenli, the chief editor of *April Fifth Forum,* who was a staunch supporter of Deng, got fifteen years; the Guangzhou editor Wang Xizhe got fourteen years. Xu and Wang, just like Wei Jingsheng before them, were to serve their entire sentences in solitary confinement.[10]

Having survived Deng Xiaoping's first crackdown two years earlier, the Democracy Wall movement was now decapitated, and any remaining activities were driven deep underground.

Although the events in Poland were always in Deng's thoughts, he was also on guard against the dangers of his rapid opening to the West. In his attack on the worker-editors, Deng encouraged the Party's reformers and conservatives to close ranks against the new common enemy of "bourgeois liberalization," a code word for Western ideas. Deng was trying to do the impossible: to break the ancient isolation of the Middle Kingdom while restricting the ideas that would flow in as a result. Starting in 1980, tens of thousands of Chinese students traveled to the United States; busloads of foreign tourists swarmed over the Great Wall and the Tombs of the Ming emperors, and they stayed in new hotels with pink and green marble atriums and glass elevators and string quartets that would not have been out of place in Dallas or Atlanta. But Deng never abandoned his illusion that foreign political influences could be filtered out, and on three separate occasions in the 1980s he allowed, even encouraged, the Party's leftists to rally their forces against the evils of bourgeois liberalization.[11]

Those who saw the events of the past five years as paving the way for an official rejection of Mao, something along the lines of Khrushchev's 1956 secret speech denouncing the crimes of Stalin, failed to understand Deng Xiaoping. In June 1981, the Communist Party issued its "Resolutions on Certain Questions in Our Party's History." Beneath the bland title, this document contained the official verdict on the entire course of the Chinese Revolution since 1949 and the final word on Mao.[12] It was the result of a hard-fought compromise between the Party's factions, but the caution of the conservatives predominated, and Deng went with them. He saw clearly enough the dangers of a thorough desanctification of Mao, and no doubt the Soviet experience was in his mind. The Soviets could strip Stalin of his halo, but (or because) they still had Lenin. The Chinese had no such luxury; without Mao there was no history. Mao himself could be held responsible for "errors," but Mao Zedong Thought, whatever it was, would continue to be the guiding principle of the Deng reforms.

A further important factor in the blizzard of official media attacks on the democrats was the Party's sense that it had partially lost control over the 1980 election process. Although they were not to suffer as harshly as the worker democrats, the Beida activists soon learned that reprisals for their campaign activities were likely. The petty harassment began within days of the vote, as posters appeared on campus attacking Wang Juntao and Hu Ping. The candidates had ordered the printing of a small book of their speeches and other election documents, but when they arrived at the printers, they found that the Public Security Bureau had got there first and had seized all five hundred copies printed. When the Beida candidates organized a seminar to conduct a postmortem on the campaign, a reporter from Hu Yaobang's office showed up. Wang Juntao readily gave her a copy of the proceedings, which later found its way to less sympathetic members of the Central Committee, who then lambasted the seminar as a "black meeting." By March 1981, a Party investigating team concluded that 30 percent of the Beida students were "rightists"; a strenuous new campaign of political education was needed.

In September, the leftist Cheng Zihua, Chairman of the National County Election Committee, delivered his formal report on the campaign. "During these elections," he told his comrades, "a tiny minority made use of the opportunity afforded by the election of people's representatives to carry out so-called 'election contests.'" There it was again, as in 1976: The enemy was a "tiny minority" with ulterior motives. "They disregarded the socialist legal system," Cheng went on, "spread anarchy and ultra-individualism, conducted secret 'link-ups' and expressed outrageous and inflammatory views, openly contravening the Four Cardinal Principles. . . . We must resolutely oppose this."

The various crosscurrents within the Party influenced how Wang Juntao's case was handled. He was quickly summoned to the office of the Beida Party secretary, who told Wang that he was being pressured by the Central Committee to extract a self-criticism from the headstrong young man. Wang declined, and, as before, his family background helped. The liberal Beida authorities did not press the point; they continued to treat him "with soft hands" as the Party's wayward child. In their report to the Central Committee, they pleaded in favor of Wang Juntao: "If you are not prepared to trust someone like this, then whom will you trust?"

The slight, mild-mannered Hu Ping fared much less well, and the line on him was much more guarded: "We have not yet discovered any evidence that he has engaged in any anti-Party or anti-socialist activities," the Beida report said. Hu had had a rough time during the Cultural Revolution, with five harsh years as a sent-down youth in the Yunnan countryside. He also came from a "bad class background," with "overseas connections," and although such classifications were supposedly a thing of the past, a cloud of suspicion surrounded him. When Hu Ping tried to assume his seat on the Haidian People's Congress, he was prevented from doing so. The Party also banned his writings on the absurd grounds that he had "resorted to a Cultural Revolution–style movement" on campus.

Chen Ziming was also blocked from occupying his seat to represent the Chinese Academy of Sciences, and his application for Party membership was denied. But, again, a sympathetic Party committee shielded Chen from worse treatment. When the annual Congress of the Communist Youth League came around, Wang Juntao was not invited, and his seat on the Central Committee lapsed. Chen told Wang that it was no longer a good idea for the April Fifth veterans to go on meeting openly. With the leftists again setting the pace, such activities risked being stigmatized as *chuanlian*. The group would maintain their contacts in a more discreet and informal way.

Wang remained stubborn, however, on the matter of a self-criticism. His friends told him that he was being foolish, that it would do no harm to make this token concession. But as he had admitted in the election questionnaire, his worst fault was stubbornness. He retorted that he saw nothing to apologize for, even though he was scared at the prospect of going back to jail. Two hundred and twenty-four days had been enough.

During this time, Wang was spending less and less time with his parents in the four-bedroom house on Wanshou Road that went with his father's teaching job at the PLA Political Academy. Although Wang adored his "old man," relations had been strained ever since the Beida elections. Characteristically, the Party had tried to use its access to the family to put pressure on Wang to conform. Sitting at home one day, General Wang had been roused by a knock at the door. It was a senior cadre. There was concern in the highest quarters about young Juntao's activities, the man explained. General Wang had always been anxious about his middle son's impulsive streak. The cadre's visit threw him into a towering rage; he had a bad heart, and the incident triggered a bout of chest pains. His wife drove to Beida to plead with her son. Would he not take his name off the electoral list for his father's sake? There was a heated discussion; Juntao was torn between filial duty and political obligation. But in the end, politics won out. After that, father and son were virtually estranged. When the 1981 Spring

Festival, the main family occasion in the Chinese calendar, came around, Wang decided to spend it on campus with Gong Xiaoxia rather than go home to Wanshou Road. His miserable year went from bad to worse in the autumn, when he came down with hepatitis, a victim, like hundreds of other students, of the deplorable sanitary conditions in the Beida dormitories.

Wang spent much of his final year at Beida in a state of nervous exhaustion. "After living for twenty-two years," he wrote in a letter to a friend, "and going through so many setbacks, successes, mad joys, great sorrows, and after thinking so hard, I have come to the conclusion that this is the standard for a human being." He struggled to reconcile the demands of his intellect and his powerful emotional drives. "Follow both Einstein and Venus," he advised a friend who was leaving to study in the United States. "I feel more and more," he wrote on another occasion, "that reason and emotion are two separate things. A person cannot only develop the side of reason and suppress emotions—the emotions will become distorted." His sense of mission even began to take on an overtly spiritual tone: "This ever-increasing thirst in the depths of my soul has forced me step by step toward religion, and I have almost got as far as 'God.'"

The months dragged by until graduation day in the summer of 1982. His career at Beida, which began with such bright promise, had become a burden. And Wang's future was also filled with uncertainty. How would the Party dispose of him? A bad attitude could be punished with a job assignment to some remote hellhole like the northwestern provinces of Xinjiang or Qinghai. Hu Ping received his doctorate in 1981, but Wang knew that Hu still had no work, despite the acute shortage of Ph.D.'s in China. (Hu waited a full two years before he was eventually assigned work.)

When Chen Ziming and Wang Juntao graduated in 1982, the Party authorities were still bickering among themselves about what to do with the troublesome crop of new graduates. But the liberals continued to shield Chen and Wang. Chen had won wide recognition in Beijing as an exceptional talent, and several departments of the Chinese Academy of Social Sciences (CASS) clamored for his services as a researcher. In the end, he chose to study philosophy there in the Department of Natural Dialectics. Despite all the gaps in his academic résumé, he still seemed to be headed for the top.

Wang Juntao learned that he had been assigned to the Number 401 Nuclear Physics Research Institute in Fangshan County, part of China's crash nuclear energy program. There was nothing to do there once one had made the obligatory tourist day trip to the nearby cave where the remains of Peking Man had been found. The atmosphere at the institute was dreary and oppressive, even though Wang did his best to enliven it by organizing discussion circles and music study groups. His job was low-level and technical, and the work was boring and repetitive—sufficiently so, Wang supposed, for the hard-liners to see it as a punitive assignment. Yet Fangshan was close enough to Beijing to allow the occasional weekend visit, and Wang kept in touch with Chen Ziming and the other veterans of the *Beijing Spring* group.

One day, Wang was surprised to hear that Hu Yaobang was visiting the facility. It seemed the General Secretary had not forgotten the young man with whom he had argued two years earlier. In fact, he recommended to the institute director that Wang Juntao be admitted to the Party as a cadre in the "Third Echelon"—the group of promising future leaders. But Wang rejected the idea. While his friend Chen Ziming hurled himself into his new work at CASS and dreamed of one day becoming an influential official, Wang decided that his path lay elsewhere.

5

Apprenticeships

It is hard for a woman to get ahead in China. A woman's place is a step behind her husband; docile and deferential, she holds the home together without complaint. Politics is a male domain. The malevolent Jiang Qing was the only woman ever to have climbed to the top of the Communist Party. After Jiang's downfall and disgrace, only the aging Deng Yingchao, Zhou Enlai's widow, enjoyed access to the top leadership.

Bai Hua had no political ambitions, but she did aspire to be a modern, independent, professional woman of the kind she read about in books on the West. The common thread that bound her contemporaries together, she thought, was rebellion against the rigid values of their parents' generation. Her own father was a low-ranking officer in the PLA, a narrow-minded and poorly educated Party hack, a man without emotional warmth or depth. The only book in the house was a bound collection of Party documents, and the only thing her father ever talked to her about was the need to become a Party member so that she could be just like him.

As a teenager during the Cultural Revolution, Bai Hua hungered for novels, for poetry, for ballet, for all the things that were banned and driven underground by the puritanism of the commissars. She shared her dreams with a friend, a young librarian whose father taught at Qinghua University, a fortress of Marxist orthodoxy. This girl's house contained secret treasures. The Red Guards' purge of her workplace was slipshod, and at night she slipped away with translations of Tolstoy and other Western classics hidden in her bag. Bai Hua borrowed them and read them under the covers at night. The librarian also had a collection of Western records, which she hid beneath the floorboards. When she and Bai Hua were alone in the house, the two teenagers huddled over recordings of Mozart with the volume turned low.

Bai Hua escaped the rigidity of her family home in 1970. She was fifteen. The Cultural Revolution and the cult of Mao were at their height. There was no question of higher education; the universities were closed. Instead, she spent eight dreary years as a maintenance worker in a supplies factory, changing fuses and light bulbs. She lived in the factory dormitory and made a token appearance at home on weekends just to wash her clothes. She applied to join the Party, not to please her father, but because it seemed to be the only way to get ahead. The Party turned her down, however; she was classified as a "free-thinker"—perhaps because, at twenty-one, she had gone with a group of coworkers to pay her respects to Zhou Enlai at Tiananmen Square. The police came to the factory a few days later and interrogated her about her movements in the week leading up to April Fifth. They said her behavior had been counterrevolutionary and that she should stop work for a few days to write a self-criticism.

But when Deng Xiaoping returned to power in 1977, Bai Hua's life was transformed. She did not make it into the first, highly competitive entry class of 1977–1978, but the following year she passed the exams for People's University. After four years, she was admitted to the graduate school of journalism. She found, however, that the journalism school was as stifling as life with her father. The essence of good journalism, her teachers told her, was to educate the masses in loyalty to the Party and obedience to the Four Cardinal Principles. One day, Bai Hua chanced to pick up a book on American journalism. On the first page she read, "What is news? Dog bites man; that is not news. Man bites dog: that is news." She laid down the book with a gasp; reading these lines was like parting a curtain to look into another world.

Bai Hua began to blossom. She was unrecognizable as the frustrated young woman who had spent eight years in the drab blue uniform of a factory worker; she now had a cool, professional demeanor that commanded respect. She was not a textbook beauty, but there was a litheness to her movements, a directness to her gaze, and a brilliance to her smile that made the textbook irrelevant. By 1984 she was in the middle of her master's thesis. The topic was the influence of mass media on the economic reforms in the country-side. Mao's collectives had been broken up, and the methods that Zhao Ziyang had pioneered in Sichuan Province were being applied nationwide; food production was booming. In the villages, the new dream was to become a "ten thousand *yuan* household" (about $3,400 at that time).[1] Most homes now had a radio, and the first television sets were making their appearance. In one village after another, the old mud-brick buildings gave way to new two-story brick houses. They were not pretty, but they represented a level of material comfort that no Chinese peasant had ever known.

Under Deng Xiaoping's new "Responsibility System," the peasants could sell their surplus produce on the open market once they had met the state's quota. They could even look for work outside the village. Enterprising farmers sold fruit and vegetables in town markets. While women and old people stayed to till the land, young men left farm life behind and headed to the cities, guided by Deng's assurance that "to get rich is glorious."

One day in 1984 Bai Hua heard of an opportunity to join a team working on a weeklong project in the countryside that sounded interesting. The new governor of Guantao County, a cot-ton-producing area of Hebei Province, was looking for a team of students to assess the needs of the county for the next five years and was offering a fee of ten thousand *yuan* for the survey—a very substantial sum for a private contract in these early days of the Chinese reforms.

Bai Hua asked who was in charge of the project. A smart little man in his early thirties, she was told, who had quite a reputation as a take-charge type and an expert fund-raiser. His name was Chen Ziming, but everyone called him "Boss Chen."

During the two years since his move to the Chinese Academy of Social Sciences, Chen had made quite a name for himself. The work for Guantao County was only one in a series of free-lance consultancies that he took on to raise money for his other activities. During the week in Guantao, Bai Hua's temporary boss displayed what would become his trademark: piggybacking one activity onto another. One day, while his team of student helpers was off doing fieldwork, Chen headed for the county library. Bai Hua went with him, since the librarian was on her list of people to interview. She wondered idly why Chen was carrying a heavy suitcase. She soon found out. No sooner was he inside the building than he threw the case open to reveal a stack of books, cornered the librarian, and tried to make a sale. Bai Hua could scarcely believe what she was seeing; a Western-style salesman doing the hard sell was, to say the least, a rare sight in China in 1984. She cringed with embarrassment and took an instant dislike to Chen. She was quite prepared to respect his shrewdness and his energy, but she found him dry, humorless, and single-minded, and quite uninterested in impressing a female colleague. This inauspicious first encounter did nothing to suggest that Bai Hua, within four years, would become one of Chen Ziming's most trusted colleagues.

Chen thrived in his years at the Chinese Academy of Social Sciences. For an intellectual in Deng Xiaoping's new China, there was no more exciting place to be. CASS was a new institution, founded in 1977. (During the Cultural Revolution, the social sciences were regarded with deep suspicion as breeding grounds for bourgeois thinking.) CASS had expanded fast, and the tall, modern building that it occupied a couple of miles east of Tiananmen Square was abuzz with the activity of bright young scholars in their twenties and thirties. Not that it was entirely a liberal stronghold; Maoist holdovers also occupied high positions at CASS, and Chen Ziming had firsthand experience of the constant tug of the Party's factional crosscurrents.

These early years of the decade reminded Chen, as he later wrote, of the period from 1941 to 1944, when the Communist Party was preparing to take power and the threat of Japanese aggression had forced the Party to moderate its policies in search of the broadest possible support. Under Deng, the Party headed off the economic crisis that had been brewing at the end of 1980. The New Helmsman's program for the "emancipation of the mind" was a promising start. There was an atmosphere of prosperity such as China had never seen.

But at the same time, Chen was alert to distinct danger signs. Chen considered the official verdict on Mao, for example, to be a cop-out by the reformers. Once disagreements about Mao's legacy surfaced, everyone sought the line of least resistance. Few high officials stood to gain from probing *too* deeply into the causes of the Cultural Revolution, and the review of the dark side of the Party's history was hastily abandoned in the name of unity. "The achievements of the past are the result of everyone's hard work," Chen complained sardonically. "The errors of the past, likewise, are everybody's responsibility." It was all to the good that Deng wanted to avoid old-style purges. But the result was that the old guard was still alive and well, even in places like CASS.

Deng required all of his considerable political skills to preserve his coalition, because the still influential old Maoists and their allies waited to pounce on the reformers the moment they went too far. They could tolerate economic reform, since they had no alternative program to offer. But they were easily scandalized by the foreign cultural influences that flooded in through Deng's "open door." Western teachers introduced exotic ideas into the universities; "foreign guests" spent as much on room service in their luxury hotels as most Chinese earned in a month; Central China Television (CCTV) carried, via satellite, the often enticing images of foreign news broadcasts. The old guard invoked the memory of Mao more and more aggressively; they bemoaned young people's *luanxue,* their "indiscriminate imitation" of the West. Chinese teenagers no longer dreamed of a future in the Communist Youth League; they seemed uninterested in emulating socialist heroes. Instead, their highest ideals seemed to be to grow their hair long, listen to bootleg cassettes of Hong Kong rock music, and neck in public. To the conservatives, it all seemed part of a larger conspiracy to drain China's moral lifeblood, an echo of the centuries in which the country was subverted and dismembered by the imperialist powers.[2]

To keep economic reform on track, the Deng faction was usually willing to make concessions to the Maoists in the areas of politics and culture. As 1983 began, the reformers agreed to a campaign to "increase political thought work" and to build a "socialist spiritual civilization." In the usual Chinese fashion, the campaign was associated with numbers. In February, Premier Zhao Ziyang announced on television the formation of a National Five Stresses, Four Beauties, and Three Ardent Loves Committee. The stresses were on civilization, courtesy, sanitation, order, and ethics; the beauties were of mind, language, conduct, and the environment; and the ardent loves were for Motherland, Socialism, and the Communist Party. By autumn, the conservatives had appropriated the campaign. Under the direction of Propaganda Minister Deng Liqun, one of the most hard-line Maoists, it mutated into a shrill, puritanical drive to eradicate "spiritual pollution"—the code word for Western cultural influences.

But what the conservatives dreaded most was any reform of the political structure that might undermine the near-divine powers of Party officials. Chen Ziming saw this cadre system as the root of many of China's problems. With no separation between Party and state, there could be no distinction between public service and obedience to the Party line. Cadres were accountable to no one, and once appointed, they had lifetime tenure. They were notoriously inefficient. It was time for a complete overhaul of the system, Chen thought, and as early as 1981 he began to outline plans for a professional civil service, one in which people would compete for entry on their merits. He studied the writings of Lenin on government personnel systems and those of Sun Yat-sen. He examined how the Nationalists had selected their bureaucrats, and how the emperors had relied on the talent that came up through the Confucian examination system. He compared the modern civil services in Japan, Taiwan, and Western Europe.

The work at CASS kept Chen in the office only part-time; he filled the remaining hours with a dizzying range of activities. In 1982, he tried to get official backing for an "Employment Group" that would study the needs of the Chinese labor market, but the government turned him down.

More serious rebuffs followed, and Chen's involvement in *Beijing Spring* and the 1980 elections continued to count against him. In retrospect, the choices made in that heady time had been like passing over a set of points that determine which track a train will follow. Although the tracks may subsequently run close and parallel to each other, it is impossible to cross over. A good friend of Chen's from the days of Democracy Wall, a former Red Guard named Zhang Gang, was now influential in the reform circles around Premier Zhao Ziyang. Zhang told Chen that he admired his sincerity and agreed with his goals but felt he had been incautious between 1978 and 1980. "To let the rice cook," he told Chen, "it is necessary to keep the lid on tightly."

Zhang Gang, with Zhao Ziyang's encouragement, now proposed to take his research into previously forbidden areas of the economy—such as a free labor market and trading in stocks.

Zhang's efforts culminated in a ten-day conference in September 1984 at the mountain resort of Moganshan in Zhejiang Province. It was a landmark in the reform process, but it was strictly for young Party insiders; there was no room for someone who carried as much political baggage as Chen Ziming.

The Moganshan proposals were extremely influential. An elite group of young scholars emerged from the conference with their fortunes tied closely to those of Zhao Ziyang, who assigned the best and the brightest of them to set up a new think tank to be known as the Research Institute for the Reform of the Economic Structure (RIRES). RIRES, in turn, gave birth to a group known as the Beijing Young Economists Association, which Chen Ziming craved to join. As a favor to a friend, Zhang Gang included Chen's name on a list of prospective members and took it for approval to the home of Bao Tong, chief aide to Premier Zhao. Bao scanned the list and frowned when he came to Chen Ziming's name. "Too dangerous," he muttered, crossing it out. "This man is still under surveillance by State Security."

Zhang Gang told Chen not to be discouraged. "After a couple of years, the government will come to trust you," he said. "Just try to be patient." But the episode set the tone for Chen's future relations with the official reform faction.

In matters of policy, Chen wrote several years later, the government's cautious approach was understandable. But the Party made a major blunder in rejecting the offers of help from young thinkers like himself: "Those who were involved in theory and research should still have been encouraged to carry out bold explorations. At that point China might have followed the experience of Hungary or South Korea, and organized a segment of reformist intellectuals inside the Party and young thinkers *outside* the Party to conduct background research on plans for reform of the political structure. If that had happened, the hearts and minds of that group would not have been lost. These people might have been in the vanguard of reform; instead they were reduced to being mere spectators, floating outside the reform mainstream."[3]

In referring to the rejected young thinkers, Chen wrote "they," but what he really meant was "we." From that moment of government suspicion, Chen himself operated on the distant fringes of the mainstream. He became convinced that the only logical course for him was to build an independent power base. This meant finding his own sources of funding, of course, which was why he took on free-lance projects like the survey in Guantao County.

The official reformers believed that the government should plan how China's new financial markets would grow, but Chen disagreed: He thought they should grow naturally out of independent grass-roots initiatives from the private sector.[4] Chen was often heard advancing arguments like this in the corridors between sessions at officially sponsored conferences on economic reform. He did not cut a dashing figure, with his poorly cut Western suits, baggy cardigans, and round shoulders. But he spoke persuasively, and usually a small crowd gathered to listen.

His real heresies, however, were political, not economic. When he spoke of new grass-roots organizations, Chen was sketching out a vision much bolder than that of even the most radical Party reformers. He envisioned a future China in which independent economic activity would lead naturally to the creation of new social groups that would organize to express their own interests; in the end they would compete freely in the political arena. If any Eastern European theorists had been paying attention to Chen Ziming, what he proposed would surely have suggested a phrase used frequently at that time in Eastern Europe—"civil society."

Those who were buttonholed by Chen at these meetings came away with the distinct impression that they were being sized up as potential collaborators. Chen made it clear that he wanted to set up his own organization. He began by convening an informal group of about twenty friends to talk about the problems of democracy and human rights. Under the motto of "Social Justice," Chen's "salon" met once a month. He pointed out one day that no scientific data existed—only the fearful mutterings of the old guard—about how Deng's economic reforms affected public attitudes and behavior, especially among the young. Why not attempt an independent survey? As early as 1983 Chen had single-handedly embarked on an inquiry into the values of Chinese youth. This was an ambitious project, and it was done with no assistance and no funding. Chen simply sent out a questionnaire to friends and contacts across the country. Less than one thousand responses came back, and Chen, without a computer, was unable to analyze the results with any accuracy. Yet, despite the limits of its modest scale, it was probably the first privately conducted public opinion poll in the history of the People's Republic.

Chen's life was a ceaseless round of meetings and conferences and conversations, and a nucleus of loyal associates began to form around him. At the core of the group were veterans of *Beijing Spring*—people like his abrasive and ambitious friend Li Sheng-ping, who was now the editor of a journal called *Encyclopaedic Knowledge,* and the boyish-looking Min Qi, a former worker-peasant-soldier student who was jailed after April Fifth and had spent a number of years, like Chen, as a sent-down youth in Inner Mongolia. Although Min Qi was sensitive about his poor academic background, he now worked at CASS, where he was editor of the prestigious *Social Sciences in China.* But no one was more vital to the team Chen was putting together than his new wife, Wang Zhihong.

Wang Zhihong was a serious and enterprising young woman who had missed out on a formal college education. When the couple married in 1981, she was the branch secretary of the Communist Youth League in a small factory. They had known each other since their childhood in Shanghai, where they were neighbors. Indeed, their parents had planned since then that the pair should marry, and though the marriage turned out to be a happy one, Wang Zhihong complained that Chen, his mind always on his work, had made no serious effort to court her.

The young couple lived frugally. Wang left her factory job in order to work full-time on her husband's projects, which left both of them technically self-employed and therefore ineligible for housing, which in China is allocated by a person's work unit. The difficulty was resolved by Chen's parents, both of whom were entitled to separate housing as cadres, and the couple moved into the cramped eighth-floor apartment that went with Chen's father's job. The apartment was in the Haidian university district in the west of the city. Books were strewn and piled over every available surface in Chen and Wang's room. Chen's brother and sister-in-law occupied the second bedroom, and the two couples shared a microscopic living room. The tiny apartment always seemed to be full of people who would drop by in the evenings, grab a beer and some cold chicken or pig's feet from the refrigerator, and make plans late into the night.

By 1984, the scope of Chen's plans had grown. The ugly leftist campaign against "spiritual pollution" of the previous year had been stalled by Party politics. Rather than take on the fight directly, Party reformers had chosen to ignore it, knowing that it would flounder without their active support. Instead, the reform faction pressed ahead with its plans to remake the economy. In the countryside, the Party encouraged "socialist entrepreneurs," which were private businesses in all but name. And in 1984 it took the crucial step of extending the economic reforms into China's urban areas.

That autumn, the Third Plenum of the Twelfth Central Committee gave its formal blessing to small-scale private enterprise in the cities. Tens of thousands of people took this as a green light to register themselves as the managers of *getihu,* or household enterprises. China's city streets filled with news vendors and trinket sellers, along with storefront clothing retailers and bicycle-repair shops. Former Red Guards, ex-prisoners, and "waiting for work" youth all seemed to catch the small business bug.[5]

Wang Zhihong used her Communist Youth League credentials to set up a business with her husband and Li Shengping. They called it the Beijing Youth Books and Journals Distribution Agency. It was a modest undertaking, but it generated their first reliable income and allowed them to expand their other activities. Chen saw the agency as a small step toward building a "Chinese Enlightenment," a movement that he claimed would be comparable in its scope to the French Enlightenment or the Italian Renaissance.

Chen and his wife were not the only ones to use the *getihu* legislation in this way. In the mid-1980s, China succumbed to "book series fever," as young social scientists rushed to take advantage of the new climate of intellectual freedom. Chen Ziming's publications were among the most successful. Ever since his first readings of Montesquieu a decade earlier in his yurt in Inner Mongolia, Chen had developed his knowledge of the classics of Western political philosophy, and his first venture was to introduce these works to a Chinese audience. He found translators to turn out quick introductions in Chinese to the life and work of Rousseau, Montesquieu, and Nietzsche, and he founded the China Northern Publishing Company to issue them. Soon afterward, Chen and Li

Shengping issued a second series, their *Treasury of Twentieth Century Writing.*

In contrast to the traditional ambitions of a Beijing scholar, Chen downplayed his own role in these activities; he preferred to be what one friend called the "Minister of Behind the Scenes," using his organizational flair and fund-raising skills to help others. He cited the young Mao, who had never traveled abroad, as an example of the necessity of staying in China and bringing about change from the inside. "I'm already over thirty," he told a friend who was leaving to study in the United States, "and I don't think I have the energy to start studying a subject from the beginning; I don't think I could catch up. I have learned a great deal through my experience in China, and if I waste this experience it will be a loss to the country." The overseas students, he believed, would provide a pool of talent to make the reforms work; he would stay behind to pave the way for them.

While Chen Ziming built his private network, his old friend from *Beijing Spring,* Wang Juntao, embarked on a venture of a rather different sort, although also with the goal of "enlightenment." At the end of 1983 Wang was still cooling his heels in the mountains of Fangshan, bored and dispirited by his work as a low-level nuclear technician. He knew that hundreds of thousands of educated people were in the same predicament, stuck in jobs for which they had neither interest nor aptitude. The old system of forcible job assignments by the Party, conducted in the name of rational central planning, led in practice to a tremendous waste of human and technical resources. Many workplaces were grossly overstaffed. But Hu Yaobang's need, as General Secretary, to recruit skilled people for the Four Modernizations led to a relaxation of the old rules, and more and more workers negotiated their own terms of employment. Complaints about *danwei suoyouzhi*—the work-unit ownership system, which treated workers as chattel—were heard less often.

Ordinary Chinese also enjoyed much greater freedom to travel, and residence regulations became less restrictive. Until the early 1980s all travelers were obliged to show a letter of introduction from their all-powerful *danwei* to spend a night in a hotel. Now only a work permit was required, and in many small *getihu* hotels, even that was often unnecessary. The cheaper "hard-class" compartments of Chinese trains filled up with individual entrepreneurs, who were encouraged to travel on purchasing and sales trips, and with young people looking for new experiences in faraway places.

In this more open climate, Wang decided to move on and gain fresh experience. He talked constantly about the need to "temper" himself, as the knight-errant heroes of the *wuxia* novels had done. Not anywhere would do; he had to find somewhere special. He chose the city of Wuhan.

At twenty-five, Wang found himself in one of China's most interesting cities. Wuhan is a sprawling, gritty, industrial metropolis of three million people, but it also has the character and charm of a lively university community. Located on the main Guangzhou-to-Beijing railroad line at the confluence of the Yangzi and Han rivers, Wuhan has always been a political nerve center, a crossroads, an entry point for foreign ideas.

Wang found traces along the Yangzi waterfront of the foreign trading concessions that dominated the city in the nineteenth century: first the British, then the Germans, Russians, French, and Japanese. He also familiarized himself with Wuhan's long tradition of dissidence and revolt. Mao made his epic swim in the Yangzi here in 1965 to dramatize his message that China's youth should "swim against the tide." Two years later, Wuhan erupted in open warfare between militant Red Guards and the PLA. The city's factories had been a seedbed for Communist labor organizing ever since the bloody suppression of a strike by workers laying the Beijing-Wuhan railway in 1923. If any single Chinese enterprise symbolized the 1950s Maoist ideal of heavy industrial development, it was the Wuhan Steelworks, or *Wugang,* a virtual city within a city, with its own colleges, hospitals, and housing projects for the plant's 140,000 workers and their families. The term "*Wugang* worker" was synonymous with lifelong employment and cradle-to-grave welfare benefits—Mao's "iron rice bowl."

In 1984, the Communist Party selected Wuhan as one of the showcases for its new urban reforms.[6] Party cadres were to withdraw from economic matters and leave them in the hands of skilled factory managers and technical experts. Wage reform and contract labor would put the first dent in the iron rice bowl. Wang Juntao arrived in a city that was in ferment; after the boredom of Fangshan, it felt like a rebirth.

Wang found an immediate friend and ally in Zhang Kaiyuan, an open-minded reformist historian who was president of the Central China Normal College. Zhang allowed his energetic young visitor to stay temporarily in the college guest house. He enjoyed the company of the young Beijinger. Wang had an expansive, open-hearted manner, as well as the streetwise male charisma that the Chinese prize as *gemer yiqi,* the "buddy spirit" that encourages male bonding and joint enterprises.

In Wuhan, Wang found a diverse group of kindred spirits, from liberal young factory managers and teachers at the Central China Normal College to drinking companions from the Wuhan Steelworks. And when he had the itch to travel, the city proved an ideal geographical base. Wang hopped trains to all over southern and central China—to Guangzhou, to the new Special Economic Zone of Shenzhen on the border with Hong Kong, to remote towns and villages in the provinces of Hubei, Sichuan, and Fujian. Preceded by his reputation as a rebel, he lectured at universities and factories, taught physics classes at night schools, held training sessions for Party cadres, and turned up uninvited at conferences where he shocked his listeners with outspoken talk about democracy and free markets. Money was never a great concern; as long as he had enough for food and a place to spend the night, he seemed content. At times, though, even this eluded him, and he would bed down in an abandoned house or in the open air on a hayrick, scavenging his food from the leftovers in restaurants and turning up at odd hours to scrounge a meal from friends, looking destitute, dirty, and half-starved.

But Wang always returned to Wuhan, and in the winter of 1984 he planned for a long stay in the bustling city. By then the Hubei provincial authorities were paying close attention to Wang, and they asked the Beijing Public Security Bureau to forward a copy of its file on the magnetic young activist. Whenever the Hubei PSB saw signs of troublesome political activity, Wang Juntao seemed to be close to the epicenter. The bureau was particularly unhappy about his connection with the editors of *Youth Forum,* a new local magazine founded under the patronage of Hu Deping, the radical son of the Communist Party's General Secretary, Hu Yaobang. ("Fire a Salvo for Freedom!" was the title of a celebrated essay that Hu Deping wrote for *Youth Forum.*)[7]

Wang Juntao often invited his friends to gather in the evenings at the college guest house on top of Luoshan mountain. The cream of the Wuhan intelligentsia came to hear him hold forth: economists, college professors, entrepreneurs, and local leaders from the arts and media world. Huang Xiang, the renowned avant-garde poet, former Red Guard, and editor of *Enlightenment* during the Democracy Wall period, also moved to Wuhan and declaimed his heated emotional verses to the spellbound audiences of the guest house into the early hours of the morning.

It was at the Luoshan mountain guest house that the bright young scholars of the province announced the founding of an independent Hubei Young Theoreticians' Association. The Party leftists found this troubling enough in itself, but to make matters worse, intellectuals flocked to the inaugural meeting from the neighboring provinces of Hunan and Shaanxi, and even from as far away as Guangdong.

At the association's inaugural meeting, Wang outlined an ambitious strategy. With the help of some teachers from the Central China Normal College, he announced, he planned to open an institution that would be called the Jiangshan School of Continuing Education. Its goal would be the "enlightenment" of young workers and officials who had been prevented from completing their formal studies. In time, Wang went on, his school would become a full-fledged training center for cadres. It would be a "Whampoa for the 1980s," he boasted, alluding to the famous military academy where Sun Yat-sen had trained his cadets in the early 1920s. "Within a decade," Wang continued extravagantly, "more than half the cadres in the five provinces of Central China will be graduates of this new Whampoa."

With such radical speeches, Wang began to outstay his welcome in Wuhan. College security personnel called on Zhang Kaiyuan, the president of the college, to caution him about the activities of his young protégé. At first Zhang tried to brush them off. But when the Wuhan Public Security Bureau warned that Wang Juntao was a bad element, Zhang explained to Wang that he could not count on his protection forever.

In the fall of 1985, when a brief flurry of protests against "new Japanese economic imperialism" stirred the campus at Beida and fueled a revival of the Party's faltering campaign against bourgeois liberalization, the Wuhan PSB pulled Wang in for questioning. He denied all involvement in the events in the capital, and the bureau eventually released him without charge. But now, official interest in Wang once again reached the highest levels, and instructions to curtail his Wuhan activities were issued from the office of Premier Zhao Ziyang himself. Even the Party's liberals thought Wang was straying too far out of line, and they waited patiently for him to make a wrong move.

When the time came to elect a president for the new Jiangshan training school, Wang put his own name forward, which gave the Party the pretext it needed to take action. On the eve of the Jiangshan election, the Wuhan authorities curtly informed Wang that his activities were illegal; he did not have a residence permit for the Wuhan municipality.

It was 1986. Wuhan had been good to Wang Juntao. The interlude had lasted for more than two years and had left him with a lifetime's worth of friendships. But nothing more could be done there. "I figured out such a lot of arguments and ways to go on doing what I was doing," Wang told a friend afterward with a mixture of amusement and exasperation. "But one thing I didn't think of—and such a simple thing—my residence permit!"

Wang, however, had learned from the Deng Xiaoping years that no Party line lasted forever. He might have fallen victim to the conservatives' latest backlash, but the overall momentum of reform continued. In the spring of 1986, the Dengists announced a New Hundred Flowers movement that would liberate China's intellectuals from their shackles once and for all. Wang heard, moreover, that his friend Chen Ziming had something new in the works. It was definitely time to go back to Beijing.

6

Going Independent

Boss Chen seemed to be everywhere. He took advantage of the first full year of the urban reforms to expand his activities at a stunning rate. In the autumn of 1985 Chen invested the earnings from his publishing operations in a new venture: a pair of private correspondence colleges. One of these, which Chen placed in the hands of his unmarried sister, Chen Zihua, handled trade and finance; the other specialized in management and administration. Courses in accountancy and auditing might sound dry, but in China the concept was visionary.

Chen's schools offered the equivalent of a bachelor's degree by mail in three years. Students would pay 250 *yuan* a year, which most of them could have reimbursed by their work units. In return, they would receive a steady flow of books, cassettes, and test questions. Chen placed ads in the *China Youth News* and other papers; his target market was not Beijing, where more students were likely to be skeptical of the value of a mail-order diploma, but the provinces, where the prestige of a degree from Beijing and courses taught by faculty from the best colleges and graduate schools was much higher.

He recruited the best people he could find. Chen Zihua, who graduated from the Beijing College of Commerce, involved a number of her classmates as teachers. Others came through friends at the city's College of Finance and Trade. Wang Wei, a young economist friend of Chen Zihua's brother, moonlighted from his job at the Bank of China.

The correspondence colleges also attracted a growing number of well-qualified teachers in provincial areas. The work was well paid: For teaching one evening session a month, or a Saturday afternoon, the fee was three hundred *yuan,* which might be three times a teacher's monthly salary. Before long, Chen Ziming's schools had more than two dozen local branches and over two hundred thousand students. Many, perhaps a quarter of them, were young and middle-aged government officials whose education, like Chen's own, had been disrupted by the Cultural Revolution.

Chen was planting the seeds of an influential nationwide organization independent of Party control. Yet ironically, his main fear of government interference was less political than economic. From 1985 until 1988, when the government finally closed the correspondence colleges down, the income generated by the schools came to a staggering fifteen million *yuan,* of which ten million was clear profit. The Chen Ziming group grew rich well beyond the dreams of the "ten thousand *yuan* household" promoted by Deng Xiaoping as an incentive to enliven the economy.[1]

No one could suggest that Chen used the profits from his businesses to line his own pockets. He paid himself a salary of just 150 *yuan* a month, and he and Wang Zhihong continued to live as modestly as ever in their cramped apartment.

In the summer of 1986, Chen decided to take the next and most important step—the launch of a think tank of his own. After two years of hard work and careful saving, he had the money he needed. He also had the connections to form a solid team of professional associates. Chen knew that the moment had never been more propitious. This was the high-water mark of the entire reform decade. The battles against the old guard were far from over, but the Maoists' position finally seemed weakened. Indeed, the Party's internal struggles were now out in the open. Maoist veterans like Chen Yun, Peng Zhen, and Bo Yibo led the militant backlash against Deng Xiaoping's policies. At one time Chen Ziming and his friends at *Beijing Spring* had seen these men as a force for tradition and continuity that would salvage the Party after the "ten years of madness." Now Chen saw that they were the dead hand of the past, weighing like a stone on the best efforts of the present.

Deng had no desire for an open break with his fellow Long Marchers, but he finally lost patience with their obstructiveness. "The old ones occupy the toilets without taking shits," the eighty-year-old paramount leader groused. The attitude of the "White-Haired Cabal" only encouraged the inertia, or outright hostility, of the vast middle tier of bureaucrats whose privileges were now threatened by potential reform. During 1986 Deng came to believe that the only effective way of surmounting the old guard's resistance to change was to bring about a full "restructuring" of the political system.

The Party reformers also realized that the old men's continued ability to veto all talk of political reform was depriving the country of the oxygen of new ideas. Without new ideas, the reforms would die. It was time to break the veto power of the *laoren bang,* the "gang of oldies," once and for all. Deng himself gave the keynote speeches, resuscitating the failed "Gengshen spirit" of 1980, and Hu Yaobang orchestrated the attack, with allies from his old "Communist Youth League clique" acting as his point men. His protégé Hu Qili led the charge. The "other Hu" told intellectuals in Shanghai that the Party intended to foster a new atmosphere of "tolerance, harmony, camaraderie and trust." On another occasion he remarked, "We cannot look upon young men with ideas as bearers of heresy and evil thoughts."

But perhaps the most outspoken of Hu Yaobang's associates was the Party's new propaganda chief, the fifty-five-year-old Zhu Houze, a man with whom Chen Ziming was to have dangerous dealings just a few years later. Zhu rose through the Party ranks in Guizhou Province. He was a mild-looking fellow, but a shrewd politician. In the year following his appointment, he succeeded in getting the better of his redoubtable hard-line predecessor, Deng Liqun. Zhu was the only senior cadre who dared to tackle the thorny issue of the degree to which China should risk what the leftists called "wholesale Westernization." He told his colleagues, "No one single country or people can monopolize all the best fruits of thought, culture, and technology." Thinly coded, this meant borrowing not only the money and scientific know-how of the West, but elements of its political system, too. Yet Zhu, who knew that the Maoists were most dangerous when roused, also had a cautious side, which expressed itself in folksy metaphors. "We must not use ginseng or deer horn to 'radically push' reform," he told his staff. "Nor must we use ox bezoar to provoke 'diarrhea.' What we need is 'gradual invigoration.' "[2]

Chen Ziming respected officials like Zhu Houze and the two Hus. He felt that if Hu Qili's comment about "young men with ideas" was meant in earnest, then surely it applied to people like himself. Perhaps the Party was finally coming around to his way of thinking. Government and intellectuals, Chen would say as he stood in a courtroom in 1991, charged with sedition, "must develop independently, recognize the common areas in their goals, each take on their particular responsibilities, each give the other sufficient weight, check each other but not clash, cooperate but not meld together."

As the Sixth Plenum, scheduled for September, drew near, Chen followed the machinations of the Party's warring factions with rapt attention. Every plenum seemed crucial, but this one, Chen thought, would be a genuine watershed. A month before the plenum began, on a sultry day in August, a sign with large black characters appeared over the rear entrance of a nondescript gray building just across the road from the imposing bulk of the Military Museum of the Chinese People's Revolution—Chen Ziming finally had a think tank of his own. Located in the basement of the Second Dragon Road Hospital for Rectal and Intestinal Medicine, its beginnings could not have been more inauspicious. What its first members recall most strongly is the overpowering odor of formaldehyde, which made them wrinkle their noses as they made their way to the small, damp basement room where the inaugural board meeting was held.

Chen Ziming addressed those assembled in the solemn and rather ponderous style that sometimes marked his public utterances: "Today, the few people gathered here are prepared to make sacrifices for this work. Although each person has his or her own reasons for feeling concerned about the future, China's political situation demands that we have some people to do the job of starting out, and so I hereby formally announce the establishment of the China Political and Administrative Sciences Research Institute." "The name," he added, "is temporary." The group around the table, many of whom had left secure jobs to embark on this quixotic new venture with Chen, looked at each other in silence.

For the next six months, the staff of the new Institute dodged the nurses, the gurneys, and the hospital smells as they ran up and down the stairs from the meeting rooms in the basement to the editorial offices and computer center that they installed on the second floor. They made plans for a new book series on twentieth-century political thought and started a bimonthly journal called *Political and Administrative Studies,* which was professionally typeset but distributed through unofficial channels.

At the core of Chen's new Institute were the veterans of earlier democratic struggles. Li Shengping, who had known Chen since 1976, lent his management skills, although his contentious personality was often a source of friction. Former Red Guard Min Qi took on editorial responsibilities. There was also an influx of new talent: a group of younger intellectuals from the Chinese Academy of Social Sciences and a number of Wang Juntao's friends from Wuhan. And, most important, there was Wang Juntao himself.

Wang returned from Wuhan in September to join Chen's new enterprise. He agreed to do menial clerical jobs at first, folding letterhead into envelopes for a salary of just seventy-five *yuan* ($25) a month. Same old Wang, his friend Chen smiled: no interest in material things. At the same time, Chen had less altruistic motives. Wang's charisma was an attractive asset, but it was also a little threatening, and Chen wanted to keep a close eye on him until the Institute was firmly on its feet. As in the days of *Beijing Spring,* it was the relationship between the two men that set the tone for the new Institute's expanding range of activities. Chen commanded respect and loyalty in his staff, and Wang inspired affection and trust. He seemed more mature, more thoughtful since his wanderings in Wuhan and the south; but his passion for the enlightenment of others was undiminished, and the spiritual side of his personality was, if anything, more pronounced.

They still struck new acquaintances as an unlikely pair, the reserved older man and the more youthful extrovert. Their friendship had never been based on the exchange of intimate confidences. What bound them together was their vision of a future China. Wang had a wide circle of other male friends, and they saw more of his gregarious side: the practical jokes, the sudden outbursts of poetry, the tears that came easily when something moved him. Chen was simply too private a personality, and Wang respected the limits. Besides, both of them were stretched to the limit by the demands of their work. Chen was bitterly disappointed when Wang Zhihong suffered the first of a series of miscarriages, but he kept his emotions to himself and went about his business at the Institute almost as if nothing had happened.

Once started, no job undertaken by the Institute was left unfinished. Chen gave the same dogged attention to the smallest details that he gave to the grandest plan. By the same token, it was not unusual for colleagues to be awakened in the middle of the night by Chen's knock, as he sought input on some pressing business matter. The tales abounded of Chen's nocturnal rambles. On one occasion, he spent the entire day and most of the night visiting Jiang Hong, an old associate who taught at a college run by the Ministry of State Security. As Chen's tinny Eastern European car drew up to the locked exit gate of the school at three in the morning, the security guard stopped him. "Why are you leaving so late?" the man demanded. "What was the purpose of your visit?"

"I'm sorry, but that's none of your business," Chen answered politely.

"But I have to make a report on everyone who comes and goes and then get you to sign it."

Chen flatly refused. The guard insisted.

"No!" Chen repeated. "What I do here is my own private affair. I insist on my rights."

And Chen sat there stubbornly in his car until morning came and the gates opened again.

Some found it strange that a liberal reformer like Chen had for a close friend a man like Jiang Hong, who worked for the Ministry of State Security. But such a connection was typical of Chen's approach. The man he hired as editor of *Political and Administrative Studies,* for example, was a researcher at the Higher Party School, where cadres are trained. Although Chen was badly rebuffed by the Party in 1979, and again in 1984, he still saw his work as vital to the efforts of the Party reformists, and he valued every insider connection that he could make.

Developing these connections was never easy. The *ti nei,* internal, circle of the official reformers was a closed world, jealous of its privileges and its access to power. The *ti nei* reformers had special clearance to pass through the ornate gateway of the Zhongnanhai compound for cozy chats with Premier Zhao Ziyang. Chen Ziming and Wang Juntao, meanwhile, lived in the *ti wai,* external, world. What Chen found so galling was that the *ti nei* and the *ti wai* intellectuals had common roots. They were all part of the Lost Generation, formed in the crucible of the Cultural Revolution. After the fall of the Gang of Four in 1976, they shared a commitment to reform, a love of scholarship. They were divided neither by age nor by ideology. There were people inside the system who believed in radical political change, just as there were cautious people in the *ti wai* world who thought that economic reform was everything.

But a distinction existed nonetheless, and one that was worn like a caste mark on the forehead. In part, it was political stigma that kept Chen Ziming and Wang Juntao locked outside the walls of Zhongnanhai. While they had edited *Beijing Spring,* contested the 1980 elections, and amassed fat files with the PSB, others had kept their noses clean. And in part, it was Wang and Chen's desire to have influence, without surrendering their independence, that kept them outsiders. In the end, Chen Ziming often said, it was more important to be a good academic than a successful bureaucrat.

One Party institution obsessed Chen: the Research Institute for the Reform of the Economic Structure (RIRES). Founded in 1984, RIRES was the very incarnation of the *ti nei* think tank.[3] It was here that the young Turks were concentrated; others, less complimentary, called them "Zhao Ziyang's stormtroopers," or his "little fleet." To the hard-line leftists, RIRES was the "headquarters for closet capitalists." Directed by Chen Yizi, a middle-aged economist, the seventy-five-member staff of RIRES was top-heavy with former sent-down youth and economics students from the Beida entry class of 1978.[4] They had concluded from their harsh experiences in the poorest rural villages that nothing was more important than what Deng and Zhao called "the development of the productive forces." They believed that if they could make the economy grow and boost gross national product, everything else would follow. Chen Yizi's team was giddy with the aura of power. A research paper written by a thirty-year-old graduate student could land on the desk of Zhao Ziyang himself. With the great man's comments scribbled in the margins, it could even become official policy overnight.

RIRES policy proposals were channeled to Premier Zhao through Bao Tong, his chief aide, a sprightly man of fifty-three. In his short-sleeved cotton-knit shirts and Western slacks, he looked as if he had just come from the tennis court. In fact, he had grown up in a poor family in Shanghai and at sixteen was a core member of the Party underground at the time of Liberation.

The young Bao ascended quickly through the Party's ranks before being arrested in the early purges of the Cultural Revolution.[5] He returned to Zhongnanhai in glory in 1978 as a personal favorite of Deng Xiaoping's and drafted the famous speech of that year in which the New Helmsman described intellectuals as "mental laborers," and therefore worthy of the same respect as the working class. In 1980, Deng himself appointed Bao Tong to be Zhao Ziyang's personal secretary. From then on, Bao remained on the cutting edge of the debate about political reform. China's central problem, he saw clearly, was the overconcentration of power. Bao believed that the Communist Party had been created to fight a war, not to run a country. Until it lost its wartime mentality, China could never hope to be a modern, democratic society.

Bao Tong and RIRES were very active in the wake of the Sixth Plenum in September 1986. The result of the plenum's session was, as usual, a hard-fought compromise. Chinese Communist Party politics was still a little like a wrestling match in which neither contestant has the strength to force a fall. The old guard managed to keep political reform off the immediate formal agenda, and Deng warned that reform would take "at least a decade" and that it would be "twenty to thirty years before national elections." Yet the implication was that reform would continue.

The reformers still felt that they were on shaky ground in a number of important areas. How were they to assess public sentiment, for example? What impact were the economic reforms having at the grass-roots level? Although the Maoists had always believed that the Party and the people were one, RIRES knew that in a complex modern society, a more sophisticated yardstick was required to measure people's true feelings. It began to look closely at the utility of Western-style public opinion surveys.

One of the RIRES researchers had a friend from People's University who was acquainted with this unfamiliar field. It was Bai Hua, the dynamic young communications expert who had been so appalled by Chen Ziming's behavior in the Guantao County library. Bai Hua did not especially care for the atmosphere at RIRES and wondered if its research was only telling Zhao Ziyang what he wanted to hear. Also, she did not like what she heard about the Institute's director, Chen Yizi. He was a brilliant economist, everyone agreed. But as a boss, he was reputed to be something of a dictator.

As a humble contract employee, Bai Hua had no particular need to deal with Chen Yizi. Beginning in 1985, she worked on a number of short-term projects for RIRES. At first her reports encouraged her new employers. In the countryside, she found widespread satisfaction with China's new prosperity. But by the summer of 1986 she heard more doubts expressed, most of them about rising prices. The peasants she interviewed complained that the government had not increased the purchase price for their rice; the price of everything they needed to buy in town, however, had risen sharply. Fertilizer and seeds were the biggest problem, they said, and the two-track economy made matters worse. What were they supposed to do: buy from the state, where the prices were controlled but the supply erratic, or from private traders, who always seemed to be able to get hold of what was required but charged an arm and a leg for it? "I spent 2,000 *yuan* on my crops last year," a typical farmer told her, "and then made only 2,050 *yuan* selling them. For a whole year's work I earned almost nothing."

In October 1986, Bai Hua persuaded RIRES to underwrite a field trip to document how peasants got their news of the outside world. How many had television sets? How many listened to the radio? Much of her earlier research had taken her to the southern parts of China; this time she settled on the desert area near Lanzhou, in the north-central province of Gansu, at the edge of the desolate plateaus of Qinghai—China's Siberia. She was secretly delighted when RIRES approved the trip, since it gave her a chance to visit the celebrated sandstone caves of Dunhuang, with their elaborate murals and painted statues of the Buddha and his bodhisattvas. As she was preparing to leave, a friend called. He knew an interesting young man who might like to accompany Bai Hua on her travels. Why didn't she call him? His name was Wang Juntao.

Bai Hua agreed to meet him outside the main entrance to the Beijing railway station at nine in the morning. Wang said that it would be easy to recognize him; he would be holding up a book. Despite the usual dense crowds, Bai Hua had no trouble picking out the tall, slightly theatrical figure. He held the book thrust out in front of his chest, and he was wrapped up against the chilly morning air in an army greatcoat of his father's, with the insignia of a general. "Get into the train," he said. "I'll meet you on board." And he turned his attention to the quiet, delicate young woman next to him. Bai Hua installed herself in the hard-class sleeper car and waited. As the train started to pull out of the station, Wang threw himself into the compartment, waving a last good-bye to the woman on the platform. "That was Hou Xiaotian," he explained breathlessly. "She's a graduate student at the Beijing College of Economics. We met this summer when I got back from Wuhan. I'm going to marry her. Can I have the bottom bunk, please? I'd like the light to read by. I have this fascinating new book on civil society. It's just been translated. I'm thinking of writing a book on the subject myself."

The trip to Lanzhou took two days and one night, and Bai and Wang argued most of the way. Wang held some strong ideas about public opinion, and he was less than impressed by the polls that Bai Hua was conducting for RIRES. It was impossible to take the pulse of the Chinese people so scientifically, he said. Besides, the findings of an official think tank would inevitably be colored by the pressures of Party politics. He outlined a different approach. A friend of his ran some correspondence schools—Chen Ziming, perhaps she had heard of him? "Yes," Bai Hua answered drily. "We met once." Wang explained that the idea was to use the students enrolled in these schools as a source of information. The young cadres in particular would be important backers of any future political reform, and Wang thought it made sense to win their loyalty and try to guide them in the most liberal direction possible. One way to do this, he suggested, was to invite selected individuals to take part in an informal program of public opinion research. His proposal was simple: Send a letter to the selected "social investigators" with a questionnaire about China's social situation, and pay them a modest fee for their cooperation. "China is like a sick person," he had once remarked to a friend, "and we should treat the whole country with acupuncture, as if it were a body. If we want to find out what disease China is suffering from, we need to test a thousand different acupuncture points before we decide on the cure that is needed."

Bai Hua detected a strong hint of elitism in all this—ironic, since the *ti wai* intellectuals often criticized RIRES for its own top-down approach to reform. "Let me tell you about a poll we did last year," Wang went on, as the train rolled across the North China plain. "One of the questions was 'What is democracy?' Fourteen percent of the respondents chose the answer 'Democracy means the masters acting on the people's behalf.' How can you talk about extending political rights when people think like that? How can you ask the country's leaders to follow opinions like those?"

"Of course," Bai Hua answered, "democracy has to have a price. You have to teach people, give them more time to understand what democracy is. You have to enlighten them."

"Yes, yes! That's right," Wang agreed. "The whole point is *qimeng,* enlightenment. That's what my friend Chen Ziming and I have been trying to do for years! But I'm not sure your kind of research will be useful. It just sounds like an intellectual trying to do things in a scientific way. I just want to go to the countryside and talk to the people."

They visited three different villages in Gansu Province, two obstinate people arguing their approaches to reform back and forth. The villages were desolate, small settlements of mud houses with a few more recent buildings of brick construction. A constant harsh wind off the desert coated everything with a thin layer of yellow dust. Bai Hua asked the village cadres to distribute her written questionnaires, but in many cases had to abandon the attempt, because too many of the peasants were illiterate.

They stayed in the home of the richest peasant in one of the villages. The man was in his sixties, a true old-fashioned patriarch, and he talked at length about the emperors. Wang Juntao asked him if he knew about Chairman Mao. "Of course I do," the old man answered with feeling. "He was the emperor. He was a great emperor, he did a lot for our people. He knew how to control the country. And this new emperor, Deng, he seems OK too. Everything the government says, I agree with. Reform—good! Very good!"

Later Wang took Bai Hua aside. "You see what I mean?" he insisted. "That's the Chinese people for you. What do you say about political reform now? Of course I believe that people should be given more rights, but at present they're at too low a level—they simply trust whoever is in authority. If we gave these people the vote tomorrow, they would simply agree to surrender all their rights to the emperor." At the end of the trip, they shook hands at Beijing station, agreeing to disagree. "But let's keep in touch," Wang said as he waved good-bye.

Back in the city, Wang threw himself into the busy schedule of the new Institute. Almost every week, it seemed, there was another spirited conference—more than a dozen in the final three months of 1986. There were sessions on the current state of research in sociology; historians gathered to discuss Marx's writings on anthropology, which had just been published in Chinese; and intellectuals met to consider their role in Chinese history and their relations to the present regime. More than once, there were seminars on administrative law, a hot topic in 1986. Of all the areas of legal reform, administrative law was the most controversial, for it dealt with the rights of the individual in relation to the state.[6] In the relaxed atmosphere of that autumn, Ziming's new enterprise enjoyed good fortune. The Institute's doings were written up regularly in the widely read journal of the Beijing Academy of Social Sciences.

But as before, the euphoria was short-lived, and after a symposium in November Chen learned that he had tacked too close to the wind. The topic of the symposium was the military: Why did the military present such an obstacle in societies attempting to make the transition from dictatorship to democracy? And why did the armed forces step in so often to abort reform in the Third World? Like anyone else who had "grown up in the big storm," Chen appreciated that reform should not move too fast lest it lead to chaos. But at the same time, he knew it was essential to block any effort by the Maoists to turn back the clock. His mistake was to believe that the Institute could hold an open discussion on the role of the People's Liberation Army.

The cosponsor of the November conference was a group of young teachers from the Central Military Academy. A staff researcher from the army's General Political Department chaired the meeting; among the others attending was the head of the Marxism-Leninism–Mao Zedong Thought Research Institute of the PLA's Political Academy—a senior colleague of Wang Juntao's father. A reporter from the *PLA Daily* covered the meeting. So did the military affairs correspondent of the *China Youth News*.

Military coups happen, the outspoken young correspondent exclaimed, when reforms are half-hearted. The only answer is to place the armed forces under strict civilian authority. He took the even more dangerous step of naming names: Control of the PLA had to be wrested away from people like the eighty-three-year-old Yang Shangkun, the former secret police operative who headed the Party's Military Affairs Commission, and his deputy, the seventy-three-year-old Long March veteran Yu Qiuli. The journalist argued that men like Hu Yaobang should be in charge instead. The army men who were present listened but said nothing. When the conference ended, they left quietly and wrote up their notes in a report to the Political Department of the PLA.

Without knowing it, the young man had blundered into a mine field. The commanders of the PLA saw themselves as Mao's truest heirs, yet no one's budgets and privileges were cut more severely by the Deng Xiaoping reforms. Now Deng proposed to retire as head of the Central Military Commission and install the iconoclastic Hu Yaobang as his successor. The generals would never have attacked Deng personally; as the veteran of the Second Field Army—*Liu Deng Da Jun*—he was still above reproach in military circles. But Hu Yaobang was another matter.

The PLA had grumbled about the ebullient General Secretary ever since his famous indiscretion a year before. A visiting Hong Kong journalist had asked Hu about the relationship between military and political affairs. Hu made no response. In the leadership's world of nuances, euphemisms, and coded signals, the conservatives interpreted his silence as an aggressive act. Now, in December 1986, the generals confronted Hu Yaobang directly. They told him that he was "weak and ambivalent" in defending the Four Cardinal Principles.

The conservatives were infuriated by news of the seminar at the China Political and Administrative Sciences Research Institute. They ordered a thorough internal investigation, and all the PLA participants were sternly reprimanded. Although Chen Ziming could hardly be held responsible for every word that was said around his conference table, the leftists' view of the matter was cut and dried: Here was a group of former political offenders, advocates of bourgeois liberalization, encouraging subversive talk about the most sacred institution of the Chinese Revolution. Bo Yibo, one of the most powerful of the elders, passed the angry word down through internal Party channels: He considered Chen Ziming to be a bad element, another black mark in his file.

Amidst the flap over the PLA conference, Wang Juntao had his mind on other things. One snowy night at the beginning of December, Wang and Hou Xiaotian turned up unannounced at a Beida dormitory room. They had come to visit Zhang Lun, a gangly twenty-four-year-old sociology student. Zhang Lun was an amiable young man who had spent a precarious childhood in the countryside, the casualty of a "bad class background." He had worked in a state chemical factory and studied briefly at Shenyang University, near the border with North Korea. In 1980, even in distant Shenyang, news reached Zhang of the exploits of a Beida student named Wang Juntao. From then on, he had dreamed of going to Beida. Now he was there, and Wang Juntao was his close friend.

"Hello," said Zhang Lun with surprise as he opened the door. "What are you two doing out here on a night like this?"

"We've got news," Wang replied. "We're getting married."

It had been a whirlwind romance. Hou was twenty-six, the youngest daughter of a Party secretary in the government bureaucracy. She had met Wang on his return from Wuhan in September at a party at his parents' house, and he had proposed within the month. Like Wang's other friends, Zhang Lun was stunned by the news. He was convinced Wang would never marry and settle down.

"Keep the news to yourself," Hou Xiaotian implored Zhang Lun. "You know I haven't graduated yet from the College of Economics, and I really want to avoid any pressure from my professors."

In China, the all-powerful *danwei* must approve the choice of wedding partners. Since neither Wang nor Hou was officially attached to a work unit, Chen Ziming agreed that the Institute would issue the necessary letters of introduction to the Beijing authorities. The couple married in a simple civil ceremony on December 4, dressed in formal Western wedding clothes that they rented from a photo studio.

It was Bi Yimin, one of Wang's closest friends, who arranged to throw the wedding party. Bi, another survivor of both the Tiananmen Incident and Democracy Wall, knew exactly the kind of gathering that would please his old friend. He called as many veterans of the movement as he could find, and more than two dozen showed up for the celebration, which was held in a spartan meeting room at the chemical factory where Bi worked. Among the guests were several whom Wang had not seen since the days of *Beijing Spring*.

It was a sentimental reunion. "These last ten years seem to have gone by in a flash," someone said. "We were young then, and now we're all approaching middle age." A second voice asked if anyone had gone to Tiananmen Square in April for the tenth anniversary of the events of 1976. "I did," said another. "I went to the square, and walked around, and remembered our struggle." The room was very quiet. Wang broke the silence. "I don't like to go out to Beida much anymore. When I do, I think of all that happened there and I realize that it's all in the past." There seemed to be too many memories in the room.

Everyone insisted that Wang Juntao make a speech. He cleared his throat. "Thank you for giving us such a wonderful party," he began. "I have been to many places and done many things. But there is not much that I truly consider worth remembering. The one thing that I value is that I have so many friends. In these times of modernization, as people's relations with each other become more and more indifferent, I value you all the more." He stopped. "I won't say anything more, but I'll sing."

He chose the *Song of Going Beyond the Northern Border,* an old melody that combined heroism and sadness.

> Please listen to my song of going beyond the northern border
> With its forgotten words and ancient phrases.
> Please let the song call gently out
> For the beautiful mountains and rivers I dream of
> For the landscape outside the Great Wall.
> Who says that the melody for going beyond the borders is too sad?
> If you don't wish to hear it,
> You are not the yearning kind.
>
> Today we sing and sing again
> Of where the grasslands gleam gold for a thousand li,

Of where the Yellow River's waves run as high as the sky,
Of where Yin Mountain lies outside the Great Wall.
Heroes ride bravely out, not knowing when they may return
In glory to their hometowns.

Everyone agreed they had never heard it sung so movingly. Zhang Lun got to his feet, a little unsteadily, to propose a toast. "I regret so much," he began, "that at the time of the April Fifth movement I was still at my home in the northeast, and that history did not give me the opportunity to stand together with you in the struggle. I hope that history will give us another chance." He raised a tall bottle of beer and drained it in one gulp.

When the partygoers awoke the next morning, it was to the news that the students of the Hefei University of Science and Technology had taken to the streets.

7

Cracks in the Fabric

When news of the Hefei protests reached them, Chen Ziming and Wang Juntao must surely have been struck by the curious way history repeats itself. In 1980, the Party's announcement of the Gengshen reforms produced an unintended consequence: victory for democratic candidates in the election campaigns that swept the Beijing campuses and threatened to catch fire in China's factories. Now, the Sixth Plenum's promises of political reform had set off a wave of campus protests that no one (least of all, perhaps, the students themselves) seemed to anticipate. Between 1978 and 1980, Chen and Wang had seen their campaign actions as a conscious effort to bolster Deng Xiaoping's faction in the Party's internal struggle. The current crop of student demonstrators carried banners praising Deng, but he was actually incidental to their protests.

The spark this time was not struck in Beijing, but more than five hundred miles to the south, in the obscure capital city of impoverished Anhui Province. The Hefei students took their inspiration from their university's president, the fifty-year-old astrophysicist Fang Lizhi. They idolized Fang for his wit, candor, and irreverence, and for his willingness to attack individual conservatives by name. In a speech on December 4, 1986, Wang Juntao's wedding day, Fang told his students that whatever Party theorists said to the contrary, "Democracy is not a favor bestowed from above; it should be won through people's own efforts." Even so, he had not intended this rhetoric to cause his listeners to demonstrate in the streets, and he was apprehensive when that was what they did.[1]

This generation was too young to remember the Cultural Revolution. It had not come to adulthood, like Wang Juntao or Chen Ziming, with a vision of Deng Xiaoping as the man who would put China back on track. Instead, it had spent its adolescence exposed to the consequences of his reforms. Wang and Chen, entering university in 1978, saw their access to higher education as a thrilling break from the past. The students of 1986 saw it merely as their right. They were bored and alienated; they suffered from what was known as the "Three Beliefs Crisis": lack of belief in the Party, lack of confidence in socialism, lack of trust in cadres. In the vacuum left by the collapsing credibility of the Communist Party, they gravitated to voices like Fang Lizhi's. They tended to idealize the West.

The protests spread rapidly to more than a dozen cities, but the Party grew most alarmed when they reached the industrial powerhouse of Shanghai and workers there threatened to join in. Here again was the threat of the "Polish disease." At first, indecision seemed to paralyze the Party. Then, at an emergency meeting of the leadership on December 26, Deng appeared to decide that stern action was needed. Any further delay would place unacceptable strains on the coalition that he needed for his economic reform program. To the satisfaction of the veteran cadres, Deng began to use the familiar language of conspiracy. The protests might have had noble motives in the beginning, he declared, but they had now been corrupted by "a handful of vicious elements."

Four days later, Deng called Hu Yaobang and Zhao Ziyang to his home. He told them that nothing was more important than Party unity and discipline. "If our country were plunged into disorder," he said, "and our nation reduced to a heap of loose sand, how could we ever prosper? The reason the imperialists were able to bully us in the past was precisely that we were a heap of loose sand." The phrase was one that Sun Yat-sen had used. China should learn from the correct example of the Polish Communists, he went on. Had they not crushed Solidarity? Fang Lizhi's conduct was "outrageous," Deng stormed. The man should be kicked out of the Party. Never mind that such an action would risk bad press abroad. After all, "Didn't we arrest Wei Jingsheng? Did that hurt China's image? When we imprisoned Wei, the West did nothing."

On New Year's Day, Mayor Chen Xitong took to the pages of the *Beijing Daily* with dark mutterings, drawn straight from the 1960s, about "class enemies" and "elements hostile to socialism." This apparently pushed the students of the capital over the edge. They responded by publicly burning copies of the detested hard-line paper. Eloquent though this was as an expression of their anger, as a political symbol it could not have been more inflammatory. Here, to orthodox Maoists and Dengist reformers alike, was the chaos of the Cultural Revolution all over again, and in the very heart of the capital.

Yet within a matter of days, the protests sputtered into silence as the students' minds turned instead to their coming exams. However, the renewed leftist campaign against bourgeois liberalization demanded its quota of victims. The students themselves would not be touched. In Shanghai, which the students brought to a standstill, the only arrests were of workers, who were vilified as the "sinister manipulators" of the impressionable young. Also dealt with sternly were those who carried the virus of "wholesale Westernization." Fang Lizhi, to no one's surprise, was expelled from the Party.

Above all, the Party had to deal with the enemy within. The liberal Zhu Houze, with his talk of ginseng, deer horn, and "democratic pluralism," lost his job as propaganda chief. And on January 16, 1987, an "expanded session" of the Politburo, packed with veteran conservatives, informed Hu Yaobang that he had decided to retire. The elders did not actually suggest that Hu was behind the student unrest, merely that he had "condoned" it. Zhao Ziyang, who was soon to be appointed General Secretary, explained that Hu had, in fact, been seriously at odds with Deng for years over the issue of bourgeois liberalization. This was an astute move by Zhao to protect his patron's reputation, not to mention to advance his own cause. But it was also the truth. Deng's striking flexibility in economic matters had never encompassed any tolerance of threats to the "leading role" of the Party.

The fall of Hu Yaobang had less of an impact at the Institute than some might have expected. In fact, it seems the subject came up only once at an Institute meeting. Chen Ziming commented that the removal of Hu, the main sponsor of intellectual freedom since

1978, was a depressing turn of events. But Min Qi, the former Red Guard, quickly jumped in to offer some cautionary words. "We have to learn our lessons from the past," he advised. "We shouldn't get involved in the Party's internal struggles." Chen Ziming was the first to agree, and no more was said about the matter.

Chen wisely had not tied the fortunes of his new think tank to any individual or faction. All its research, he stressed repeatedly—the conferences, the books, the opinion polls—was geared toward the long-term goal of reform, not to any immediate political payoff. Besides, Hu Yaobang accepted his downfall so meekly that there could be no question of rallying to his defense now. As the Party quickly pointed out, the disgrace of one General Secretary did not mean the end of the reforms. The conservatives still had no alternative economic strategy of their own; Zhao Ziyang might be a more cautious figure than the fiery Hu Yaobang, but he was still in favor, still in place.

The Institute made no attempt to involve itself in the December protests. Although Wang and Chen had graduated only four years earlier, they felt no common bond with the new generation of students. Their ideas seemed vague, their organizing amateurish. To Chen and Wang, the burning of *Beijing Daily* seemed a perfect symbol of the students' immaturity. If you poked a stick at the snake, how could you be surprised when it bit you?

Chen's Institute also had to cope with growing pains of its own. With its operations barely four months old, it was still smarting from the PLA affair. Worst of all, there was a festering dispute between Chen and his old friend and colleague, Li Shengping. There seemed to be fault on both sides: Li, most agreed, was hot-tempered and self-seeking. But Li had complaints about Chen's management style that others echoed. Li said it was unfair that Chen had placed his sister in charge of the trade and finance college and then given her husband control over the finances of the two correspondence schools without so much as a word to any of his colleagues. Was he bent on creating an old-fashioned Chinese family business empire? Min Qi, for one, thought Li had a point.

The combination of politics and personality had a corrosive effect. In an atmosphere of conspiracy and back stabbing, several all-night meetings were held to resolve the crisis. People took to sleeping over in the hospital basement. In the end, Chen and Li called upon the affable Wang Juntao to mediate their quarrel. Wang was reluctant to get involved. "But they both seem to trust me," he told Bai Hua, "so I suppose I have to try and help."

There was also the matter of Deng Pufang, the patriarch's crippled son. Like Wang Juntao, Deng Pufang had been a promising physics student at Beida—until 1969, when the Red Guards shoved him into an abandoned dormitory room, locked him in a closet, and dragged him out for repeated beatings in an attempt to make him confess that his father was a traitor and a capitalist roader. Eventually, semiconscious, Deng Pufang fell, or was pushed, from a fourth-floor window. The fall left him a paraplegic, confined to a wheelchair for the rest of his life.[2]

In the era of reform, Pufang became a notable political actor. He set up the China Welfare Fund for the Handicapped, whose charitable work countered thousands of years of Chinese cultural hostility to those with physical disabilities. He also headed the giant official trading company known as Kanghua Enterprises, and by late 1986, when Chen Ziming opened his new Institute, Pufang had achieved ministerial rank. The *taizi dang,* the "party of princes," had no more elevated member.

Pufang was much more radical than his father and became a noted patron of the most outspoken reformers, both inside and outside the Party. He was also his father's favorite. It was said that the patriarch had a liberal ear on one side and a conservative one on the other; Deng Pufang had his father's liberal ear.

Chen Ziming often beat a path to Deng Pufang's door. This practice was in line with Chinese tradition: It was customary for the intelligentsia to seek patrons in high places. Chen's Huaxia Publishing Company was officially registered under the auspices of the younger Deng's fund for the handicapped. On the title page of each volume in the book series on Western political thought appeared a list of all the leading names on the Huaxia editorial advisory committee; Deng Pufang's name was at the top of the list.

Access to Pufang was one of the main issues of contention between Chen and Li Shengping. It was clear to everyone that Li was jealous of Chen's successes, although people were puzzled about what he hoped to achieve by provoking an open split. Did Li want to squeeze Chen out of the new Institute and seize control himself? Wang Juntao speculated that Li was trying to create a breakaway group. In the end, it seemed that Wang was closer to the mark. Li finally went his own way early in 1987, taking most of the Institute's junior staff with him. Eventually he set up an institute of his own. But the key figures, those with the greatest talent and the thickest files with the Public Security Bureau, remained with Chen.[3]

For reasons that are unclear, Deng Pufang let it be known that his sympathies lay with Li, which was one more blow to any hopes Chen had of crossing over into the *ti nei* world of the official reformers. As much from necessity as for philosophical reasons, he went on working at the margins of the system.

One day in May 1987, Bi Yimin came into Chen's office and told him that he had found a three-year lease on new quarters for the Institute—not as centrally located, perhaps, but spacious, cheerful, and above all cheap. Money was always an issue with Chen. His frugality was legendary. Although he was willing to sink 150,000 *yuan* of the profits from his correspondence schools into this new center, he favored a move to the suburbs. The Institute, even shorn of those who had left with Li Shengping, had outgrown the rented space in the hospital, and rents in central Beijing had risen quickly with the urban reforms and the recent construction boom.

The building that Bi Yimin found was on the northern outskirts of the capital, in a neighborhood called Shuangquanpu, beyond the old Desheng city gate. It seemed ideal—a new four-story building of red brick that belonged to the Beijing Number 2 Vehicle Repair Factory. Chen agreed at once to rent the third and fourth floors. After the cramped and smelly quarters at the hospital, the factory building seemed luxurious. The corridors were broad and airy, and the offices were sunny. There was space for a library, a computer center, and two meeting rooms.

On the top floor, in an arrangement that is not uncommon in Chinese work units, six or seven rooms were set aside as living quarters. Visitors could sleep over here. So could staff, on the frequent occasions when they worked too late to catch the bus home. Min Qi moved in altogether. For several weeks, so did Wang Juntao and Hou Xiaotian, although Hou cursed the arrangement: Her excellent cooking was always in demand from colleagues who got bored with the unchanging stodgy fare in the canteen that the Institute shared with workers from the factory downstairs.

The longish bus ride from central Beijing, admittedly, was far from ideal for the growing number of people who now worked for Chen. By now, the Institute had almost fifty staff members, including a dozen full-time researchers and more than two hundred affiliates—a mix of graduate students, college professors, and staff from government-sponsored think tanks like RIRES. Although Chen paid generous salaries, he had difficulty hiring clerical staff: typists, secretaries, computer operators, data processors, librarians, and archivists. The commute was part of the problem, but people were also nervous about working for a private outfit, especially one with such a dubious political reputation. The Institute promised neither long-term job security nor the fringe benefits that came with a government job—pensions, health care, housing, or special food at festival time.

Chen Ziming formally unveiled the new Institute headquarters in May 1987, which was an auspicious time. Zhao Ziyang had just delivered an electrifying speech that effectively buried the leftists' latest Campaign Against Bourgeois Liberalization. For the rest of the year the Maoists were in full retreat. The Institute's new Chinese name translated as the Beijing Social and Economic Sciences Research Institute (SERI). But Chen also had a few English-language business cards printed up with another title, Social and Economic Studies, with the organization's logo, a large eye, symbolizing openness to the outside world, formed from the letters SES. It was Wang Wei, the young man from the Bank of China, the only member of Chen's group to speak English, who chose the new name.

At Shuangquanpu, Chen rounded out his team. Power in the new Institute operated on three distinct levels. First, there was Chen Ziming himself. He gave himself no formal title at first, but he was the mastermind setting the overall direction, holding the purse strings, dispensing his patronage. Then there was a second track, occupied by Wang Juntao. Wang's charisma and energy made him the ideal public face, the ambassador, the headhunter. It was Wang who attended all the key conferences. And finally, there was the nominal hierarchy. Chen appointed Min Qi to be general secretary, overseeing the Institute's day-to-day activities. And as SERI's first director, he chose the young economist Fei Yuan. Given the uncertain political climate, Chen wanted to be as discreet as possible about the names on his masthead. Those with bad political backgrounds were to be kept out of the limelight. Fei Yuan was close to squeaky clean.

Fei was from Zhenjiang, an ugly, midsized industrial town on the Yangzi River, near Nanjing. He had a graduate degree in economics from Beida, and the only black mark on his record was a marginal role in the 1980 campus elections, when he acted as campaign manager for one of the other candidates. At SERI, he was well liked, although no one felt they knew him intimately. He was a notorious workaholic, a good manager, a problem solver. If you wanted to approach Chen Ziming on a sensitive matter concerning money or policy, you went to Fei Yuan for advice. He was like an older brother. "Leave it to me," he would say with an earnest smile. "Trust me." Was his manner a little devious? some wondered. But Fei's easy smile, his obvious sincerity, soon dispelled any doubts.

Min Qi, whose only studies were as a worker-peasant-soldier student, still smarted from his lack of academic credentials. For that reason, perhaps, he was inordinately proud of the attention that the Institute soon commanded in Beijing intellectual circles. He erected a long bulletin board at the third-floor entrance to display covers of SERI's new books, photographs of its conferences, and copies of reports of its latest public opinion surveys from the official press or the liberal Shanghai *World Economic Herald*. Colleagues joked about Min Qi's compulsive need for order. He even posted a set of office rules on the wall and hung a banner that bore the three characters of the Institute's slogan—*Gongzheng, Kexue, Xiaolu:* Justice, Science, Efficiency. Chen Ziming placed total trust in Min Qi, who handled all hiring and firing. He even decided on the salary that Boss Chen himself received.

The only other person who dared to challenge the boss directly over money questions was Chen Xiaoping. The younger Chen, who taught at Politics and Law University, came from a poor family in southern China and had studied at Beida. Chen was the country boy made good. He was hyperactive, silvery-tongued, and a little vain, constantly taking out a pocket mirror to pat his hair and study his appearance. He liked to socialize with Wang Juntao, and the two of them often spent their weekends driving around from one university party to another, looking for pretty women to flirt with, even though Wang was now a married man.

Chen Xiaoping always seemed to be broke. "I've worked for you for months now," he complained to Chen Ziming one day.

"Why don't you pay me more? Look, I can't even afford to buy a refrigerator or a sofa or a TV for my apartment."

"How much do you need?"

He did a quick mental calculation. "Three thousand."

And just like that, Ziming wrote him a check.

Yet there was also a much more serious side to the young southerner. Chen Xiaoping was well known to the Chinese authorities for his role in the angry student demonstrations against the "second Japanese occupation of China" that had rocked Beida in September 1985. Having failed repeatedly to subjugate China by force of arms, the students had said, Japan was now realizing its dream of an Asian Co-Prosperity Sphere with Sony cassette recorders and Honda motorcycles.[4] Chen Xiaoping had not played a role in the protests until the government declared them illegal, when he wrote a celebrated wall poster at Beida that denounced the ban as being "in violation of the Constitution." Chen even took the bold and unusual step of signing his name to the *dazibao*, which won him instant celebrity among his fellow students. At Politics and Law University, he became an expert in the Chinese Constitution and taught a popular class in administrative law, where he argued for reforms to protect the civil rights of ordinary citizens.

Chen Ziming was happy to encourage the young lawyer to pursue his research in a new setting. But after a few months, Chen felt that SERI's academic work was getting a little scattershot and that it could benefit from hiring a research director. Wang Juntao recommended a close friend from his Wuhan days. Liu Weihua, the same age as Wang, had been a teacher at Central China Normal College. He was one of those who had flocked to the Luoshan hilltop guest house to listen to Wang spin his dreams. For Liu, Wang was a Pied Piper, and he dropped everything to follow him to Beijing. Liu Weihua was an asset in every way: big-hearted, well read, with the enthusiasm of a schoolboy. Chen's team was virtually complete.

Downstairs at the Number 2 Vehicle Repair Factory, things were not going so well. The plant was having financial problems, which was the reason the managers had decided to rent out their two upper floors. As a friendly gesture, Chen Ziming offered them his team's advice on some management questions, all on a pro bono basis; by the end of the first year the factory's operations were in healthier shape.

The managers complained to Chen that they, like other state enterprises, were now obliged by the urban reforms to take responsibility for their own profits and losses. In a number of cities, the Communist Party was even planning to allow bankruptcies on an experimental basis, all in the name of improving efficiency.

If the Party was troubled by the grumbling of factory managers, it was even more disturbed by the mounting signs of unhappiness on the shop floor. Chinese workers were taught from birth that they were the "masters of the house." That being the case, there was no need in China for labor unions to agitate for higher wages. The role of the official All China Federation of Trade Unions (ACFTU), therefore, was to provide welfare and political education. But for two years now, evidence showed that workers no longer found these services sufficient.

The first real danger signal was the bus strike that brought Beijing to a near-standstill over the National Day weekend in 1985. It was an early response to the urban reforms of the previous year. The reforms of October 1984 had ushered in an economy that was not in any sense free market; it was rather a chaotic hybrid of market forces and central planning. Some people were better placed than others to navigate the chaos. In a two-track economy with a two-tiered pricing system, personal connections—guanxi— became the currency of survival; if you had the guanxi, then guandao— corruption, official profiteering—usually came next.

The removal of the "iron rice bowl" had serious consequences. With the relaxation of price controls taking effect faster than the increase in wages, workers quickly found their living standards under siege. The new mood of material expectation that the Party encouraged mingled with a certain nostalgia for the old social leveling of the Maoist era. "We are grateful to Deng Xiaoping for raising wages," went one song that made the rounds. "But we remember Mao Zedong for not raising prices." This odd mix of acquisitiveness and egalitarianism left the Party unsure of what it was facing. Were the rumblings of discontent to be classified as a new manifestation of bourgeois liberalism, or as a breeding ground for leftist reaction?

Over the summer of 1985, Zhao Ziyang's think tank, RIRES, began to assess working-class opinion. But the survey was incomplete when the buses on Route 336, serving Beijing's northern and western sections, started a "go-slow" on September 28. By October 1, which was a payday as well as National Day, a holiday, the entire city bus network was affected. The issues that prompted the action were small ones: One worker discovered that his work unit had reneged on an offer of housing; a university student assigned to the bus depot was given a job as a stoker, which his workmates found demeaning; older, less-productive workers found that they were being sent home on a meager part-time salary instead of being retired on full pension. Nevertheless, these seemingly small complaints were enough to set the bus crews on a collision course with the government.

Zhao Hongliang was typical of the strike leaders. He was a natty, slightly built, streetwise twenty-year-old working on bus Route 336. After graduating from his Beijing high school, Zhao was a "waiting-for-work youth" (that is, unemployed) for two years. And when he finally got work, in 1985, he earned just thirty-four *yuan* ($11.60) a month as a ticket collector. When he took the bus crews' wage demands to the leaders of the work unit, Zhao felt that he and his workmates were not politically motivated but were simply reacting to an unsettling change in their own circumstances. The larger historical import of the strike did not cross their minds. Nor did they try to enlist outside support, although some workers, like the coal miners of Mennagou whose shifts were disrupted by the bus stoppage, gave quiet signals of sympathy.

The Communist Party, on the other hand, fully understood the significance of the bus strike. But it chose to handle the conflict with kid gloves, while keeping quiet about it in the official media for fear it would escalate. When payday arrived again, on October 15, the bus crews found they had been given a fat increase. As protection against the harsh winter ahead, each worker was also issued a pair of high leather boots and a new down jacket. Once the buses were running again, the Public Security Bureau sent its agents into the bus depots. "Who made you do this?" they asked workers coming off shift. "Who were the ringleaders?" Everywhere they received the same answer: The action was spontaneous; there were no leaders, there was no organization. Even so, the official line soon emerged in the press: The strike was the work of a handful of bad elements. Activists like Zhao Hongliang learned that their cases were "under review" by the PSB.

After 1985, the symptoms of insecurity only increased. A new contract labor system, introduced in 1986, deprived newly hired workers of their traditional job security. Those who entered a state factory on a contract basis knew that their jobs were threatened by a huge reserve labor army of underemployed peasants. For every worker who embraced the get-rich-quick mentality of the 1980s, there was another, imbued with the Maoist ideal of equality, who mistrusted Deng's policy of "letting some people get rich first." In a series of polls conducted between 1986 and 1988, RIRES asked workers to comment on a number of "negative tendencies" in contemporary Chinese life. The widening gap between rich and poor ranked higher with each new survey. One of the pieces of popular doggerel now heard on the streets was a parody of the old paean to Mao, *The East Is Red*. The new version ran:

> The West is Red,
> The sun has set,
> A Deng Xiaoping has come.
> He serves the privileged very well,
> And tells the rest to go to Hell.

At the top of the list of complaints, however, was that factory managers behaved like the vilified capitalists of the old China. Lacking any institutional grievance procedures, more and more workers simply took the law into their own hands.[5] Many managers installed iron bars on the windows of their apartments, and some hired bodyguards.

Deng Xiaoping had amended the Constitution in 1982 to outlaw strikes, on the grounds that socialism had removed all possible sources of antagonism between the proletariat and its employers. But strikes now became commonplace. One ACFTU survey showed that there were at least 129 during 1987.[6] More than half of those called for greater workplace democracy and wage increases, or protested unfair management practices. To fulfill the demands of propaganda, the ACFTU sent its investigators out to a number of cities to assess workers' attitudes to the strikes. The findings came as no surprise. A handful of bad elements were to blame;

most workers craved the order and tranquility necessary to carry out socialist modernization.

Zhao Hongliang threw back his head and laughed when he read the report of the 1987 ACFTU survey in the *Beijing Workers Daily*. "Hey, look at this," he called to a colleague, another veteran of the 1985 bus strike, when he clocked in at the depot that morning. "They're still on our case. I wonder what those guys really told the ACFTU survey people," Zhao mused. "Maybe we should find out."

Zhao was unhappy in his job. With bonuses, his pay had risen to about fifty-five *yuan* a month. But it didn't keep up with rising prices; pork alone, a staple of the Chinese diet, had gone up to 4.80 *yuan* a pound. Furthermore, the petty harassment that followed his involvement in the bus strike had never really ceased, and Zhao requested a transfer to another work unit.

Now he had a better plan. What if he and a group of friends from the bus company quit their jobs and retraced the steps of the ACFTU investigators? If they asked the same questions, would they get the same answers? None of them had any savings, but once word of the idea got round, Zhao was amazed at how many colleagues agreed to chip in with a few *yuan* to finance the trip. Zhao told his superiors that new government regulations allowed him to quit his job. When they said the most they could do was to study his request, since his case was still not clarified, Zhao told them to go to hell.

In the spring of 1987, a small group of bus workers left Beijing by train. They traveled west to Shanxi Province, checking in first with their counterparts at the Datong Bus Company at the northern tip of the province, near the boundary with Inner Mongolia, and they visited the city's vast coalfields. From Datong, they worked their way southward, staying in small hotels in half a dozen smaller towns, traveling through the barren Taihang mountains, ending up in Yuncheng, on Shanxi's extreme southwest edge.

An obligatory stop on any trip through Shanxi was the village of Dazhai, the model commune of Mao Zedong's glory years. In 1963, Dazhai, which stands on the bleak loess plateau, had been washed away in a single night of floods. The village Party chairman,

Chen Yonggui, galvanized the peasants into rebuilding the commune with such energy that Mao himself was impressed. Dazhai, an obscure settlement of several hundred souls, became the incarnation of the New China, and Chen Yonggui was rewarded with a meteoric rise to the Politburo. Until it was quietly dropped in 1977, all Chinese learned the slogan:

> In agriculture learn from Dazhai
> In industry learn from [the oilfields of] Daqing.

Mao invested millions of *yuan* in his dream, building aqueducts and reservoirs and rice terraces and a vast five-story hotel for visiting VIPs that was surrounded by simulated cave dwellings.

By the time Zhao Hongliang arrived, the hotel was empty, the slogan forgotten, and much of the nearby hillside occupied by real cave dwellers. Zhao wandered around in an angry daze as the peasants of Dazhai told him of the deceptions, the routine falsification of grain production figures. What about those famous pictures in the newspapers, he asked, of the giant corn grown in Dazhai? The peasants showed Zhao how the trick worked: Trim the tapered ends off two or three separate ears and then string them together on a length of wire for the benefit of the photographer. What of the overflowing storehouses of grain? Again, the villagers showed him: A wooden board was set into the granaries, midway up, to form a false floor. Now, reduced to its normal standing as one dirt-poor village among thousands, Dazhai could not even feed its people rice or white flour. They got by on coarse cornmeal porridge.

In one village after another, the same story: starvation, homelessness, people wearing rags; villagers bullied and exploited by local Party officials but not daring to protest; women harassed; children with no opportunity to study. In the provincial towns, workers expressed support and sympathy when they heard the story of the Beijing bus strike and shared their own complaints of insecurity, inflation, and inequality.

From Shanxi, Zhao and two of his coworkers headed west, stopping off in the ancient capital of Xi'an and the city of Lanzhou, where Wang Juntao and Bai Hua had traveled the previous autumn. Finally, Zhao boarded a train and headed as far west as he could go, to Golmud.

Golmud is, in every sense, the end of the line. It stands in the center of the vast wastes of Qinghai Province, a garrison town and supply station for the Chinese occupation of nearby Tibet. Zhao discovered that Qinghai was also home to thousands of people who had been caught up in the great anticrime campaign of 1983. Exemplary sentences of five to seven years for theft were not uncommon, coupled with the loss of urban residence permits. These were the kind of young men Zhao had gone to school with, who had turned from unemployment to petty crime and now found themselves abandoned in Qinghai in the name of an official policy of "opening up the border areas." Zhao found them living in roofless lean-tos, at the mercy of the elements. They told of friends who had died of cold, starvation, or exposure. As soon as they built a shelter and succeeded in coaxing crops from the harsh land, they said, the police moved them on as vagrants. Zhao Hongliang stayed in Qinghai for a month. Then, sick at heart, he caught the train back to Beijing.

Arriving in Beijing, Zhao took a job as a salesclerk at the Xidan Department Store, a few hundred yards west of Tiananmen Square. The pay was sixty *yuan* a month, which was no fortune, but the job was secure. And with bonuses, Zhao's real wages usually crept closer to one hundred *yuan*. In fact, as he quickly learned, it was easy for an employee at Xidan to increase his or her earnings tenfold by striking an informal deal with the suppliers: For every ten electric fans, or ten cassette players, that the factory supplied, have them slip in an extra one without an invoice. Otherwise, no deal. Then it was simple to sell the eleventh item off the books and pocket the proceeds. Some salesclerks made a cool two thousand *yuan* a month this way, sometimes even up to five thousand. Why not, they reasoned, since all the managers and cadres were doing the same thing? Cynicism about official corruption was pervasive.

Wherever they looked, it seemed, ordinary workers like Zhao saw a system in disarray, with the Party's credibility at an all-time low. On the face of it, this might be thought ironic. The Deng years had seen none of the monstrous dramas of his predecessor's rule: no human suffering on the scale of the "three difficult years"—the famines of 1959 to 1961 that followed Mao's Great Leap Forward, no street violence or mass political purges like those of the Cultural Revolution. But the change in expectations about prosperity and the strictness of the Party line over the ten years of Deng's rule had been incalculable. The Party had lost its iron grip on daily life. Deng's Four Cardinal Principles were so liberally interpreted that few Chinese any longer had a clear idea of what Marxism was supposed to be. Even Zhao Ziyang was said to have declared that there should no longer be any formal insistence on "upholding socialism," since no one really knew what it was.

At the same time, the Chinese economy was fast overheating. The *People's Daily* acknowledged officially what workers already knew: Real wages had stagnated. Inflation, virtually unknown before Deng's reforms, soared to more than 30 percent during 1988.[7] The ACFTU could no longer hide behind the bland optimism of its 1987 survey of working-class opinion. All its internal polls now indicated similar trends: resentment at income inequality, anger at official profiteering, fears that Zhao Ziyang's theory that China was in "the primary stage of constructing socialism" was no more than a fraudulent cover for restoring capitalism.

The most common form of protest was passive resistance on the job. In one ACFTU survey, 89 percent of factory managers complained that workers did not work as hard as they used to. And strike actions increased as well. One official estimate showed more than seven hundred strikes in the first ten months of 1988. The largest, involving fifteen hundred workers, was at Number 3 Cotton Mill in the eastern coastal province of Zhejiang. The longest was a three-month conflict at the Northwest Medical Instruments Plant in the city of Xi'an. These might have been localized affairs, but the official unions took them seriously, for they suggested that some workers were now prepared to organize against the Communist Party.

By the summer of 1988 it seemed as if Deng's reform alternative to classic Maoism had stalled. The reform-minded economists agreed that two measures were necessary to break the impasse, but they disagreed over which should come first: Subject the state-owned industrial behemoths to market discipline, or remove price controls from vital raw materials. Everyone knew that inflation would increase if prices were freed. The optimists believed that ordinary Chinese would accept this and find comfort in the reduced scope for corruption, which thrived on the two-track pricing system. The pessimists countered that the risks were too great, given the present state of public anxiety.

In June, Deng Xiaoping unexpectedly announced that price reform would come first. It was the month before the annual retreat to the sunny bathing resort of Beidaihe, where Party chiefs gather each year to escape the heat of Beijing and thrash out their differences. But on this occasion the eighty-four-year-old patriarch overplayed his hand. The pessimists were right. Chinese rushed to the banks to withdraw their savings for a spree of panic buying. The psychological impact was devastating. Within two weeks, the Party announced that it had changed its mind; price reform would be introduced at the much slower pace favored by the old guard. The reversal was a huge personal triumph for Li Peng, the Soviet-educated technocrat who was the conservatives' standard-bearer in the younger generation. And it was a devastating blow to the prestige of Zhao Ziyang, whose career would never fully recover.

8

The Blueprint Faction

"In a famous cancer hospital," wrote Su Xiaokang, a well-known investigative reporter, "the doctors' incomes are no greater than that of an old woman who sells baked sweet potatoes at the entrance. Those who operate on skulls make less than those who shave heads, and those who play the piano make less than those who move pianos."

Inflation does not affect everyone equally. It is, in its own way, a method of redistributing resources. Factory workers certainly lost ground during the mid-1980s, but perhaps no group felt the decline in their economic status so acutely as China's intellectuals.

Su Xiaokang's bitter remarks came from his script of a six-part television documentary called *River Elegy,* which riveted the attention of Chinese viewers from the airing of its first episode on June 14, 1988, just a month before the Beidaihe meetings. Su called grandly for *River Elegy* to be "an expression in collective soul-searching in which we ponder the history, civilization, and destiny of our nation." It was certainly that, and it showed that the disillusionment of the intelligentsia had plumbed new depths. After the death of Mao, China's independent intellectuals had tried first to make sense of the horrors of the Cultural Revolution, then the abuses of centralized power by Mao's successors, and finally the continued relevance of the Communist Party as an institution. With *River Elegy,* the intellectuals, or at least the most pessimistic of them, seemed to throw out the four decades of Communist rule as just one more illustration of China's failure to cope with the modern world.

Su Xiaokang and his coauthors offered the bleakest reading of China's identity as an inward-looking society that had never broken the iron shackles of agriculture. Ransacking the stock footage in the CCTV archives, they put together a dizzying montage of vignettes of Chinese backwardness and Western progress. The images of China were worker ants "hearkening to the will of Heaven," water buffaloes knee-deep in a patchwork of rice paddies, the endless slow turn of a bamboo irrigation wheel, the horse-drawn "honey cart" with its buckets of night soil. The West boasted whirring train wheels, giant shipyards, children playing volleyball under palm trees, Coke bottles, the Manhattan skyline. "We are standing at the crossroads," said Su Xiaokang's voice-over.

Like many of their twentieth-century predecessors, the filmmakers presented China's intellectuals as its only salvation. "Their literary and artistic talents could be subverted," Su wrote. "Their will could be misrepresented; their souls could be emasculated; their backs could be bent; and their bodies could be destroyed. However, they held in their hands the weapons for wiping out ignorance and superstition.... It was they who could sprinkle the sky-blue, sweet spring water of science and democracy on the yellow soil."

Thoughts like these could never have been expressed on prime-time state television, of course, without explicit encouragement from the highest quarters. In this case, the backing came from Zhao Ziyang himself, who staved off the fury of conservative elders such as the seventy-nine-year-old Vice-President, Wang Zhen, a former Long March commander known as the "big cannon," who took great pride in his illiteracy. Zhao was now actively seeking support from China's independent intellectuals as his fortunes in the Party wavered. The makers of *River Elegy* returned the favor of Zhao's backing by heaping praise on his new "Gold Coast strategy" of development, which allowed a number of China's maritime provinces, in Zhao's words, to "join the great international circle."

In his search for talking heads for the program, Su Xiaokang contacted SERI to invite Wang Juntao to appear. But Wang, as so often those days, was on the road, attending to a variety of SERI projects. In the early spring of 1988, the *River Elegy* film crew caught up with him on a visit to Yan'an. Wang was there to talk to local officials about setting up a training school and developing the rich natural resources of this poor area of Shaanxi Province.

The cameras panned across endless dry, dusty brown hills that had once been terraced for agriculture. Nowhere was there a starker contrast between the founding values of the Chinese Revolution and its present predicament. Yan'an had been the Communists' headquarters from 1936 until Mao abandoned it to the Guomindang in March 1947. The very name echoed with all that was most noble in the Maoist tradition: modesty and courage, austerity and self-sacrifice. Now, as Wang tramped through the poorest areas of Yan'an's poorest counties and visited the caves where the survivors of the Long March had lived and fought for a decade, he was overcome by oppressive feelings of gloom. There seemed to be nothing here: no money, no technology, no technical skills.

Wrapped up in a belted overcoat against the chilly spring wind, Wang explained to the *River Elegy* interviewer that Yan'an was a perfect example of China's problems in building a modern society. Prosperity, such as it was, never reached these western hinterlands. "This means," he said, "that a population of one hundred million and vast resources will be relegated outside the structure of China's economic development." He continued, "China is a land with a large population, infertile soil, and scarce resources. It is scientifically backward, education has declined, and the quality of labor is low." The dull monotony of life was worst of all, creating "a powerful inertia in people's cultural concepts that results in the lack of an enterprising spirit."

Wang's gloomy response to Yan'an at first appeared to mirror the extreme pessimism of the filmmakers, who seemed to despair of the Chinese as a race, as if there were some inherent feebleness in the bloodstock.[1] The implicit message of *River Elegy* was that China could only be saved by what the Party conservatives called "wholesale Westernization." But Wang Juntao's habitual optimism had not altogether deserted him. He still seemed to believe that China could pull itself up by its own bootstraps. "We intend to challenge such a system of development," he told the interviewer. Projects like the SERI cadre school, he explained, were designed as a practical alternative to the failure of central government programs—and, never forget, the project had not been SERI's idea; the suggestion came from the Yan'an cadres themselves.

———————

Wang Juntao and Chen Ziming continued to believe they could build a constructive relationship between enlightened Party officials and independent thinkers. It must often have seemed futile, but Chen was a persistent man. And SERI's track record of activities grew more impressive by the month.

By early 1988, Chen had organized the Institute into four separate departments—political science, psychology, economics, and sociology. SERI's four departments had, in turn, spawned offshoots and subsidiaries, many of which were designed to generate income for the work of the main think tank. "The independent kingdom," some called Chen's network.

With an eye to security, Chen kept the various parts of his operation highly compartmentalized. No one was told more than they needed to know. Chen's colleagues called him *guandaogong:* the maker of connections, the "plumber." Keep things separate, and join them when necessary. Even so, it was impossible for any Beijing intellectual to ignore the scope and influence of Chen's work. Even a few American China specialists began to call at the Shuangquanpu offices. One of them suggested a spell at a U.S. university. "Thank you," Chen replied politely, "but that doesn't interest me. My place is in China. Things here are very exciting."

Chen's decision to go independent might have been forced on him by the mistrust that his political record inspired in official circles, but that was fast becoming academic. His "independent kingdom" had become, de facto, the leading example in China of a thriving private sector. Or, to use the term that a number of the intellectuals picked up from Eastern Europe, it was an example of a "civil society" independent of the state. There were dozens of conferences, scores of research projects, hundreds of publications.[2] Among them, they offered a remarkable X ray of a society at the edge of crisis.

SERI's Political Science Department was especially productive. It published Chen Ziming's *Guide to Contemporary Politics* and a twelve-volume series entitled *Famous Thinkers,* which introduced Chinese readers to such Western giants as Nietzsche, Weber, Sartre, and Freud. In late 1987, under the direction of Wang Juntao and Fei Yuan, the department carried out a "Survey of the Political Psychology of China's Citizens," based on more than a million and a half items of response data. The survey, whose findings were extensively reported in the liberal Shanghai-based *World Economic Herald,* revealed a desire for greater freedom, though SERI concluded that ordinary Chinese citizens "basically know very little about democracy." And although a large number expressed pride in living in a socialist country and faith in the Communist Party's leadership, the great majority believed that people should be able to speak up when the Party made mistakes.[3] Min Qi summarized the results in book form. Sounding rather like Wang Juntao, he concluded that "China's democracy movement must begin, first of all, with a process of cultural renewal and enlightenment."

SERI's polling activities became more professional after March 1988, when the Sociology Department set up the Opinion Research Center of China (ORCC), the country's first independent public polling organization. Chen Ziming appointed Bai Hua as its first director.

Wang Juntao had kept in touch with her ever since their argumentative trip to Lanzhou eighteen months earlier. Bai Hua told him of her frustration at RIRES, which had now grown to a staff of two hundred. She tended to agree with what Wang had once said: RIRES told Zhao Ziyang what he wanted to hear. She was fascinated with scientific Western polling techniques like those used at the University of Michigan, but RIRES was not interested. "You already know what I think of that stuff," Wang told her. "But Chen seems to like it. Why don't you come over and work for us?" Bai Hua said she would think about it. But first she wanted to finish teaching her People's University class in public relations, the first course of its kind in China. At the end of 1987, she called Wang. RIRES was still unresponsive to her ideas; she would be happy to come to SERI. When her RIRES friends heard the news, they treated her like a traitor. "Going to work with Wang Juntao and Chen Ziming?" one said snidely. "You're getting to be a dangerous person these days."

Chen Ziming offered Bai Hua the best computer systems in China and a team that would use far more advanced and scientific polling techniques than anyone else in China. He promised her the funds to hire three recent Chinese graduates of Michigan's Survey Research Center and to bring in ten of Beijing's brightest academics as consultants.

Bai Hua's first project for ORCC was an April 1988 "Survey of the Views and Aspirations of Delegates to the National People's Congress." Privately, she and Chen hoped to prove scientifically what was already common knowledge: that the three thousand or so "people's representatives" were in fact poorly educated Party appointees who were largely unfit for their jobs. Eleven hundred of them replied to ORCC's questions about the level of their political and legal knowledge. (Finding: "extremely low.") Even with some of the more embarrassing details deleted, the survey placed ORCC on the cutting edge of the movement for political reform.

Bai Hua followed up this early success with a survey of *shehui shisuhua,* the secularization or, literally, the "making worldly" of society—meaning, in the Chinese context, the problem of ending the widespread prejudice against money as something "dirty." Next came a summertime poll on the "Thoughts and Ideology of Today's University Students." This questioned young Chinese about their attitudes toward everything from love, sex, and Western culture to their career goals, the job allocation system, and the student movement of 1986 to 1987. The students said that the winter's demonstrations had left them feeling disillusioned. "There's no point," was a common response. "We just want to get on with our studies now." Wang Juntao was unimpressed with the picture that emerged. He found the current crop of students superficial and quite unripe for political action.

At this time, Wang took on a crippling work load. His marriage to Hou Xiaotian was less than two years old, but it was already experiencing strains. After their initial whirlwind romance, the couple had taken to staging unpleasant arguments in public. Hou was a strong-willed woman who refused to be a traditional Chinese wife; Wang liked to spend his limited free time with his male friends. Although he usually left Saturday nights free for a trip to the cinema, since Hou loved the movies, more often than not he would nod off to sleep in the middle, exhausted. He was working on three books at once: a dictionary of the Cultural Revolution,[4] a history of the democracy movement, and a long theoretical essay on civil society. He was also assisting Min Qi and Chen Xiaoping on a seven-volume *Handbook of Chinese Politics.* This monumental work, covering the period since 1978, was to be the first unofficial study of the Chinese political system ever published. But none of the manuscripts would survive the events of 1989.

Wang also wore another, unfamiliar hat: that of a journalist. In March 1988, the SERI Economics Department, headed by Wang and Fei Yuan, paid three hundred thousand *yuan* to buy a newspaper called *Economics Weekly.* The moribund paper belonged to an affiliate of the Chinese Academy of Social Sciences, which was eager to sell it off to improve its financial position. Under SERI ownership, *Economics Weekly* carried a mix of news, editorials, and long theoretical articles, but the main attraction was the regular feature by deputy editor Wang Juntao on the political and social problems associated with Deng Xiaoping's decade of reforms.

The paper even came to rival the influence of the celebrated Shanghai *World Economic Herald,* and the editor of the *Herald,* Qin Benli, paid the *Weekly* a generous and perhaps excessive compliment. "In terms of predicting and analyzing the economic situation," Qin said, "providing critique and comment on the economic reforms, and in the quantity of its output of articles on economic theory, the *Weekly* went way beyond the *Herald.*"

One person who followed the paper with interest was Hu Yaobang. Although technically Hu had kept his seat on the Politburo after his "retirement" from office in January 1987, he was really in political limbo. A heart attack in 1988 further diminished his influence. Some people said that Hu's commitment to independent journalism was less than wholehearted; in the self-criticism that he was obliged to write after his downfall he said—under duress, perhaps—that the investigative journalist Liu Binyan had "never moved from his 'rightist' position," and was "not suitable as a reporter." But Hu had never lost his reputation as the fiery champion of the intellectuals, and he sent clear signals of support for this new enterprise of the promising young man who had once knocked on his door in Fuqiang Alley. The ailing Hu asked his wife, Li Zhao, to write a warm letter to the editors of *Economics Weekly.* "Not only does the *Weekly* contain scholarly research," Li wrote for her husband, "but it also has a clear sense of direction and realistic ideas, and this will gain it the trust of society."

The Economics Department won more friends in official circles than any other division of SERI. The Higher Party School bought one hundred copies of Chen's *Famous Thinkers* series to use as textbooks; the official press praised SERI's research in front-page editorials; and a six-volume set of books on financial reform was warmly praised by the National Commission on Science and Technology and sold out its first printing of thirty thousand in less than a week.

Chen knew that his work would have only a limited effect on the reform process unless these channels to officialdom existed. But he faced an uphill battle on any topic that was not pure economics. Chen tried unsuccessfully to forge ties to the State Commission for Reform of the Economic Structure, whose director, Bao Tong, sat on the Central Committee. After several unsuccessful overtures, Chen invited two senior members of Bao Tong's staff to visit SERI for the day. They listened politely and left. Chen heard later that one of the men remarked, "I don't think we can use these reports from SERI. You just don't know what will happen to them in the future. Maybe they'll be closed down someday. I prefer not to get involved with them." For even in the most reform-minded circles of the government such as this, Chen Ziming's political record still haunted him. He and Wang Juntao had been rehabilitated years ago, but no firm rules existed in China, no legal framework, for expunging a "bad record." And the security services still brimmed with unreconstructed leftists who had served the Gang of Four without complaint. The Public Security Bureau, and then the Ministry of State Security, never stopped their monitoring of Chen and Wang after the days of the hidden surveillance booth behind Democracy Wall.[5] Chen was alerted that SERI had been reported four times to the Party's Central Secretariat since 1987; on two occasions, "situation feedback" reports about the Institute had been issued at the highest levels. Although they had no way to prove it, people who worked at the Institute took it for granted that their phones were tapped. There was also the ever-present possibility that SERI had been infiltrated, that one of its staff was a security agent. But when anyone expressed these fears to Chen, he was cool and low-key. "Of course we should be cautious," he told Zhang Lun one day, "but that mustn't stop us doing our work. Besides," he added, "we're not doing anything illegal."

But the storm warnings grew stronger in the summer of 1988, especially around the time of the June screening of *River Elegy* and the Beidaihe meeting of the Party leadership the next month.

The authorities signaled their displeasure about a number of SERI projects. A study of corruption since 1949 was designated "reactionary." In June, news came abruptly that the State Education Commission would no longer recognize the credentials of Chen Ziming's two correspondence schools. His cash cows had to be closed down.

The impetuous, knight-errant side of Wang Juntao's character also continued to antagonize the Party. Wang's excursion into the world of journalism exposed him to innumerable instances of the petty harassment that ordinary Chinese faced in their dealings with those in power, and it was typical for him to feel obliged to get involved. "I can't bear to see people mistreated," he would retort to friends who told him it was a poor use of his time. "If I can even save one person, then others will have hope." Wang passed on the stories that crossed his desk to friends in the official media and appeared in court to plead as a kind of people's advocate. He must have known this was a quixotic enterprise, for the verdict in Chinese trials is decided upon before anyone sets foot in the courtroom.

Wang made these forays into civil rights with his close friend, the energetic young SERI lawyer Chen Xiaoping. But their mentor was Gong Xiangrui, a law professor at Beida and a consultant to SERI. Professor Gong was a true maverick. He was in his mid-seventies then, an irrepressible, balding little fireplug of a man who had pioneered the vogue for administrative law in 1986. His mission in life was to use the courts to give the individual citizen redress against wrongful actions by the state.

One case that particularly bothered Gong concerned a young man in the impoverished eastern province of Anhui who had fallen victim to an obscure personal vendetta by the local police chief. In the winter of 1988, Wang, Chen Xiaoping, and Gong Xiangrui traveled together to Anhui to find out more about the case. The accused man's brother, who was the manager of a local car factory, paid their train fare. The more Wang learned, the more he was convinced that it was a frame-up. But when he returned to Beijing to review his notes, he learned that their intervention had succeeded only in getting the man's sentence increased—almost certainly on the grounds that he had involved outsiders in his case and had shown no willingness, as the Chinese system demands, to repent.

The local police chief reported that Wang and Chen had "disrupted stability and unity" (the Party's battle cry of the day) and "incited" opposition to the government. The report went all the way to Beijing, where the official Xinhua News Agency issued another damning report, for internal circulation, that described Wang and Chen as "bad people." Under other circumstances this might have been a minor affair; it was certainly not the first time Wang Juntao had been described in this way. But by the winter of 1988, there was a palpable sense of political crisis in China, and the Party was not inclined to look at Wang's most recent legal escapades in isolation. At the end of the year, Public Security Minister Wang Fang issued a secret report that identified the ten most serious threats to Communist Party rule. He singled out three potential sources of revolt: the dissident astrophysicist Fang Lizhi, the makers of *River Elegy,* and the independent network headed by Chen Ziming and Wang Juntao.

Of all SERI's activities during 1988, none worried the authorities so much as a December survey by Bai Hua's Opinion Research Center of China (ORCC). The topic was "Political Participation Among China's Citizens." The survey was restricted to the capital, but SERI planned to use it as the pilot for a nationwide survey the following year. In the event, however, it was to be three years before this could happen.

For the first time, Chen Ziming looked abroad for funding and obtained the financing for the ORCC survey from the U.S. National Science Foundation, the Ford Foundation, and the Fund for the Reform and Opening of China. The last was the brainchild of Hungarian-born financier George Soros, who had met a group of Chinese economists in Budapest in 1986. It was Bao Tong, wrote Soros, who "cut through the red tape and approved the foundation on the spot." The Soros connection alone would have been enough to interest the Ministry of State Security in the ORCC survey, since the ministry had already begun to compile a dossier on Soros, whom it later accused of using the U.S.-based fund as a cover for CIA-backed espionage activities.[6]

The ORCC survey was directed by one of Bai Hua's three Michigan-trained colleagues. Some of the findings might have come as a relief to the government—over half the respondents, for example, said they would expect to receive fair treatment at the hands of government bodies. But in other respects, the survey challenged a number of the Communist Party's most basic assumptions and provided explosive evidence of the country's frustrated mood. Of those polled, 72 percent agreed that "Democracy is the best form of government," and 79 percent disagreed with the proposition that "If we implement democracy in our country now it will lead to chaos." "A country can't be run well if it has too many political parties," was one of the statements in the poll; 62 percent disagreed. "If people's thinking isn't unified, society will be turbulent"; 55 percent disputed this. Were the Chinese in fact prepared to risk becoming the "heap of loose sand" that Deng Xiaoping so feared?

Wang Juntao usually loved parties. At most of them, he was the center of attention. But on New Year's Eve 1988, he was sullen and withdrawn. He looked exhausted; his face was ashen. Several friends asked what was the matter. Toothache, he replied, terrible toothache. He had been laid up in bed for several days. He had a drink. It seemed to improve his humor. As always, a single beer was enough to bring a flush to his cheeks.

Toward midnight, there was the usual call for everyone to deliver a song. For Chen Ziming, this was always a painful embarrassment. He forced himself to come to these parties because he thought it was important for his colleagues to see him socially. But he had none of Wang's social graces; in truth, he would rather have stayed home with a book. What he hated most was to sing in public, but tonight they would not take no for an answer. In the end, he agreed and struck a stiff pose. There was awkward laughter when someone recognized the melody: It was the "Song of the Scissors-Grinder" from one of Jiang Qing's model operas of the Cultural Revolution. It was the only song Chen could remember.

Wang Juntao, by contrast, burst into song or recited a poem at the drop of a hat. He had an uncanny memory for the classical literature he had learned as a child, the songs and poems from the Long March that he had listened to at his father's knee. For this New Year's Eve, he chose two songs: the melancholy "Song on Leaving My Country" and the stirring "In the High Aspirations of Youth, Sorrows Are Left Unsaid." Even with the toothache, he sang with a special intensity that night. He sat down to applause, clutching his painful jaw. Someone made the obvious suggestion:

Why not see a dentist? For the first time that evening, Wang smiled. "No," he said, "I need to test my ability to withstand pain."

Everyone at the party agreed that China seemed to be falling apart. Factionalism paralyzed the leadership. The mood on the streets was ugly. Crime was on the rise. Shoppers picked fights with each other for no reason. And the theoreticians, whatever their political coloration, agreed that the reforms had reached a roadblock. Chen Ziming and Wang Juntao had a powerful premonition that a storm would break in 1989, and they decided that it was time for emergency measures.

At the end of 1988, they invited all the leading young intellectuals in Beijing to a series of special meetings, those from both the internal groups like Zhao Ziyang's think tanks and the external groups such as their own. They rented a number of rooms at the State Council's Number 2 Hostel at Xizhimen, near the Beijing Zoo. Chen Ziming himself chaired the meetings. Zhang Gang, the former Red Guard who had organized the hugely influential Moganshan conference in 1984 and was now a deputy director of RIRES, acted as deputy chair. And as general secretary of the conference, Chen chose Zhou Duo, a forty-one-year-old economist with the Stone Corporation, the successful Beijing computer company. The specific aim was to discuss the best way to mark the coming seventieth anniversary of the May Fourth movement of 1919. But the larger purpose was to put forward proposals for keeping the reform process on track. Chen Ziming had no patience with those who came bearing high-flown theoretical papers; what he wanted were practical, nuts-and-bolts ideas.

Although many of the members of the internal groups continued to rebuff Wang and Chen, the turnout at Number 2 Hostel was better than they had hoped, and the meetings quickly attracted the watchful eye of the security services. Economists and political scientists came to offer their views on the crisis of Deng's reforms; historians analyzed the lessons to be learned from earlier revolutionary periods; artists and writers were invited to make their contribution to the cultural enlightenment of which Wang Juntao spoke so often. It was the first time that such a systematic exchange of views had been held, because the state-run research institutions, such as RIRES, had never been willing to collaborate with outsiders; among the unofficial groups, only SERI had the necessary resources and the network of contacts.

Chen knew that Zhao Ziyang and the reformers were in disarray. Since their triumph at Beidaihe in July over Zhao's ambitious program of price and wage reform, Li Peng and the conservatives had been threatening to gut the reform process altogether. But even in this atmosphere of crisis, Chen pleaded for caution. At the Number 2 Hostel meetings, he strongly criticized many of the main policies that had gotten the Zhaoist program into trouble, such as deficit financing and the over-hasty release of price controls. The reform spirit could be rescued, he went on, only if everyone kept a cool head. This meant keeping all lines of communication open to the more conservative, Soviet-trained "techno-bureaucrats," even the unpopular Li Peng. Chen believed that China would never get anywhere as long as its next generation of leaders "stood on a one-plank bridge, slaughtering each other."

There was a great deal wrong with the way the reforms had been carried out, Chen said, especially after they had spread to the cities in 1984. There was too much improvisation, too much short-sightedness, too great an obsession with satisfying the immediate demands of consumers. He quoted a witty aphorism: If the Cultural Revolution was ten years of *dongluan* (chaotic turmoil), then the reform period was ten years of *luandong* (a flurry of movement without direction).[7] The only way out of the present impasse was for the scholars assembled at Number 2 Hostel to work out a detailed, hardheaded blueprint. It was time for technicians, not dreamers. Until the runaway economy was tamed, talk of democracy was irrelevant.

The partisans of Zhao Ziyang used these meetings to push their own newest idea: the theory of "New Authoritarianism," as laid out in the writings of Harvard political scientist Samuel P. Huntington and put into practice by South Korea, Singapore, and Taiwan—Asia's new economic "tigers." Huntington had denied that his ideas were applicable to China, but this did nothing to deter the Zhaoists. New Authoritarianism was central to their effort to revive the General Secretary's flagging fortunes. In the words of Wu Jiaxiang, a young economist who worked for the Party's Central Committee, the theory meant "using a liberal totalitarianism to maintain stability and to eradicate the obstacles to freedom." Antidemocratic, perhaps, but all in the name of (eventual) democracy.

Chen Ziming found the idea of New Authoritarianism half-baked and dangerous, but Wang Juntao was not quite so quick to dismiss it. Like Chen, he knew that China could not become a democracy overnight. Culture and history made that impossible. Under Deng Xiaoping, the vast nation had moved from traditional dictatorship to enlightened autocracy. But in the last few months the traditionalists had threatened to derail the next stage, the transition to democracy. Wang could not see how to refocus the process other than through a period of benign "elite" (*jingying*) politics. Trying to move too fast, he told the conference, would open the doors to chaos, as it had during the Cultural Revolution. The elite would again be swept away by the "scum" (*pizi*).[8] Listening to Wang's speech, some members of the audience muttered that he was "betraying democracy."

In the first months of 1989, SERI worked around the clock on Chen Ziming's detailed reform proposals. People even gave Chen's team a nickname: the "Blueprint Faction." But if Chen thought the meetings at Number 2 Hostel had taken him any closer to the inside track, he was in for an unpleasant surprise.

On April 3, Chen Yizi of RIRES invited four hundred young scholars to a hotel in Daxing County, on the outskirts of Beijing. He was initially opposed to the SERI team being involved, but Zhang Gang argued their case eloquently. When the SERI contingent arrived, they saw that the distance between the groups was greater than ever. The proceedings were dominated entirely by the *ti nei* think tanks. Outsiders like Chen Ziming and Wang Juntao were allocated little time at the microphone. As they walked from one meeting room to another, their anger mounted. Almost every room was reserved for a discussion of economic theory. Desultory knots of people trotted out the same old, clichéd arguments. Only one session was given over to political reform, and it was packed to overflowing. Chen Yizi seemed completely out of touch with the scale of China's crisis.

The meeting went on all night, and by 4:00 A.M. Wang and Chen were fuming with frustration and prepared to walk out. Zhang Gang urged them to be patient. "Don't think of your personal insult," he told Chen Ziming. "Think of the national interest." Zhang Gang was a trusted friend, almost the only insider who had consistently encouraged SERI. He had prevailed upon his boss at RIRES not to exclude the SERI group altogether. When Chen Ziming calmed down, he agreed to stay for the remainder of the conference so that his friend and sponsor should not lose face.

Besides, Zhang Gang told him, he had good news. SERI's blueprint for the next stage of reform had been brought to the attention of the highest levels of the Party. There was agreement in principle to meet with the authors. It was possible they might even be received by Zhao Ziyang himself.[9]

Chen thanked Zhang effusively. This was a last, slender thread of hope, but had it come in time? The unspoken question was whether the intellectuals alone could break the slide into social upheaval. SERI was set up as a long-term ally of peaceful reform, but history had begun to move to a different timetable. Chen and Wang knew all about the strikes, the factory slowdowns, the biting hurt of inflation. Their own polls showed the depth of mass discontent and alienation. And they understood the inner workings of the Communist Party well enough to know that its deadlocked factional struggle would be broken only by the press of outside events. But what could that mean other than protest on the streets, which was the last thing they wanted? Chen and Wang still had one thing in common with Deng Xiaoping: a deep and abiding fear of chaos. "What good has ever come from mass insurrection?" Wang Juntao often asked.

Wang had very few dealings with the foreign press, but one reporter sought him out several times over the course of that winter.[10] During one of their conversations in November 1988, Wang made a prediction. "With the current economic problems," he said, "social unrest is inevitable in China next year, and I expect that at least one leader will fall—probably Zhao Ziyang. But you can't look to the students to do anything, they are too immature." Wang was half right.

BOOK TWO

Tiananmen

9

"A Planned Conspiracy"

Wang Juntao's low opinion of the state of campus politics was based on more than just his reading of SERI's gloomy survey of student attitudes that summer of 1988. He also kept informed through his personal contacts at Beida; of these, one of the most important was a new acquaintance named Liu Gang.

Liu Gang was the temperamental opposite of Wang, who was three years his senior.[1] He was serious-minded to a fault, belligerent, and something of a loner. But in other ways, he and Wang had much in common. Like Wang, he was a physicist by training, and after receiving his master's degree from Beida, he was assigned, as Wang had been, to a dull job in a provincial town—Ningbo, on the coast south of Shanghai. And like Wang, he worked for only a short time before quitting to explore the back roads of China. "I believe in my own abilities," he said on that occasion. "I don't like that 'safe and secure' but dull and colorless way of life. The 'iron rice bowl' lets you eat even if you do nothing. I would rather earn a living based on my own efforts and accomplishments. I don't want anything given to me. I just want to test how far our society will let people go by themselves."

After returning to the capital, Liu supported himself with a variety of temporary factory jobs. In 1988, he worked with a corporation that made wear-resistant fabrics and lived in the factory dormitory. He often returned to Beida, however, where he had quite a record as an activist. Liu had first made a name for himself in the anti-Japanese protests of September 1985. After that, he became something of a hero on campus as one of the thirty-three Beida students arrested in Tiananmen Square on New Year's Day 1987. Later that year, in April, he successfully organized Beida students to nominate their own independent candidates in the district elections of "people's representatives." As in the case of Wang Juntao, the Party tried to pressure Liu through his father, who was a Public Security officer.

Liu Gang was undeterred, and he became a pivotal figure in the new democracy movement that sprang up at Beijing University during 1988. May 4 of that year was the ninetieth anniversary of the founding of the university. The authorities invited all alumni to return for the celebration, but not all of those who came stuck to the official program. On a shady lawn near the entrance to the campus, under the statue of Miguel de Cervantes, a group gathered to debate the significance of the occasion. They discussed academic freedom and the historic importance of the May Fourth movement of 1919, which is commemorated at Beida by a simple stone monument that intertwines the letters D and S—Democracy and Science.[2] Liu Gang was the driving force behind this meeting.

As the summer of 1988 wore on, these "lawn salons" became a regular Wednesday institution. Western journalists often dropped by to listen to the invited speakers, who included Fang Lizhi and his wife, the physicist Li Shuxian, as well as the celebrated activist of the Democracy Wall period, Ren Wanding. Among the students attending was Zhang Lun, the graduate student in sociology who now worked closely with SERI. Liu Gang struck Zhang as an unusually talented young man, but he seemed at loose ends; why not come out to the office, Zhang Lun suggested, and meet Wang Juntao and Chen Ziming? Liu agreed, and he and Wang became fast friends.

Over the following winter, the democracy salons not only continued at Beida but appeared at several other universities. The *shalong* idea spread to Qinghua, China's leading university of technology, to People's University, and to Beijing Normal College, the country's main teacher-training institution. At Beida, a second group was formed by Shen Tong, a slight, good-looking third-year student who read Martin Luther King and listened to Simon and Garfunkel records. Shen Tong called his salon the Olympic Institute, as a tribute to Albert Einstein's group of the same name. ("We should take a name connected with the Greek gods," he told his friends, "because they have human weaknesses."[3])

The original Wednesday salons at Beida were now led by Wang Dan, a twenty-one-year-old history freshman whose father was a Beida professor. Wang Dan, a scrawny young man with olive skin, lank black hair, and thick glasses, was perhaps the most intellectually impressive figure among the leaders of the 1989 student movement, and he quickly became a favorite of the foreign press corps.

When the Communist Party eventually compiled its official report on the events of 1989, it singled out the democracy salons as having "prepared, in terms of ideology and organization, for the turmoil that ensued." The great irony in this was that Wang Juntao and Chen Ziming saw the salons in a quite different light. Liu Gang told them that most of the student body was shallow, politically apathetic, and interested only in traveling abroad. Wang Dan also expressed this pessimistic view, but with eloquence. As the seventieth anniversary of the May Fourth movement drew near, he lamented, "We cannot help recognizing the fact that the 'TOEFL [Teaching of English as a Foreign Language] School' and the 'Mahjongg School' are in vogue, and that business fever has suffocated all other interests."

Wang and Chen cast a benevolent eye on the salons but saw nothing in them to arouse special interest. They valued them less as a serious political movement than as the source of a good friend and useful collaborator in Liu Gang, who came to work for a couple of months in the spring of 1989 with Bai Hua at her Opinion Research Center. The authorities, however, saw the salons as a serious security threat. Liu Gang became the target of harassment by agents of the Ministry of State Security; if he stayed a night at a certain Beida dormitory, he could count on a visit from police or campus security officials the following morning. As the anniversary of May Fourth approached, the atmosphere at Beida grew more tense. The salon leaders were warned to exercise care in their choice of speakers and subjects; Fang Lizhi and Li Shuxian were considered especially inappropriate visitors.

Wang Dan bridled at these new restrictions, and his name headed a list of fifty-six signatures on a *dazibao* pasted to the notice board at the Triangle on the morning of April 3, 1989. The poster was written as an open letter to the authorities, and it complained that seventy years after the May Fourth movement Beida's role as "the birthplace of this extraordinary movement of democratic enlightenment" was threatened: "This legacy of academic freedom and freedom of speech is in danger."

Wang Dan's views were not formed solely by events on the Beida campus, however. He also realized that 1989 was a year full of auguries: not only the seventieth anniversary of May Fourth, but the two hundredth of the French Revolution, the fortieth of China's Liberation, and the tenth of Wei Jingsheng's imprisonment. (The young man was one of the few among the current student body who remembered the jailed electrician. The Party had done a good job of silencing any news about earlier generations that might provide the democracy movement with a sense of continuity.) What may have alarmed the Party most about Wang Dan was the first issue of an independent student magazine that he edited, called *New May Fourth*. In contrast to the Democracy Wall period, the written output of the 1989 democracy protests was tiny. Whatever the reason for this—the crush of day-to-day events or the intellectual poverty of this latest generation of students—Wang Dan's *New May Fourth* was one of the few intellectually substantial publications of the 1989 movement, despite the fact that only a single issue was published. The magazine carried a preface by Li Shuxian, the main champion of the Beida salons, and an article by Hu Ping, the winner of the 1980 Beida elections, who was now living in New York. Most explosive of all, it included a short essay by Wang Dan that touched Deng Xiaoping's most sensitive nerve—his fear of "the Polish disease." "The freshness of the 1956 [Hungarian] spring is again permeating the air," Wang Dan wrote. Poland, where the Communist Party had legalized Solidarity and ended its own monopoly of power, showed the way forward. "Only if China sets its steps on the road of development of Eastern European countries in the near future will it be possible for her successfully to build a highly democratic and advanced country," the young history student continued.

Wang Dan did not even remotely consider SERI a source of guidance for the nascent democracy movement. One of his earliest encounters with Chen Ziming and Wang Juntao took place during Spring Festival in February 1989, at a "winter jasmine gathering" at Beijing's Friendship Hotel, where Fang Lizhi was the guest speaker. Chen Ziming sensed right away that Wang Dan was unimpressed by SERI's cautious and circumspect approach. In his speech, the Beida freshman went so far as to describe people like Wang Juntao as "the first in the first category of the five 'conservative forces' in Chinese politics." This was an early hint of the problems that Chen and Wang Juntao would have in attempting to moderate the course of that spring's democracy movement.

For Wang Dan, Fang Lizhi, who now described socialism as a failed system, was much more of a mentor, although technically, it was the old campaigner Ren Wanding who first ignited this new phase of the democracy movement. After his 1979 arrest and eventual release from jail in 1983, Ren had buried himself in a new job as an accountant for a machine installation company. He now resurfaced, every bit as outspoken as he was when he founded the China Human Rights League in 1979. Ren appealed to the international community to take up the cause of human rights in China. In December 1988, he published an essay that challenged the Communist Party to "let the people decide their future through the ballot box," and he called publicly for the release and pardon of Wei Jingsheng, who had been imprisoned for ten years.

Fang Lizhi took up this call for Wei's freedom in the unprecedented form of an open letter to Deng Xiaoping himself.[4] To Deng, this was the height of impertinence. Then, on February 13, the poet Bei Dao led a group of thirty-three intellectuals in issuing an appeal to the National People's Congress and the Central Committee that echoed Fang's demand. The release of Wei Jingsheng, they wrote, "would create a positive atmosphere advantageous to reform as well as being consistent with today's steadily growing trend across the world of respect for human rights." This was the first time that Chinese intellectuals had banded together in such direct criticism of the Communist Party. The signatories included the makers of *River Elegy* and members of both *ti nei* and *ti wai* think tanks. The letter snowballed, leading to a petition campaign that eventually gathered more than three thousand signatures, including almost all the leading members of SERI.

———

Wei Jingsheng's case was one of the items on the agenda of a Politburo meeting scheduled for April 8. Hu Yaobang was present, though he cut a forlorn figure. His attendance at Politburo meetings was still tolerated, although he was stripped of all portfolios in

1987 and had no real power. Hu had never fully recovered from his heart attack in 1988 and had spent much of the winter confined to bed with a bad case of the flu. But there were still echoes of his old brash and outspoken manner, and some believed that he became angry and upset on April 8 at the Party's intolerance of this new round of intellectual protest. Whether or not this is true, Hu collapsed in the middle of the discussion and was rushed to Beijing Hospital, where he remained for a week. He died at 7:53 A.M. on April 15.

Had Hu lived, the events of 1989 would surely have taken a different course. But with his death, all the latent pressures in Chinese society burst forth. A single common thought permeated the posters and leaflets and the spontaneous cries of anger that filled the streets: "Those who should have died live; those who should have lived have died." Grief is a powerful force for revisionism. In life, Hu's shortcomings were well known. But Hu the vacillator now became Hu the champion of freedom of thought; the General Secretary who had accepted his removal from office so meekly was now transformed into the tireless campaigner against bureaucratic orthodoxy, and the erratic and clownish sides of his character were all forgotten in the general mourning for "the soul of China."

In one crucial respect, however, no rewriting of Hu's life was necessary. He was still the man who, even when close to the pinnacle of his power, had been capable of the common touch—such as receiving Wang Juntao into his modest home in Beijing. Hu was the only Party leader who did not have a son or daughter working or studying abroad, and his family was free of the rumors of scandal and corruption that beset so many others. It was common knowledge that Hu's personal worth when he died was just a few hundred American dollars. In the seven days between Hu's death and the official memorial service, tens of thousands of people took to the streets in mourning, united in disgust at the stench of corruption that enveloped the Communist Party.

Nowhere was the shock at Hu's death deeper than at SERI. Liu Gang went to Beida to help with the frenzied preparations for what would shortly become the Beijing Federation of Autonomous Student unions. Nearby, at Politics and Law University, constitutional law expert Chen Xiaoping and a group of his fellow teachers worked late into the night to make an elaborate wreath. Early the next morning, April 16, Chen loaded the wreath, which measured two meters across, onto the back of a flatbed tricycle and pedaled off, accompanied by several hundred students, to Tiananmen Square. There he placed the wreath at the base of the Monument to the People's Heroes; the scene was an uncanny replay of 1976 after the death of Zhou Enlai. By dawn on April 16, the Monument was already dotted with white paper flowers and elegiac verses.

At the offices of *Economics Weekly,* Wang Juntao and his fellow editors remade the front page to carry a large portrait of Hu, edged in black. As his epitaph, they printed a statement that Hu made during the dark days of the 1981 crackdown on the democracy movement: "When contradictions among the people are dealt with in the wrong way, when they are sharpened, we must absolutely take a rational attitude, and not follow along and exacerbate things. . . . If you believe that you are right, why must you push yourself in the direction of mistaken aspects? If you think you may not be absolutely right, why must you still insist on the mistaken things? If we are right, then others will not be able to oppose us, and will not be able to overthrow us; if we have failings, and other people point them out, we should admit our mistakes. This is very good, and a relatively easy way of solving problems."

Hu's remarks were intended as a direct rebuttal of the classic Maoist line on class struggle. But they also reflected with great accuracy the philosophy that would guide Chen Ziming and Wang Juntao in the political crisis now erupting, not only in their attitude toward the Communist Party but toward the angry and impulsive student movement as well.

Beida was the core of the movement, but by April 17, 1989, events had begun to move with dizzying speed on every campus in the city. That night, thousands of students from Beida and People's University converged on the square, singing the *Internationale;* they stayed all night to make sure their freshly laid wreaths would not be removed. The next morning they handed in a petition to the National People's Congress. At the top of the list were demands to reevaluate Hu Yaobang's life and work and to end the Party's campaigns against "spiritual pollution" and "bourgeois liberalization." The Party did nothing to halt the demonstrations; in fact, word filtered down that Zhao Ziyang's faction supported the students. Sympathetic crowds gathered, and they grew as the week went on. By April 21, Deng Xiaoping decided that this was "no ordinary student movement."

The seven weeks of protests in Tiananmen Square moved through a number of discernible phases, and the climax of the first phase came on the night of April 21. The state memorial ceremony for Hu Yaobang, in itself a remarkable gesture to a man who was officially disgraced, was scheduled to occur in the Great Hall of the People the next day, a Saturday. The authorities curtly informed the crowds that the square was to be sealed off; but in an audacious tactical stroke, tens of thousands of students moved into the square under cover of darkness to preempt any action by the police.

Every member of the SERI steering committee was at the square to demonstrate support. Wang Juntao, who had been out of town in Xi'an for a two-day conference on enterprise reform, arrived in Beijing that evening in time to join the students. He ran into his colleagues at the square. The bold confidence running through the young demonstrators made him nervous, he remarked, given how things had turned out the last time crowds had staged an all-night occupation of Tiananmen in 1976. "I remember it all so clearly," he told Zhang Lun. "It happened at dawn, around four or five A.M. The police arrived and sealed off the square. Next they formed lines—one north-south, another east-west—and split the crowd into four separate, smaller groups. Then the beatings started, and the arrests. You can't believe how many troops there were, tens of thousands. They massed at the south end of the square, down by the Qianmen gate."

"What about tonight?" the younger man asked. "Do you think the same thing could happen again?"

"I don't know. Maybe not," Wang answered. "Old Deng is getting on, he's losing his grip. Maybe old age is even making him stupid."

They walked across the square to the Great Hall of the People. "The main thing," Wang continued, "is to avoid provocations, anything that might give them an excuse to crack down on the students. Like that, for instance," he added with irritation, pointing to a crowd at the foot of the steps of the Great Hall. They jogged over to see what was happening. A thin line of police was struggling to hold back the jostling crush of students. "Calm down!" Wang cried. "No confrontations!" And he quickly organized a group of students to link arms to form a protective picket line that could hold back the mob and defuse the angry moment.

Dawn was approaching. "Come on," said Zhang Lun, putting a hand on Wang's arm. "You ought to leave. You shouldn't be here, not with your record. If anything goes wrong, the first thing they'll do is to look for 'black hands' like you." As Wang went home, the peaceful mood in the square held.

The morning of Hu Yaobang's memorial service found the square still occupied by a substantial crowd and the police still standing off. The Party seemed paralyzed. Defying city regulations banning unauthorized demonstrations, thousands of ordinary Beijing citizens—the *laobaixing,* or "old hundred names"—now poured into the square in a display of solidarity with the students. At midmorning, the crowd was riveted by the sight of three students prostrating themselves on the broad staircase of the Great Hall, one of them holding aloft a long paper scroll in a parody of the manner in which feudal petitioners submitted their requests to the emperor in the Forbidden City.

The next day, April 23, student leaders from the various Beijing campuses gathered secretly at the ruins of Yuanmingyuan, the "garden of all gardens," the great palace of the Qing dynasty that had been looted and burned by Anglo-French forces in 1860. Here they set up the Provisional Students Federation of Capital Universities and Colleges and elected a steering committee. Most of its members, like Wang Dan, were undergraduates; a few others were graduate students. The twenty-eight-year-old Liu Gang, although no longer technically a student, was elected to the committee as a more experienced adviser. That evening, Chen Ziming drove to Beida to read the big-character posters on campus. He also carried a check for three thousand *yuan* ($800), which he handed to Liu Gang, the first outside donation to the new federation. (Some sources suggest the check was much larger, perhaps even one hundred thousand *yuan* [$26,000]).[5]

The Party at last began to prepare its official pronouncement on the crisis. On April 24, Beijing Party Secretary Li Ximing and Mayor Chen Xitong, both leftists, prepared an internal report for the five-man standing committee of the Politburo. They described the disturbances as "an anti-Party and anti-socialist political struggle" and urged an immediate crackdown. The following morning, Premier Li Peng and President Yang Shangkun paid a call on Deng Xiaoping to tell him that they agreed vigorously with this assessment. The eighty-four-year-old Chen Yun, regarded as the "godfather" of the conservatives, weighed in with a letter of his own to Deng. "We must take strong action to suppress the student movement," he wrote. "Otherwise it will only grow bigger, and if workers join in, the consequences will be unimaginable." Other senior conservatives accused a small number of bourgeois liberal intellectuals of inciting the students, offering an early hint of what would become the Party's line on "black hands."

The conservatives may have imagined that this lobbying effort was necessary to sway Deng's opinion. But they were probably wrong. For when Deng responded in his remarks to Li Peng and Yang Shangkun on April 25, it was apparent that he needed no one to fan his fears, especially of working-class involvement in the protests. The speech was like a catalogue of Deng's fears: his belief in behind-the-scenes conspiracy; his inability to distinguish between peaceful dissent and the nightmarish upheavals of the last ten years of Mao's life; his morbid, decade-long fascination with the collapse of socialism in Eastern Europe.

"This is turmoil," Deng declared. "We must take a clear stand, adopt effective measures, and not let them succeed in their aim. These people have been influenced by the liberals of Yugoslavia, Poland, Hungary, and the Soviet Union. Their aim is to overthrow the Communist government and make the future bleak for China. We must act swiftly. We should not be afraid of others cursing our mothers, or of international reaction." Deng noted the "potential for instability" among Chinese workers. "This turmoil is a planned conspiracy," he went on. "They are using the same old tactics used by troublemakers during the Cultural Revolution. They won't be satisfied until all is chaos." And again he made reference to the country that so haunted him. "We must quickly put an end to this turmoil. The more the Poles gave in, the greater their turmoil became. The opposition is very powerful in Poland, and there is Solidarity."

That evening, the highlights of Deng's remarks were broadcast on radio and television. So that no one should miss it, the message was repeated the next morning in an editorial in the *People's Daily,* which informed the population that all further demonstrations were illegal. But Deng's age and his obsessions had blinded him to reality. He and his fellow elders had defeated the warlords, the Guomindang, the Japanese, the Gang of Four. Were they now to be stymied by a bunch of twenty-year-olds with Sony Walkmans? Put the fear of God into them, Deng must have thought. They are sure to back down.

Some did. Zhou Yongjun, the first chair of the recently formed Beijing Students Autonomous Federation and one of the three students who had knelt in supplication on the steps of the Great Hall, spent April 26, the day of Deng's editorial, huddled in a fetal position, frightened out of his wits. But most students were infuriated by the harsh language of *People's Daily*. On April 27, instead of backing down, a four-mile-long column of students, cheered on by sympathetic bystanders, broke through the halfhearted police lines along Chang'an Boulevard and made its way to Tiananmen Square. Echoing earlier struggles half a world away, the chant on campuses that night was "We shall overcome!"

The middle-aged bourgeois liberals, whom the Party thought were masterminding the movement, did not share the students' euphoria. Chen Yizi, the head of the official think tank, RIRES, was in a hospital bed on the day the *People's Daily* editorial was read over the radio. At that moment, he saw clearly the dangers of escalation. The Party's hard line was foolish, but the protesters' behavior was also worrisome. Signs of divisions within the student movement began to appear, and their displays of zealous self-assurance provoked a nagging sense that the young demonstrators might be carried away by the grandiose comparisons they drew between themselves and the historic May Fourth movement of 1919. On the eve of the April 27 march, hearing rumors that the 38th Army was poised to move into Beijing, hundreds of students had written their wills. Talk of blood sacrifice was thick in the air. In this overcharged atmosphere, how could confrontation be avoided?

As student anger mounted in the days after Hu Yaobang's death, the question on everyone's mind at SERI was how to defuse the developing situation. The SERI staff also wrestled with the question of the role the older intellectuals should try to play in the movement. The Shanghai *World Economic Herald* and the liberal biweekly *New Observer* called a meeting on April 19 to evaluate the legacy of Hu Yaobang. Many of the key members of the Beijing intelligentsia, including Chen Ziming, attended. The participants agreed that the student movement merited their full support, and they endorsed the two main demands that had emerged so far from the student protests: a revision of the Party's verdict on the dead Hu and an end to the hostile campaigns against bourgeois liberalization.

Four days later, on April 23, Chen convened a meeting of his top associates at SERI to assess the situation. They feared that the Institute might be under surveillance, but they had no idea at the time of its extent. The meeting that took place at Shuangquanpu that day was recorded and later used as the state's first exhibit when Chen and Wang Juntao came to trial. According to the official court dossier, Chen told the meeting that "the historic duty of the intelligentsia, the advanced elements of the intelligentsia in particular, is rapidly to complete the process of organizing" to "form a new source of leadership for the common people."[6]

Wang Juntao, always more blunt than Chen, spoke next. "The government no longer has any social foundation which would enable it to control the crisis," he announced. "It has no remaining base of support." Wang went on, "China's leadership is once again caught in the midst of a transition period. Over the next several years, the old politicians who were previously forces for stability will successively depart from the scene. This is a period of great opportunity." He ended by reiterating many of the arguments he made in *River Elegy:* "China is on the verge of a brand-new civilization [and] present circumstances attest to the fact that the old methods are outdated. All the old methods employed by Chinese civilization must be transformed, and the basic tendency of this transformation will be toward mainstream world civilization." Finally, in the statement that must have most infuriated the Party, Wang declared, "After several decades of peaceful competition, socialist civilization has proved the loser."

After the April 23 meeting, events moved so fast that the SERI staff found it impossible to keep on top of the political situation and simultaneously deal with the normal work load of the Institute. Chen decided it was time for his team to get out of the office for a few days, to go somewhere quiet, somewhere without distractions and with fewer worries about security. The following Sunday, April 30, SERI's eleven-member executive committee headed for a small conference center at Xiangshan Villa, in the Fragrant Hills Park, on the northwestern outskirts of Beijing. Chen and Wang were both there, of course. So were Min Qi and Chen Xiaoping, Fei Yuan and Wang Zhihong. Bai Hua and Bi Yimin came from the Opinion Research Center. Zheng Di, who worked with Wang Juntao at *Economics Weekly;* Liu Weihua, SERI's director of research; and Xie Xiaoqing, another member of the Wuhan group and the director of SERI's Human Resources Testing and Evaluation Center, rounded out the committee.

Mao Zedong had always appreciated the attractions of the old imperial pleasure gardens of Xiangshan and had holed up there for six months in 1949 before moving into his new headquarters in liberated Beijing. Under other circumstances, it would have been a delightful place for SERI to meet. The hillsides were spotted with winter jasmine and peach blossom against the lush spring greenery. A path from the villa led first to the pretty Spectacles Lake, which was laid out in a figure eight with an arched stone bridge in the center; from there the path wound uphill to the curious Tibetan-style Luminous Temple and the seven-tiered Glazed Tile Pagoda. But the members of the SERI committee did not notice their surroundings. For two days, in a haze of cigarette smoke, they talked and argued about what to do: throw the Institute into the heat of political battle, or keep their distance from a conflict that seemed likely to end in bloodshed?

No one disputed that the 1989 student movement would be a turning point in China's long struggle for democracy. A watershed for the decade-long reform program, ideally it should also act as a spur to the Communist Party to carry out its own much-needed housecleaning. But there were two distinct schools of thought on what SERI's role should be. Some, like Min Qi, argued for caution. They stressed how hard it had been for SERI to overcome official hostility and surveillance and to build an institution that was economically self-sufficient and politically influential. SERI now operated with its own news media and employed several dozen full-time researchers. Plunging into the student movement would risk everything they had worked for, giving the Ministry of State Security a pretext to close SERI down. A second group, headed by

Wang Juntao, took a different view. The whole point of SERI, this group argued, was that it brought together people who had worked since 1976 to bring freedom and democracy to China. A historic opportunity to advance the cause of democracy now presented itself, and the choice should be clear. If SERI hesitated about supporting the students in Tiananmen Square, surely it would forfeit its reputation and prominence in the democracy movement.

The argument seesawed back and forth. Finally, Chen Ziming brought the matter to a vote. The committee members agreed that SERI would give the students its full support and guidance but would not take a visible, public role. These movement veterans were acutely sensitive to the reference in the April 26 *People's Daily* editorial to "an extremely small number of people with ulterior motives [who] continued to take advantage of the young students." Thus, there was general agreement that it was essential for SERI to do nothing that might lend credence to the official conspiracy theory.

At the time, this position seemed to be a sensible compromise, but in fact it placed Chen Ziming and Wang Juntao on a collision course with the authorities. Chen and Wang saw their decision as a matter of discretion, an effort to avoid confrontation. The Party, however, was later to present it as evidence of their sinister intent to manipulate events from behind the scenes.

10

Masters of the House

While SERI anxiously debated its responsibilities to the students in Tiananmen Square, Party conservatives had been anxiously monitoring an ominous development just a few hundred yards away from the square. As the aging Chen Yun had feared they would, the workers were beginning to join in. The first sign of their participation actually appeared on the first day of the protests, April 16: a white paper wreath laid at the foot of the Monument to the People's Heroes by an anonymous group of textile workers. That evening, the former bus conductor Zhao Hongliang, who had kept his distance from politics since the 1985 bus strike, decided to ride down from his parents' home in Hepingli, in northeast Beijing, to see what was happening on the streets.

As Zhao got off the bus, he saw soldiers on Chang'an Boulevard lining the northern approaches to Tiananmen Square. But the mood was quiet, even festive, in the cool evening air. Every so often as he walked through the crowds on Chang'an Boulevard, he was stopped by a smile or a handshake. It would take a moment to place the face; then he would recognize some coworker from the 1985 strike. They would exchange a few sad words about Hu Yaobang, shake their heads over rising prices, and wonder out loud what ordinary workers could do to register their anger.

The next day was Monday, April 17. After work at the department store on Xidan Street, Zhao walked the mile or so to the square, and gasped as he saw thousands of students rounding the corner by the Great Hall of the People and striding toward the Monument. Down by the west side of the Monument, a small knot of workers had gathered; Zhao joined them. There were heated voices, as one worker after another rose to speak. They talked of the moral courage of the students, but they also talked about inflation and corruption, and about the Party's remoteness from the concerns of ordinary workers like themselves. Finally, a tall, striking young man with a thick mass of wavy black hair rose to speak. From his first words, something in his manner fixed the crowd's attention on him, and other conversation quieted. The students only expressed what Chinese workers had in their hearts, he said. And the Constitution granted workers the right to organize freely, he went on, although in practice that right had been usurped by the official labor federation (ACFTU), which seemed as paralyzed by the economic crisis as the Party itself. The young man focused his speech on the army, waving his hand toward the troops who stood menacingly at the edges of the vast square. "How could they ever attack the likes of us?" he asked. "The army and the people are like fish and water."

Zhao Hongliang rushed over to congratulate the striking young man after the speech. "I thought that was very brave," Zhao said. "You have many good ideas, and you speak so well. What's your name?"

Although many workers preferred in these early days of the movement to keep their identities secret, the bushy-haired young man introduced himself as Han Dongfang, a worker at the Fengtai railway yards in Beijing's southwestern suburbs.

Han came from a wretched farming village of two thousand people called Nanweiquan ("Delicate South Spring") in the barren Taihang mountains of Shanxi Province, four hundred fifty miles southwest of the capital. He was among the poorest of the poor. These were Mao's people, the ones for whom he had made the revolution. By 1963, when Han was born, rural regions like eastern Shanxi had been devastated by the "three bad years" of largely man-made disasters. For parents of those times to call their newborn son "Dongfang" took real loyalty to Mao. The name translates as "East" and is one of the proudest terms in the Maoist canon. It was the very first word in the great anthem to Mao that was played everywhere while he was alive:

Dongfang hong,
Taiyang sheng.
Zhongguo chule ge
Mao Zedong!

The East is red
The sun is rising.
In China a Mao Zedong
Has appeared!

Han's mother was a strong and determined woman. Although pregnant, she left her husband in 1962 and moved to Beijing, where her first child was born. The boy spent his first three years in the home of an uncle, a cadre in the People's Liberation Army, in Xibiaobei *hutong,* a narrow alleyway a mile or so east of Tiananmen Square. But in 1966, in the early days of the Cultural Revolution, his uncle was denounced as a "capitalist roader" and sent to a remote province to perform manual labor.

The uncle's disgrace forced Han's mother to go back to Shanxi and to her husband, although she was unwilling to relinquish her much-prized Beijing household registration permit. In the harsh atmosphere of the Cultural Revolution, this marked her as a "black resident." Black residents were not entitled to grain coupons, and Han Dongfang's earliest childhood memory was of creeping into the fields in the dead of night to help his mother gather the chaff from the harvest, which she would press into coarse pancakes. This activity was fiercely denounced by the local Party cadres as "extra-collective consumption." The grain should be left to rot in the fields, they told the villagers, rather than fall into the hands of such "capitalist elements."

Han quickly came to feel that he was different, at the bottom of the heap even in a miserable place like Nanweiquan. When news filtered back to the village of his uncle's political troubles, neighbor children hung a heavy slate around the boy's neck, scrawled slogans on it, and jeered insults at him, in imitation of the official "struggle sessions" against counterrevolutionaries.

By 1970, when Han was seven, his mother could take no more of this life. She moved back to Beijing for good, leaving the boy's father behind in the ancestral village to toil over his maize fields. She found work on a construction gang, earning just thirty *yuan* a month. But she remained a devoted Party loyalist, for she could still remember the days when mothers in the Shanxi countryside had been forced to sell their children in order to survive. Growing up in the 1930s, she and her three sisters still had their feet bound; but she had thrown off her bandages and, as a result, was the only one of the four who could walk properly.

Mocked by his city teachers for his slowness in the classroom, Han grew proud and rebellious. During the Qing Ming festival of 1976, at the age of twelve, he slipped off to Tiananmen Square and filled a notebook with the poems he found pasted up in honor of Premier Zhou Enlai. In the schoolyard, he and his friends played the game of *xiao pingtou*—"Crewcut Shorty"—picking on any child with short hair for resembling the counterrevolutionary villains they saw in the government propaganda broadcasts about the Tiananmen Incident. The arch-villain in these schoolyard games was the *xiao pingtou* with dark glasses—that is to say, Chen Ziming.

When Han graduated from the run-down Beijing High School Number 124 in the summer of 1980, his prospects were bleak. Under Deng Xiaoping's new regime, "degree fever" was all the rage, yet Han decided not to try for college. Instead, he took his mother's advice and joined the *Gong An Bing,* the Public Security Soldiers Corps—predecessor of the modern People's Armed Police. After basic training at the Qinghe prison labor camp, near Tianjin, he spent three years as a guard at Tuanhe, a similar camp south of Beijing.

Han proved an excellent soldier, and he was soon put in charge of a squad of twelve men. His superiors forecast a rosy future—until the time came for the camp's annual review. This was designed as a ritual. Squad leaders were expected to come up to the platform, in front of all the officers and men, and deliver themselves of suitable platitudes. But Han got straight to the point. "My men's main problem is food," he announced. "The officers are stealing a third of our food allowance. This is in direct contravention of Chairman Mao's line that officers and men are equal and must share both sufferings and good times. My second point concerns cruel punishment. My men are beaten and abused at will by their superior officers." Looking around the hall, Han could see expressions of delight and amazement on the faces of his squad, and black rage on the faces of the officers. The next day, the battalion commandant pulled out Han's application for Party membership and tore it into small pieces. "Han Dongfang will become a Party member over my dead body," he said.

Han served out his three years at Tuanhe, fighting to the end for the rights of his men. When he left in September 1983, his squad members nominated him for a commendation as an "advanced individual in building socialist spiritual civilization."

It was his younger sister, Dongmei ("Winter Plum"), who found him his next job as an assistant librarian at the Beijing Teachers College. Although a humble position, the post still carried a certain prestige in China, since Mao Zedong himself had once worked as an assistant librarian at Beijing National University, more than sixty years earlier. Han performed well, but he found the work dull and used his free time to read voraciously—Freud, Hemingway, the Chinese classics, the Greek myths, anything he could lay his hands on. Neighbors would point to the piles of books at the home of his illiterate mother and ask whose they were. "Dongfang's?" they would say in amazement. "How can he read such things? He's only a worker."

After six months at the library, Han felt himself at something of a crossroads. His sister tried to persuade him to return to school to get some professional qualifications. But Han worried about the family's economic situation, and the library job paid less than manual labor. The family had returned to its old home at Number 33 Xibiaobei *hutong*. The house was a few yards off the busy thoroughfare of Jianguomenwai, the eastern extension of Chang'an Boulevard; if you listened closely, you could just hear the martial tones of *The East Is Red,* every hour on the hour, from the giant clock over the nearby Beijing Railway Station. But to enter Han's *hutong* was to enter another world, to make one of those abrupt transitions that are so common in Beijing. Grass grew on the roofs of the mean brick-built courtyard houses, which still had no sanitation of their own; every fourth or fifth building in the *hutong* was a foul-smelling public latrine. Han's was an ordinary worker's home, a dismal contrast to the home of a "golden child" of the Party like Wang Juntao.

For the sake of a higher salary, Han decided in 1984 to take a job at Beijing's huge Fengtai Locomotive Maintenance Section, working on the antiquated, sooty goods trains of the Chinese National Railways. He became an electrician on a mobile repair and maintenance crew for the big diesel refrigeration cars that transported fruit and vegetables all across China. Work conditions were hellish. Temperatures in the engine room rose above 70 degrees centigrade; coolant fumes hung thick in the air; the noise was deafening. But there was time to read and scenery to admire, and the work schedule—a month on, followed by twenty days off—gave Han long stretches of time at home with his mother and sister.

Each trip home there seemed to be some new incident that gave shape to Han's budding sense of political injustice. On one occasion, he found that elections to the local People's Congresses had been held while he was away from Beijing. He asked his work-unit leader if anything could be done about this. The man grinned and said, "Don't worry; we had someone vote for you." "But isn't that a violation of my rights?" Han asked. This time the man laughed out loud. Another time, in 1986, his coworkers suggested that he approach the representative of the official union to pass on their grievances about working conditions. "Why are you coming to me?" the official asked. "My hands are tied." "As far as I can see," Han retorted, "the ACFTU does nothing except organize the occasional film show and hand out soap so that we can wash our hands."

In January 1987, at the height of the Beijing student demonstrations, Han was back in the capital once again. He strolled to Tiananmen one evening, arriving just in time to see two squads of police beating up a crowd of demonstrators. He saw one student kicked in the face and trampled; another was picked up and flung into the back of a jeep. It reminded Han of how the peasants of Nanweiquan would toss a slaughtered pig on the back of a flatbed truck.

When he met Zhao Hongliang in the square that night in 1989, Han Dongfang was only twenty-five, but he had a maturity and an air of wisdom that belied his boyish appearance. There was a quietness to his passion and a conservative cast to his thought that made him deliberate hard, lips pursed, before answering a question. There was an almost scholarly air to Han, an innate caution in his gestures, but at the same time he had a dry wit and a ready sense of humor.

When the speeches were over, the group of workers agreed to convene again the next day, April 18, at 5:00 P.M. Among those who emerged as the early leaders of the group were: Wang Dengyue, in his mid-thirties, a worker at the Xuanwu District Construction Company; Xiao Delong, a man of about the same age, who was a cook at Qinghua University;[1] and Zhao Pinlu, a boilermaker in his late thirties. A good-humored, hard-drinking man with bony features and a scraggly beard, Zhao often looked much older. Everyone called him *Lao Zhao*—Old Zhao.[2]

As they looked around, they remarked wryly that their motley group of a few dozen souls was hardly a threat to the powerful monolith of the ACFTU. They did, however, come from work units with thousands of members. Why not go back to their workplaces the next day to canvass support, someone suggested, and tell anyone who was interested to meet here on April 20?

But that proved to be difficult. By April 19, the student marchers were better organized, and when the first workers arrived outside Tiananmen Gate near the giant portrait of Mao, they found a student picket line blocking the northern side of the square along Chang'an Boulevard.

"What's going on here?" Zhao Hongliang asked a picketer who seemed to be in charge.

"What college are you from?" the man replied.

"We're not students, we're workers. I work at the Xidan department store."

"Then you'll have to move along," the student answered. The tone was polite, but the message was not. "This is our movement, and it has nothing to do with you. We students are the vanguard. If we let you into the square, things might get out of hand. We're afraid bad people might stir things up."

The workers looked at each other. They were annoyed, even a little shocked. Some, however, felt the students had a point: Beijing was, after all, full of angry, unemployed young men, and it was reasonable for the students to guard against any incident that might give the government an excuse to point the finger at "ruffians" or "hooligans," as it liked to call working-class dissenters.

As they mulled over this first incident of worker-student unpleasantness, the workers walked away from the square, toward a spot known as Xiguanlitai, the West Reviewing Stand. The great gate, and the portrait of Mao at its center, are flanked on both sides by broad banks of red-painted seats, which fill with cadres and dignitaries on special occasions. At the west end of the reviewing stand, just across the street from the walled Party leadership compound of Zhongnanhai, the seats meet the ground at a sharp angle; there the space beneath provides shelter from the rain. The workers decided this place was better than nothing and set up their headquarters. They posted a notice on the wall, inviting people to join a new, independent workers' organization; then, they threw their overcoats and cotton jackets down on the concrete and prepared to sleep.

Sleep did not come easily that night, because hundreds of the student demonstrators left the square to stage a sit-in at Xinhuamen, New China Gate, the ornate gateway to Zhongnanhai. The mood was angry, and the chants suddenly became vitriolic. At the very entrance to the citadel of power, nineteen- and twenty-year-old students pounded at the gates, yelling "Down with the Communist Party!" and "Let Cixi retire!"—referring to Deng Xiaoping and equating him with the aging dowager empress Cixi of the final years of the Qing dynasty. Han Dongfang observed the protest with concern. He told the students that it was absurd for them to demand that Li Peng come out and talk to them. He pleaded for them to show restraint, not to goad the guards into a confrontation. But it was all in vain. Mixed in with the crowd were some street toughs who smashed a few parked bicycles and exchanged blows with the police when they forcibly broke up the sit-in around 3:30 in the morning.

All sides drew their own lessons from the skirmish at Xinhuamen. At a tense Politburo meeting on the morning of April 20, Li Peng began to advance the conspiracy theory: "I think the students were instigated by a small group of people," he said, "and that this entire affair is aimed at the Party, especially the elderly leaders." Not so, retorted Zhao Ziyang. "There are so many people involved, it's doubtful that a 'small group' of people could have been behind it. I think we should be very cautious. We should try to solve the problem through dialogue."

In the makeshift quarters under the reviewing stand at Xiguanlitai, news of the melee was spread quickly by a small group of workers who had been caught up in it. The dilemma was clear. The students obviously had sound reasons for their ambivalence about working-class support; at the same time, however, the workers had their own agenda, their own reasons for protest, and, in light of what had happened at Xinhuamen, a desire to do what they could to protect the students on the square. A small delegation decided to go to Building Number 48 at Beida and confer with the students' interim leadership to discuss how the two groups could work together. The students agreed to help print the workers' handbills, but on the matter of the square, they refused to budge: No one but students would be allowed to set foot there.

The workers' first posters came out later that day. A short "Letter to the People of Beijing" expressed support for the students, demanded wage increases and price stabilization, and extravagantly compared the violence of the previous night to the suppression of the April Fifth movement in the square thirteen years earlier. The letter was accompanied by a sardonic list of "Ten Polite Questions for the Chinese Communist Party." "How much did Deng's son [Pufang] bet on a horse race in Hong Kong," asked the first, "and where did he get the money to place the bet?"[3] Second question: "Mr. and Mrs. Zhao Ziyang play golf every week. Who pays the greens fees and other expenses?" And so on down to number ten: "Would the Party be so kind as to explain the meaning and implications of the following terms: (a) Party; (b) Revolution; and (c) Reactionary?"

The students largely ignored the workers, and no foreign reporters came by to ask them questions. Over the next few days, however, the workers at Xiguanlitai took their first hesitant steps toward becoming a more solid organization. By April 21, they had divided up their tasks. Zhao Hongliang was put in charge of logistics, including the provision of food and water to the students. The federation issued its crude credentials for membership, stating that only bona fide workers carrying work-unit identification would be accepted. After April 21, the first slogans raised by the workers at Xiguanlitai could be heard among the shouting crowds: "Down with official profiteering, eliminate corruption!" "Stabilize prices and raise the wages of the workers." "Publicly reveal the wealth and assets of Deng Pufang and the sons and daughters of leading cadres."

None of this activity went unnoticed in official quarters. When the April 26 *People's Daily* editorial appeared, it referred pointedly to the Party's "tolerant, restrained attitude to certain inappropriate words and actions of emotionally excited young students." But it left no room for tolerance of worker dissent and complained that "an extremely small number of people with ulterior motives" were "making unauthorized use of the names of workers' organizations [and] distribut[ing] reactionary leaflets."

It was the Qinghua cook, Xiao Delong, who went on April 27 to the Ministry of Public Security on East Chang'an Boulevard to inquire whether the new workers' group could legally register under Article 35 of the Constitution, which guarantees the freedoms of speech, press, assembly, and demonstration. He came back despondent; since the workers' group was designated an illegal organization, the ministry reasoned with perfect bureaucratic logic, how could it be legally registered? Each day someone else made a new attempt, trekking off to the ministry again or to the Beijing municipal authorities. The answer was always the same: You are class enemies; stop stirring things up; you will be arrested if you keep this up. Public Security agents began to make threatening visits to the cramped quarters under the reviewing stand.

But the workers persisted. They saw themselves neither as unusually brave nor unusually militant. They simply acted out of deep moral indignation and a sense of puzzlement about the government's obtuseness. Their attempts to broaden their membership were amateurish: Delegates canvassed strategic factories, such as the huge Capital Iron and Steel Works in western Beijing, where they were given a warm welcome but were warned by friendly workers that they were taking a serious risk. A number of reform-minded cadres from the ACFTU quietly contacted the group at Xiguanlitai and let it be known that the workers' views were shared by many in the official unions. But when the Xiguanlitai group marched one day along Chang'an Boulevard to the headquarters of the ACFTU, they found their way barred and did little more than mill around outside and pass out leaflets to the security guards at the gate.

Yet slowly their infrastructure grew. Members of the group brought tables and chairs and bedding to Xiguanlitai and helped themselves to supplies from a nearby public washroom. A donation of heavy waterproof cloth made a primitive tent. A notice went up asking for the loan of a diesel generator. Someone even brought

a small van from his work unit; a loudspeaker rigged on top blared
out the workers' slogans during the huge student march of April 27.

Although Deng Xiaoping and the conservatives thundered against
turmoil and conspiracy, the Party also spoke with a second, softer
voice. The mixed signals that Han Dongfang and other worker
activists received on May 1, a public holiday in China, were confusing in the extreme. On that day, the hard-line Beijing Party
Committee issued a stern directive to all workplaces in the capital,
advising factory managers to do whatever they thought necessary
to break the link between workers and students. The higher levels
of the Party, however, seemed to take pains to sound more conciliatory. At a May Day rally for model workers in the Great Hall
of the People, the main speaker was Hu Qili, the sixty-year-old
Politburo member in charge of propaganda. The choice of speaker
may have been a little surprising, for Hu was a former liberal ally
of Hu Yaobang's and was linked in many people's minds with the
moderate line of Zhao Ziyang. Hu's speech was full of boilerplate
phrases, which satisfied the conservatives, but a close reading revealed a more subtle message. "While we emphasize stability and
unity," he said, "it does not mean that we do not want to foster
democracy. Stability and unity are the prerequisites for propelling
the building of democratic politics." Chen Ziming and Wang Juntao would certainly have echoed these sentiments. *People's Daily,*
in a retreat from its brutally hard line of five days earlier, echoed
Hu's remarks in a front-page commentary. "The workers have
made great contributions to society," it added, "and yet have received little in return."

While Hu Qili was delivering his ambiguous greeting to model
workers, an official aircraft was bringing his patron, Zhao Ziyang,
back to Beijing from a weeklong state visit to North Korea. On
his arrival, he listened to reports from his aides. Zhao became
convinced that the moment had come to pull the Party back from
the confrontational mood of the April 26 editorial, which had been
written during his absence. Zhao was not a great democrat; his
cause was economic reform, and he was no political liberal. But
he did have more tolerance than his older colleagues for the intellectuals' demands for change. And as a politician with ambitions,

he still smarted from the reverses he suffered the previous summer when he had taken personal blame for the overheating of the economy.

When Zhao looked out at the crowds in the streets, he saw a source of political leverage for his own comeback—a little, perhaps, as Deng Xiaoping had seen the crowds at Democracy Wall in 1978. Zhao felt that his hand was strengthened by the coming anniversary of the May Fourth movement, which was certain to mark a new climax for the student movement. This year the date was important for another reason, too: Hundreds of international bankers would flock to the Great Hall of the People on that day to hear Zhao's keynote speech to the Asian Development Bank. He felt confident that the hard-liners would not risk a crackdown at such a time. Zhao decided to make his move.

Zhao's decision to confront the hard-liners would have a monumental impact on the remaining weeks of the battle for control of Tiananmen Square, and especially on the fate of Chen Ziming and Wang Juntao. The Party's divisions were by now painfully apparent to the two men, who saw a frightening downward spiral developing. These divisions caused paralysis, which left the Party incapable of responding to the students' demands. The protesters' tactics became only more radical as a result. The danger of a bloody outcome therefore increased, and no one stood to benefit from that but the hard-line conservatives.

Ever since *Beijing Spring*, Wang Juntao had seen an independent press as an essential part of any democratic opening. Now, from his contacts through *Economics Weekly*, Wang knew that hundreds of journalists in the official media were sympathetic to the democracy movement but were forced by their editors to doctor their reporting about it. Since 1949, with rare, honorable exceptions such as Liu Binyan, Chinese journalists had acted as a conveyor belt for the Party leadership, printing each gyration in the official line as it was fed to them. But during the late 1980s, this tradition was shaken, thanks to publications like *Economics Weekly* and the *World Economic Herald* in Shanghai, whose editor was the gnomish seventy-year-old Qin Benli. After the April 19 forum, organized by the *Herald* and attended by Chen Ziming, the Party stepped up its vigilance of Qin; by April 27, it decided he had gone too far.

The Shanghai Party boss, Jiang Zemin—another Soviet-educated conservative technocrat, like Li Peng—ordered that week's issue of the *Herald* seized because of its "inflammatory" reporting of the death of Hu Yaobang. Qin Benli was summarily fired.

But the very next day brought a different signal, as propaganda chief Hu Qili delivered the softer line. On April 28, Hu invited the editors of nine major newspapers to discuss press coverage of the student demonstrations. Reversing his instructions of the previous week, which had been to ignore the students, he now told the editors they could report on "the actual state of affairs" so that readers could form their own conclusions. He added, reassuringly, that the Party shared many of the demonstrators' feelings about inflation and corruption.

The city's reporters were confused by these mixed signals, and on April 30 they held a meeting to discuss how the media could keep the reform process on track. They met in the Beijing office of the Guangzhou-based *Asian and Pacific Economic Times,* in a room above the small museum dedicated to the memory of the great Chinese writer Lu Xun. Despite Hu Qili's assurances, many reporters found that when their copy reached the printer it was shorn of the street voices they had tried to capture. Press freedom, a growing number of reporters concluded, should not be a matter of official whim but of legal guarantees. Otherwise, journalism would continue to be as Liu Binyan once described it: "In China, what a reporter writes and does not write, or even the way he chooses to approach a subject, is not for him to decide. A good part of the reporter's working life consists of hanging around official doorsteps waiting for approval for his pieces."

Wang Juntao, a recent, passionate convert to the journalism profession, was invited to give his views to a second gathering of concerned reporters in the office above the Lu Xun Museum on May 3. In the spirit of what was agreed to the day before at Xiangshan Villa, Wang acted in his own capacity and did not advertise his connection to SERI. Bai Hua, who taught a journalism course at People's University in addition to her work on public opinion at ORCC, called several of her friends and encouraged them to come. In the end, more than one hundred people from some thirty Beijing media organizations crowded into the room.

Wang still seemed optimistic that the government would back down and cited the example of the 1980 Kwangju student massacre in South Korea. "It would be dangerous for the Party to crush the students as the Koreans did, because then they would only nurse resentments and the problem wouldn't go away unless the government were overthrown. But the Chinese government is not so stupid."

The journalists drafted a petition to the Central Committee urging the reinstatement of Qin Benli, the removal of the Party "rectification group" that had been attached to the *World Economic Herald,* and a dialogue with the government. Fei Yuan was at this second meeting, and on behalf of *Economics Weekly,* he and Wang agreed to help organize a contingent of reporters who would participate in the next day's march under banners demanding press freedom. For more and more of SERI's members, the magnetic pull of Tiananmen was getting harder and harder to resist.

Early the next morning, in bright sunshine, two columns of students converged on the square, one from the university district of Haidian, another from the colleges in the eastern part of the city. It was the seventieth anniversary of the May Fourth movement. Today the marchers showed a new level of discipline, and student marshals barred anyone who could not produce a college identification. The police lines across Chang'an Boulevard melted like butter, and the two columns of marchers met under the giant portrait of Mao before filing into the square to the strains of the *Internationale.* There they listened to Wu'er Kaixi, the new chair of the Beijing Students Autonomous Federation, as he read an emotional manifesto that declared the demonstrators to be the spiritual inheritors of the "May Fourth spirit of science and democracy."

But by midafternoon, as the temperature reached into the eighties, the energy seemed to dissipate. What next? Some students decided to denounce the official media. On the way back to campus, one group paused to chant slogans outside the offices of Radio Beijing and CCTV. Another headed east to the headquarters of *People's Daily.* To the tune of *Frère Jacques,* the marchers chanted:

> *People's Daily, People's Daily,*
> *Really strange, really strange.*
> *Always printing lies, always printing lies,*
> *Really strange, really strange.*

If one was looking for an emblematic expression of the students' self-absorption—their lack of real attention to other social groups involved in the protests—it was this, because they failed to notice that the editorial offices of *People's Daily* were almost deserted; in fact, a hundred of the paper's staff were marching in the streets that day, under banners that read "A Press Blackout Doesn't Help Stability" and "Our Pens Can't Write the Articles We Want to Write, Our Mouths Can't Say the Words We Want to Say."

The students paid even less attention to the contingent of several thousand young workers, who were segregated from the main march by the efficient young student marshals. As on previous occasions, the workers came not only to show their admiration for the students but also to press their own demands. In many cases, these were less about civil liberties than about economic justice. The workers were less likely than a history student like Wang Dan to have read about the events in Poland, but they were more likely to be in sympathy with Lech Walesa's remark that "Everybody has to fill their belly, be they a minister or a cleaning lady."

In an air-conditioned conference room in the Great Hall of the People, Zhao Ziyang offered his guests soothing words about the clamor in the sunshine outside. "I am firmly convinced that the situation will gradually quiet down," he told the Asian bankers. "China will not experience any major turmoil," he went on, pointedly using the term that Deng Xiaoping had chosen to stigmatize the protests. "I think that we must use democratic and legal avenues to resolve [the reasonable demands of the students]. We should resolve them through reform and reasonable, orderly methods. If you analyze for a moment the specific situation, it becomes quite clear: What the students are most upset about is the phenomenon of graft and corruption. As a matter of fact, this is a problem the Party and government have been working on for several years now."

Zhao's remarks to the Asian Development Bank were broadcast on national television that evening on the seven o'clock news. The Party's "divided sovereignty" (in the phrase of the scholar Andrew Walder) was now on full public display.[4] The media launched into an extraordinary week of honest, open coverage, and the student movement realized that it now enjoyed the support of one faction of the Party, which was an unexpected turn of events whose dangers were not immediately apparent. As students watched the evening news broadcasts on May 4, they erupted in applause. "Zhao Ziyang's speech is a relatively objective and realistic one," one student from Politics and Law University told a reporter from *People's Daily*. "I agree with his eight-word principle: Be Calm, Be Reasonable, Exercise Restraint, Keep Order."

Following Zhao's prescription, however, was to prove more easily said than done, for two reasons. One was that the hardliners' view of events was now transformed; Zhao Ziyang's speech, in their view, verged on treason—and the traitor was looking to enlist mass support to fight his factional battles. The other reason was that the student movement found itself at a crossroads; its tactics so far might have won public support, but they had not achieved tangible results.

Over the following week the mood on campus faltered. May Fourth had been a catharsis, but now fissures appeared in the student leadership. Some argued for a return to classes, which many students were doing anyway, and formed a moderate "Dialogue Delegation" that asked the government for talks that would be broadcast live on television; more radical leaders, however, feared the movement was losing its momentum and pleaded for new, more aggressive tactics to force the government's hand.

On May 8, the standing committee of the Politburo met in emergency session. The meeting ended in a shouting match between Zhao Ziyang and Li Peng when Zhao announced that he intended to visit the students in the square. "Do that," Li Peng warned, "and you will be held responsible for splitting the Party." Three days later the Politburo was in session again. This time, Zhao suggested that the Party accede to some of the protesters' demands, especially those that concerned corruption. As a sign of good faith, he said he would allow his own sons' activities in Shenzhen to be the first target of a probe.[5] Zhao also boldly proposed that press freedom be expanded; Li Peng raged that Zhao was straying from Party policy. With his outspoken remarks on press freedom, Zhao had deliberately moved a step closer to the expressed position of the independent intellectuals like Wang Juntao. The journalists' petition, which Wang had helped draft at the Lu Xun Museum, had now been submitted to the government with more than one thousand signatures.

On paper, the Chinese Communist Party was an immense machine, engineered according to Leninist principles. From the humblest work unit to the various Party commissions, to the Central

Committee, the Politburo, and the Standing Committee of the Politburo, it was a pyramid of minutely detailed regulations and procedures. In practice, Deng Xiaoping acted much as Mao had, which was to ignore the whole elaborate decision-making process when it was inconvenient for his goals. The Politburo went through its deliberations, as the rule book demanded, but Deng had begun simultaneously to consult with his own secret conclave of elders, most of whom had no formal powers.[6] Assisted by Li Peng, the old men—Deng, Peng Zhen, Chen Yun, Yang Shangkun, and others—resolved to crush the democracy movement and silence the Party's "splittists."

Although Zhao Ziyang had been in politics a long time, he had failed to learn some basic lessons about the realities of power in China; the inexperienced students, however, grasped even less than Zhao. The Dialogue Delegation had given the government until May 8 to answer its demand for live broadcast talks; but the Party, still locked in its internal conflicts, stalled until May 12. That evening, it agreed to a meeting on May 15—but only "an informal discussion," not a dialogue, and with no live media coverage, just "a partial news report." A small group of radical student leaders was infuriated by the stalemate.

On the night of May 12, a crowd gathered as usual at Beida to listen to speeches. They were enraptured by the words of a frail, diminutive twenty-three-year-old psychology student named Chai Ling. The young woman declared that it was time for a new and more confrontational strategy to force the Party's hand. What she proposed was to begin a hunger strike. "Why am I doing it?" she asked rhetorically. "Because I want to see the true face of the government. . . . We only want the government to talk with us and say that we are not traitors. We, the children, are ready to die. We, the children, are ready to use our lives to pursue the truth. We, the children, are willing to sacrifice ourselves." This kind of language left the Party moderates with little room to maneuver.

11

Pushed to Center Stage

No one was pausing for breath. Every day, around the clock, the meetings went on. Student leaders, both moderate and radical, met to ponder their next step; allies of Zhao Ziyang met to improve their leverage against their conservative rivals; Chen Ziming, Wang Juntao, and their colleagues at SERI met for daily situation reports on the showdown in the square.

The newly formed student Dialogue Delegation was headed by Xiang Xiaoji, a law student at Politics and Law University, and Shen Tong, who had formed the Olympic Institute. The Dialogue Delegation hoped to offer a bridge between Zhao's supporters in the government and the "illegal" Beijing Students Autonomous Federation. Delegation leaders scrutinized Zhao's speech to the Asian Development Bank, as well as every word uttered by his opponents, trying to read between the lines, to fathom the split between Zhao and Li Peng, and to plan their next move accordingly. But the group found it hard to present a coherent negotiating position, since the student movement too often spoke as a babble of discordant voices.

Meanwhile, one of Zhao's closest allies, a fifty-eight-year-old member of the Central Committee Secretariat named Yan Mingfu, talked himself hoarse in a series of marathon sessions with reform-minded intellectuals in an effort to find common ground with the students. Yan brought a distinguished political résumé and high-level connections to the task. Born in 1931, he had known Yan'an as a child; his father had been a high Party official and a close associate of Zhou Enlai. Later, as a precocious young man in his mid-twenties, Yan was appointed Mao's Russian translator during the Chairman's dealings with Khrushchev. In 1966, at the onset of the Cultural Revolution, he was thrown into Qincheng prison as a Soviet spy and traitor. In the next cell, held on the same charges, was the veteran Yang Shangkun, who was now China's President; the two men were rehabilitated together in 1979.

By May 9, Yan Mingfu had worked himself into a state of collapse and was hospitalized. From his sickbed he made known his desire for a substantive dialogue with the unofficial student leaders. The threat of a hunger strike, and the rhetoric that accompanied it, threw Yan into something approaching panic, because it injected a completely new intensity into the crisis—a language of blood and sacrifice that had deep and damaging roots in China's political history.

On the morning of Saturday, May 13, Yan, barely recovered from his illness, met a group of friendly intellectuals at the Central Committee's United Front Work Department, which he headed.[1] He anxiously asked Zheng Yefu, a young researcher at the Chinese Academy of Social Sciences, for advice about how best to approach the students. Zheng shrugged; personally, he had no special influence with the students. But he thought that SERI, the private research institute where he was an occasional collaborator, might be an appropriate intermediary. Several of SERI's staff kept their fingers on the pulse of the campus movement, and they were the kind of people who made things happen quickly. Yan Mingfu turned to an aide and ordered a minibus and driver to be placed at Zheng's disposal right away. "See if you can find these SERI people," he told Zheng, "and ask them if they will act as a bridge to the students, find a representative group of them that we can talk to, and help us defuse the situation. Above all, let's see if they can find a way of getting the hunger strikers to end the strike before Monday." The historic Sino-Soviet summit, putting an end to thirty years of hostility, was to begin on May 15 and had attracted the world's media to the Chinese capital. Now the student hunger strikers were encamped at the base of the Monument to the People's Heroes, just yards from the Great Hall of the People, where Deng and Gorbachev were to meet.

At three o'clock, Zheng Yefu's minibus sped off to the SERI offices at Shuangquanpu. Zheng found the leading members of SERI preparing for their weekly board meeting. He explained the situation to them briefly. They did not need to be told that the hunger strike and Yan Mingfu's request for them to act as intermediaries altered their decision to remain detached; the careful compromises they had reached at the Xiangshan Villa retreat less than two weeks earlier were now overtaken by events. If one of Zhao Ziyang's closest allies, presumably acting with the authority of the General Secretary himself, was pleading for them to become involved, how could they refuse? As Chen Ziming later remarked, SERI did not choose its own destiny; it was "pushed to center stage" by the Party's request.

The board decided that Wang Juntao should lead the SERI contingent to the talks while Chen Ziming remained in the background. It would be rather like the Communist Party in the 1930s and 1940s, someone said, when the Red Army Marshal Zhu De had supplied the troops and materiel and Mao Zedong the public face and the ideas. The Red Army had had its "Zhu-Mao leadership"; now SERI would have its "Chen-Wang leadership."

Wang Juntao, Chen Xiaoping, and Bai Hua piled into the waiting minibus and told the driver to head for Beida. But finding the campus quiet and none of the student leaders around, they pressed on to People's University. There was no one there either. The next stop was Politics and Law University, where Chen Xiaoping taught. He jumped out of the minibus and ran off to see who he could find. He returned a few minutes later with a hastily assembled group of Dialogue Delegation members, led by Shen Tong. Wu'er Kaixi and Wang Dan were not there; they had gone to a restaurant to enjoy a last lunch before beginning their fast.

At about five o'clock, the minibus drew up outside the headquarters of the United Front Work Department. A second vehicle arrived moments later with Chai Ling, Wu'er Kaixi, and Wang Dan on board; all wore the dramatic headbands of the hunger strike. They made their way upstairs to the conference room. Yan Mingfu, still looking pale and unwell, was at the head of the long oval table. He gestured for the students to sit down. A dozen seats were allocated for the students, but word of the meeting had spread and more than three times that number were milling around. The members of the Dialogue Delegation sat down to Yan's left, the hunger strike leaders to his right. A number of leading figures from the Beijing Students Autonomous Federation also showed up, and they stood around the edge of the circle. Wang Juntao took an empty seat next to Wang Dan.

"So," said Yan Mingfu, "before we start, who is representing the students here?"

"We all are," said Wu'er Kaixi with breezy self-confidence. "The fact that we've come in three groups doesn't mean we're divided. It only means that we have three different positions."

Yan considered this piece of logic. "As you wish," he said with an indulgent laugh. Then he became serious. He began by reminding the students that Gorbachev's arrival was a great plum for China, an important symbol of the success of Deng's economic reforms. Nothing should be done to jeopardize this, or to give the conservatives grounds for a crackdown that would set the reform process back for years. "If you must divide the Central Committee into factions," he went on, "then your action is not helpful to the pro-reform faction. Zhao Ziyang's intentions would be very hard to realize."

Wang Juntao spoke next, making a long, eloquent appeal for moderation. Although he echoed all that Yan Mingfu had said, he left no doubt that his sympathies lay with the students. It was up to the government, he argued forcefully, to defuse the situation. And it was up to the students to stay cool and negotiate for some compromise, since their intransigence would only benefit the conservatives.

The angrier voices among the students objected. The students had already reduced their original list of demands to just two: Recognize the students as a legitimate patriotic movement, and repudiate the April 26 *People's Daily* editorial and its description of the protests as "turmoil."[2] Now it was the government's move, they said. The meeting broke up after more than three hours. Nothing had been achieved.

Outside, Wang Juntao cornered Wang Dan and Wu'er Kaixi. Did they think there was any realistic chance of ending the hunger strike before Monday morning? he asked. Yes, they thought there might be, if Chai Ling agreed. But Chai Ling was nowhere to be found. She had slipped out of the meeting early and had headed back to the square.

Chai Ling, it turned out, had never heard of Wang Juntao. Like many of the student leaders, she appeared to subscribe to the view that no one over thirty was to be trusted. (Wang was now two months short of that fateful birthday.) Zheng Yefu had in fact been too optimistic about Wang's chances of influencing the student leadership. Wang's reputation was secure among his fellow intellectuals. And, on campus, his name was known to the older graduate students, some of the teaching staff, and those who remembered the 1980 Beida election campaign. But Wang Juntao and Chen Ziming, despite their fat political dossiers and the frequent denunciations of them in internal Party documents as bad elements, had never been publicly vilified in the official media. This meant that, unlike a Fang Lizhi or a Liu Binyan, they had little name recognition and influence among the younger students.

Chai Ling's rhetoric of sacrifice and the selflessness of the hunger strikers triggered a new mood on the streets. Over that weekend, tens of thousands of Beijing residents flooded into the square. The foreign press, on hand for the Gorbachev visit, recorded their every move. The *laobaixing* were drawn to Tiananmen out of curiosity at the spectacle of these skinny kids defying the monolith. People wanted to help, so they brought umbrellas to shield the hunger strikers from the fierce sunshine, and quilts and blankets to ward off the sudden chill of the spring nights. They responded to the image of Chai Ling; they did not necessarily pause to think of the political consequences, as did Wang Juntao.

On Sunday, May 14, as the hours ticked by to Gorbachev's arrival the next day, the students waited anxiously for Yan Mingfu to summon them to a second meeting. Word finally came that he would see them at 6:00 P.M. This time, Wang Juntao and his SERI colleagues were not invited; they had already served their purpose, which was to bring the two sides together.

As on Saturday, there were again more than forty students in the room but only a dozen seats reserved for them. The students argued among themselves and scuffled with security guards. Although the members of the Dialogue Delegation strove to stick to their agenda, other students interrupted them or thrust notes suggesting new topics and tactics into their hands. When Yan Mingfu proposed an early end to the hunger strike, open discord erupted, with several voices shouting at once. A militant group of hunger strikers suddenly drowned out the talks altogether by turning on a tape recorder to play Chai Ling's histrionic "last words": "Even though our shoulders are still soft and tender, even though death seems to us too weighty, we have gone—we could not but go!" At this, several students burst into tears. Then, a second group of hunger strikers burst into the conference room, elbowing aside the guards and demanding that the meeting end immediately because the loudspeakers in the square were silent; the government had broken its promise to broadcast the proceedings live. Yan Mingfu, unable to offer a satisfactory explanation, led the official delegation out of the room.

Wang Juntao and the other intellectuals waiting outside were frantic at the news that the talks had broken down. They proposed to Yan that the loudspeakers be turned on immediately and that an edited version of the talks be broadcast on state television that evening. Yan said this was impossible; it was clear that his hands were tied by someone higher up in the Party.

The last, best chance for a peaceful settlement vanished. Senior Party conservatives had deliberately antagonized the students by their refusal to broadcast the dialogue. The students, through a mixture of inexperience and impetuosity, had allowed that single sticking point to sabotage the entire process. No one with Wang Juntao's skills of persuasion was present at the second meeting to restore calm. The moderates in the Party could not deliver what they had promised.

A group of a dozen intellectuals (but not Wang Juntao) went back to Tiananmen in a vain attempt to persuade the hunger strikers, who now numbered six hundred, to call off their protest.[3] At nine o'clock that night, the group gave up. Yan Mingfu, pallid and dripping with sweat, came back to the meeting room and announced tersely that the talks were dead. As rumors flew that the army would use force to clear the square at midnight, the leaders of the Dialogue Delegation raced to the Monument and pleaded for an end to the hunger strike. Shen Tong broke down in tears. But it is doubtful that many hunger strikers even heard him over the puny microphone. The hunger strike went on, and the only compromise made was that Wu'er Kaixi moved the strikers to the east side of Tiananmen, away from the entrance to the Great Hall of the People, where Gorbachev was due to be greeted the next morning.

Up until the last days before Gorbachev's arrival, most of Beijing's older intellectuals had displayed the kind of reticence that was their most striking historical trait. But on the morning of May 13, a big-character poster, tellingly entitled "We Can No Longer Remain Silent," appeared at Beida. At the head of the list of signatories were two middle-aged scholars, Bao Zunxin, a philosopher in his early fifties who edited an avant-garde journal called *Pacific Review,* and Yan Jiaqi, a good-natured and self-effacing political scientist in his late forties and the author of a history of the Cultural Revolution that was banned in China. Yan had Zhao Ziyang's ear by virtue of his work at one of the General Secretary's think tanks, the Research Institute for the Reform of the Political Structure. Over the next several days, Bao and Yan emerged as the leaders of a group that issued a series of increasingly radical statements. They followed up their first *dazibao* with an "Urgent Appeal" on May 14. Timed to coincide with Yan Mingfu's second session of talks, the appeal called for the government to recognize the Beijing Students Autonomous Federation and acknowledge its patriotic motives. At the same time, it pleaded with the students to let the Sino-Soviet summit proceed without incident. "We beg you," they wrote, "to make full use of the most valuable spirit of the student movement, the spirit of reason, and temporarily leave the square."

But the appeal fell on deaf ears. The students stayed where they were, and at the last minute the government altered its plans for receiving Gorbachev. Instead of being welcomed formally in the square, as protocol demanded, the Soviet leader was spirited into the Great Hall of the People by a back entrance. All three U.S. television networks were on hand, as were CNN, the BBC, and dozens of other international news crews; the government's loss of face was broadcast live to the world. Li Peng and the conservatives were incensed.

The open split in the Party was no doubt what accounted for the more outspoken tone of the appeals from Yan Jiaqi and Bao Zunxin's group. Yan in particular was the personification of the moderate internal *ti nei* faction that had long stressed the primacy of Party rule. Yet he knew by May 15 that his patron, Zhao Ziyang, was now locked in the final, decisive battle for his political future. And Yan agreed to be openly enlisted in that cause. On the evening of May 14, in despair at the breakdown of his talks with the students, Yan Mingfu called Bao Zunxin to plead for a more massive display of support for his efforts from the intellectual community. The next day, as Gorbachev arrived, Bao and Yan Jiaqi marched to the square at the head of a vast, chanting column of writers, teachers, scientists, and other professionals.

On May 16, which was also the twenty-third anniversary of the Maoist purge that had launched the Cultural Revolution, Yan and Bao's group issued a further statement, mainly authored by the famous writer Zheng Yi, and bearing more than one thousand signatures. It attacked Mao's famous desire for the "one-voice chamber." "A society with only one voice is not a stable society," the group declared. It was now the job of the intellectuals "to step forth boldly to push forward the development of democracy."

Wang Juntao, despite having been thrust into half-unwanted prominence over the weekend by his attempt to mediate the ill-fated talks with the students, still kept his distance from Bao Zunxin and Yan Jiaqi's more radical message. Along with Chen Ziming and Zhou Duo, he continued to spend time at the United Front Work Department, encouraging Yan Mingfu not to abandon his efforts at dialogue. By now, the barriers that had long divided Wang and Chen from the Party reformers had begun to fall. On May 15, Wang and Chen Ziming chose not to join the thousands of intellectuals who marched to Tiananmen. Instead, they honored a long-standing invitation to take part in a one-day conference on political reform and China's labor unions that had been organized by the official ACFTU and was being held at the editorial offices of the newspaper *China's Labor Movement*. In a modern society under the rule of law, Wang told the audience, popular demonstrations should not be seen as abnormal. "There is a view which maintains that simply by taking to the streets one is being highly radical. This is absolutely not so. As long as guns are not fired and artillery is not used . . . I feel that none of this can be construed as radical."

Chen Ziming added that though the young students might be headstrong, the organized ranks of intellectuals were an important force of sanity and reason. "The journalists took to the streets on May Fourth," he pointed out, "forming a force that is better organized, more conscious, better educated and better able to cope with the situation." Chen went on, "We have witnessed a new phenomenon: the teaching staff and the scientific research institutes have taken to the streets."

"But aren't the students being manipulated by people behind the scenes," someone asked, "like the Party says?"

"If it's really a case of setting up a political party," Wang Juntao replied, "then behind-the-scenes manipulation can, indeed should, still be conducted within the scope of the law." He hastened to add that he spoke here in his capacity as a social scientist, not as an activist. But the remark, captured by the Party's hidden tape recorders, would be enough to damn him when it was introduced as evidence in his trial.

Many of those listening were sympathetic to the idea of the organized working class joining the democracy movement. But Chen was convinced that this was not something to be encouraged. "I propose," he said, according to the Party's transcript of the discussion, "that at the present moment, it would be best for us not to play the ACFTU card. We should play our cards one by one, and not all at once. If you play all your cards, you would have no deterrent left whatsoever. The best way is to use the deterrent skillfully and wield your power sparingly. . . .

"A hero of world stature like de Gaulle was blown away by the May 1968 storm," Chen mused in conclusion. "What ranking people will this May storm blow away?"

As believers in moderation, Chen and Wang now faced an enormous dilemma. The student leadership, with its insistence on continuing the hunger strike, seemed bent on self-destruction. On the other hand, the most circumspect official reformers, forced to take sides in the power struggle between Zhao Ziyang and Li Peng, seemed to throw caution to the winds. Even segments of the ACFTU were beginning to talk of throwing the muscle of the industrial working class behind the democracy movement. And men like Yan Jiaqi, the very soul of moderation, now spoke the language of confrontation. Chen and Wang decided that it was time to bring together a roomful of what they called "elite individuals" to consider their next step.

They rented space at the Jimen Hotel in the northern part of the city, around the corner from the Beijing Film Studios. The first meeting took place on Wednesday, May 17, with Wang Juntao as chair. It was quickly apparent how angry the mood had become. Bao Zunxin asked to present the draft of a new declaration that he and Yan Jiaqi had drawn up together. Wang told him to go ahead. It was fiercer than anything published up until then. "Because the autocrat controls unlimited power," the May 17 Declaration read, "the government has lost its own obligation and normal human feelings." It went on, "Despite the death of the Qing dynasty seventy-six years ago, there is still an emperor in China, though without such a title, a senile and fatuous autocrat." Bao Zunxin passed the document around to collect signatures, but Wang, who disagreed with its harsh language and the personal attacks on Deng Xiaoping, demurred.

Instead, that night Wang wrote an anonymous essay for the coming issue of *Economics Weekly,* combining Olympian calm and dreadful foreboding. He wrote, "The government is in a situation in which its functions, powers, and responsibilities are severed. It is unable to go either backward or forward while its back is to the wall. It has become a government that refuses to take responsibility."

Wang also gave a glimpse of his frustration with the students' intransigence. "The fact that the people have to use self-destructive methods to express their aspirations is a very sad thing. However, whatever the eventual outcome of the student movement, it has marked the end of the old era and the beginning of the new. Relying on traditional thinking to deal with the situation will only bring catastrophe to the nation and hardship to the people."

This "traditional thinking," Wang went on, was rooted in the deepest experience of the Communist Party's leaders. "The old generation of revolutionaries won the empire on horseback, and after the founding of the nation in 1949, they continued to rule it on horseback, using the methods of war as the model for their system." But those methods, Wang argued, could never create a modern society. The stability that the Party spoke of so obsessively could only come from "a democratic, constitutional political system," involving the inalienable human rights of the individual, a representative system of universal suffrage, political pluralism, the separation of powers, and a system of checks and balances.

Was there a way out of the impasse? Perhaps not—unless the independent intellectuals could find a way to cool tempers. "The situation in society in the past few days has already led to splits in the emotions of the masses, and there is no lack of angry people. In the absence of the thoughtfulness of the intelligentsia, and with the government delaying any response, these angry feelings could easily develop into unreasonable behavior. This would give retrogressive forces in society an opportunity to intervene and to provoke disturbances, risking everything in a single venture, and proceeding to exacerbate contradictions, causing all parties to abandon restraint. This is what the students and intellectuals must guard against."

The hunger strike had dramatically altered the mood of the city, and it was hard for Wang and his colleagues to keep up with the rush of events. During the week that the strike lasted, Bai Hua sent two teams of young ORCC researchers to take the pulse of public opinion. She asked them to conduct two separate surveys—the first of the students themselves, and the second of the ordinary residents of Beijing, the *laobaixing*. The pollsters fanned out across a carefully chosen cross section of Beijing neighborhoods, knocking on doors and asking residents for their views on the movement.

The eventual crackdown prevented ORCC from ever carrying out a scientific study of its poll findings, but the general trend was obvious to Bai Hua as she examined the returned questionnaires: The great mass of Beijing residents actively supported the students. Even so, some important differences emerged in how the *laobaixing* saw the battle for Tiananmen. What the students wanted was democracy, but for most of those who answered the ORCC surveys, the more important issues were high prices and corruption among government officials. The *laobaixing* also seemed more wary than the students on the question of where the movement was likely to lead—nowhere, most of them thought. The majority, hardened by years of watching the Party refine its monopoly of power, agreed with the statement "The student movement won't be able to achieve anything." Even many of the students interviewed expressed the fear that the government would "settle accounts after the autumn harvest," when the dust had settled.[4]

In a sense, the polls told Bai Hua little that was not readily apparent to anyone who looked at the streets. The students had rapidly won the battle for public opinion after beginning their fast. Three hundred thousand people took to the streets to show their support on May 16; the next day, there were a million; the next day, despite cooler weather and a rainstorm, a million again. What the government was confronting was no longer a protest movement; it was the specter of mass insurrection.

On May 17 and 18, all the factories in the capital seemed to empty. The group of workers in their makeshift quarters under the West Reviewing Stand no longer felt so isolated as the working class of Beijing poured forth from all sorts of workplaces: the small independent *getihu,* the medium-sized factories, and the giant heavy industries with their 1950s-era Soviet technology. They came from the newly legal private sector, the gargantuan state monopolies, and the new joint ventures between Chinese and foreign capital. Workers entered the central precincts of the capital in an armada of trucks and buses, waving red flags and banging drums, gongs, and cymbals. It was the government's worst nightmare come to life.

At Xiguanlitai, Zhao Hongliang and his friends wrote down the names on the factory banners. They read like a roll call of the elite of Chinese industry: the Beijing Rubber Manufacturing Plant, the Beijing Coking Factory, the Beijing Boiler Factory, the Petroleum Chemical Products Corporation, the Civil Aviation Administration of China, even the giant Capital Iron and Steel Works. There were familiar faces from the Beijing Workers Union in many of the *danwei* contingents. Zhao Hongliang grinned as he saw a group of workmates from the Xidan Department Store, and then, more broadly, when he spotted the banners of the Beijing Bus Company. The drivers, some of them old friends from the 1985 strike, had driven several of the company vehicles into the square. There they sat, immobilized, with their tires slashed, to serve as secure quarters for the hunger strikers. Such gestures of support from ordinary workers were all the more remarkable, since the students had done absolutely nothing to encourage them.

The worker-activists from Xiguanlitai moved among the dense crowds, distributing their leaflets and handbills. A "Notice to All Chinese Compatriots," printed on May 17, listed senior Communist officials who, the handbill said, should be "investigated with regard to their material consumption and use of palatial retreats." They were all there: not only the most notorious hard-liners, such as Peng Zhen, Chen Yun, and Li Peng, but also the beleaguered Zhao Ziyang and his liberal ally Wan Li, the man who had supervised the construction of modern Tiananmen Square and was about to play a crucial role in the drama in his present post as Chairman of the Standing Committee of the rubber-stamp National People's Congress.

The workers, in other words, had no interest in taking sides between the Party's warring factions or becoming pawns of the inner-Party struggle. This was a vital development, and it set the 1989 protests apart from every other previous stage of the democracy movement. "We must now be on our guard," the handbill went on in a none-too-veiled reference to Zhao Ziyang's fight for survival, "against political careerists within the Chinese Communist Party who will use the current democracy movement to usurp power for their own purposes." The workers had learned the bitter lessons of history. "Deng Xiaoping used the people's movement of April 5, 1976, to obtain power. Afterward, his evil intentions were exposed."

In fact, the Party leadership was doing all it could to redirect the frightening upsurge of working-class anger. Reports from the provinces told the Party that independent worker-led groups had raised their banners in support of the student protests in a number of other cities—in Xi'an and Wuhan, in Lanzhou and Hangzhou, in the pulsing southern metropolis of Guangzhou, where Western influences were strong, and in the industrial powerhouse of Shanghai. Worse, there were signs that the democratic disease had even infected the safe precincts of the official ACFTU.

Like every other Party organization, the ACFTU was riven from top to bottom along factional lines. Its president, Ni Zhifu, was an enigmatic figure. A round-faced Shanghainese in his mid-fifties, he had risen through the ranks as a model worker. On April 5, 1976, he had headed the workers' militia that cleared Tiananmen Square. Later, after Mao's death, he was even rumored to have been plotting a pro–Gang of Four coup.[5] But since then he had shifted with the political winds and was no longer regarded as a flaming leftist.

As the student hunger strike began, Ni left on a poorly timed official trip to the Soviet Union. That placed union affairs temporarily in the hands of Zhu Houze, a man with a very different political history. His liberal credentials dated back to his punishment as a rightist in the campaign of 1957. In 1985, Hu Yaobang had brought him from far-off Guizhou to be the Party's new Chief of Propaganda. The capital's independent thinkers rated Zhu second only to his mentor, Hu. Wang Juntao and Chen Ziming, for example, respected Zhu as the driving force behind the new climate of freedom that their new think tank enjoyed in 1986. The name of Zhu was inseparably bound with the three catchwords he used constantly: *kuanrong* (tolerance), *kuansong* (relaxation of control), and *kuanhou* (benevolence). When Hu Yaobang was "retired" in January 1987, it was inevitable that Zhu should fall with him. But the purge was incomplete. The conservatives were not strong enough to silence their adversaries completely, and by the end of 1988 Zhu Houze had bounced back to a slightly less visible job on the national leadership of the ACFTU.

With Ni Zhifu out of the country, Zhu abruptly found himself in a position of great influence. Like many second-tier Party officials, he was privately sympathetic to the students. And like many top cadres, he could hardly ignore the rumblings of support he heard from his staff in the corridors, or the vivid, enthusiastic reports of the protests published each morning in *People's Daily*. Zhu quietly gave the nod for ACFTU officials to take part in the great million-strong march of May 17. Officials from *China's Labor Movement,* the same people who invited and listened to Chen Ziming and Wang Juntao as their guest speakers two days earlier, marched alongside. And on May 18, the sixth day of the hunger strike, Zhu shocked the leftists by writing out a check for one hundred thousand *yuan* ($26,600) to the students.

The final throw of the dice by Party moderates had a note of desperation about it. All through the week of the hunger strike, Yan Mingfu worked feverishly to salvage something from the wreckage of his talks with the students. At dusk on May 16 he even turned up in their midst and offered himself as a hostage as a guarantee that there would be no reprisals once the strike was called off.[6] His visit had been suggested by Chen Ziming, Zhou Duo, and some of the other moderate intellectuals who were spending time at the Party's United Front Work Department. Wang Dan, perhaps the most levelheaded of the student leaders, presented Yan to the crowd as "a true Communist, an upright Communist, and a very good person" and begged the hunger strikers to listen to him. Wu'er Kaixi, weakened by four days without food and using an oxygen mask, hailed Yan's offer and urged the strikers to call off their action. Then he fainted. In the uproar that ensued, the voices of compromise were all but drowned out. It was all a trick, the angry radicals yelled. Why leave the square when nothing had been accomplished?

On May 17, Zhao Ziyang made his final stand. He must have known by now that his position was hopeless. Through indecision he had achieved the worst of both worlds. To shore up his faltering position, Zhao had turned to the people in the streets, but this only marked him as a traitor in the eyes of the conservative leadership and did not make a real difference to the people. His turn to the masses looked more like an attempt to secure his position in history than a principled search for an alternative to Communist Party rule. Even in extremis, Zhao was still the gray bureaucrat who lacked the stomach for real political reform.

In the eyes of "the veteran proletarian revolutionaries," Zhao was guilty of a series of offenses against Party discipline, each one more serious than the last. First, his May 4 speech to the Asian Development Bank had seemed designed to fan the protests by exposing the Party's divisions in public. Then on May 16, Zhao made his worst blunder when he revealed a "state secret" to the visiting Soviet president—namely, that a secret Party accord had granted effective veto powers over important policy questions to Deng Xiaoping, despite the patriarch's formal retirement from virtually all his official posts in 1987.[7]

Yet Zhao remained a creature of the Party, not of the streets. One of the few real weapons he still wielded as General Secretary was the power to demand an emergency session of the National People's Congress, which, at least on paper, had the power to remove Li Peng and appoint a new government. But here perhaps was the greatest measure of Zhao's failure. Instead of using his powers, he merely dispatched the faithful Yan Mingfu to put a word in the ear of President Yang Shangkun, apparently hoping that the two men's friendship, based on their shared experience of persecution as "Soviet spies" in the 1960s, would be enough to avert a disaster. It was not.

Deng could wait no longer; the situation had to be resolved. On May 17, he called a number of top officials to his heavily fortified private residence in Miliangku *hutong* to discuss imposing martial law in Beijing. The masses in the streets called for the downfall of the government; the students were like the Red Guards reborn, wild-eyed with the sense of their own purity, refusing to give an inch in compromise; the alien banners of an entity calling itself an "independent" workers' organization were snapping in the breeze over Tiananmen Square. "Retreat?" Deng asked testily. "Where do you think we can retreat?" Yang Shangkun, his comrade for almost sixty years, agreed. "This would be the last breach in the dam. If we retreat, everything will collapse." Yang did not mention a word about Yan Mingfu's friendly overture.

Zhao Ziyang found himself a minority of one. "I cannot carry out this policy," he muttered. "I have difficulties with it."

But what about Party discipline, Deng wanted to know. "The minority must obey the majority."

Zhao sighed. "Yes, that is Party principle. I will obey the majority." Yang Shangkun thought he was being evasive.

At eight o'clock that evening, the Standing Committee of the Politburo met to finalize the decision. It was a last, bitter lesson for Zhao in the difference between the Party rule book and the realities of power. All five members of the Standing Committee were there. But they were not alone. The old men, the "proletarian revolutionaries," were well represented too. At this time of crisis, as in January 1987, those who called the shots were not the Politburo, but the retired veterans: the eighty-four-year-old Chen Yun, the eighty-seven-year-old Peng Zhen, the eighty-year-old Li Xiannian, the eighty-two-year-old Yang Shangkun. And, of course, Deng himself.

Zhao's fight was lost. "My assignment is finished," he told his colleagues. "I cannot continue to function, because I disagree with the majority of you. How can I act as the General Secretary and carry out a policy with which I do not agree? I therefore resign."

12

State Secrets

Of all the fevered days and nights in and around Tiananmen Square, the forty-eight hours after May 17 may have been the most decisive in determining the outcome of the protests. If the 1989 democracy movement were seen as Greek tragedy, then that was the moment in which all the characters laid bare their inner flaws, the moment when the positions of every faction hardened fatally, when every misunderstanding and every failed communication escalated to catastrophic proportions. From the night of Wednesday, May 17, to the early hours of Saturday, May 20, the circuits of reason and logic overloaded, and mental fuses blew. People of goodwill, trying desperately to head off an inevitable horror, put their names to documents, plans, and agreements that later sealed their fates as the black hands of the whole affair.

On the surface, there was the shadow play that captivated the television cameras. In the predawn darkness of May 18, Zhao Ziyang and Li Peng, the grotesque pairing of good cop and bad cop, went to the Beijing Hospital and the Tongren Hospital to visit the fasting students who had been carried there from the square, less than a mile away. At 11:00 A.M., with Zhao absent, Li Peng hosted a surreal meeting with a motley group of student leaders in the Great Hall of the People. Wu'er Kaixi, fresh from his hospital bed and dressed in pajamas, controlled the discussion. The quieter, more reflective Wang Dan was thrust into the background by Wu'er Kaixi's ebullience and arrogance. Flustered by the young man's interruptions, Li Peng failed even to set an agenda for the meeting. But as Li suppressed his fury and mouthed platitudes—"To us, you are like our own children"—he heard the most damaging possible admission from his student guests: The mass of protesters in the square were beyond the control of their own leaders.

"We would very much like to have the students leave the square," Wu'er Kaixi told Li. But, he went on to say, "right now, what's happening in the square is not so much a case in which the minority follows the majority, but one in which 99.9 percent follow 0.1 percent, so if one hunger striker refuses to leave the square, then the other several thousand will not leave either." The most intransigent voices, in other words, exercised veto power over the students' actions.

"Yesterday," Wang Dan added, "we conducted a poll among over a hundred students, asking whether or not they would agree to withdraw from the square after our conversation with Secretary Yan Mingfu. The poll showed that 99.9 percent of the students were against withdrawing."

To someone of Li Peng's character, this was the perfect confirmation of the hard-liners' belief that it was useless to talk to these people. Did they not function according to the same hysterical rules of implacable self-righteousness as the Red Guards had two decades earlier?

———

Han Dongfang was one of a growing number of people who felt that the hunger strikers were running out of ideas. He had been going to Tiananmen every day for a month now, making his impromptu speeches; he was usually accompanied by Chen Jingyun, his wife of six months. Each night, when they returned home, she would tell him how well the crowds had reacted to his words.

Yet Han's calm, articulate manner also worked against him. He still thought of himself as a worker, a man of humble means and modest education. But the crowds who gathered to listen often seemed to suspect him of some hidden agenda. Even when he tried to quiet the skeptics by displaying his work-unit identification from the Fengtai Railyards, he could hear their cries: "It's not true! He's concealing his true identity! You can tell he's an intellectual by the way he talks!" The students, meanwhile, would shout him down angrily at the sight of the identification: "What right do you have to tell us what to do? You're just an ordinary worker!"

Until now, Han had kept his distance from the loosely organized group of workers at Xiguanlitai, preferring to try to influence the students. On the night of May 18, his persistence seemed to have been rewarded when he was invited to spend the night in the van at the north end of the square that served as the hunger strikers' command post. But all night he sat there as self-important aides bustled past, ignoring him completely.

At dawn, angry and frustrated, Han walked down to the Monument to the People's Heroes and made a short, impassioned speech on the need for students and workers to join forces and stop bickering. When he finished, he was stunned to see someone else take the microphone and deliver a speech along similar lines. Afterward, the second speaker strode across to introduce himself.

The two men could not have been less alike—Han tall, quiet, and reserved; the newcomer short, wry, and garrulous, as he lit one cigarette after another. The characters scrawled on his headband read "Doctor of Constitutional Law." His name was Li Jinjin. Li was yet another member of Wang Juntao's circle of friends from Wuhan, the thirty-four-year-old son of a conservative official in the city's Public Security Bureau. As a teenager, he served in the army. After the end of the Cultural Revolution, he obtained an undergraduate law degree at Wuhan's Central South Finance and Economics College, which had been closed down for the previous ten years. During the mid-1980s, he divided his time between Beida, where he enrolled in the graduate law program, and Wuhan, where he became friendly with Wang Juntao, working with him there on a research project exploring ways to protect citizens' rights under the law. By 1987, Li was back at Beida, this time in the Ph.D. program. But he had political ambitions, too. He decided to specialize in constitutional law—thus the designation on the headband—and was elected chair of the Beida Graduate Students Association. His term of office was ending just as Hu Yaobang died.

Li was scheduled to defend his doctoral thesis on June 3. The topic was administrative detention, the Chinese system under which the police can sentence offenders to up to three years of "reeducation through labor" without the benefit of trial. But Li's mind was on matters other than his academic career. Since April

17, when he had joined Wang Dan on the first march of Beida students to Tiananmen Square, he had sought his niche in the movement. Now, he told Han Dongfang, he had found it—with a group of workers over at the West Reviewing Stand.

Li explained that he had made contact with the group only the previous day. Already he had worked with them on drafting two documents. But the group lacked a charismatic leader, Li felt, someone who might play the same role in China that Lech Walesa played in Poland. As he looked at Han Dongfang, Li wondered if perhaps he had found his man.

One of the documents that Li Jinjin had helped to draft was a call for a general strike by Beijing workers. In the early hours of May 19, a worker read out the strike call in Tiananmen Square. But few people heard the announcement, for even as the worker began to speak there was a flurry of excitement a hundred yards away and the sudden bright glow of klieg lights.

Zhao Ziyang had appeared in the square unannounced, shadowed once again by the grim-faced Li Peng. It was Zhao's final public appearance. Ashen from lack of sleep, his Sichuan accent thicker than ever, his voice breaking with tears, Zhao admitted to the students, "We have come too late. We deserve your criticism."

Li Peng and his cohorts might have won the inner-Party power struggle, but they failed to keep their greatest secret: the plan to place the capital under martial law the following night. That failure led to the government's greatest humiliation and to a full-blown constitutional crisis. And as the drama in the Party leadership unfolded under the lights, the parallel drama of the black hands was played out elsewhere.

The first news of the conservatives' plans leaked out on May 17, after Zhao Ziyang offered his resignation to the Politburo and the Party elders. According to the government's later version of events, the principal culprit in the leak was fifty-seven-year-old Bao Tong, the senior aide to Zhao Ziyang. Bao was secretary to the Politburo and a member of the Central Committee of the Party. He was also head of the Research Institute for the Reform of the Political Structure (RIRPS) and deputy director of the State Commission for Restructuring the Economy. He was the man who had smoothed the way for the Hungarian-American financier George

Soros to set up his operations in China. Bao had always been more of a political liberal than his boss. While Zhao spoke of his admiration for the chilly doctrines of "New Authoritarianism," Bao argued for democratic reform at the grass-roots level and for an increase in *toumingdu,* transparency, roughly the Chinese equivalent of the Russian concept of *glasnost.*[1]

The conservatives had detested Bao Tong for years. During the great Campaign against Bourgeois Liberalization of 1987, they had demanded his head. But that campaign ran out of steam, and Bao survived. Now he had been under surveillance for weeks, ever since the start of the student protests. As secretary to the Politburo, he had routinely attended meetings of the Central Committee. But at the end of April, those privileges were abruptly denied, and he was no longer allowed to see important Central Committee documents, although he was Zhao's top aide.

According to the government's later charges, when Bao Tong learned of his boss's fall from grace, he hurriedly informed a group of colleagues at RIRPS. In what he called a "farewell speech," he warned that no one should breathe a word of their discussions. Anyone who talked would be a "Judas." For the next day and a half, there is no evidence that Bao Tong told anyone else of what he knew.

But the rumor of Zhao's downfall had begun to filter out in other ways; an event of such magnitude could not be kept hidden, and the Party lost its former tight control of information. At the offices of the United Front Work Department, Zhang Gang of RIRES waited anxiously to hear the outcome of the May 17 Politburo meeting. With him was Zhou Duo, the forty-two-year-old economist from the successful computer company, the Stone Corporation. In the early hours of the next morning, Thursday, the telephone rang. An aide picked it up. She listened for a few moments, then quietly put the phone down. She said just two words: "It's over." Those present agreed to say nothing publicly for the time being; it was too dangerous. But Zhang Gang immediately began to call his colleagues at RIRES to try to organize an emergency meeting of the Institute's senior staff. He did not succeed. RIRES director Chen Yizi was still in the hospital nursing a broken leg. Others were at Tiananmen Square and could not be located. Zhang Gang failed to assemble a quorum, and the meeting was postponed until the following day, May 19.

On that morning, about twenty representatives of RIRES and other official think tanks gathered to pool their information on the crisis. Chen Yizi came from his hospital bed to chair the meeting. Someone suggested calling in Gao Shan, a thirty-three-year-old economist who was Bao Tong's deputy at RIRPS. When Gao arrived, he confirmed that there had indeed been a split between Zhao Ziyang and Li Peng, and that Zhao had lost his post. By four o'clock that afternoon, those attending the meeting had hammered out an urgent six-point statement whose demands included "disclosure of the behind-the-scenes maneuvers and the disputes within the top leadership," warned that martial law was now a real danger, and urged the students to end their hunger strike "at the earliest opportunity."[2] But the statement was worded discreetly; only oblique references were made to what its authors now firmly believed: It was only a matter of hours before the PLA would move in to retake the streets of Beijing. At no time, say those who attended the meeting, did Bao Tong divulge any secrets to them. His only comment on reading the six-point statement was: "At last somebody is telling the truth."

The real center of political gravity of the democracy movement shifted that afternoon to the modest Jimen Hotel, in the northwestern district of Haidian. The meetings of "elite individuals" that Chen Ziming and Wang Juntao had launched two days earlier on May 17 were now in virtually permanent session. SERI occupied several rooms in the hotel. There was a wartime atmosphere as telephones rang incessantly and new arrivals picked their way over the sleeping bodies of exhausted participants.

The cast of characters in these meetings changed continually. SERI always provided the core participants: Chen and Wang chaired the meetings themselves, and Min Qi and Chen Xiaoping were often on hand as well. Beida graduate student Zhang Lun sometimes turned up in the company of Liu Suli, a twenty-eight-year-old professor at Politics and Law University, who was a recent recruit to SERI. The two young men shuttled back and forth between the hotel and Tiananmen Square, where they helped their good friend Liu Gang, the physics graduate turned factory worker, with a range of practical tasks in support of the students.

There was also a floating population of younger intellectuals who cycled out to the Jimen or flagged down one of the Beijing taxis that were carrying passengers for free as a gesture of support for the protesters. There was Liu Lichun, a bright young economist from whom Wang Juntao borrowed many of his ideas; Yuan Zhiming, one of the writers of *River Elegy;* and Wu Jiaxiang, perhaps the leading exponent of the theory of New Authoritarianism. A few of those in attendance were a little older. Zhou Duo attended several meetings, as did Lü Jiamin, also in his early forties, a veteran of *Beijing Spring* who taught at the Workers Movement College of the ACFTU and provided one of the first real links between Chen Ziming, Wang Juntao, and the organized working class. A representative of the student leadership was also generally in attendance. On the morning of May 19, the student liaison was the skinny, bespectacled Wang Dan.

That day Wang Juntao and Chen Ziming felt that their customary capacity for calm and reason was stretched to the limit. They saw the students and the Li Peng government locked in a fatal dance. Voices of moderation and compromise seemed, as in a dream, to produce no sound.

Chen Ziming was the chair on this occasion. What was the latest from the square? he asked.

"We are still insisting on our two basic conditions being met," Wang Dan reported.

"Do you really intend to stick to your original policy, given where things stand now?" Chen wanted to know. "Don't you think the hunger strike could stop, just temporarily? Can't the students be persuaded to start eating again?" He seemed exasperated. There were just so many unknowns, so many dangers. "Will revisions to the student movement affect what happens inside the Party? If you don't change, what will be the consequences? If Deng Xiaoping were to step down, what would that mean? A new political beginning, or a period of military rule?"

Wang Juntao arrived late for the May 19 meeting; he had spent the morning at the hospital, having caught his hand in a car door. When he finally reached the Jimen, the room seemed paralyzed by indecision. Many of those present believed it was time for the students to call off their hunger strike in order to head off the danger of bloodshed. But no one dared openly challenge the hunger strikers' moral authority.

The sense of deadlock magnified some of the subtle differences between Chen and Wang.[3] Chen, normally the embodiment of doggedness and reason, appeared unusually frustrated. Wang, a few years younger, a little more impetuous, personally closer to the students, was still looking for new tactics, new ways to put pressure on the government.

"Look," Wang argued, "the hunger strike group has neither increased nor lessened its conditions. We should be doing anything we can to open up new space for political activity. We have to look for new strategies. We should be using the news media, using the law. We should lobby for an emergency session of the National People's Congress. All the parties involved should do whatever they can to link up." There it was again, *chuanlian*—linkup: that fatal phrase from the Cultural Revolution that set off every alarm bell in Zhongnanhai. "There should be joint pickets organized," he went on, "to include workers, ordinary Beijing residents, students. . . ."

Wang Juntao pressed his case further as the day wore on, arguing persuasively for setting up a single joint advisory center to coordinate the Tiananmen protests, advise the students, and find more channels for applying pressure—though all still in the name of seeking an eventual compromise.

Yet as Chen's questions to Wang Dan suggested, no one could predict clearly what was likely to happen. No one even knew who in the Party was really calling the shots. Everyone was red-eyed with exhaustion. The group at the Jimen Hotel was getting by on a couple of hours of sleep a night, sometimes none at all. Even the coolest heads could change their views with almost schizophrenic speed.

Whatever their differences, Wang Juntao and Chen Ziming did concur on two key points. First, this was no longer simply a student movement; the mass of the population was involved. Second, all channels of communication between the students and the government were now closed. "This crisis cannot be resolved on the streets," Wang remarked. "We need to bring democracy off the streets and into the Great Hall of the People." Chen nodded: "It's time to allow the democracy movement to expand to encompass the whole of society. So if the government is to be persuaded to enter into another round of dialogue and negotiations, it must talk to representatives of all social sectors."

Looking around the room, it was clear to the two men that their meeting of "elite individuals" was as representative a body as any that existed in the movement. Someone suggested a cumbersome name for the Jimen Hotel group: the Preparatory Committee for the Federation of All Circles in the Capital. Whatever name this group might choose, the Communist Party would see it as the germ of a Chinese *Solidarnosc.*

At about 2:00 P.M., Chen Ziming was told that he had an urgent telephone call. He came back to the conference room after a few minutes, grim-faced. Holding up his hand for silence, he announced, "I have just been told by an extremely authoritative source that martial law is about to be imposed in Beijing." He refused to name his source—although it was presumably someone who had been present at the RIRES meeting that morning. Chen said only that the group should issue an immediate public statement based on his extensive notes of the phone conversation.

The new document, entitled "A Letter to the People," gave a blow-by-blow account of how the showdown in the Politburo had unfolded.[4] For a brief moment, the old chasm between the official reformers and the outsiders was a thing of the past. The struggle for survival was a common endeavor.

The "Letter to the People" took up Wang Juntao's earlier proposal for a special session of the National People's Congress (NPC). The elderly head of the NPC, Wan Li, was reputed to be a staunch ally of Zhao Ziyang. But Wan Li was abroad on official business. His immediate recall was grasped at as a final, desperate chance to remove Li Peng from office and rescind his martial law decree. "The imposition of military rule is now imminent, and the dark days following the April 5 crackdown in 1976 are about to be repeated," the letter read. The last phrase was added at the suggestion of the Beida graduate student Zhang Lun, too young himself to remember the seminal event that had launched Chen Ziming and Wang Juntao on their political careers. By early evening, the document—the first explicit public warning of martial law—was circulating in Tiananmen Square.

As scholars know, history often turns on tiny textual amendments, on footnotes added and afterthoughts crossed out. In addition to Zhou Duo's original draft, there were in fact at least *two* separate later versions of the "Letter to the People." One, unsigned, was rushed into type as an unauthorized supplement to *People's Daily,* a kind of samizdat edition of the iron flagship of Communist Party propaganda. The other version was signed by "a group of cadres from leading state organs."[5] Both versions agreed that all citizens should do their utmost to remain nonviolent and avoid bloodshed. But there they parted company.

In the most explosive line of an explosive document, the cadres' version of the letter called on "all workers, students, and citizens to launch an immediate general strike [and a] nationwide class and market boycott." The milder, unsigned version said only that "All sectors of society must unite to protect and uphold the Constitution." It is not clear who made the changes, although the reference to the Constitution in the milder version contains language that was often used by Chen Ziming and Wang Juntao's group.[6]

To the government, such niceties were irrelevant. The damage was done. Here, the Li Peng faction had the nub of its conspiracy: Senior Party officials, embroiled in a factional struggle, had leaked state secrets to outsiders, who used the information to call for a general strike that would topple the government. But the night was not yet over, and for the Communist Party worse was still to come.

At midnight on May 19, there was an unearthly stillness in Tiananmen Square. Western television crews had set up at the two northern corners of the square, pointing their cameras east and west along Chang'an Boulevard to film the expected contingents of the PLA. Students were bedded down all around the Monument to the People's Heroes, but few of them slept. The whole square was listening, straining to catch the distant sounds of the approaching army.

Some came to the square after watching Li Peng on television. Many thought that the Premier had never looked more foolish, more mediocre. His voice was strained and reedy. Shoulders hunched, eyes blank, fists occasionally jabbing the air as if he thought this the appropriate gesture for a hard-nosed revolutionary, Li Peng stood before a massed audience of Party cadres and military men, who seemed dazed at being pulled before the television cameras at such a late hour.

"It is becoming clearer and clearer," said Li, "that an extremely small number of people want to achieve through turmoil their political goals, which are to negate the leadership of the Communist Party and to negate the socialist system." The students were not the problem, he emphasized. "As our Party and government have stated many times, the intentions of the great majority of the students are good and honest; the students themselves do not wish to create turmoil." In Li's eyes, the problem was, of course, the black hands behind the movement. Wang Juntao and Chen Ziming heard the Premier's speech in the tent of the student leaders, where they had gone to spend the night; they knew immediately that he meant people like them. Li also had no doubt of where the conspirators' actions were heading. "They stir up trouble everywhere," he droned on, "secretly link up with others, encourage the establishment of all sorts of illegal organizations, and attempt to force the Party and government to recognize them. What they want to do is to lay the foundation for the establishment in China of opposition factions and an opposition party."

On the balustrade at the foot of the Monument, a nervous young man struck up a conversation with a foreigner.[7] He seemed eager to practice his English. He glanced frequently at his watch.

"What college are you from?" the foreigner asked.

"I'm not a student," the young man replied with an uneasy smile. "Do you know who I am?" he asked, after a long pause.

"Who are you?"

"I'm a military officer," he beamed. "But please don't tell anyone here, will you."

He said that he was on leave from his unit, visiting relatives in Beijing. More likely he was an agent sent by the PLA command to gauge the amount of opposition the troops could expect when they arrived to clear the square. But he seemed an unlikely candidate for such a delicate mission. Perhaps he was just a very bad spy.

As he discussed the impending arrival of the PLA, the young man's face lit up with professional pride. He related the various routes the troops would take to enter the capital, the types of trucks they would use, how fast they would travel, and (checking his watch again) when they would arrive.

The minutes passed, and they stretched into hours. In the silence and the darkness, the PLA man's chatter grew more surreal. "It's a funny thing, you know, but in Chinese we have two different words for the tomato: *fanqie* and *xihongshi*. And the tomato is not even indigenous to China! The fact is, the tomato comes from

Brazil—or maybe it's Iraq? Anyway, how is one to explain the Chinese language having two different terms for this vegetable?"

The foreigner confessed that he was mystified by the eccentric quirks of Chinese vocabulary. The minutes dragged on. Still, no soldiers came. The PLA man consulted his watch.

Then, abruptly, at about 3:30 A.M., the student loudspeakers on the Monument crackled to life. "Students! The people of Beijing have stopped the advance of the People's Liberation Army at the Hujialou intersection!"

"It's not possible, don't believe it," the PLA man stammered. "The students are just spreading rumors now."

Half an hour later, another announcement came. "The people of Beijing have blocked the army in the west, at Wukesong." Other announcements followed thick and fast. Army units were blocked at Fengtai and Liuliqiao—Six *Li* Bridge—in the southwest, at Donggaodi in the south, at one strategic point after another on the great ring roads that circle Beijing.

Peering at his watch, the PLA man was deep in his own calculations—numbers of troops, types of transport trucks, road speeds, distances, times. Suddenly he looked up, frowned, and said, "They should have been here by now. Damn it, perhaps it's true!" And he grinned broadly.

The lights still burned in Zhongnanhai, where the same information was reaching the Party leadership from the PLA unit commanders. The troops could not get through. The news left Li Peng and his cohorts enraged and humiliated. Again, as with the April 26 editorial, they had grossly misread their ability to cow the people into submission. Now they could not even manage to impose martial law in their own capital city.

The leak of "state secrets" had been effective. Word of martial law had reached the student headquarters on the Monument late the previous afternoon, May 19, a little after it had reached Wang Juntao and Chen Ziming in the Jimen Hotel. By early evening, the "Letter to the People" was circulating. As the night wore on, another, anonymous document also hit the streets. It listed the key Beijing intersections through which the incoming troops would have to pass and urged citizens to block them.[8] At 9:00 P.M., an hour before Li Peng went on television, Chai Ling and the hunger strike group called off their fast, converting it to a peaceful sit-in. At that late hour, however, it was too much to expect that the Party would see this as a gesture of good faith and compromise; given the maneuvering by Zhao Ziyang's allies, it is likely that the Party saw it only as one more factional trick.

Late that night, Chen Ziming took a vehicle from the SERI car pool and drove out along Beijing's Number 3 Ring Road. An amazing sight greeted him. Long columns of army trucks stood halted. Citizens argued with the troops, pleaded with them, offered them food and water. The young soldiers seemed dazed. Some wept; others laughed and embraced demonstrators.

By some estimates, two million Beijing residents took to the streets on the night of May 19–20. The *laobaixing,* forewarned of martial law, fanned out to block every intersection they knew the troops must use. At intervals, Chen Ziming saw a motorcycle swerve to avoid the dense crowds, its driver flashing his hand in a V-for-victory sign as he sped past. These motorcycle riders were part of an impromptu network of bikers who crisscrossed the sprawling city to observe and report to the populace on the troop movements. At first called the Iron Mounted Soldiers, and later better known as the Flying Tigers, these bikers provided the crowds with the critical, up-to-the-minute intelligence that enabled them to countermaneuver effectively. They were a quintessential product of the reform years; most were the owners of Deng's private *getihu,* or "household enterprises."

May 20 dawned fine. The spring sky was cloudless, the light brilliant as the first rays of sunshine crept over the square from behind the Museum of Chinese History and fell on the dark, huddled shapes of the student tents. From the direction of Chang'an Boulevard, a sound of chants and singing was heard, quietly at first and then growing louder as a great column of marchers, ten abreast, swung around the corner and into Tiananmen. There were burly worker pickets and, in the front row, factory workers with headbands that read *gansidui*—Dare to Die. Historically, the phrase is associated with Tan Sitong, the scholar-philosopher, reformer, and student of the martial arts who was beheaded on the orders of the Dowager Empress Cixi in 1898. The Citizens and Workers Dare-to-Die Corps circled the perimeter of the square several times in a victory march. Suddenly, anything seemed possible.

China Spring

Wang Juntao, as a sixteen-year-old high school student, poses in front of the Monument to the People's Heroes during the Tiananmen Incident of April 1976.

Tangtai

An official photograph of the seventeen-year-old Wang Juntao on his release from prison in November 1976.

Courtesy of Bao Pu

Premier Zhao Ziyang (left) and his top aide, Bao Tong, confident and relaxed at the height of their power and influence in 1986.

Han Dongfang's father in the ancestral village of Nanweiquan, Shanxi Province, 1991.

Courtesy of Han Dongfang

Courtesy of Han Dongfang

Members of Han Dongfang's extended family congregate at home in Nanweiquan, 1991.

Cheng Yu

Tangtai

Above: Chen Ziming and Wang Zhihong on their wedding day, 1981.

Left: Members of the *Beijing Spring* group, 1979. Chen Ziming is in the center of the back row; Wang Juntao is seated, second from left.

Cheng Yu

Chen Ziming working at home in 1986, at about the time of the opening of the China Political and Administrative Sciences Research Institute.

Xinhua

Student leader Wang Dan, center with glasses, and Li Shuxian, the wife of Fang Lizhi, conducting a meeting of students at Beijing University under the famous statue of Cervantes.

Gloria Fung

Xiguanlitai—the West Reviewing Stand—where the Beijing Workers Autonomous Federation had its headquarters before moving into Tiananmen Square.

Outside Han Dongfang's house in Xibiaobei *hutong,* protesters burn copies of the leftist *Beijing Daily,* June 1, 1989.

In the aftermath of the June 4 massacre, troops patrol the abandoned square.

Above: Prior to their execution, condemned workers—or, in the official parlance, "burning, smashing, and looting elements"—are paraded before the television cameras.

Right: After his release from jail in April 1991, Han Dongfang begins his slow recovery from tuberculosis.

Below: At his first public appearance since the Beijing massacre, paramount leader Deng Xiaoping salutes the commanders of the martial law troops for their "resolute action."

Robin Munro

Above: The main gate to Qincheng prison.

Left: Liu Gang in prison with his father.

Below: Prison watchtower as seen from the streets of Beijing.

Robin Munro

Robin Munro

Tangtai

In his attempted escape, Chen Ziming's first destination was Inner Mongolia. Here, on June 8, he stands in front of a yurt—presumably in the capital city of Hohhot—of the sort he would have lived in as a "sent-down youth" during the Cultural Revolution.

Heishou de heishou: "the black hands behind the black hands." Wang Juntao (left) and Chen Ziming.

Tangtai

But in the tents, few of the students stirred. Some awoke and stretched. Most, sitting amid the debris of the weeklong hunger strike, seemed too exhausted to react. No one came running out to thank the marchers or to join their ranks. Those who were awake glanced at them incuriously, almost as if this show of solidarity were the students' birthright. In this euphoric dawn, their blank stares were a sour and troubling note, an omen of trouble yet to come.

13

The Eclipse
of Reason

In the makeshift quarters of the workers under the West Reviewing Stand, Zhao Hongliang and a number of his colleagues had
somehow managed to sleep through the tumultuous night. But at
dawn on May 20, they awakened to the news of martial law. They
rubbed the sleep from their eyes and sat down to an emergency
meeting.

Everyone agreed that it was necessary to place the Beijing
Workers' Union on a firmer footing. By now the group comprised
a reliable core of perhaps thirty to forty activists, and hundreds
more had written their names on the sign-up sheets at Xiguanlitai.
But the organization was still loose, even chaotic. It was time to
turn the informal preparatory committee into something more
solid.

A number of new leaders had risen to prominence in the
workers' organization in the month since its first ragged meetings.
Most of them had at least a smattering of higher education,
although it was not quite accurate to think of them as "worker-
intellectuals" in the same sense as their predecessors of the Democracy Wall period; after all, these men were born in the early
1960s, too late for their education to have been seriously disrupted
by the Cultural Revolution. Shen Yinhan, for example, a twenty-
nine-year-old university graduate, was head of the official union
at the Bureau of Civil Aviation. He Lili, the same age, taught at

the Workers' University run by the Beijing Bureau of the Ministry of Machine Industry. Another member of the group, Liu Qiang, was three years younger. After three years of service in the navy, Liu took some correspondence courses in economics and psychology. Now, he worked at the city's Number 3209 Printing Factory. A beefy young man usually in need of a shave, Liu was physically fearless, and the BWAF placed him in charge of the workers' pickets. Zhao Hongliang continued to handle logistics in the square, and a twenty-six-year-old railway attendant named Bai Dongping was placed in charge of signing up new members for the federation.

At first light, as the group discussed its future, a tall figure appeared and asked to be admitted. Li Jinjin looked up and recognized the young man he had met twenty-four hours earlier at the Monument. It was Han Dongfang, paying his first visit to the workers' headquarters, and Li ushered him inside enthusiastically. Han tried to impress on the group the need for calm and order. One misstep could lead to calamity, he warned. The previous day's call for a general strike, for example, must now be withdrawn, given the new reality of martial law. Besides, the group did not have the strength to enforce its demands. Han Dongfang's quiet charisma gave the group's discussions some much-needed focus.

The Xiguanlitai group also acquired a name that morning. Its members painted the words "Beijing Workers Autonomous Federation" in large black characters on a red banner, hung it on the side of a Number 130 Beijing bus, and drove the bus once around the city center to the beating of drums and gongs. The new BWAF handed out copies of a handbill that it called its first manifesto. Written by Li Jinjin the previous day, May 19, it was phrased in strikingly traditional Marxist terms. "The proletariat is the most progressive class in society," it began. "Through the democracy movement, we have nothing to lose but our chains, but we stand to gain the whole world," it ended.[1]

By noon, Han and Li had also written an urgent appeal for workers and students to join forces, and in the midafternoon, Li tried to read it to the crowds in the square. He saw the lamppost-mounted surveillance cameras swivel in his direction, but a strong wind carried his words away, unheard. That evening he asked permission to read the BWAF documents over the loudspeakers at the Monument to the People's Heroes, but the students were hostile to the idea, so the workers pooled their meager savings to rig up their own primitive broadcasting system, complete with hand-cranked generator, at Xiguanlitai.

At ten o'clock that morning—the time when martial law took formal effect, the dull throb of rotor blades filled the skies over Tiananmen Square as five PLA helicopters made a series of low, threatening passes over the student encampment.[2] At almost the same moment, across town at the Jimen Hotel, Chen Ziming and his colleagues commenced a day-long emergency session of their new group. The mood at the Jimen Hotel was angry. Wang argued passionately that martial law changed the whole picture; SERI, whatever its members may have felt in the past, whatever their qualms about the wisdom of the students, now had no alternative but to throw its weight fully behind the democracy movement and help protect the square as the movement's living symbol. It was a matter of simple historical obligation. No one disagreed.

That evening, Wang and Liu Gang borrowed a car and drove through the streets of Beijing to observe the results of the first full day of martial law. Everywhere they went, they found that the human barricades of the previous night had held firm and that no troops or army vehicles had been able to enter the city; and all this without violent incident. It seemed too good to be true. The next morning, May 21, the two drove down to the square. This time Liu was carrying a bulky package of handbills, and while Wang sat in the car outside the Museum of Chinese History, Liu jumped out to deliver the handbills to the students. Wang claimed later that he was unaware that Liu's package contained copies of the angry and inflammatory version of the "Letter to the People."

Over the next few days, Wang remained plagued by the fears he had expressed in his most recent article for *Economics Weekly*. What if, as seemed likely, martial law were to radicalize the protests and cut away any middle ground that might remain? How then was the absolute principle of nonviolence to be maintained? He was particularly disturbed by the reports of a violent clash in the early hours of May 22 at Fengtai, where a large convoy had been blocked by crowds since May 20. The whole episode had been a misunderstanding. An angry crowd had seen a movement of trucks and soldiers and had assumed, wrongly, that they were headed for central Beijing. Blows had been exchanged. Antiriot squads of the People's Armed Police had rushed to the scene. Heads were bloodied on both sides.

By now Wang and Chen had used the Jimen Hotel as their contact point for nearly a week. But it was time to move. The place had begun to feel unsafe. The evidence mounted of twenty-four-hour surveillance by State Security: The cars of SERI's leaders were followed, and plainclothes personnel dogged the footsteps of SERI members. As many as three hidden video cameras, it later was revealed, had recorded the meetings of key democracy movement leaders. The office telephones at SERI were tapped, and Chen and Wang's personal beepers were monitored.

After the meeting on May 20, the police had showed up at the Jimen. They searched the hotel and questioned the staff, but Wang and Chen had already moved on. Over the next ten days they shifted their meeting place several times, never staying in one place for more than two or three days at a time. They used quiet, inconspicuous hotels, the kind not frequented by foreigners. For more formal meetings, Wang and Chen borrowed rooms in the bland, modern skyscraper that houses the Chinese Academy of Social Sciences (CASS), a couple of miles east of Tiananmen.

The group changed its name several times as well. In two open letters dated May 21 and May 22, it described itself as the "Preparatory Committee for the Conference of All Circles in the Capital."[3] These two documents were very dissimilar in tone, and no clear evidence exists of who wrote them. The first, very unlike Wang Juntao and Chen Ziming's usual calm in its harsh language, was full of the fresh rage provoked by martial law. "If Deng Xiaoping, Li Peng, Yang Shangkun, and their fellow degenerates continue to act foolishly," it began, "it will provoke genuine turmoil, perhaps even to the extent of creating a warlord-style civil war and a splitting asunder of the nation." More radical yet, the letter proposed arresting Deng, Li, and Yang, stripping them of their posts and Party memberships, and placing them on public trial. It is almost inconceivable that Wang and Chen, after a decade of critical support for Deng's policies, would have signed off on anything so incendiary. By the next day, the tone was calmer, and the focus was on "Li Peng and the rest of his tiny band of degenerates."

There was no mention this time of Deng and not a word about a public trial.

Chuanlian—linkups. That word was on Wang Juntao's lips for the whole week. It was one thing to issue appeals for concerted action by all sectors of society, as Chen and Wang had done several times, but how could they make these appeals more than empty words? For Chen and Wang, veterans of a thousand meetings, martial law made it imperative to bring together as many organizations as possible in a single room. This was the idea behind the "Conference of All Circles," which, during the first week of martial law, evolved into an entity called The Joint Liaison Group of All Circles in the Capital.

On May 22, Wang Juntao was unusually subdued. His doubts and anxieties had grown. Two days had passed, and the martial law troops still held back from the city center. After hearing about the clash at Fengtai the previous night, Wang had gone to the headquarters of the students' federation to express his alarm. Why not instruct the students, he suggested, that if they find someone picking a fight with the troops, they should make a citizen's arrest and take the person straight to the nearest police station?[4] But even as he spoke, Wang knew that the students' powers to do anything of the sort were extremely limited.

The square by now was full of wild rumors about splits in the army, an impending coup by reformers, the imminent fall of the villainous Li Peng, the triumphal resurgence of Zhao Ziyang. Although Wang saw little of his father these days, he may have heard through his family connections that unhappiness existed at high levels in the army over the martial law decree. But his sense of history also warned him of the dangers of rash action on the streets, propelled by nothing more than wishful thinking. "When has a government ever been overthrown by street marches?" he asked with a frown at the May 22 meeting. "Except for the French Revolution, no one has ever done it. Social change is a much slower process."

For a moment, roles were reversed. This time, Chen Ziming stilled the doubts of his more impulsive friend. "You know that in principle I agree with everything you've said," he told Wang sympathetically. "All the same, we have a responsibility to go on. We can't turn back now."

They continued the discussion over lunch. For both men, the dilemmas of conscience had reached agonizing proportions. Since the start of the hunger strike nine days earlier, the democracy movement had turned into a tidal wave that threatened to wash away all their timetables, all their blueprints, all the patient years of work to create the independent intelligentsia that China lacked. If they put themselves forward as advisers to the students, were they merely offering to climb on the back of the tiger? All the evidence suggested that the students did not take kindly to counsel from outside voices, especially moderate ones such as those of Wang and Chen. Also, given how polarized the situation had now become, it was hard to know what moderate advice could consist of, other than the suggestion that the students abandon Tiananmen altogether.

If the crackdown came—and logic told them it would—would the subsequent "settling of accounts after the autumn harvest" destroy all that Chen and Wang had worked for? If, on the other hand, they chose to stand aloof, could they ever look in the mirror again? Would they not go down in history as one more stale example of all they had condemned—the refusal of Chinese intellectuals to make a principled moral stand in times of national crisis? Over lunch that day, they very likely glimpsed the full potential for tragedy in their situation.

The situation in the square swayed them in the end. Whenever possible, Chen and Wang went there themselves and argued with the student leaders in their tents. More often, they listened intently to the latest news from Zhang Lun, Liu Gang, and Liu Suli—the SERI staff who had the closest day-to-day involvement with the students. These three brought vivid reports of disarray: The end of the hunger strike had caused a loss of momentum and leadership; martial law had led to a minor exodus of students; and heat and rainstorms were turning the colorful tent city into a reeking squatter settlement that stank of human waste and uncollected garbage. "The students just don't have the maturity to control the situation," Zhang Lun insisted. "You have to admire their bravery, but they often act so foolishly. For a lot of them, being in the square is like playing house. They have no idea of what they're up against." By the afternoon of May 22, Wang and Chen had overcome any reservations they may have had about becoming formally involved.

At ten o'clock that night, the two men gathered together a group of about thirty people on the second level of the Monument to the People's Heroes. Security was tight. Zhang Lun, who was running the meeting at Chen Ziming's request, placed his pickets in a protective circle. But after a few minutes, he leapt to his feet to remove an unauthorized photographer who was perched on the third level. The square, as everyone knew, was crawling with government spies.

Each of the organizations that had emerged in the course of the protests was present. The students were on hand, naturally—though not their top leadership. So was the Beijing Intellectuals Union, newly set up by the outspoken Bao Zunxin and Yan Jiaqi. There were also leaders of the Dare-to-Die squads and several members of a new group that called itself the *Beijing Shimin Zizhi Hui,* the Beijing Residents' Autonomous Federation. And that night, for the first time, a formal link was established between Chen Ziming, Wang Juntao, and the BWAF, represented by Liu Huanwen, a former employee of the giant Capital Iron and Steel Works who was now in charge of the workers' pickets. The only group missing was RIRES. Chen Ziming had asked Bai Hua to use her influence there, hoping against hope that the official think tank would agree to attend. But no one came, and the next morning there was a message for Bai Hua: Chen Yizi still thought it was too dangerous for RIRES to get involved.

On the morning of May 23, Chen and Wang arranged for a large van to pick up the same group, with the addition of Chai Ling, who had missed the meeting the night before at the Monument, and drive them out to the CASS building. There was an eerie stillness along Chang'an Boulevard and its eastern extension, Jianguomenwai. There were still no troops to be seen.

They met, with fine irony, in the offices of the Institute of Marxism-Leninism–Mao Zedong Thought. It was time to pull loose ends together, assign responsibilities, set up subsidiary committees, and choose a name. They settled on an awkward one: The Joint Liaison Group of All Circles in the Capital to Protect and Uphold the Constitution. The final phrase was added as a token of their desire to overturn the martial law order through an emergency session of the National People's Congress; Wan Li, its chair, was expected to return to the capital at any moment.

Veterans of SERI were distributed strategically throughout the eight newly created sections of the Capital Joint Liaison Group.[5] Liu Gang became head of logistics. Liu Suli headed the liaison section. Zhang Lun, by now in a state of nervous exhaustion, was given overall charge of the worker, student, and citizen picket teams. He set up his headquarters in two vehicles parked on the northern edge of the square. There he marshaled his forces, issuing them code names, walkie-talkies, binoculars, and maps to help pinpoint the location of the martial law troops.

Bai Hua took control of the Capital Joint Liaison Group's propaganda operation. She proposed to produce a weekly journal, *People's Voice,* but its first issue, published on June 2, proved also to be its last. Chen's wife, Wang Zhihong, agreed to help Bai Hua by running off one thousand copies of the group's daily broadsheet, *News Flash.* The first number carried the statement that the Capital Joint Liaison Group issued at the end of its inaugural May 23 meeting. Drafted by the well-known scholar Gan Yang, "The Final Showdown Between Darkness and Light" was an impassioned rejection of all the rules by which politics had traditionally been conducted in China.[6] "The era of fighting evil with evil is coming to an end," Gan Yang wrote. Since Luther and the Reformation, the document went on, political movements in the West have been about the expression of high ideals. In China, they have been only about survival and food. Until now.

In one sense, the May 23 meeting at CASS must have appeared to Wang Juntao and Chen Ziming as the culmination of their political careers. Everything they had done since that first, inauspicious meeting in the smelly hospital basement three years earlier had pointed logically in the direction of an independent political party. And that, in embryo, was what they had created. But in another sense, the Capital Joint Liaison Group was the derailment of all their caution. It was an unplanned child, an unwanted accident of history.

The problem was the students. What had begun as their protest had become a nationwide mass movement. Workers and ordinary citizens had organized themselves, not only to support the students but for interests of their own. Now, with the Capital Joint Liaison Group, the movement had a coherent advisory body in which all social groups were represented. But the students still exercised veto power. It was all very well for Chen Ziming, Wang Juntao, and their colleagues to debate the wisdom of continuing the occupation of Tiananmen Square. In reality, however, only the students encamped there had the power to make that decision. All that Chen and Wang could do was offer advice, and that, more often than not, was spurned.

Until 1988, Xie Xiaoqing had been an associate professor at Central China Normal College in Wuhan. He was one of the close friends that Wang Juntao had made during his stay in the central Chinese city in the mid-1980s. Xie helped Wang start the short-lived Jiangshan School of Continuing Education. When the time came to assemble the team at SERI, Wang tapped deeply into the Wuhan talent pool, and Xie accepted his invitation to come to Beijing as head of SERI's Human Resources Testing and Evaluation Center.

In a manuscript smuggled out of China a year after the June 1989 Beijing massacre, Xie wrote with deep sadness of the obstacles that Wang and Chen had faced in trying to moderate the behavior of the students. For all that the students spoke of democracy, Xie wrote, "the last third of May [in Tiananmen Square] closely resembled a Jacobin dictatorship. Those who were applauded loudest were the most radical."

The root of the problem existed from the very beginning. As early as April 27, the student federation's first leader, Zhou Yongjun, was ousted for opposing that day's mass demonstration and suggesting a return to classes.[7] Then, as Wang Juntao had painfully witnessed, the Dialogue Delegation negotiations of May 14–15 collapsed, in large measure because its student leaders had no control over the purist, emotional language of the hunger strikers, who had brought the masses onto the streets.

The spirit of the hunger strike was embodied by Chai Ling, who had launched it in the first place. She was the Joan of Arc of the democracy movement, a tiny, frail figure who, with a faraway look in her eyes, spoke of streets washed clean, of a nation redeemed, by the blood sacrifice of her fellow students. She melted arguments among her devoted male colleagues with her tears, which came easily and often. She could still a political disagreement by picking up a leaf and musing wistfully on the beauty and fragility of existence. During the hunger strike, with her parchmentlike skin, her cracked lips, and the cotton jeans hanging loose around her boyish hips, she seemed too feeble to survive. The banner of the hunger strikers was a triptych: Two agonized female nudes flanked bold characters that read "Save the Children." How could such purity of spirit be criticized? How could anyone speak of compromise with the government without betraying the innocence of Chai Ling?[8]

The leadership of the student movement shifted with bewildering speed. Each time the leadership changed, those who lost out were those who spoke of compromise. The spirit of pluralism began to erode. Dissent came to be equated with treachery. After the breakdown of the Dialogue Delegation, Wang Dan and Wu'er Kaixi had told Wang Juntao that there might be a chance of ending the hunger strike—if Chai Ling would make the appeal. But she refused. As the strike went on, Wang Dan, notably lacking in charisma in his zippered jacket and grubby T-shirt, began to lose influence to the more macho and magnetic Wu'er Kaixi. But neither of them could contest Chai Ling's authority.[9]

The momentum of the student movement also began to shift away from the Beijing students. As the fainter hearts abandoned the square after martial law, droves of new arrivals from other cities took their places. These newcomers had left their real constituencies behind in Xi'an and Shanghai and Guangzhou; any power they now wished to exercise had to be derived from the magic talisman of the square. Chai Ling and her husband of a year, Feng Congde, were now constantly seen in the company of a good-looking young man with thick black hair and steel-rimmed, tinted glasses. This was Li Lu, a student from Nanjing who had come to the capital at the end of April. He had become Chai Ling's loyal lieutenant.

Li Lu had little patience with the older intellectuals who presumed to give the students advice. When Bao Zunxin, Yan Jiaqi, and a group of ten colleagues visited the square on May 14 and tried to persuade the students to call off the hunger strike, Li Lu thought he saw right through them. "It sounded good," he later recalled. "They were voicing our main demands. But when we calmed down and thought, we realized that they were actually acting on behalf of the government." Li Lu felt a mistrust bordering on contempt for those who had not actually lain on the cold flagstones of the square and fasted, and his attitude more and more defined that of the student leadership as a whole.

On May 22, after a sleepless night spent waiting for the soldiers to arrive, the exhausted students decided that the defunct hunger-strike group had left a dangerous vacuum. Leaders met that evening; the talks went on all night, which was the reason Chai Ling and the top student leadership missed the meeting that Wang Juntao and Chen Ziming had convened at 10:00 P.M. on the steps of the Monument. Wu'er Kaixi delivered a characteristically rousing speech to the students, urging them, for safety's sake, to retreat to the embassy district a few blocks away. He was shouted down, denounced as an alarmist, a defeatist, even a traitor, and removed from the Tiananmen leadership.[10]

When Wang and Chen reassembled their group the next morning at CASS for the inaugural session of the Capital Joint Liaison Group, they found that they had to contend with two student bodies, not one. Wang Dan came as the elected delegate from the Beijing Students Autonomous Federation. But the hunger-strike group had been reborn during the night as the Command Headquarters of Tiananmen Square. Chai Ling now had the resplendent title of commander in chief, and Li Lu was her deputy commander. It was this group that called the shots.

Li Lu, again, was unimpressed with his elders. "The joint conference began disappointingly," he wrote later. "The intellectuals were good at analyzing the situation and making proposals, but were weak and indecisive when it came to action. Many organizations existed in name only, like the independent workers' union [the BWAF]. The leaders of several organizations had changed many times. The organization of intellectuals consisted of only a few members and other groups had even fewer. Other than the square headquarters, these organizations had little power." Li Lu went on impatiently, "Some of the intellectuals were still debating whether any crisis existed in China. . . . But those of us who were at the forefront of the struggle knew what was in store for us, and that moderation could not be expected."

Deng Xiaoping and the Party elders had taken one look at the students and decided that this was the Cultural Revolution all over again. And as Wang Juntao and Chen Ziming listened to the students that day and during the week that followed, they too must have caught at least a whiff of the zealotry they had witnessed as teenagers. Even Li Lu thought that many of the newcomers from the provinces were "a bunch of troublemakers with no clear leadership." Too many of them were filled with that driving moral certainty that had led the Red Guards to condemn as a capitalist roader anyone who owned so much as a radio or a foreign book.

However vehemently the students repudiated Mao and his legacy, those who moved into the ascendancy after the hunger strike were also, in a curious way, his children. There was no room for self-doubt in their eyes. They believed that the struggle is all, and that battle lines are drawn in black and white; history is made by mass action; compromise equals cowardice; and moderation is betrayal.

Chen Ziming chaired the first full meeting of the Capital Joint Liaison Group. But the next day, May 24, he turned the proceedings over to Wang Juntao. When the group met on the tenth floor of the CASS building, everyone seemed overwrought. There was yet another fresh rumor that the troops were about to move in. "This is nothing but a talking shop!" someone shouted. "We're wasting valuable time here when we should be out in the streets organizing resistance. The fate of a billion people is at stake!"

Wang Juntao did all he could to maintain a sense of calm and order, and Li Lu, almost despite himself, was impressed. Wang was "the soul of the conference," he decided, the only one who kept its energies from spinning off in a dozen fragmented directions. He resolved to emulate Wang's style when it next fell to him to chair one of the fractious meetings of the students in the square.

"We need to make a decision," Wang announced. "Are we going to unveil this organization publicly or not?"

"It's too dangerous," someone replied. "If we do that, we'll be labeled as *heishou*—the black hands."

"The time for that kind of caution is past," another voice broke in impatiently.

"I tend to agree," Wang said. "The question is no longer what they call us. The question now is whether we'll all be killed."

As the argument raged back and forth, Li Lu's respect for Wang Juntao grew. He knew that he was witnessing a landmark in Chinese history. For the first time, the intellectuals had placed themselves on the firing line; for the first time, they had overcome their fear of how the Party might label them. If this was no longer just a student movement, but a broad movement of the Chinese people, perhaps it was acquiring here an embryonic leadership to reflect that new reality.

The meeting broke for lunch. Wang Juntao called out for a delivery of Kentucky Fried Chicken from the recently opened franchise at the southern end of Tiananmen Square. "Eat your fill," Wang urged the students. "You've been hungry for so long." It was the first time Li Lu had eaten this Western delicacy; he thought it was inedible. Chai Ling, thinking of her student budget, found it extravagantly expensive.

When the meeting resumed, the group agreed to Wang Juntao's proposal.

The Capital Joint Liaison Group decided to announce its existence at a press conference that same afternoon. Everyone piled into a waiting minibus and headed for the Monument to the People's Heroes, where the members of the Command Headquarters swore an emotional blood oath to defend the square. Zhang Lun, Liu Gang, and Liu Suli, in their appointed capacity, joined in. Finally, Chai Ling led the crowd of one hundred thousand in a mass reading of the oath.

It seemed to Wang Juntao that the only question that remained was when, not whether, the troops would move in to retake the rebellious city. At the next morning's meeting, Wang raised the possibility of a withdrawal from the square. He suggested a simultaneous display of good faith: Let the troops pull back from their positions, and the students would march out of Tiananmen in good order. Wang Dan, who chaired the meeting that day, agreed. But how was such a thing to be negotiated, given the breakdown of every channel of communication with the government? Liu Gang, who also thought it was time to end the occupation of the square, thought the situation might be defused if the out-of-town students went back to their home campuses to "exchange experiences." The discussion broke up with no decision.

At the end of the meeting, the Capital Joint Liaison Group issued its most formal public statement to date. It described itself, in terms that must have made the government's blood run cold, as "a mass organization of the workers, intellectuals, cadres of the state apparatus, young students, patriotic-democratic elements, peasants, and people engaged in business"—the germ of a political party, in other words; Wang Juntao and Chen Ziming's old dream of a functioning civil society in China.

Given the mood of the students in the square, however, the Capital Joint Liaison Group was severely restricted. Its only option was to protect and support them, whatever Chen and Wang may have felt. "The immediate goal of the Capital Joint Liaison Group," the May 25 statement continued, "is to mobilize all patriotic people actively to assist the Beijing Students Autonomous Federation and other autonomous organizations in the higher education field and resolutely to support the present patriotic-democratic movement to the very end." In practical terms, the document explained, this meant "to mobilize the masses from all sections of the community to do everything possible to resist martial law and thoroughly defeat the conspiracy of military rule imposed by the small clique of autocratic elements."[11]

That evening, Li Lu presided over an emergency meeting to discuss the students' next move. More than three hundred universities around the country were represented. Li Lu placed four proposals before them: (1) stay in the square, treat the government as an enemy, and try to foment strikes, even a military coup, to overthrow it; (2) hold talks with the government, gradually withdrawing from the square as the students' demands are met; (3) "keep the movement pure" and persuade the government to withdraw the April 26 editorial; or (4) withdraw from the square, as Wang Juntao had suggested.

As the arguments flew back and forth, Li Lu groped for analogies from the board game of *go*. What was the opponent's strategy? What pieces did the government hold? How should the students plan their defense? But the board kept dissolving in his mind. It was impossible to assess anyone's next move, because it was not even clear how many players were involved. Each day some new envoy arrived at the Command Headquarters, claiming to represent one or another faction of the Party. The square was awash with contradictory rumors. Li Lu heard his own confusion echoed in the voices that swirled around him in the darkened square.

"If we leave now, the troops are certain to move in."

"If we stay, perhaps they won't come. After all, they haven't come yet."

"Even if the military does retake the square, there won't be any killing. They won't dare, not with all the foreign press about. Let's stay put."

"The masses on the streets are the best guarantee against violence. They've kept two hundred thousand troops out for almost a week now, haven't they?"

"Nonsense! The masses on the streets are our biggest problem. They may provoke the PLA to attack!"

"The movement outside Beijing is gathering strength; that should encourage us to stay where we are."

"How do we know that? Maybe we're deluding ourselves. We should be sending people out from Tiananmen to get things moving outside the capital."

"What is the worst that can happen if we stay where we are?" another voice asked. "Won't it be like April Fifth all over again?"

In the fog of the present, the past offered at least this one precedent: the Tiananmen Incident of 1976. Chen Ziming had talked at length about April Fifth, Li Lu remembered, about how Jiang Qing and her cronies had used their thugs to clear the square with tear gas and cudgels. On the first day of martial law, a young PLA colonel had slipped into the students' headquarters with a similar message. April Fifth will be the Party's model, he had told them. Lay in plenty of cotton face masks; have wet towels and handkerchiefs on hand to protect yourselves against the tear gas.

Shortly before dawn, after the debates ended and the vote was taken, Li Lu announced the results: 162 for a frontal attack on the government; 80 for remaining in the square and attempting a dialogue; 38 for keeping the movement pure; and just 8 for withdrawing. Cotton face masks were duly issued.

Wang Juntao and Chen Ziming were depressed to hear the results of Li Lu's show of hands. But they were not immune to the pressure that everyone else was feeling. Wang felt he was being torn apart by indecision. One moment he would see the force of Chai Ling's emotional appeals: Perhaps, as she said, this deadlock would only be broken by bloodshed. But then his horror of disorder would regain the upper hand, and he would try to find fresh arguments for a moderate solution. Wang reminded the students of China's lamentable history. For example, he argued, the overthrow of the Qing Dynasty in 1911 inflicted thirty-eight years of turmoil on China—*dongluan,* he called it, using the same word the government now used to slander the student movement. After the repeated disasters of Maoism, how could China afford another era of upheavals?

At other times Wang resorted to parable, as if he were speaking to children. "Don't we often see maggots and garbage in our homes?" he asked one student leader that week. "But we wouldn't think of burning down the house to get rid of them. If we burn down the house, it will be a calamity for 1.1 billion people. We have the lesson of the Cultural Revolution always before us. We can't retrace those old, well-trodden paths again. We have to do our house-cleaning one step at a time."

Wang Dan seemed receptive to these arguments, but his influence had been eclipsed since the end of the hunger strike. The majority of the students remained deaf to Wang Juntao's appeals. In one final article in *Economics Weekly,* Chen Ziming pleaded for all sides to seek compromise. But in the end, his frustration with the students exploded. "Don't you see," he cried in despair, "this strategy of driving the government into a corner, of giving them no way out, is stupid. It's just plain ignorant."

The students' stubbornness contained a paradox, however. Although they refused to give the Communist Party a graceful exit, they seemed nevertheless to be waiting for it to pull a solution out of the hat, as if by magic. Between May 24 and May 26, one ominous development after another made it clear that this expectation was a pipe dream. Wan Li, the aging "savior" who was supposed to convene a special session of the NPC, made an anticlimactic return to Shanghai from his trip abroad. Citing "health reasons," he remained in Shanghai. Military units commandeered press and broadcasting outlets, and the reporters, for all their earlier brave words, did nothing to resist. General Xu Qinxian, commander of the elite 38th Division of the PLA, was arrested for refusing to endorse martial law.[12] President Yang Shangkun tersely informed the Central Military Commission that the entire episode of turmoil was rooted in Zhao Ziyang's insubordination; Zhao was placed under house arrest. There would be no coup and no miraculous comeback.

The squalor of Tiananmen mounted as temperatures soared into the mid-nineties and the bursts of heat were punctuated by sudden, heavy rain showers. The uncompromising mood of those who remained at the square threatened to engulf even Chai Ling.

On the morning of Saturday, May 27, the Capital Joint Liaison Group met as usual at the CASS tower. It was the best attended meeting of the entire 1989 movement, and in many ways the most representative. The main item on the day's agenda was the draft of a major statement that reviewed the course of the movement so far and outlined its next moves. Crafted by the radical poet Lao Mu and by Gan Yang, author of "The Final Showdown Between Darkness and Light," the May 27 statement was perhaps the most significant document of the entire 1989 movement. As Chen Ziming read through the draft, he could not help recalling the course of his adult political life. In 1976, as a young man of the same age as today's students, he had hurried to the square to lend his support to Deng Xiaoping in his mortal struggle against the Gang of Four. At Democracy Wall, he had offered *Beijing Spring* as a weapon for Deng and his fellow reformers in their battles with the die-hard Maoists of the Whateverist faction. Throughout the 1980s, Chen had beaten vainly on the doors of the reformers with offers of help. But now he had to concur with the May 27 statement: The greatness of the present movement lay in its independence from all inner-Party struggles. Chen had learned the painful lesson that no good could ever come of allying the democrats with any faction behind the walls of Zhongnanhai. On the contrary, leaders would now be judged by their attitudes toward the cause of democratic reform. "No leader can sway the course of this movement," the statement declared with pride. "Those who flow with it will prosper," it continued, echoing a famous remark of Sun Yat-sen's, "Those who oppose it will perish."

Chen and Wang were still uncertain, however, about what to do next. As long as the students refused to budge, was there any alternative but to call vainly for the NPC to remove Li Peng, something they knew would never happen? With a feeling of impotence, they agreed to a meaningless ultimatum—the eighth in a list of ten points in that day's document. It represented the views of the Tiananmen Square Command Headquarters. If the NPC did not call an emergency session within the next few days, "then the large-scale peaceful petition activities in Tiananmen Square will continue at least until June 20"—the date of the next regularly scheduled session of the NPC.

Wang Juntao opened the meeting by calling on the students to give their daily report. A member of the Beijing Students Autonomous Federation announced that the BSAF had resolved the previous night to end the occupation of the square. They would stage a triumphant withdrawal on Sunday, May 28, timed to coincide with worldwide demonstrations of support. On the face of it, this was dramatic news, but it was common knowledge by now that there was a bitter split between the BSAF and the more powerful Tiananmen Square Command Headquarters, without whose approval nothing could be done. At this point, Chai Ling and her husband, Feng Congde, entered the room. What was their view?

Chai Ling said she was exhausted and confused. Much as she might want to prolong the occupation, the practical obstacles were becoming insurmountable. There was a steady exodus of students from the square; they were running out of supplies; and how much longer could one expect the citizens to go on blocking the martial law troops? Perhaps the BSAF proposal made sense after all, she said dejectedly.

A ripple of approval passed through the room. Could it really be that the impasse was to be resolved without bloodshed? The new proposal would allow the movement to claim a resounding moral victory. Intact and undefeated, it would have written a shining page in China's history. The Capital Joint Liaison Group suggested only one amendment to the proposal. May 28 was the next day; perhaps it would be better to wait until Tuesday, May 30, to prepare a final citywide victory march. After that, the students would return to their campuses. "Let's vote on the proposal," said Wang Juntao. All eyes were on Chai Ling. After a moment's hesitation, she raised her hand in favor. The vote was unanimous. The meeting broke up amid relief and embraces. Catastrophe had been averted.

Everyone rushed back to Tiananmen Square to report to the Command Headquarters. At the Monument, Chai Ling met her lieutenant, Li Lu.

"What's the news?" he asked.

"We're leaving," Chai Ling replied. "It's all agreed. Here's the statement that's going to be issued today in the name of the Capital Joint Liaison Group."

"What are you talking about?" asked Li Lu, dumbfounded. His voice rose. "It's less than two days since three hundred colleges took the vote to stay in the square. How can that decision be overturned so quickly? It's against democratic procedure."

"People just can't hold out any longer," she answered. "The next meeting of the NPC isn't until June 20. That's more than three weeks."

Li Lu grew more agitated. "It's too dangerous," he yelled. "If we leave, they'll stop the NPC. Beijing will be under army control. We won't be able to demonstrate. They'll surround the colleges and block the exits. They'll throw us in jail. You're talking defeat. They've given us nothing we asked for. All our hopes will be gone!"

Li Lu turned angrily to Wang Juntao. "What's going on here?" he snapped. "The Capital Joint Liaison Group has no power to make a decision like this."

Wang frowned. "That's right," he said. "You know that we've said right from the start that we're only an advisory backup group. But it was the students who said they wanted to leave; all we're doing is reflecting what you've decided."

"What do you mean? Which students?"

"The Beijing Students Autonomous Federation. And Chai Ling told us that the Command Headquarters couldn't hold out any longer."

The two men turned to face Chai Ling. She broke down in tears.

Someone grabbed a pen and added new wording to the ten-point statement. Someone else crossed it out again. By the time Wang Dan read the statement at a press conference that evening, the paper was a mass of illegible scribbles. When Wang Dan reached the eighth point, he paused for a moment, then softly read on, "It has been proposed to the Capital Joint Liaison Group that the students evacuate Tiananmen Square on May 30." He then walked away from the microphone and handed in his resignation. Pandemonium broke out. Another emergency conclave; another re-write. When the students emerged, the document had been re-written again: "Unless a special meeting of the National People's Congress is convened in the next few days, the occupation of the square will continue until June 20."

In the name of democracy, the most radical voices had triumphed. Wang Juntao and Chen Ziming knew now that nothing could hold back the storm that hovered over Beijing any longer. They had failed for thirteen years to convince the government of the need for moderation; now, after barely thirteen days, they had failed to curb the excesses of the students. They had placed them-selves in the jaws of a vise, and it was now about to crush them.

Chai Ling spent the next day, May 28, in a state of nervous ex-haustion, racked with grief and guilt. In the evening, she returned to the square. "I've come to the end of my strength, both physically and mentally," she told the students. "Please forgive me, and ap-prove my resignation." The student movement was slipping into chaos, she said in tears. She no longer knew whom to trust. People had begun to steal money from the students' strongbox. The old leadership—Wang Dan, Wu'er Kaixi, and now Chai Ling herself—was finished. It was time for someone else to clean up the mess. She begged Li Lu to try to straighten things out.

The provincial students congratulated themselves for reviving the moribund movement. The garbage in the square was cleared away, and the stinking portable toilets were removed and cleaned. A new consignment of tents and large injections of cash arrived from well-wishers in Hong Kong; the brightly colored tents, square nylon domes on sturdy tubular frames, soon went up in neat, or-derly rows. A visitor from Hong Kong took Chai Ling to a nearby hotel, let her take a shower, and gave her a change of clothes. In better spirits, she told Li Lu that she felt ready to return to the fray. Meanwhile, a group of students prepared a scaffold at the northern end of the square, directly facing the great portrait of Mao; it was to support a statue that was being sculpted from Sty-rofoam at the Central Academy of Fine Arts. The statue—the God-dess of Democracy—arrived on the night of May 29 on a half dozen flatbed Beijing bicycles. It was the final symbol of the movement's refusal to yield. That night, strong winds lashed Tiananmen

Square, bringing sudden gusts of rain. But work on the Goddess went on.

The statue, staring defiantly across at the Great Helmsman, was an affront to the Party. So was the sparkling new tent city. But the die had already been cast. The government stripped Zhao Ziyang of his official posts on May 26 and rooted out the faint hearts in the PLA command. This time the troops would not be humiliated; the square would be retaken. Yet even with this decision made, the Party continued to have kind words for the students—the whole Party at that, even eighty-seven-year-old Peng Zhen, the oldest and crustiest of the elders. If the students didn't trust anyone over thirty, then Peng Zhen probably trusted no one under eighty. Even so, he quavered, the government had nothing but praise for the students' "good, pure, kindhearted, and constructive motives." They would be spared in the coming crackdown. The workers and the *laobaixing* would not.

14

The Polish Disease

Deng Xiaoping remained transfixed by his nightmarish vision of a Chinese Solidarity in the making. According to the reports reaching him from State Security, workers had become a fixture of the conspiratorial meetings taking place each day in the Jimen and other small Beijing hotels and at the Chinese Academy of Social Sciences. They seemed, in fact, to be benefiting from the advice and guidance of the shadowy counterrevolutionary forces, the black hands behind the turmoil.

It was true that since May 22 the BWAF had attended the meetings of the Capital Joint Liaison Group. They had sent three representatives, who varied from one meeting to the next. Usually Liu Huanwen was there, sometimes Shen Yinhan. The workers tended to cluster at one end of the table, and for the first couple of days they said little, speaking only when they were spoken to. At times Chen Ziming or Wang Juntao would turn to one of them and ask the BWAF's opinion on some point. They would say a few words in reply, and the discussion would move on.

Before martial law, there had been little to suggest that Wang or Chen was actively seeking to involve the workers as major players in the democracy movement. Indeed, they seemed nervous that the slumbering giant of the industrial working class would awaken and aggravate an already tense situation. Chen and Wang's main interest was in controlling all that muscle. Above all, they wanted to be sure that the workers' patrols were smoothly coordinated with Zhang Lun's picket headquarters. Wang worried that angry worker pickets might provoke further unpleasant incidents like the scuffle at Fengtai in the dawn hours of May 22. The BWAF leaders assured him that everything was in hand.

Nevertheless, the BWAF found the meetings useful. For one thing, they brought the workers some much-needed legal advice on how to avoid trouble with the police by adhering to the letter of the Constitution, which was Han Dongfang's particular concern. A number of people offered their expertise. There was Chen's old friend from *Beijing Spring,* Lü Jiamin, who now taught labor law. There was Zhou Yongjun from Politics and Law University, one of the first generation of leaders of the Beijing Students Autonomous Federation. But no one was more helpful than Wang Juntao's old friend from Wuhan, Li Jinjin.

During these final days in Tiananmen Square, Han Dongfang and Li Jinjin became inseparable, and the BWAF formally appointed Li as its legal counselor. "We can't be your leaders, but we can be your advisers," he told Han, with whom he had struck up an easy friendship. They shared private jokes in the workers' tent. Li helped Han with the wording of the BWAF's statutes and advised him on his infrequent interviews with the press. (Few journalists were paying any attention to the workers.)

The BWAF was still plagued by schisms and personality conflicts, and by May 25 it was clear that the only way to resolve these problems was for the federation to hold its first leadership vote. The members elected a five-man standing committee, with Han Dongfang, an informal first among equals, given the title of "convenor." Li Jinjin drafted its inaugural statement. "Our old unions," it read, "were welfare organizations. But now we will create a union that is not a welfare organization but one concerned with workers' rights."

Later that day, the two men rode together at the head of the BWAF contingent in a huge march, organized by the Capital Joint Liaison Group, that started from the square and wound its way along the Number 2 Ring Road. "Welcome back Wan Li! Remove Li Peng!" was the slogan of the day. Li Jinjin had explained to the BWAF that Wan Li, and a special session of the NPC, was the last slender hope of resolving the crisis through constitutional means.

When the march was over, Li took Han Dongfang aside. "It occurred to me," Li suggested, "that you might cancel whatever plans you have for tomorrow morning and attend the daily meeting

of that new group that my old friend Wang Juntao has organized.
I think you'd find it interesting."

Han agreed to go, a little reluctantly.

He was unimpressed by the meeting; its discussions didn't seem
grounded in reality. But when the talk turned to the question of a
general strike, he spoke up candidly. It was a subject that Chen
Ziming and Wang Juntao had always shied away from, although
recently Chen had begun to put out discreet feelers to Zhu Houze,
the acting head of the ACFTU. Liu Weihua, SERI's director of
research, had been Chen's main envoy. Liu did not get as far as
Zhu himself, but he did speak to several of his aides. Some of them
were enthusiastic about the idea, but Zhu himself drew back at the
last minute. Liberal though he was, he did not ultimately want to
"use ox bezoar to provoke diarrhea."

Chen and Wang mentioned none of this in the meeting, but
they were eager to hear Han Dongfang's opinion. Han explained
that the BWAF had dropped its earlier appeals for a general strike.[1]
He admitted that the federation had made no real inroads into
Beijing's factories. It might be useful, he suggested, for the students
to make greater efforts to reach out to the working class. After all,
Tiananmen Square could not be the focal point of the democracy
movement forever. Sooner or later the occupation would end; it
was time to look to the future, and the next stage of the movement
would inevitably take a different form.

"You theoreticians," he said, waving a hand around the table,
"can go on acting as the brains of the movement, and the students
can give it its emotional spark. But unless the workers are the main
force, the struggle for democracy will never succeed.

"Don't misunderstand me," Han went on. "I'm not trying to
spout the old Maoist dogma about the working class being the
leading force in society. But I hear you talking a lot about the
'citizens' [shimin] who are out on the streets, when what I think
you mean is 'workers' [gongren]. I don't know if that's a deliberate
evasion on your part, but it's important to call these people by
their true name. Only if they think of themselves as workers and
band together in a new trade union will they develop the strength
that is required. Otherwise the movement will be too loose, too
formless to succeed—as it has been this time."

When Han got back to the BWAF headquarters, he told Li
Jinjin that one of these meetings was enough. He didn't plan to
go back.

Han Dongfang persisted in his efforts to raise the profile of the independent union. On May 28, the BWAF again revamped its five-person standing committee. More than one hundred members took part in the vote, squatting on the ground in the near darkness at Xiguanlitai. After the vote, Han turned the meeting over to Li Jinjin, who laid out the provisional charter he had drafted.

> The Federation shall be an entirely independent and autonomous organization, built up by the workers on a voluntary basis and through democratic processes; it should not be subject to control by other organizations. The Federation shall perform the role of monitoring the Party of the proletariat—the Chinese Communist Party. Within the bounds of the law and the Constitution, it shall strive to protect all legal rights of its members.

These were bold words, and perhaps a little hyperbole was involved. True, the BWAF had grown impressively in the six weeks since Zhao Hongliang had listened to Han Dongfang's first moving speech. But it was still far short of being a trade union in the classic sense. There was nothing in Li's statutes, for instance, about restoring the right to strike, which had been suspended from the Constitution since 1982. Han agreed strongly with Li that the BWAF should raise no demands that were illegal, even if the law was wrong. The federation's sole objective at this stage, the two men thought, was legal registration. Han even said he was prepared to explore the idea of registering the BWAF as a subsidiary of the official ACFTU.

A tour of the main industrial quarters of the city earlier that day convinced Han and Li that their goals must be modest. The scene was as before. Workers swarmed to the factory gates to listen to the speeches, erupted in applause, brought out cold drinks, and then drifted back to work. The sympathy was palpable, but sympathy alone would never bring down a government.

That was not, however, how the government saw it. Where workers were concerned, molehills were mountains. If the BWAF described itself as an independent organization of the working class, then the "party of the proletariat" would take it at its word. The Communist Party also saw working-class dissent radiating outward to the big factories and to the rest of China. It paid inordinate attention to even the most trivial cases, like that of Yi

Jingyao, a twenty-year-old driver assigned to a large municipal construction company. On the first night of martial law, Yi, an impulsive young man, drove to the giant Capital Iron and Steel works to urge the workers there to help block the incoming troop transports. He was apprehended by security guards at the factory gate. The case had attracted the interest of the Capital Joint Liaison Group, which set up a task force to investigate Yi's arrest.[2] For Wang Juntao, it was a reprise of the role as people's advocate that he had pursued the year before in Anhui and elsewhere. For the government, the Yi Jingyao case was sinister evidence of linkups between the Capital Joint Liaison Group and the core of China's heavy industry.

Enterprises like Capital Iron and Steel were the source of Deng Xiaoping's greatest anxiety; the Party could not afford to lose their support. The Capital Iron and Steel plant, extending over hundreds of acres on the western outskirts of Beijing, employed two hundred thousand workers and turned out three million tons of steel a year. On May 26, the official press issued an unusual report: Rumors that the plant had been placed under military control were groundless;[3] annual production quotas were right on target; everything was normal. The report was the surest sign that something was seriously amiss at Capital Iron and Steel.

The government also saw dangerous signs of worker discontent in the provinces. By the fifth day of martial law, the same trains that brought the out-of-town students to Beijing were also carrying hundreds of workers from other cities who quickly made their way to the scruffy tents at the northern end of the square. News of the BWAF has reached our cities, these workers reported—Shanghai, Nanjing, Changsha, Xi'an, Hangzhou, Wuhan.

The government was most concerned about unrest in Shanghai. The history of the great port city was one of repeated turmoil. It had been the scene of the slaughter of thousands of Communist and labor militants by the Guomindang in 1927. And it had been the seedbed of the Cultural Revolution in 1966, home to the ultra-radical Rebel Workers Headquarters, and birthplace of the Gang of Four.[4] Now, the Communist Party again saw it as a potential powder keg.

Angry workers had joined in the January 1987 protests in Shanghai, something that never happened in Beijing. The economic crisis of 1988 hit Shanghai as hard as any city in China: Of its 14.5 million people, one in seven was a displaced peasant. Almost as soon as the 1989 democracy movement began, the Shanghai authorities began to evict this angry "floating population" back to the countryside. But the feared workers' protests happened anyway. Led by Cai Chaojun, an unemployed officer in the Public Security Bureau, the Shanghai Workers Autonomous Federation made its appearance on May 17.

Lü Jinghua was one of the few women who rallied to the banners of the BWAF. On the surface, there was nothing extraordinary about her. She was, in fact, quite typical of the *laobaixing* who got their first taste of politics through the great, emotional mass rallies of mid-May.

Lü, twenty-seven years old, was the daughter of Party loyalists. Her father had become a Party member before Liberation, and her mother was a neighborhood activist during the Cultural Revolution. Lü attended the highly respected Yucai Middle School, where most of her classmates were the sons and daughters of PLA officers. She attended art school for a year and then held one job after another, none of them lasting for long: in a trading company in Guangzhou, on a chicken farm in the countryside near Beijing, and, most recently, as manager of a privately owned dress shop.

Lü rode past Tiananmen on her bicycle every day on her way to work. After the hunger strike began, she often stopped there in the afternoons on the way home. Like innumerable other women, she started to bring plastic bags of food to the student pickets: a few cucumbers, a bowl of rice porridge, a dozen pork *baozi* (dumplings). Even the students who were not fasting seemed to be half-starved. In return for her kindnesses, they told her the latest hair-raising stories of corruption among the Party elite. Lü began to march with the students. She had a powerful voice, and she chanted their slogans until she was hoarse.

On May 17, she was looking for a friendly group to march with when a huge banner caught her eye: "Elder Brother Workers from Capital Iron and Steel." She fell into step behind it; it somehow felt more natural to be with other workers. Each day she stayed in the square a little longer, worried only that she was not seeing enough of her one-year-old daughter.

Another banner caught her eye several times, the one that read "Beijing Workers Autonomous Federation." On May 26, she spotted it again outside Xinhuamen, the ornate gateway to the Zhongnanhai Party compound. Curious, she looked for someone who was connected with the group. A marcher pointed her toward a burly young man in a checked shirt who introduced himself as Liu Qiang. He explained that he was a printing worker and was helping to organize the workers' pickets. Lü asked if she could help. Liu Qiang frowned. "I don't know," he answered. "The situation isn't good. The government says we're an illegal organization. I feel like things are getting dangerous for us." They walked back toward the West Reviewing Stand.

Lü looked around. "The place is a mess," she said. "I'll help you clean it up."

The next day, she took up a collection from her friends at the dress shop and came back to Xiguanlitai laden with buckets, soap, washbasins, towels, and detergent. When the cleanup was done, she offered to correct some of that day's batch of BWAF handbills, carving neat characters laboriously onto mimeograph sheets.

"Do you know anything about broadcasting?" someone asked. "No," said Lü, "but I'll give it a try."

Papers piled up next to her microphone. She turned nothing away unread: manifestos, announcements of marches, appeals for material help, songs, poems, open letters. All day and into the early hours of the morning, Lü's strong, clear voice echoed across the northern part of the square. She read a satire of a poem of Mao Zedong's, contributed by an official from the Ministry of Trade and Economics. The crowd loved it. She read another poem dropped off at her table by an anonymous Beijing resident:

A red garbage can, it took many years to cast its form.
The power of the party, government, and military is the shell,
But with whose blood was it dyed red?
A red garbage can, filled up with feudalism and autocracy.
Deceptive policy is the shell,
And what's inside is anyone's guess.

The audience whooped. She read a letter from an eighty-five-year-old peasant in Hebei Province. "I have been a Party member for forty years," the old man wrote. "The cannon booming at Marco Polo bridge [during the Japanese invasion] did not scare me; the butchers' knives of the Guomindang did not intimidate me; likewise, the injustice and terror of the present puppet government cannot scare me at all. . . . I am holding out these two fingers: as I heard from my grandson, this means victory." Han Dongfang stopped by the broadcasting table to congratulate Lü on the magnificent job she was doing. She was a little awed by him; she felt she had never done anything more important in her life.

But as Liu Qiang had warned, there was danger in the air. On the evening of May 29, Lü's broadcasts prompted a visit from the Public Security Bureau. A plainclothes officer snapped at her that the BWAF's presence at Xiguanlitai was illegal. She sent someone to fetch Han Dongfang, but by the time Han arrived, the agent was gone. He had left an official notice pasted to the wall. Han deciphered it with difficulty under the dim, flickering street lamps. "This facility is the property of an important state organ," he read. "Occupation is forbidden. It must be vacated immediately, or those present will be responsible for the consequences." There were some jeers of bravado. "Stay where you are," a group of workers shouted.

Han, weighing the options, frowned anxiously. The West Reviewing Stand was too isolated a location anyway, he reasoned. Tucked away off the square as it was, it limited any influence the workers could hope to have, besides offering an easy target for the security forces. Perhaps it was now time to abandon the site and move the BWAF headquarters into the square—whether the students liked it or not.

Zhao Hongliang was sent to negotiate. He had little hope of getting near Chai Ling or any other top student leaders, for they were sealed off by bodyguards, picket lines, and a confusing system of passes that seemed to change by the hour. So Zhao made do with Guo Haifeng, a friendly twenty-two-year-old from Beida, one of the three students who had knelt in supplication on the steps of the Great Hall of the People back on April 22. As far as Guo was concerned, the workers could move into a corner of the square, although he could not speak for the top leadership on this. But he was certain that a move to the Monument was out of the question. The student leaders would never agree to share that pinnacle with any outsiders.

The following dawn, however, brought chilling news. All through that night, the students had labored to piece together the six sections of the Goddess of Democracy. The police did nothing to interfere. But at about 1:30 A.M., Shen Yinhan, a member of the BWAF standing committee, cycled past to take a look. When he got as far as the Beijing Hotel, several men leaped out of a parked jeep, grabbed Shen, and bundled him inside. Shen had the presence of mind to drop two notebooks on the ground. A passerby picked them up and scribbled down the jeep's license number as it sped away. By dawn on May 30, the notebooks had found their way to the BWAF headquarters at Xiguanlitai. As Han Dongfang digested the news, a pregnant woman arrived at the tent in tears. She explained that she was the wife of Bai Dongping, a BWAF leader who worked in the maintenance section of the Beijing Railways. Bai had not come home all night. She was frantic with worry. Next came word that one of Bai's coworkers, Qian Yumin, had been picked up by two policemen as he left for the railyards in his work-unit uniform. The arrests were like the first drops of rain that announce a coming storm. And as Peng Zhen had hinted, the students were not the target.

Han Dongfang led a group of two dozen BWAF activists to the offices of the Beijing Public Security Bureau on Qianmen Street, just off Tiananmen Square. A line of police blocked the entrance. Some of them taped the BWAF delegation with video cameras. Behind the police line, the PSB building itself was blocked off by the customary wide screen wall with its gold inscription—"Serve the People!"—in the slanting calligraphy of Mao Zedong. These screen walls have ancient origins. They were long believed to ward off the evil spirits that swept down from the northern deserts. Evil spirits, as all Chinese know, cannot turn corners.

The crowd swelled as hundreds of students rushed over from the square in a rare display of solidarity with the workers. A small convoy of trucks with armed police was spotted driving into the rear entrance of the PSB. Then someone recognized the license plate number of the jeep that had sped away with Shen Yinhan. The crowd went wild, and a Dare-to-Die squad pounced on the vehicle, bouncing it up and down on its springs and smashing its windows. Police with bullhorns ordered the crowd to disperse. The students and workers sat down instead, holding up placards that read "Secret arrests show your true face" and "If we don't dare to descend into the jaws of hell, who will?" As the sun beat down on the crowd and the police threatened to use force to remove them, the mood turned ugly. There was talk of storming the building. A group of Zhang Lun's pickets from the square rushed over to keep the two sides apart.

Han Dongfang tried to calm the frayed tempers. "We are under a state of martial law," he said, microphone in hand. "Just by coming here we risk being accused of attacking the PSB. The people under arrest are members of the Beijing Workers Autonomous Federation. They are not students. It is up to us workers to negotiate. The rest of you, please disperse." Remarkably, they did so.

Eventually, the police allowed Han Dongfang, Li Jinjin, and three bodyguards to enter. A cadre strode out and demanded to know what they wanted. "I am the legal adviser to the BWAF," Li announced, "and I have three questions for you. First, can you confirm the arrest of our members? Second, were these arrests carried out in due legal fashion? Third, what were the grounds for their detention?"

The PSB official looked at Li as if he had descended from another planet. "You represent an illegal organization," he snapped. "By coming to quibble with us on these matters, you are in violation of martial law. You must leave right away."

Li pressed on with his legal arguments, but to no avail; the audience was over. The three returned to the crowd outside, and Han took up the microphone to propose a compromise. Since the authorities would not respond to their demands, the workers should move to the nearby Ministry of Public Security and maintain a token sit-in there until Shen, Bai, and Qian were released. The crowd broke up quietly. They had been there for seven or eight hours. Han had not raised his voice once. But the incident marked him in the minds of the authorities as the workers' ringleader.[5]

Amid the celebration and festivity that accompanied the unveiling of the Goddess of Democracy, it is doubtful whether the student leadership even noticed the scruffy table and chairs that were installed that afternoon in a newly roped-off area in the far northwest corner of the square. The workers' new site was still on the periphery, but it had a number of advantages: It was relatively secure, thanks to the roads and railings that flanked it on two sides; and it afforded a supply of free electricity, since it was right next to a lamppost that was rigged up with a set of government loudspeakers. A worker quickly shinned up the pole and cut the wires. Over the course of the afternoon, the BWAF members hauled some more of their furniture through the underpass beneath Chang'an Boulevard, leaving a notice at Xiguanlitai that told people of their new location.

Han had been impressed, but also somewhat alarmed, by the students' show of support outside the PSB offices that morning. They seemed so much more truculent than the earlier crop, those he had visited every day in their tents during the hunger strike. Han had come to believe that it was probably time for the students to evacuate the square, but he realized that the latest round of student leaders, those from outside Beijing, had other ideas. That evening, he had a further bitter taste of their behavior.

Li Jinjin asked an unusual favor of the new student leadership. Would they allow the BWAF to hold a press conference that night on the steps of the Monument to report on the arrests of the three workers? The students agreed, and Li delivered a fine, lawyerly analysis of the PSB's conduct. But when he passed the microphone over to Han for him to announce further information about the BWAF, the atmosphere quickly curdled. There were cries of "Who is this guy?" "We are the vanguard!" "Get down, leave!" There was a skirmish; someone grabbed the microphone from Han's hand and shoved him aside. The press conference broke up in disorder.

Han spent much of the next day, the last of May, in his tent, exhausted and doubled over with stomach cramps. But more troubling still were his fears about what might come next. The students might eventually be persuaded to leave Tiananmen, he supposed. But after the events of the previous day, he wondered whether the workers *could* leave. All the signs were that the government intended the students no harm, no matter how radical their positions became. But would the BWAF have anywhere to hide? More ominous news of the impending crackdown had arrived that day: The police had rounded up the Flying Tigers, the daredevil motorcycle squads that had tracked the movements of the martial law troops. That night, for the first time, Han began to consider the need for the federation to go underground.

The first three days of June seemed to pass in a giddy carnival atmosphere, as if the students believed themselves immune from harm in the charmed circle around the Monument to the People's

Heroes. Crowds flocked to see the Goddess of Democracy. Right outside Han Dongfang's tumbledown courtyard house on Xibiaobei *hutong,* jeering demonstrators burned copies of the hated leftist *Beijing Daily,* whose offices were on the other side of the alleyway.

On the afternoon of June 2, an unlikely group of four men began a fresh seventy-two-hour hunger strike on the Monument. One of them, a maverick young scholar named Liu Xiaobo who had recently flown in from New York, explained that they were taking this step because the students refused to trust intellectuals unless they were prepared to put their own lives on the line. The hunger strikers added that one of their number, the rock star Hou Dejian, would only be able to fast for forty-eight hours, since he had to get back to Hong Kong in time to meet his recording obligations.[6] The crowd joined Hou in rousing renditions of his greatest hits.

On the night of June 2, Han Dongfang gave what was to be his last interview with a foreign journalist for almost three years. She asked him whether he thought the Party could ever be reformed. As usual, Han chose his words with care: "I believe that the Communist Party will still be able to overcome its difficulties, that it will accept the people's suggestions and keep its officials honest and uncorrupted. The Constitution is the highest law, it is the highest embodiment of the people's will. Everything should be done subject to the rule of law."[7]

Events were now moving, however, in a different direction. Only hours later, a People's Armed Police jeep jumped the kerb and hit three people in the western suburbs of Beijing, killing all three. A crowd of several thousand enraged local residents quickly formed, many of them suspecting foul play and calling for revenge. Shortly before dawn on June 3, a contingent of PLA troops jogged into Beijing all the way from Tong County, 25 kilometers to the east, where Chen Ziming had once been held for reform through labor. They wore white shirts and green pants and carried only water bottles. The crowd halted them, roughed them up a little, and escorted them back out of the city. In the early afternoon, news reached the BWAF tents that the PLA was using tear gas on crowds at the Liubukou intersection, a few hundred yards west of the square. Zhao Hongliang grabbed the BWAF flag and sprinted to the spot. Finding two battalions of troops, he sought out the officer in charge. The man seemed dazed as he explained that his troops had been told they were engaged in a training exercise. He had not seen a newspaper for two weeks. Then he promised that his men would not be seen again for forty-eight hours. In a bizarre ceremony, Zhao and three Beida students signed an agreement to that effect with the PLA officer, then added their thumbprints.

The evening was balmy. The students inaugurated a series of open-air meetings, like grand-scale versions of the old Beida salons, which they called the Tiananmen University of Democracy. A smiling young father strolled across the square with his baby riding piggyback on his shoulders. An English businessman in a three-piece business suit pedaled his bicycle slowly along Chang'an Boulevard. And then it began.

15

Power Comes from the Barrel of a Gun

The phrase "Tiananmen Square massacre" is now fixed firmly in the political vocabulary of the late twentieth century. Yet it is inaccurate. There was no massacre in Tiananmen Square on the night of June 3. But on the western approach roads, along Chang'an Boulevard and Fuxingmen Avenue, there was a bloodbath that claimed hundreds of lives when the People's Liberation Army found its path blocked by a popular uprising that was being fueled by despair and rage. To insist on this distinction is not splitting hairs. What took place was the slaughter not of students but of ordinary workers and residents—precisely the target that the Chinese government had intended.

"Tiananmen Square massacre" is the shorthand that observers in the West distilled from the hours of dramatic television footage and thousands of column inches of press reporting. Although hundreds of journalists were in Beijing that night, few were present for the army's climactic clearing of the square itself in the predawn hours of June 4. Many of the press were on the real killing grounds of western Beijing, several miles away, and they reported vividly and accurately on what they saw. Some who tried to remain in the square were arrested and did not see the final PLA assault. Others were pinned down behind roadblocks. Still others were working in their hotels to meet early-morning filing deadlines for media in distant time zones. But most of the reporters who remained near the square after one o'clock in the morning, when the first army units got there, left in haste and out of legitimate fear for their safety.

The lack of eyewitnesses was the first problem in establishing what happened on that fearsome night in Beijing. But there were other, more profound questions about how the foreign media saw their role in the Beijing spring.[1] The pacifist idealism of the young students triggered memories of the 1960s and America's civil rights movement, and the students' adept use of Western symbols, like headbands inscribed with Patrick Henry's "Give me liberty, or give me death," riveted Western attention on the students, which caused the crucial role of the workers and the *laobaixing* to be largely overlooked.

There was more: some predisposition, perhaps, to believe in the massacre in the square, even though no one actually saw it. Whether or not it happened in reality, it was the necessary consummation of an allegory of innocence, sacrifice, and redemption. To this, the rhetoric of the students themselves contributed mightily. On the first day of the hunger strike, they declared, "Our bodies are still tender and not full grown, and the prospect of dying frightens us all; but history calls and we must go." Chai Ling, such a magnetic presence for the foreign news cameras, spoke of sacrifice in almost mystical terms. On May 28, with the students in disarray over the issue of withdrawing from the square, she said that "it would take a massacre, which would spill blood like a river through Tiananmen Square, to awaken the people." One Western sinologist recalled a student telling him in the final hours: "We are now ready to face death, and we don't want you to have to be part of that. Please go home."[2] And the media, for the most part, did so.

Imagination filled the gaps. Into the vacuum rushed the most lurid tales of the supposed denouement in the square. Wu'er Kaixi, flamboyant to the last, reported that he had seen "about two hundred students" cut down by gunfire in the army's predawn assault, but it was revealed later that he had been spirited away to safety in a van several hours earlier. A widely recounted eyewitness report, purportedly from a student at Qinghua University, spoke of the students on the Monument being mowed down at point-blank range by a bank of machine guns at four in the morning. The survivors had then either been chased across the square by tanks and crushed, or clubbed to death by infantrymen. But it was all pure fabrication.

By the time historians began to correct the record, the episode was enshrined in myth: Hundreds, perhaps thousands, of students had died in a massacre in Tiananmen Square. As Tom Hayden would write in the *Los Angeles Times,* it was the equivalent of the slaughter of the entire graduating class at the United States' top universities.

No one had been listening to what Peng Zhen said: The students were not the problem. Indeed, the Party's line never varied after Deng Xiaoping first defined it for the April 26 *People's Daily* editorial. "Emotionally excited young students" were never the issue. The official conspiracy theory demanded other threats and other scapegoats—"outside elements" with "ulterior motives." This meant dissident intellectuals and workers. After their ruthless repression under Mao, the intelligentsia had been granted a kind of historic compromise by Deng. But by the spring of 1989, they had come to be seen as the agents of bourgeois liberalization, of China's "peaceful evolution" toward Western-style pluralism. After Tiananmen, they would be singled out for punishment. The working class, meanwhile, had become the carrier of an even more dangerous virus—the Polish disease.

The Beijing Workers Autonomous Federation, tiny though it may have been, was the "cancer cell" the authorities feared. The Goddess of Democracy represented the arrogant intrusion of decadent Western values into the symbolic heart of Chinese Communism, rupturing the sacred cosmology, the *feng shui* of the great square. But the crude red and black banner of the BWAF, less than a hundred yards away, signified the more terrifying power of the workers awakened.

The students initiated the Tiananmen movement, and they brilliantly outmaneuvered and embarrassed a leaden-footed government. But after the mass demonstrations of mid-May, the threat from the students was dwarfed by the intervention of much broader social forces. This threat was like a pyramid. At the base were the *laobaixing,* with their outpouring of spontaneous human sympathy, a million or more ordinary people, like Lü Jinghua with her cold drinks and her pork dumplings. The second level was the ideological defection of the Party apparatus itself. By mid-May, much of the Chinese press had rallied to the cause of democracy;

even sections of the Public Security service, the law courts, and the military—the very backbone of the People's Democratic Dictatorship—had begun to break free of the Party's iron grip.

Faced with the crumbling of its power, the Party imposed martial law on May 20. But again it miscalculated. Its inner defections had progressed further than anyone realized; it did not even have control over its own secrets, and it failed to anticipate that its tanks would be halted by a human wall of protesters. Age, and years of unchallenged authority, had atrophied the Party's judgment, leaving it incapable of foreseeing the action groups that now formed spontaneously throughout Beijing. After May 20, the pickets, the Dare-to-Die squads, and the Flying Tigers virtually took over the day-to-day running of the city. The PSB and the traffic police disappeared from view.[3] And, finally, there was the apex of the pyramid: the specter of an incipient organization of all classes, symbolized by the Capital Joint Liaison Group.

The students, in the final analysis, were marginal to the threat. But ironically, one of their main arguments for prolonging the occupation of Tiananmen was that they had nothing to lose: Since they were the heroes and focal point of the movement, the incarnation of all the government hated, it therefore followed that they would suffer the fiercest repercussions. Chai Ling had been shaken by a conversation with a plainclothes police officer in the early days of the movement. She had asked him what the maximum sentence was for counterrevolution. Seventeen years, the man answered.[4] Chai Ling gasped. Seventeen years? She would be forty by the time she got out.

But the government saw the matter quite differently: To deal with the students, it was enough to drive them from the square and herd them back to their campuses. Mass self-criticisms would follow, and probably bad job placements. In the case of the more obstinate ringleaders, those who refused to repent, short jail sentences might be necessary. But the larger threat could be eradicated only by the application of brute force, terror, and exemplary punishment. The specter of organized popular unrest had to be exorcised not for a year or two, but for an entire generation.

In the dim light of the workers' tent, Han Dongfang was calm. He had been up for much of the previous night giving an interview to a young Dutch reporter. Despite his exhaustion, he maintained his stoicism. He told the woman that he fully expected the authorities to "take action" against the BWAF. "Our federation has taken certain precautions," he explained. "But if they use violence against us, then we are unarmed, and we will not resort to the use of violence against them. We are prepared to go to prison, and we are not afraid to die."

In fact, the BWAF had taken only minimal precautions. There was some reckless talk about heading to the mountains and becoming guerrillas, like the Communists in the 1920s. There was talk of remote hideouts in the province of Hubei. But the agreed escape plan, such as it was, was much simpler: If the army used force, everyone would try to meet at Beida at dawn the next day. They could either try to hide out on campus or make for the Fragrant Hills on the outskirts of the city. Although the official media had denounced the BWAF the day before as a counterrevolutionary organization, more new members than ever were signing up.[5] A steady stream of workers continued to arrive at the federation's headquarters to have their work-unit IDs verified and to add their signatures to a list that now contained some three thousand names. Even after 6:30 P.M. on June 3, when the government loudspeakers in the square broadcasted dire warnings that the army would use force that night, the workers simply cut the wires on as many speakers as they could and stayed put in their tents. Lü Jinghua remained at her post and continued her broadcasts, pouring gasoline into the temperamental generator at hourly intervals. As the evening wore on, however, she found that most of her news consisted of the latest casualty reports filtering in from the outskirts of the city.

The first serious violence came at around 10:30 P.M., at Gongzhufen, five miles west of the square. Here, vanguard contingents of the assault force used about twenty armored personnel carriers (APCs) to smash through a line of buses that blocked the huge circular intersection. Many people were crushed to death as the APCs burst through the barricades and troops fired indiscriminately on the crowd. Two soldiers armed with AK-47 assault rifles who had jumped off an army truck were attacked and killed by the enraged crowd. The pattern of the night's conflict, then, was set from the start: random and brutal killings by the PLA came first, followed swiftly by a small number of revenge killings by distraught, and increasingly insurgent, citizens.

Why did the troops behave with such savagery? At Gongzhufen they had been alerted to the lethal realities of mass resistance, provoked by the army's violent invasion of the city and by its evident determination to avoid the humiliations of the first night of martial law. Once the troops saw that their initial terror tactics clearly had failed to subdue the crowds, they feared for their lives, and as they advanced along the great east-west artery of Chang'an Boulevard they responded by escalating the level of terror. The hospitals in western Beijing that night resembled abattoirs.

Unexpected factors, too, may partially account for the army's paroxysm of killing. The troops had planned to converge at Muxidi, two miles from the square, with an escort unit of the People's Armed Police. But the PAP detachment, which was familiar with the layout of Beijing, never made the rendezvous. It had been surrounded, blocked, and in the end dispersed by the *laobaixing* as the unit made its way through the alleyways around Yuetan Park, about a mile and a half north of Muxidi. The army also had political reasons for not being found wanting. After all, General Xu Qinxian, commanding officer of the elite 38th Army, was arrested for refusing to carry out martial-law orders; this no doubt left other units eager to prove their zeal against the "counterrevolutionary rebellion" that now erupted.

At the workers' tents, Han divided his pickets into five contingents and dispersed them to key intersections along Chang'an Boulevard. He continued to counsel scrupulous nonviolence. As rage drove out reason, however, many of his comrades began to waver. With the troops pressing closer to Tiananmen and the reports of casualties mounting, several workers prepared for a show of armed resistance, no matter how pitiful. They fashioned wooden staves out of the BWAF's tables and chairs and siphoned off the last of Lü Jinghua's precious gasoline to turn soda bottles into Molotov cocktails. Then they swore a final oath: "For democracy, for freedom, we are prepared to sacrifice until the last drop of our blood is shed and fight until the last person falls."

Most of the leading members of SERI were absent from the square on the evening of June 3.[6] There had been too many all-night sessions, and their moderating influence seemed to have been offered in vain. Since the collapse of the May 28 plan to evacuate the square, the Capital Joint Liaison Group had dwindled to the hard core of SERI people—Chen and Wang, Liu Gang, Chen Xiaoping, a handful of others. Certain that force would be used to clear the square, Wang Juntao had tried over the last few days to procure forged identity papers to help the student leaders escape. But the only firm plan to come out of the remnants of the Capital Joint Liaison Group was for a series of small, seventy-two-hour hunger strikes—a final gesture of good faith to the students, to convince them that others were also prepared to risk their lives for the cause. The economist Zhou Duo and the literary critic Liu Xiaobo were among the few outsiders to attend these final meetings, and they agreed to be part of the first group of hunger strikers. Once this plan was set in motion, Chen Ziming and Wang Juntao felt there was little more they could do but go home and wait.

Only Bai Hua ventured out on the night of June 3. She hurried to the Monument at about 11:30 P.M. to warn the students that the ominous messages they had heard earlier over the loudspeakers were no bluff. Her sources in the Party told her the threats were for real. But by the time she arrived the warning was academic. News of the first killings had already reached the students. They gave Bai Hua the same answer as always. No one was leaving; they had decided to stay where they were and die for the sake of democracy.

Bai Hua cycled west as fast as she could along Chang'an Boulevard. Her normal elegance and composure had vanished; she was utterly distraught. At Xidan, there was a line of buses barricading the eight-lane avenue. She climbed on top of one for a better view, but an advancing tank rammed the bus so hard she jumped off again. The sky out toward the Muxidi overpass was lit with fires from burning buses. There was the rattle of gunfire. She stood, frozen, in the middle of the Avenue of Heavenly Peace and watched the massed ranks of soldiers moving toward her. When they were twenty yards away, they began to yell, "Go home or we'll kill you!" Bai Hua stood her ground. Half a dozen soldiers broke off from the main formation and headed in her direction. They carried guns in one hand and electric cattle prods in the other. "Out of the way, counterrevolutionary!" a soldier screamed and rammed her in the shoulder, sending a jolting shock of electricity through her body. A man and a woman dragged her onto the sidewalk and into the crowd of bystanders. Like so many people that night, anger stilled her terror, and she strode along the avenue in step with the troops, screaming at them. Again she was pulled back to safety. She continued to scream. When the crowd picked up stones from the flower beds and began to hurl them at the advancing troops, she joined in, screaming "Fascists! Murderers!" Without realizing it, she was back at the square again. The entrance was blocked by troops. It was now close to 1 A.M.

At the workers' tent, Lü Jinghua issued a last, despairing call for a general strike the next day. But it is doubtful that anyone was listening. Back at the Monument, Wu'er Kaixi was yelling into the microphone, "The citizens have a right to defend themselves, and the only way to do so is with force." An anonymous BWAF member pleaded with the students to carve out their place in history by remaining faithful to the highest pacifist principles of the democracy movement. "When the Dare-to-Die squads find themselves face-to-face with the soldiers," he shouted hoarsely, "the first thing they must try is persuasion. With our songs, our truth, and our sense of justice, persuade, persuade, and persuade again."

The lights in the square began to pulse on and off, creating macabre effects. The workers' broadcasting station was now silent. Zhao Hongliang, silhouetted against the glow at the entrance to one of the BWAF tents, saw two APCs barreling toward him from the south, crashing through a line of improvised barricades outside the Great Hall of the People. The membership lists, Zhao thought. Thousands of people could face jail or worse if the lists were found. He poured the last drops of gasoline over the papers and set a match to them, but it was a thick pile and some refused to catch. Those that burned he tossed into a metal garbage can. The rest he stuffed into his pockets. (Duplicate membership lists existed, however, the fate of which is still unclear.)

Many of the BWAF's most important leaders remained in the darkened tents until the end. The burly Liu Qiang was still there. So was Xiao Delong, the grizzled cook from Qinghua University, and Zhou Yongjun, the ruddy-faced twenty-two-year-old from Politics and Law University who was the only one of the student leaders to have consistently stood by the BWAF. Han Dongfang lay in a deep sleep. His wife, Chen Jingyun, knelt by his side, her delicate features drawn tight with fear. Han stirred to the sound of gunfire. "Don't wake me until the tanks reach our tent," he mumbled, and drifted off to sleep again. He awoke a second time. Three masters of the ancient martial art of *qigong* were standing over him. "You must leave now," they said. Han refused: "I must stay to the end." But strong hands laid hold of him, and half carried, half walked him out of the tent, away from the advancing line of tanks. "You no longer have the right to decide your own fate," a voice said in the darkness. "We can't afford to lose you. You are China's Walesa."

The two APCs had drawn level with the workers' tents. As the lead vehicle swerved to the left to enter Chang'an Boulevard, it hit a young woman, hurling her into the air like a doll. A crowd—strangers, *laobaixing*—swarmed over to the spot and began to hurl petrol bombs at the stalled APC. The vehicle tried to inch forward, but the crowd blocked its path. Some of them burst into the workers' tents and grabbed whatever they could lay their hands on—articles of clothing, cotton quilts—set fire to them and flung the burning rags over the sealed hatches of the APC. The driver threw the vehicle into reverse and screeched away to the south, with the crowd running behind. Zhao Hongliang, drawn outside by the din, joined them. But at the end of the street he found his way blocked by a phalanx of troops with submachine guns. Beyond the PLA lines there was the chaotic noise of street fighting. Tracer bullets and red flares illuminated the night sky.

As the troops facing him aimed their weapons, Zhao hurled himself to the ground. When the burst of firing ceased, he stood up and looked back over his shoulder. There was a bright glow at the northwestern corner of the square. The workers' tents were in flames. A menacing line of about two hundred heavily armed troops stood facing them. The first units of the PLA invasion force had entered Tiananmen Square, and the red and black banner of the upstart BWAF was their first target. It was 1:15 A.M.

The northern end of the square was now almost deserted.[7] Another APC, its tracks jammed with iron bars, blazed in the northeast corner, near the Goddess of Democracy. Three of its crew had been beaten to death; the fourth was escorted to safety by student pickets. Several dead bodies lay under the portrait of Mao on Tiananmen Gate.

The students' tent city appeared abandoned. The southern part of the square, below the Mao Mausoleum, was littered with burning cars and buses but empty of people. In the north end, almost the only sign of life was the emergency tent of the Beijing United Medical College. Surrounded by a thin circle of student pickets, doctors worked feverishly to save a steady stream of casualties. By then, almost all the students had withdrawn to the three tiers of the Monument: between three thousand and five thousand of them, perhaps, huddled tightly together. They seemed calm, almost resigned. Some quietly wrote their wills. There was no sense of panic, though the steady chatter of gunfire could be heard on the fringes of the square and in the darkness beyond. Abruptly, the remaining loudspeakers burst to life with an endlessly repeated warning: A "serious counterrevolutionary rebellion" had broken out; everyone was to leave the square immediately.

The main invasion force, entering the city from the west, arrived at the smoldering ruins of the BWAF tents at 2:00 A.M. The first column of troop transport trucks entered the square hesitantly, moving forward at walking pace. Groups of infantry escorted them, at first just a thin line, but soon increasing to a dense column, thousands of troops, all wearing steel helmets and carrying assault rifles. They took about an hour to deploy fully along the northern edge of the square. Several hundred troops moved across from Tiananmen Gate to seal the northeast entrance to the square. A student named Ke Feng, one of the main organizers of the Goddess of Democracy project, was hiding in the small park outside the Museum of Chinese History. In the first five minutes or so, he saw about twenty people in the vicinity of the pedestrian underpass hit by stray bullets, including "five people who fell and couldn't get up again." The soldiers, Ke Feng recalled, were "jumping for joy, as if playing a game." The PLA sealed off the entire square by 3:00 A.M. Thousands of silent troops, each carrying an AK-47 and a long wooden cudgel, positioned themselves along the steps in front of the museum. On the other side of the square, in front of the Great Hall of the People, it was the same. Only a small exit corridor in the southeast would be left open.

At the stroke of 4:00 A.M., all lights went out. Like everyone else in the square, Bai Hua, who for the last three hours had crouched in the bushes by the Great Hall of the People, assumed that this meant the worst. She slipped away into the darkness toward Xidan, where Democracy Wall had once stood, until she found a functioning public telephone. Her first call found Chen Ziming at home, awake, alert, oddly calm. His phone had been ringing off the hook since midnight, he told her. Bai Hua asked where Wang Juntao was; he had no telephone at home, and she couldn't try his beeper until morning. But Chen had no idea where Wang was. They said good-bye, quickly and formally. Bai Hua was never to see Chen—or Wang—again.

But still the attack on Tiananmen Square did not materialize. For a quarter of an hour after 4:00 A.M. there was nothing but darkness and silence. The students remained seated on the Monument, as before. No one made any move to leave. Noiselessly, as if in a dream, a busload of student reinforcements appeared from the southeast. The loudspeakers on the Monument crackled back on and a voice announced—deadpan, as if reading a railroad schedule—"We will now play the *Internationale,* to raise our fighting spirit." The famous words, "Arise, ye starvelings of the earth," floated across the square to the soldiers, who had been taught to sing them by the Party.

At about 4:15 A.M., an array of lights suddenly came on all across the front of the Great Hall of the People, filling the west side of the square with a soft, luminous glow. At the same time, floodlights went on along the facade of the Forbidden City. Next, the southernmost doors of the Great Hall swung open, releasing a river of gun-toting troops, many of them with fixed bayonets. These soldiers formed an L-shaped blocking line across to the front of the Mao Mausoleum. Troops fired warning shots at the Monument from the steps of the Museum of Chinese History, and sparks flew from the obelisk, high above the students' heads.

Just after 4:30 A.M., the loudspeakers came on again, and someone who introduced himself as a leader of the Beijing Students Autonomous Federation took the microphone. "Students! We must on no account quit the square. We will now pay the highest price possible for the sake of securing democracy in China. Our blood shall be the consecration." There was a tense pause, and another voice, less educated, rang out. It was an anonymous leader of the BWAF. "We must all leave here immediately," he cried, "for a terrible bloodbath is about to take place. There are troops surrounding us on all sides and the situation is now extraordinarily dangerous. To wish to die here is no more than an immature fantasy." The struggle between immolation and compromise—or, as some of the students would have it, between principle and surrender—continued to the last.

On the government side, every vestige of reason seemed to disappear. But in the end reason triumphed, after a fashion, among the protesters who held on in the square. For that, the four members of the seventy-two-hour hunger strike could take the greatest credit. In the final predawn hours, they went among the crowd at the Monument, persuading some demonstrators to surrender their sticks, chains, and bottles, arguing with them that resistance was futile. To their horror, they discovered one fifteen-year-old at the foot of the Monument with a machine gun, hidden in padded quilts, trained on the advancing army. The boy was incoherent with grief. Someone said they had killed his brother. The gun was wrested away from him, and Liu Xiaobo, the professor who had recently returned from New York, took it and smashed it to pieces.

The hunger strikers then confronted the ragged remnants of the student leadership—Chai Ling, Feng Congde, and Li Lu. They told them that there was no choice but to negotiate with the army. The rock singer Hou Dejian and the economist Zhou Duo, an unlikely pair, walked across the darkened expanse of the square to seek out the officers in command.[8] Chai Ling declined the invitation to go with them. She was commander in chief, she told them; she could not abandon her people.

Two men came forward to meet Hou and Zhou. They introduced themselves only as Commissar Ji and Commissar Gu. "There is only one way the troops will not, by mistake, do any harm to the students in the square while carrying out our orders," they told the hunger strikers tersely. "The students and other people must leave unconditionally. You have until daybreak. The southeast corner of the square has been left open. If you could persuade the students to leave," the officers added, "you will be praised."

While the negotiations went on, Chai Ling and Li Lu made their final appeals to the students. Li Lu, feeling helpless, urged everyone to be calm. "We will stick to the principle of nonviolence to the very end," he said, echoing what the BWAF leader had said four or five hours earlier, what seemed like a lifetime ago. "We won't swear when sworn at, we won't hit back when hit." But Chai Ling's last speech was more wrapped than ever in the mystique of blood. "There is a story," she began, "about a clan of a billion ants who lived on a mountain. One day there was a terrible fire on the mountain. The only way for them to escape was to hold each other tight into a ball and roll down the mountainside. But the ants on the outside of the ball would be burnt to death. We are now standing on the Monument. We are the ones who stand on the outside of our nation. Only our sacrifice can save it, only our blood can open the eyes of our people and the rest of the world."

Zhou Duo and Hou Dejian came back. They told the students the outcome of their talks; there was no option but to leave immediately. They had no bargaining chips left. Too much blood had already been shed. Hou promised that the hunger strikers would guard the retreat and would be the last to leave. There was a momentary silence, then furious shouts of "Shame!" and "Surrender!" From the northern sector of the square came a distant rumble; the tanks had started their engines.

Minutes passed with nothing to break the spell until Li Lu proposed taking a final vote. Given the darkness, a show of hands would not work. They would have to make do with a voice vote. There were two choices: "Evacuate!" or "Stand Firm!" Some swear to this day that the "Stand Firm!" voices were louder; others say opinions were equally divided. But Li Lu, opting this time for wisdom over the clamor of the masses, announced that those who favored evacuation had won. The occupation of Tiananmen Square would end.

What happened next? The belief in a "Tiananmen Square massacre" is, at root, tied up in the problem of television news. At the best of times, the medium has a wretched relationship to historical truth, saturating its audience with powerful, instantaneous images that are not easily revised. But television, paradoxically, is never more powerful than when the screen goes blank.

There were, perhaps, a dozen foreign journalists in the vicinity of the Monument that night as dawn approached. The footage shot by a crew from Televisión Española and by a Hong Kong film crew perched on top of the public toilets on the west side of the square was not widely seen outside their home countries. The last American crew on the scene was from CBS News. The network's correspondent, Richard Roth, had time to file one final report before he was arrested and frog-marched into the Great Hall of the People. As the camera lurched skyward and the picture went black, the voice-over was dramatic: "Soldiers have spotted [cameraman Derek Williams] and myself and are angrily dragging us away. And a moment later it begins: powerful bursts of automatic weapons, raging gunfire for a minute and a half that lasts as long as a nightmare. And we see no more."

The impression of a student massacre without witnesses is stronger still in the reports of John Simpson of the BBC. Simpson was one of the media stars of the Beijing spring, and his team won several awards for its reporting. He was filled with remorse at having left the square so early. "Someone should have been there when the massacre took place," he wrote later in *Granta*. Simpson remembered that from a safe vantage point on an upper floor of the. Beijing Hotel, "We filmed as the lights in the square were switched off at four A.M. They were switched on again forty minutes later, when the troops and the tanks moved forward to the Monument itself, shooting first in the air and then, again, directly at the students themselves, so that the steps of the Monument and the heroic reliefs which decorated it were smashed by bullets." The problem with this report is that the Monument and the entire lower half of Tiananmen Square are hidden from view from the Beijing Hotel, half a mile away.[9]

The gunfire that Roth and Simpson heard was not directed at the students at all. By 5:05 A.M., the top level of the Monument swarmed with commandos. The writer Lao Gui saw the whole thing. "A small detachment of soldiers dressed in camouflage uniform rushed up to the Monument, occupied the top of it, and fired incessantly into the air. . . . Soon, there was no more sound from the broadcast station. The soldiers had shot the loudspeakers apart." The Spanish television crew was also on the spot; they saw no killing.[10]

For the next twenty-five minutes, the students filed out of the square. They moved back at the same pace as the advancing APCs, extracting every last ounce of moral victory from their retreat. Many in the ten-deep column, each contingent under the banner of its college, had tears rolling down their cheeks. All looked shaken; many were trembling or unsteady on their feet. "Down with the Communist Party!" one group shouted. In the east, the sun was just rising in a red sky.

BOOK THREE

Scapegoats

16

"A Conspiratorial Clique"

Nothing in Hong Kong stays as it is for very long. Before the construction of a new skyscraper even begins, the architect can spend months simply planning access to the site through the colony's maze of alleyways and densely packed apartment buildings. Still, new building goes on endlessly.

In the glory days of the British Empire, the heart of the colony was Royal Square. Flanked by the Hong Kong Club and the headquarters of the Hong Kong and Shanghai Bank, it commanded a fine view of the bustling waterfront. It took its later and more popular name, Statue Square, from the bronze figures of the British monarchs who surveyed the scene from their stone plinths.

The statues did not survive World War II. During the Japanese occupation, Hong Kong's new masters found them an odious reminder of the colonial past and shipped them off to Tokyo to be melted down. But the statues languished in a warehouse instead and were recovered intact when the war ended. Only one of them—that of Queen Victoria—was brought back, and she was not restored to her earlier vantage point, but to the large open playing fields known as Victoria Park. Today, the only statue that remains in the square is that of Victorian financier Sir Thomas Jackson, chief manager of the Hong Kong and Shanghai Bank. What war did not destroy, commerce transformed. Statue Square is now a tiny oasis, hemmed in on all sides by the towers of a financial district that rivals those of New York and London. The old Hong Kong Club, with its leather armchairs and slow-turning ceiling fans, was torn down to make room for a hulking skyscraper. The forty-eight-story Hong Kong and Shanghai Bank has yielded pride of place to the glittering postmodern needle of the Bank of China, twenty-two floors taller, designed by the Chinese-American architect I. M. Pei to symbolize the influence of the People's Republic in Hong Kong's business affairs. On the weekends, the colony's thousands of Filipina maids gather in the shade of the square's Palladian colonnades to share box lunches and exchange gossip. In May 1989, however, the maids abandoned Statue Square, yielding to a series of mass demonstrations such as Hong Kong had never seen.

Hong Kong Chinese, who make up 98 percent of the territory's population, have rarely involved themselves in politics. Until 1997, when the colony will be absorbed into the People's Republic, the formalities of government remain under a British colonial administration. At the head is the governor; under him are an appointed executive council and a partially elected legislative council known as EXCO and LEGCO, respectively. Successive governors have done their best to avoid confrontations with Beijing, and on the whole they have succeeded. Only in 1968, when students staged angry demonstrations against British rule and in support of Mao's Great Proletarian Cultural Revolution, was the colonial calm disturbed.

But the 1980s brought slow, subterranean processes of change. Illegal immigration from southern China pushed the population of Hong Kong ever higher. Guangdong Province, across the border, went its own way from Beijing, following the giddy logic of capitalism in preference to the rigid dictates of Marxism-Leninism. Deng Xiaoping selected the border town of Shenzhen as one of his new Special Economic Zones, where the laws of the free market would prevail, and the once sleepy village came to resemble Hong Kong. The British recruited Gurkha soldiers from Nepal to patrol the border, but it nonetheless became more and more porous. Businessmen, with headquarters in Hong Kong and branch offices in Guangdong, ignored the border altogether. And fugitive Cantonese have now driven the population of Hong Kong close to six million.

Also during the 1980s, a small but vocal political class, headed by LEGCO member Martin Lee Chu-ming, emerged in the colony. Mistrustful of Beijing's official slogan of "One country, two systems," Lee and others demanded a stronger and more independent political voice for the colony to prepare it to withstand the impact of absorption into China in 1997.

When the hunger strike began in Tiananmen Square in May 1989, as many as two hundred small groups of Hong Kong activists organized to show their support. They raised more than $2 million in local donations for the Chinese students, and after martial law was declared in Beijing, more than a half million people marched from Victoria Park to Statue Square. The cenotaph in Statue Square, which honors the dead of two world wars, became a rallying point for supporters of democracy in China; the cenotaph is considered by many a small-scale counterpart of the Monument to the People's Heroes. After June 4, it was turned into a place of mourning, covered with white paper flowers and wreaths and elegiac poems.

Many of the demonstrators were first-generation migrants who had disappeared into the alleyways and sweatshops of Hong Kong's Kowloon district, keeping their noses clean and staying out of politics. But the obvious divorce between the Communist government and the masses in the 1980s prompted these Hong Kong Chinese to condemn the Beijing authorities and express their fears about 1997, even while they maintained their basic patriotism as Chinese.

Politicians like Martin Lee moved quickly to channel the angry mood that swept through the territory. In May 1989, while Hong Kong students and small grass-roots groups struggled to define themselves and coordinate their protest actions, Lee and a group of other prominent figures announced that they were setting up an umbrella group called the Hong Kong Alliance in Support of the Patriotic Democratic Movement in China. The Alliance quietly sent envoys to Beijing late that month; they made contact with the student leadership and even attended a couple of meetings of Wang Juntao and Chen Ziming's Capital Joint Liaison Group. One of their point men in Beijing was a colorful character, a plump, balding actor-singer-entrepreneur named John Shum. As tensions heightened in the square, Shum and a few colleagues—whose identities and roles in the operation remain, even four years later, a closely guarded secret—began to think of how Hong Kong could offer sanctuary to any protest leaders who might need to escape in the event of a crackdown. They knew that the Alliance could expect little help from the colonial authorities. Indeed, after June 4, Governor David Wilson was unwilling to condemn Beijing directly; he referred to the massacre only as "these tragic happenings." The Alliance faced other problems, too. Arranging for escapes was an expensive business. This meant giving priority to the most urgent and important cases. Immediately after June 4, the Chinese government said that the effort to overthrow it was the work of "a tiny handful of people." But who were they? Who would be singled out by the Communist Party as the black hands of the Beijing spring?

In his final commentary for the June 4 issue of *Economics Weekly,* Chen Ziming, using a pen name, wrote that the search for this tiny handful of people was rooted in the worst and most outdated habits of Communist Party thinking. The Party did nothing to acknowledge the reality of social conflict; it merely tried to explain it away. It was not interested in "seeking truth from facts," as Deng himself had so often preached, but followed the reverse logic: starting from a dogmatic conviction and then finding the facts to fit. The old guard, Chen wrote, failed to understand how profoundly China had changed. They thought the democracy movement had emerged because the struggle against bourgeois liberalization had been conducted with insufficient zeal, and they were incapable of seeing that after a decade of reforms, "our society is moving toward pluralism, and it is no longer in the stage of life-or-death class struggle." For one group to try to eliminate another, as Mao had done in his innumerable political campaigns, could only bring disaster to the new, more open China of the 1980s.

The doctrine of waging war against enemies in the name of "class struggle"—so ironic in men who, like Deng Xiaoping, had survived the madness of Mao's final years—rested on a conspiracy theory of history. Since the interests of the Party and those of the people were by definition the same, the masses could never be wrong. They could only be deceived and misled. Thus, if the people dissented from the official line, the Party maintained, this was the consequence of manipulation by tiny minorities, bad people, black hands. Of course, Chen freely acknowledged, "a mass movement cannot be kept entirely pure." He had made this argument many times since 1976.[1] There were always going to be bad apples in any mass movement, however admirable its goals. Surely the Communist Party itself would admit that there were plenty of rogue elements in its own ranks. But that was not the point. "To argue that the million students and the masses of people in the capital and the tens of millions in all the provinces and cities in the nation have been 'incited' by others is a gross exaggeration," Chen wrote. "Why has a 'small handful' of people been able to 'provoke' chaos which has spread throughout the country, while under the leadership of the ruling Party and the government, the 'overwhelming majority' have not been able to prevent this and calm the people down?" The Communist Party had to admit either that it was totally inept, or that its world view was bankrupt.

The Party, needless to say, refused to countenance either possibility. Instead, it set about documenting the history of the sinister plot against it, not just any conspiracy, but one so immense that it would explain how China had been brought to the verge of insurrection. Detailing this plot would take several months and the efforts of thousands of cadres: historians and propagandists to shape the theoretical backdrop; agents of the security system to pore over the *dangan* of those under suspicion; lawyers to find the constitutional basis for prosecuting them; top officials to sift through the evidence and decide on the verdicts. The effort was not simply a matter of finding scapegoats or of using terror to crush dissent. The aim was to construct a seamless, linear account of events—stretching back to the end of the Cultural Revolution, if possible—that would confirm the frozen prejudices of old men about how history is made.

Deng Xiaoping himself sanctioned the process. At first, for five days after June 4 he was silent, and Beijing was alive with wild rumors that he was incapacitated, even dead.[2] Then on June 9, just as chipper as usual, Deng suddenly appeared at a gathering of martial law commanders. "You comrades have been working hard," he beamed. The paramount leader was in an expansive mood, but his remarks were a textbook illustration of the intellectual poverty that Chen Ziming had warned against. "This storm was bound to happen sooner or later," Deng told his commanders. "It was just a matter of time and scale. It has turned out in our favor, for we still have a large group of veterans who have experienced many storms and have a thorough understanding of things." Deng stressed that the events in Tiananmen Square were the result of an inevitable battle between his Four Cardinal Principles and the pernicious influence of bourgeois liberalization.

"There's nothing wrong with the Four Cardinal Principles," Deng assured the PLA leaders. "If there is anything amiss, it's that these principles haven't been thoroughly implemented; they haven't been used as the basic concept to educate the people." But no one should make any mistake about what was at stake here, he went on. "The key point is that they wanted to overthrow our state and the Party. Failing to understand this means failing to understand the nature of the matter. . . . Their goal was to establish a bourgeois republic entirely dependent on the West."

But who were the "they"? Deng did not say. He spoke only in the usual coded phrases: "a tiny minority," "bad people," "a rebellious clique." The identities of the conspirators were not yet revealed.

China waited another three weeks for the first hint of who the Party thought the conspirators were. It was not until June 30 that Chen Xitong, the dour, fifty-nine-year-old leftist mayor of Beijing who had signed the initial martial law decrees, rose to give his report to the Standing Committee of the National People's Congress, the same body in which the democracy movement had placed such illusory hopes. The mayor's two-hour address added substance to Deng Xiaoping's earlier speech. And for the first time it named names—a whole string of them. This speech was, so to speak, the rough draft of the Party's black hands theory.

Like most first drafts, the report was short on clarity and polish. The principal conspirators seemed to flit in and out of Chen Xitong's story, like enemy soldiers glimpsed in a forest at night. Some of those he singled out for blame were downplayed in later versions. Yet the general outlines of the Party's case became clear at this point. The story reflected, as Chen explained, the views of Deng Xiaoping and the "proletarian revolutionaries of the older generation." The *laoren bang*, the gang of the old, and their supporters in the mayor's generation, were convinced that the conspiracy had originated outside China. "Some political forces in the West," Chen stressed, "have always attempted to make the socialist countries, including China, give up the socialist road, [in order to] eventually bring these countries under the rule of international monopoly capital and put them on the course of capitalism. This is their long-term, fundamental strategy." A more immediate context was what

Mayor Chen called "the policy mistakes and temporary economic difficulties" in certain socialist countries. Mikhail Gorbachev's program of *glasnost* and *perestroika* was now four years old, and the fall of the Berlin Wall was only five months away.

"The entire course of brewing, premeditating and launching the turmoil," the mayor went on, "bore the salient feature of mutual support and coordination between a handful of people at home and abroad." Next came a rambling list of those who had acted as the agents of the West in China, and of the actions that constituted their plot.[3] Zhao Ziyang, who had "committed the serious mistake of supporting the turmoil and splitting the Party," was known to have met with the Chicago economist Milton Friedman in September 1988. Unnamed newspapers in Hong Kong were said to have close ties to Zhao Ziyang's "brains trust." Hu Ping, who edged out Wang Juntao in the 1980 election at Beida, now lived in New York, where he headed the Chinese Alliance for Democracy. Hu had written in support of the protests, Chen asserted; his Alliance was "a reactionary organization groomed by the Guomindang" in Taiwan.[4] The Voice of America had fanned the flames of turmoil with its broadcasts.

Next in the pyramid of conspiracy, according to Chen Xitong, were the members of Zhao Ziyang's "brains trust." His top aide, Bao Tong, who headed the list, had been arrested at the end of May. The Party singled him out for a number of reasons: He was the author of Zhao's conciliatory May 4 speech to the Asian Development Bank, which Chen Xitong cited as "the turning point in escalating the turmoil." He was also suspected of being the source of the vital leak on May 19 about the imposition of martial law on the following day. And he was Zhao's intermediary to the financier George Soros, whose Fund for the Reform and Opening of China was a CIA front, according to the security services.[5]

The ripples of the conspiracy theory spread outward to include a number of scholars from Zhao's *ti nei* think tanks, notably Yan Jiaqi of RIRPS and Chen Yizi of RIRES. Then there were the independent figures who moved in the same circles: Bao Zunxin, the outspoken founder of the Beijing Union of Intellectuals; Wan Runnan of the Stone Corporation; Su Xiaokang, screenwriter of *River Elegy*. Of the score of plotters denounced by Chen Xitong, none was more hated by the Party than the astrophysicist Fang Lizhi, who had taken refuge in the U.S. Embassy with his wife.

"What he termed as 'reform,' " the Beijing mayor blustered, "actually is a synonym for total Westernization."

Although Wang Juntao was not mentioned by name at all in the mayor's speech, and Chen Ziming cropped up only once, named as a participant in the *World Economic Herald*'s April 19 memorial meeting for Hu Yaobang, ominous signs foretold what lay in store for them. Chen and Wang themselves were not singled out, but the speech harshly criticized the groups with which they had been associated. Their newspaper, *Economics Weekly,* in fact, was named first in Chen Xitong's listing of hostile domestic institutions. At the end of 1988, he complained, the paper had published a dialogue on the political crisis between Yan Jiaqi and "another person." This, in the eyes of the hard-liners, was evidence of intent "to coordinate with the drive [in the Hong Kong press] to 'topple Deng and protect Zhao.' "

Chen Xitong pressed on with his report. Hu Yaobang's death was just the spark that lit the fire, he insisted. A small group of "elitists" had set their plans in motion long before. Looking back over the winter of 1988 and the early spring of 1989, anyone involved with SERI would have found the idea absurd. Those months had been filled with failed attempts to bridge the gulf between the internal and external think tanks, with one display after another of the timidity and passivity of most Chinese intellectuals, and with the gravest doubts about the wisdom of getting SERI involved with the students.

But Wang Juntao and Chen Ziming clearly belonged to the group the mayor had in mind, those who "clung stubbornly to their position of bourgeois liberalization." These were the same people that Chen Ziming so often spoke of as the *jing ying*—elite individuals, the "heroic essence" of China. After April 15, Chen Xitong charged, these elitists had controlled the course of events in Tiananmen in league with Zhao Ziyang and his aides. They had intensified the "turmoil" little by little, siding with Zhao in his divisive efforts to paralyze the Party by creating "two headquarters" and using the student hunger strikers as "hostages" in the sinister plan.

The most serious charge was that the elitists had actively planned acts of sedition, which is a capital offense. "The plotters of the turmoil attempted to use the chaos as an opportunity to seize power," Mayor Chen continued sternly. In a prelude to their later acts of violence, the "agitators of the rebellion" had attacked the Public Security Bureau after the arrest of leaders of a certain illegal workers' group. This statement drew Han Dongfang and Li Jinjin into the plot. The conspirators also brought in *liumang* elements, such as the Flying Tigers and the Dare-to-Die squads, to act as their shock troops; they had offered to pay "local hooligans, ruffians, and criminals" a bounty for any attacks on martial law troops and military vehicles.[6]

The government also possessed documents, Chen claimed, to back up the charge of sedition. Pronouncements of an organization that called itself the Joint Liaison Group of All Circles in the Capital had been found. This body had been "engaged in such underground activities to topple the government as organizing a special team in charge of molding public opinion and making preparations to launch an underground newspaper." Thus, Bai Hua's propaganda group became part of the seditious plot. The agitators also issued the call for a general strike in a "Letter to the People" published on the eve of martial law. Printed demands to prolong the occupation of Tiananmen Square in defiance of the martial law decrees had also been found. These were the bare bones of the government's case. Over the next several weeks, as Party investigators studied the origins of the documents cited, they would bring their attention to bear more closely on Wang Juntao and Chen Ziming.

The cast of villains in this first version was too diffuse. The script still demanded real black hands, individuals whose careers would sum up the threat to the regime more convincingly than the tenuous line linking heretical university professors, senior Party officials, overseas plotters and spies, and overheated student radicals. Much work remained to be done before all the facts could be forced into the procrustean bed of the official conspiracy theory.

Perhaps the most important consideration in designating the black hands was a purely pragmatic one: They had to be caught. The Party was not prepared to risk the embarrassment of naming its principal enemies only to see them slip through its fingers. With the exception of Bao Tong and the three leaders of the BWAF, there had been no move to arrest the leading figures in the democracy movement prior to June 4. After the slaughter of that night, the activists scattered. The Chinese government was incensed that Fang Lizhi and his wife, Li Shuxian, had already become international celebrities from the safety of their refuge at the U.S. Embassy. It soon became apparent that this situation could be resolved only by allowing the couple to depart, almost a year later, for exile in the United States.

Escape was a matter of connections. The Hong Kong border was fifteen hundred miles away, a thirty-six-hour train ride from Beijing. The railway stations in every major city were crawling with police and soldiers. Networks of neighborhood committees, trained to inform, maintained tight surveillance all over China. Those who had taken part in the Beijing movement knew little definite about the public mood outside the capital after June 4. There were anecdotes about sympathetic peasants, like the horseman who had ridden all the way from Inner Mongolia with five thousand *yuan* ($1,330) in his saddlebag as a gift from his village to the students.[7] But would the countryside really offer a safe haven, or would most peasants consider fugitives from Beijing to be criminals who should be handed over to the authorities?

Workers, isolated in their workplaces, had fewer connections than anyone, and the BWAF and its counterparts in other cities were the first targets of the post–June 4 crackdown. A defiant BWAF leaflet appeared at Hufanglu, south of Tiananmen, on June 7, but this was the last flicker of life from the outlawed organization. Two days later, Public Security Bureau agents burst in on the workers' secret printing press, arresting the elderly couple who ran it until the end. In other cities, the same harsh treatment was meted out to any workers who dared to raise a voice against the massacre in the capital.

Some of the worst violence occurred in Shanghai on the evening of June 6, when a police officer on a train from Beijing ordered the engineer to plow into a crowd of demonstrators who were blocking the tracks, killing at least six people. The crowd rioted and burned the train. In Guangzhou that same night, military police ended three days of protest rallies with a roundup of dissident workers. At the huge Number 1 Car Manufacturing Factory in the northeastern city of Changchun, a young auto engineer named Tang Yuanjuan organized a crowd of several thousand demonstrators. Tang had formed a small group at the plant in 1987, one of the hundreds of similar salons that sprang up all over China at that time. He said his hopes were to "wipe out feudalism, respect human rights, carry out people's rule, reform China." After the June 6 demonstration, Tang was arrested and charged with forming a counterrevolutionary group. He was sentenced to twenty years in prison.

The Shanghai protesters suffered swift, exemplary punishment. Three of them, all workers, including one who was mentally retarded, were sentenced to death and shot on June 21. In other cities, at least fifty workers were executed on similar charges of "burning, smashing, grabbing, and looting." Just enough *pour encourager les autres.* Countless others died anonymously from a bullet to the base of the skull, but their deaths were not made public, because a confidential directive curtailed the open reporting of arrests and executions in the Chinese media. The leaders of the BWAF heard little, if anything, of all this, since they were all on the run.

17

Rest in a New Forest

In the early hours of June 4, a weakened and exhausted Han Dong-fang was helped to a friend's house close to the square. After hiding out there for a few days, he fled the city by bicycle, heading for northeast China. Lü Jinghua slipped out past Tiananmen Gate, beneath the portrait of Mao, and melted into the crowds in the predawn darkness. Zhao Hongliang, after burning the BWAF's membership lists, hopped aboard an ambulance carrying the wounded from the square. A young doctor gave him a white coat to pull on over his work clothes. "You don't have to tell me anything," the doctor told Zhao. "I know you're from the workers' federation. There's some money in the pocket of that coat, and some grain coupons. Now get going."

Zhao went on foot from the hospital to the Beida campus, which was the BWAF's prearranged meeting point. But Liu Qiang, the beefy printing worker, was the only other member to show up.

"Do you think we should leave together, or split up?" Zhao asked him.

"Split up," Liu answered without hesitation. "It's much too dangerous for you and me to be seen together."

"OK, let's fend for ourselves, then." The two men exchanged a brief handshake. This was the last they saw of each other.

Zhao ran over the possibilities in his mind. Xiao Delong, the grizzled cook from Qinghua University, had mentioned one likely place, a restaurant run by a friend of his at the beach resort of

Nandaihe. Too risky; it was right next to the Party leaders' summer retreat at Beidaihe. Try to pick up a change of clothes and some money at home? Out of the question; the place was sure to be watched.

Zhao linked up with a group of people on campus, most of them fleeing students, who said that one possible exit they could take from the city would be the ring road at Dongzhimen, by the huge Workers' Stadium. But Dongzhimen, they could see from a distance, was swarming with troops.

Suddenly a garbage truck pulled up beside them. "You students?" the driver yelled.

"No," said Zhao, "workers' federation."

"Well, whoever you are, we're all Chinese," the driver replied. "Jump in and sit in the back if you don't mind the filth." Thirty or more of them crammed in with the rotting mountain of garbage. Eight were workers, the rest students.

Zhao's group stuck together for more than a month. The garbage truck took them as far as Badaling, where thousands of tourists regularly come to visit the most famous reconstructed section of the Great Wall. From there the group made their way to Inner Mongolia. The local people did not speak Mandarin, but they pointed out caves where the fugitives could hide. After three weeks, Zhao heard that military search parties were closing in on them. It was time to move on. But at least there would be train fare. When the time came to leave Inner Mongolia, a delegation of villagers announced that they had taken up a collection for the fugitives; they handed over four thousand *yuan* ($1,065), a huge sum for such a poor region.

The group pushed on, first to Shijiazhuang and from there southward to Anhui, each time a step closer to the Hong Kong border. They traveled discreetly, keeping each other in sight whenever they had to go on foot but breaking up into twos and threes each time they boarded a train. At each stop, some split off from the main group to take their chances alone. By the time the group reached Huaibei, a middle-sized city in Anhui Province, five hundred miles south of the capital, it included only a dozen members. They hid at the Coal Mining Normal College. After a few days, Zhao risked a long-distance phone call to Hong Kong.

"It's no good anymore," he told the voice at the other end. "I want to bring my younger brothers and sisters to visit their relatives."

"Where are you calling from?"

"Huaibei, in Anhui Province."

"Give me your number and we'll call you right back."

Zhao hung up and waited. Finally, the phone rang.

"Could you bring your family to a place a bit nearer to Guangzhou?"

"I'll try." The booming capital of South China was still a full day's journey by train.

While Zhao Hongliang wound his way south, others were less fortunate in evading the Public Security Bureau's dragnet. One after another, the BWAF leaders fell into police traps. Li Jinjin, the federation's legal adviser, was picked up on June 12 at his home. Liu Huanwen, the former steelworker who had attended the early meetings of the Capital Joint Liaison Group, evaded capture only until the following evening, when he was turned in by local residents in Shijiazhuang. The police said that he was carrying a security pass signed by the student leader Wu'er Kaixi, a dagger, two rounds of ammunition, and a "picket certificate." Liu was accused of "engaging in reactionary rebellious activities."

On June 14, the PSB issued its Most Wanted list of workers. The faces of Han Dongfang, He Lili, and Liu Qiang were flashed on national television. He Lili managed to evade capture, but within hours someone informed on Liu Qiang. He had made it as far as Wuchuan in Inner Mongolia. That same evening, the former leader of the Workers' Picket Team appeared on television again, this time in dramatic fashion. The PSB had sent a camera crew along to Wuchuan to film Liu being dragged off a train. He was accused of "distributing knives stolen from military vehicles to his pickets, inciting his followers to take iron bars from the railings on both sides of Tiananmen Square, ordering the preparation of a number of gasoline bombs, participating in a secret meeting with leaders of the Beijing Students Autonomous Federation, and leading pickets in setting fire to twelve military vehicles and two tanks and in frenzied beating, smashing, and looting."

The man at the top of the Most Wanted list, Han Dongfang, pondered what to do for four days after hearing his name read out over state radio. Where was he to go? He had never wanted to leave China. His future lay there. Beijing was his home, where all his friends and much of his family were. His mother, prematurely aged by her arduous years of manual labor, had died of cancer nine months earlier, and Han still felt the loss painfully. His sister, Dongmei, was doing nicely in her job with a foreign trading company, but since their mother's death it seemed more important than before for the two siblings to look out for each other. Han had a new wife now, too, a beautiful young woman named Chen Jingyun. Han's mother opposed the match at first, but Jingyun had visited her each day in the hospital, bathing and massaging her to ease the pain. As she lay dying, the old woman gave her blessing to the couple, and they were married a few days later. One day, they hoped to have a child. Besides, Han reasoned as he weighed his options, what do I have to fear? I have committed no crime. Nothing we did at the workers' federation violated the letter of the Constitution. Li Jinjin helped us make sure of that.

Han's mind was made up. On June 19, he cycled back to Beijing from his hideout and headed straight for the Public Security Ministry, where he had led a sit-in just three weeks earlier. "My name is Han Dongfang," he told the guard at the main gate in his mild-mannered way. "I believe you're looking for me."

At about the same time, the authorities issued another Most Wanted list, this one with the names of six "important criminals" who had "incited, organized, and directed the counterrevolutionary riot in Beijing." Wang Juntao and Chen Ziming headed the list. "These important counterrevolutionary criminals," the notice read, "may have concealed their identity and disguised themselves. The broad masses are urged to sharpen their vigilance." Descriptions and photographs accompanied the notice.

> Wang Juntao (alias Wang Xiaojun), male, 31, native of Henan Province, head of the privately operated Beijing Social and Economic Sciences Research Institute, deputy editor of *Economics Weekly*. Height 1.75 meters, rather plump, dark complexion, round face, large eyes, rather thick lips, speaks with a Beijing accent.

In the mug shot, Wang looked youthful and self-assured, half smiling at the camera, his black hair combed forward thickly across his forehead.

> Chen Ziming (alias Li Bin), male, 37, native of Haiyan County, Zhejiang Province, head of the privately operated Beijing Social and Economic Sciences Research Institute. Height 1.68 meters,

rather plump, with parted hair, round face, rather thick lips, slightly round-shouldered, walks with toes turned outward, speaks with a Beijing accent. On the run with his wife, Wang Zhihong.

Chen, dressed in a Western business suit, peered out stiffly from hooded eyes, his lips pursed in a characteristic expression that could be read as either a frown or a smile.

Wang Zhihong (alias Liu Hong), female, 32, native of Shanghai. Height 1.62 meters, short curly hair, rectangular face, double-fold eyelids, wears dark brown sunglasses.

The wanted notice pictured Wang in her Western-style wedding dress with a full white veil. Her "double-fold eyelids" were a Western feature, a supposed sign of beauty and sophistication, acquired through a simple, inexpensive operation that was much in vogue with Chinese women in the 1980s.

In the hours that followed the massacre, the leading personnel of SERI, unlike the workers, behaved as though they believed they led charmed lives. Some, however, discussed hiding places and escape routes, and others fixed themselves up with fake IDs. Liu Gang was dispatched to the south of China a few days before June 4 to set up a network that could forge documents, and even arrange for plastic surgery.

Despite Bai Hua's dramatic 4:00 A.M. phone call on June 4, Wang and Chen went to work as usual the next morning at the Shuangquanpu offices. The following day they did the same. They told their colleagues they felt a responsibility to remain at their posts; at the same time, they wanted to monitor the situation in the capital, which was still confused. Not until the morning of June 6 did Chen and Wang heed colleagues' warnings for their safety and leave the city. Bai Hua, for the time being, stayed put. Chen still had warm memories of the grasslands of Inner Mongolia, where he had spent his teenage years, and decided to take his chances there. Wang opted for Wuhan and the good friends he had made there in the mid-1980s.

They fled from Beijing just in time. On Saturday morning, June 10, a squad of armed police and soldiers burst into the SERI offices, seizing manuscripts, files, and computer disks and loading everything into waiting trucks. Two days later, in Martial Law Proclamation No. 14, the government formally declared the Joint Liaison Group of All Circles in the Capital to Protect and Uphold the Constitution—the group founded by Chen and Wang on May 23—to be "an illegal organization . . . involved in the turmoil and counterrevolutionary rebellion in Beijing."[1] The group's leaders were ordered to turn themselves in to the PSB immediately or face severe punishment. The material that was confiscated included the complete text of Chen Xiaoping and Min Qi's pathbreaking *Handbook of Chinese Politics*. Within days, an index of banned books went out to all Beijing booksellers; it included anything ever written by Chen Ziming and Wang Juntao.[2] The police also demanded all data from the opinion polls that Bai Hua had conducted during the week of the hunger strike. She told them innocently that the survey had been abandoned; there was nothing to give them.

Bai Hua realized that she was taking a huge risk by remaining in Beijing. On June 9, she heard that several of her friends had been arrested. Although several weeks would pass before a wanted list would be issued with her name on it, she knew it was only a matter of time. Everything she had done, from RIRES to SERI to the propaganda operations of the Capital Joint Liaison Group, had marked her as a black hand in the government's eyes.

Bai Hua spent the next six months in Beijing, tucked away in friends' vacant apartments, under the very noses of the martial law troops. Until it was time to move on, she never left whichever building she was hiding in. Often she saw soldiers march right past her door. Friends would leave groceries for her on the doorstep. She exercised to keep in shape for the escape attempt she would make when the time was right, and she recited poetry out loud to keep her vocal cords working. She did not speak to a soul.

Occasionally in the first weeks after June 4, a scrap of information would filter in to her from the outside world, a note slipped under the door with news of another colleague arrested. One by one, the police picked up the main figures in SERI. Zheng Di, who had worked closely with Wang Juntao at *Economics Weekly,* was the first. On the Saturday after the massacre, Bai Hua's two friends from Politics and Law University, Liu Suli and Chen Xiaoping, fled to Wenzhou, a bustling open port on China's east coast that was a boat ride away from Taiwan. But they stayed there only a few days before heading back to Beijing, where they were soon arrested.

Wang Juntao's close friend Liu Gang, who had been in charge of logistics for the Capital Joint Liaison Group, ranked number three on a new State Security Most Wanted list of twenty-one students issued on June 13. Only Wang Dan and Wu'er Kaixi ranked higher. Liu had fled immediately after the massacre, moving from one hideout to another in the Beijing suburbs. On June 19, he made his way to the railway station in the town of Baoding, in Hebei Province. Disguising himself as a worker, he asked for a ticket to a distant part of western China. But the clerk there was trained to be suspicious. This young man spoke like a worker and dressed like a worker, but look at his hands: They are too white and uncalloused. Within minutes the station was full of police. Liu was arrested and charged later with "conspiracy to subvert the government."

Bai Hua occasionally wondered what had happened to Fei Yuan, the personable young economist who had been SERI's first director and had worked closely with Wang Juntao on *Economics Weekly*. Fei Yuan did not have the troublesome political past of SERI's other leading members, but a warrant was issued for his arrest after the Beijing massacre, just as it was for every other member of the SERI executive committee.

Other activists who remained at liberty, however, began to hear perplexing stories about Fei Yuan. Word was that the police had taken him in twice for questioning and then released him without charges. Several times he turned up on the doorstep of Hou Xiaotian, Wang Juntao's wife. It was never clear to her what he wanted, but something in his manner made her uneasy. There were also reports that he was traveling a lot and was often seen in Guangzhou, the capital of Guangdong Province.

The Chinese intelligence services had set up a special joint operation in Guangzhou, even though the Guangdong–Hong Kong route was not the only one the escapees were using. Some intrepid activists were risking the dangerous overland passage through the mountains of Yunnan Province and were heading for the high plateaus of Tibet or the steamy rain forests of Burma. Others aimed for Macao, farther along the coast from Hong Kong, but that was very risky. The ramshackle government of the old Portuguese colony was deeply infiltrated by Chinese security, and very little happened there without the knowledge of the vicious "Three in Accord Society," the Triads. Any fugitives falling into the hands of the Triads might end up wishing they had surrendered to the Public Security Bureau.

There were other important reasons for basing the sting in Guangzhou. The intelligence operation after June 4 had been something of a fiasco, as one democracy leader after another slipped through the net. A press report in Hong Kong told of Premier Li Peng barking at his senior intelligence officials, "There are only three people I really want after Tiananmen: Chen Yizi, Chen Ziming, and Wang Juntao."[3] But Chen Yizi soon reached safety, hidden in a secret compartment beneath the water tank of a small cargo ship. Su Xiaokang, who had so infuriated the authorities with his documentary *River Elegy,* escaped in a powerful speedboat that outran machine-gun fire from Chinese patrol craft.[4] The flamboyant student leader Wu'er Kaixi had the audacity to make one leg of his escape in a Chinese Air Force jet, protected by sympathetic military personnel, before being spirited away to Hong Kong by smugglers. President Yang Shangkun flew into a rage, saying that it would be "a major shame and disgrace" if any other criminals were to escape.

The security services badly needed a success to polish their tarnished image. All the better if the sting could net conspirators from Hong Kong as well as mainland democrats, thereby proving the Party's case of collusion with foreign anti-Socialist elements. The services could not rely on the Guangdong branch of the PSB to conduct an operation of this magnitude. The provincial authorities were riddled with corruption and incompetence. Many cadres were openly disaffected from the hard line in Beijing, and several were known to have fled to the West; others succumbed to the lure of South China's new, easy money. One of the more common sights on the streets of Guangzhou was smuggled Mercedes-Benzes without license plates. The local authorities seemed uninterested in investigating where the cars were coming from. The Triads were active through wide stretches of Guangdong Province. And the discreet collaboration of PSB, People's Armed Police, and Border Guard officials was one reason for the success of the smuggling networks that the Triads and enterprising local fishermen operated in the Pearl River delta. Those same networks became a vital link in the democrats' underground railroad.

With people like Chen Yizi, Wu'er Kaixi, and Su Xiaokang coming out of China, it was a hot summer in Hong Kong. The Hong Kong Alliance's Kowloon safe houses were full of fugitives, and the British authorities, reluctant to anger Beijing, were being less than helpful. Until the early 1980s, refugees arriving in Hong Kong were subject to the "touch base policy": If they got as far as Hong Kong island or Kowloon, across the harbor, they could stay. If they were intercepted at sea or in the New Territories that bordered on China, they were sent back. But more recently patrols along the border were stepped up, and anyone looking like a new arrival was subject to spot identification checks by the Hong Kong police. The police knew how to spot a mainlander: the cheap clothes, the bad haircuts, an unworldly demeanor that contrasted markedly with the street-smart savvy of the Hong Kong Chinese.

John Shum and his colleagues had other anxieties, too. The Hong Kong Alliance was shelling out huge sums on the escapes, as much as $70,000 (U.S.) or more apiece for certain key figures. And there was still the problem of knowing which fugitives should be given priority. All the Alliance had to work with was the official wanted lists, and many of those had not reached Hong Kong. That was the case, for instance, with the lists that named Wang Juntao, Chen Ziming, and Wang Zhihong—lists that the Chinese government never, indeed, made public.

Wang Juntao, in fact, felt that he had been left to twist in the wind. More than four months had passed since he had left Beijing, fleeing with the historian Bao Zunxin and the student leader Wang Dan. Wang Juntao had grown fond of the serious-minded twenty-three-year-old Wang Dan, but the older man was not the easiest of companions; he tended to get nervous and agitated under pressure. The three of them traveled together for more than a week, first to Harbin, in the far north near the Soviet border, and then south again to Shanghai and to Wuhu, a shabby port on the Yangzi river. Wang Juntao was eager to reach Wuhan, which had been his home for nearly three years. The three agreed that Wang would go on alone.

Wang reached Wuhan on June 19—the same day that Han Dongfang turned himself in to the Beijing PSB. Immediately he felt safe. The city was full of memories. It also seemed a promising refuge, with its bustling crowds and row upon row of featureless six-story apartment buildings. Wang's first stop was the Central China Normal College, whose president, Zhang Kaiyuan, had shown him so many kindnesses in the past. For the second time in his life he found sanctuary there.[5] But the circumstances were very different. In 1984, Wang had been put up in the college guest house; this time, he hid for three weeks in a windowless basement chicken run.

The dragnet, however, was beginning to close in on Wang, and a friend who had agreed to shelter him worried about police surveillance. Sure enough, on July 12 the friend was pulled in for questioning, and Wang was passed on to the protection of a group of sympathizers from Wuhan's Dajiang Institute of Applied High Technology. The institute's director, Wu Litang, promised to find him a more secure hiding place, but for the time being Wang had to stay put at Dajiang and await further instructions.

He did not have to wait long. Wu came back the same evening and told him they were going to try to move him into the labyrinth of heavy industries on the east bank of the Yangzi. They took him first to Heping township, where he hid out in a liquid acetylene plant. On Sunday, July 16, Wu sent an intermediary to brief Wang on the next step. Under the new, looser contract-labor arrangements of the urban reforms, they thought it was possible that Wang, even with his heavy Beijing accent, could pass as a worker at the nearby Temple Vanadium Rolling Mill. He was to report to work the next day. His name from now on would be Liang Bin.

For two months, in the broiling heat of Wuhan's late summer, "Liang Bin" went quietly about his daily tasks at the rolling mill, receiving no news about plans for the next stage in his escape. The trail seemed to have gone cold for State Security, but the underground railroad also appeared to have forgotten about him. Then, one evening toward the end of September, the envoy from Wu Litang came to find Wang. The man was greatly agitated. PSB agents were sniffing around the Dajiang Institute, and Wu felt it was no longer safe for Wang to stay.

"What do you expect me to do?" Wang demanded.

"I'm sorry," the envoy said. "Things are getting too hot for us. As we see it, you'll either have to leave town and take your chances, or give yourself up to the police."

"No," said Wang. "That's crazy. I can't do that. Go and tell Wu that I'm staying here at the factory until he can come up with a better alternative."

Another three weeks went by. Wu Litang felt trapped by indecision. September passed, and the first two weeks of October. The first chill of autumn crept into the smoggy air. On October 16, Wu Litang was visited by a short, neatly dressed young man with a Beijing accent. He introduced himself. "My name is Fei Yuan. I understand from a friend that you have been sheltering an old colleague of mine, Wang Juntao, and that things are getting hot for you around here. I wonder if I might be of any assistance?"

Wu was cautious. He asked Fei Yuan for the friend's name who had given Fei this news. "Liu Danhong," he replied. Wu recognized the name. She was a young woman who had worked for SERI as business manager of the Human Resources Testing and Evaluation Center, and she could certainly verify Fei Yuan's identity.[6] Better still, she now lived in Xiangfan, just a half day's travel from Wuhan. Wu picked up the phone and asked her to come to the city as soon as she could.

Liu had summoned Fei Yuan to Wuhan with a carefully coded letter and telephone call. Now that he was there, she quickly confirmed to Wu that Fei Yuan was indeed who he said he was. "That's settled, then," Fei said. "Why don't I go on ahead to Changsha, and meet Wang off the Friday afternoon train?" Wu was mightily relieved, and he imagined that Wang would be as well. Wang could now begin the next leg of his journey south, confident that he was in the hands of a trusted colleague.

The train Wang took was supposed to be the Beijing to Guangzhou express, but the ride south into Hunan Province seemed to take forever. At last the train creaked and groaned its way into Changsha station. Wang picked his way through the crowds in the cavernous, grimy station hall, straining to catch sight of his friend. Then he spotted Fei Yuan. But not until it was too late did he also spot the PSB agents closing in on him. Wang's wife, Hou Xiaotian, was arrested in Beijing a few days later.

Fei Yuan had been traveling around a lot the last few months, especially in South China. In early September, John Shum of the Hong Kong Alliance received word that the former director of SERI wanted urgently to make contact with the underground railroad. He needed to pass on a list of names of the people who most desperately needed the network's help in fleeing China, and he proposed a meeting with an Alliance courier in Guangzhou.

For security reasons, the escape network was a highly compartmentalized operation. Individuals were involved on a need-to-know basis, and escape plans were never discussed in Alliance board meetings.

The man chosen for the delicate job of making contact with Fei Yuan was a forty-two-year-old Kowloon businessman, Luo Haixing.[7] Luo was a quiet, thoughtful man, not given to grand gestures or an exaggerated sense of his own importance. He held a British Hong Kong passport, but he knew China well. From 1986 to 1989, he had been Beijing representative for the quasi-governmental Hong Kong Trade and Development Council. Luo was not particularly political, but like most Hong Kong Chinese, he was moved by the student protests. He had not joined the new Alliance, but he did get to hear of it quickly because John Shum's wife was an old family friend. So when Shum asked Luo if he would like to take on a delicate job to help the students, Luo readily agreed.

He met Fei Yuan in Guangzhou on a warm Saturday afternoon, September 9, in the Baiyun Binguan, the White Cloud Guest House, a nondescript tourist facility near the railroad station, named for the range of hills, the Baiyun Shan, that rises behind it. Luo Haixing introduced himself. "You know," he told Fei Yuan, "I'm no escape artist. I'm just here to do a favor for a friend." Glancing discreetly around him, Fei pulled out a list of names and passed them across the table. The names meant nothing to Luo, who had not followed the intricacies of the democracy movement closely. But Fei told him that these were China's most important fugitives. Luo scanned the list. At the top were three names: Wang Juntao, Chen Ziming, Wang Zhihong. Next to each name were details of the person's present hiding place. Wang Juntao, apparently, was holed up in Wuhan. Fei explained that Chen and his wife would soon be ready to set off on the final leg of their journey to Hong Kong. Luo promised to hand the list over to John Shum that same night. The two men agreed to meet again when Shum was ready to propose the next move.

Having found his courier, Shum's next problem was to select the operatives who would transport Chen and Wang Zhihong across the border. The Alliance had in mind two good men who had accumulated several months of experience. Li Peicheng and

Li Longqing, two Kowloon workers in their early thirties, had made four or five separate trips into China since the end of July, not only making contact with activists on the run in Guangzhou but penetrating much deeper inland, to Changsha and even to Lanzhou in the far northwest. Li Peicheng had rented a safe house in a Guangzhou *hutong,* where the escapees were sheltered in small groups. They included several people who were high on the government's Most Wanted lists. Li Peicheng and Li Longqing were not altruists; they were paid well for their assistance in these escapes—several thousand Hong Kong dollars for each trip. The work was full of dangers, and they knew they could expect no help from the Alliance if anything went wrong. In this kind of enterprise, any agent who was caught would be disowned.

John Shum lived with the fear that the network was infiltrated by Chinese intelligence. One of the most difficult parts of any escape was to verify the identity of the people involved—not just the intermediaries, like Fei Yuan, but the escapees themselves. How was Shum to know that Chen Ziming was indeed who he claimed to be? For that, a second meeting in Guangzhou was necessary. Luo Haixing crossed the border again on October 8. This time the meeting with Fei Yuan was short—only a half hour—and to the point. Fei reported that Chen Ziming was now in Zhanjiang, three hundred miles west of Hong Kong.

Zhanjiang is a pleasant little town of narrow streets and low, whitewashed houses. But it was not a safe refuge for very long, since it was a common escape route to Hainan Island, a Special Economic Zone where Communist Party authority had broken down altogether. Chen Ziming was eager to get moving. Leaving China went against all his principles, but there seemed to be no alternative.

Fei Yuan laid down the rules for the next stage. He gave Luo Haixing the address of the house where Chen and Wang Zhihong were staying, the aliases they were using, and the secret password by which they would identify themselves. Luo was to arrange for a car to be sent to Zhanjiang on the night of October 12; the rendezvous would take place the next morning. The car would then take the couple to a drop-off point halfway between Guangzhou and the Shenzhen border.

Li Peicheng was designated to carry out the plans. He left the safe house in Guangzhou in sufficient time for the long, tiring drive to the coast. He spent an uneventful night in Zhanjiang, and the next morning he drove to the address that Fei Yuan had specified. A man opened the door, and Li looked him over. He was short and stocky, no more than five foot six, but powerfully built, with a distinctive waddling gait. The man introduced himself with the correct alias. Then the password. That was correct, too. Everything seemed to be going according to plan—that is, until police burst into the room and announced that everybody was under arrest. Luo Haixing was picked up the following day by the border police at Shenzhen.[8]

The arrests were a traumatic blow to the Hong Kong Alliance, and the democracy movement in exile was engulfed by rumors and recriminations. In the United States, where more than forty thousand Chinese students had traveled since Deng Xiaoping's easing of travel restrictions in the early 1980s, the finger of suspicion was pointed at one person after another. For example, there was the mysterious forgery of Wang Juntao's signature on certain cash receipts smuggled out of Tiananmen Square, which some said gave the forger a motive for preventing Wang from reaching safety. There was also the curious case of the group of self-proclaimed defectors from State Security who appeared before the movement one day to express remorse for their activities and to allege that two of the longest-standing Chinese democracy activists in the United States were Wang's betrayers. But as time wore on and the authorities laboriously prepared their legal case against Wang Juntao and Chen Ziming, one name came up continually in the inner circles of the movement—that of Fei Yuan. Why had he been released after questioning? Why was he never brought to trial after aiding the blackest of the black hands to escape? How was his timely appearance at the scene of both arrests to be interpreted other than in the worst possible light?

More charitable interpretations were possible, as some people pointed out. The Chinese security services are past masters of the art of plea bargaining; who knew what terrible power they might have had over Fei Yuan, what obscene threats they might have held over his head? After all, some said, look at what happened to Liu Gang after his arrest. His mother was dying of cancer, but the prison authorities denied Liu the right to see her in hopes of breaking him and forcing a confession. Liu himself had been threatened with death. Under circumstances like those, what might a person not do? Or perhaps State Security, well aware of the movement's weakness for rumor, and hoping to raise doubts and stir up division, had leaked misleading information about Fei's role.

Whatever the truth of the matter, the Hong Kong Alliance never recovered its earlier brio, although isolated escapes were still carried out. For example, Chai Ling, the heroine of the hunger strike, suddenly turned up one day in May 1990, together with her husband, Feng Congde, aboard a Hong Kong subway train.

Bai Hua, after six months alone in a room in Beijing, picked her way laboriously south, disguised in glasses and a short haircut. She aborted a plan to escape to Taiwan by boat from the open port of Wenzhou, where her friends Chen Xiaoping and Liu Suli had gone earlier. From Wenzhou, she hopscotched her way down the coast from one dangerous village to another, many of them PLA outposts. Once she was in Guangdong Province, Bai Hua descended into the murkiest circles of the human traffic between South China and Hong Kong. Arrangements were made to get her out through local smugglers, who were told that she needed to go to Macao for business. Fine, the smugglers replied; they would take her out at night in a boat in the company of two Guangdong prostitutes. They swam two rivers, crossed two coastal islands on foot, and finally stumbled into a swamp. Bai Hua sank into the oozing mud to her waist. On the horizon she could see the lights of Macao twinkling in the darkness. For an interminable moment she thought she was going to die.

In Macao, Bai Hua fell into the hands of the Triads. A 2:30 A.M. telephone call from a prodemocracy intermediary in Hong Kong to a Manhattan apartment said that if $10,000 (U.S.) could be guaranteed within half an hour, Bai Hua would be taken out of Macao to safety. Otherwise the operation would be canceled. The money was found within twenty minutes. It was also necessary to confirm Bai Hua's identity. Her boyfriend in the United States provided what the intermediary needed: a short poem he had written for her, which only she would understand.

Pretty little tree,
You will no longer be alone

In a corner of the big forest.
The cold winter is almost over.
Come and let the strange bird sing to you,
Come and rest in a new forest.
We are waiting.
(No need for old clothes.)

In late March 1990, a small boat carrying Bai Hua nosed its way into Hong Kong harbor.

Zhao Hongliang's group of fugitives had numbered more than thirty when they set out from the Beida campus on June 4. By the time the group reached Guangzhou, it had dwindled in number to two. But there they were joined by a woman who claimed to have been a reporter for *People's Daily*. From a safe telephone, Zhao placed a call to Hong Kong. The voice at the other end proposed a meeting at one of the city's glittering new Western-style hotels, a place with a waterfall in the atrium. When the contacts arrived, Zhao was overjoyed; they were people he remembered from Tiananmen Square. They gave him a little money and his first change of clothes in weeks.

Most of the money was used to hire a car and a driver to take the three of them as far as Shenzhen. The rest was spent on haircuts and new clothes. Shenzhen people were China's nouveaux riches, and they dressed flashily. Neither Zhao nor the *People's Daily* reporter spoke a word of Cantonese, so on no account, the Hong Kong people told them, were they to open their mouths.

An ancient, decrepit car picked them up at Shenzhen that night and deposited them on the seashore. A searchlight swept the beach in slow circles. They boarded a small speedboat in the shallows and slipped out into the dark waters of the Pearl River delta. Just as Zhao was beginning to feel safe, his breath stopped as a larger vessel loomed up before them in the darkness. On its side Zhao could decipher the Chinese characters for the Public Security Bureau. Along the rail stood a line of unsmiling uniformed men with automatic weapons. Zhao spun around. "We've been betrayed!" he gasped. "Don't worry," he was told with a smile. "They're friends. Their boat will take you a little further. When it drops you, walk a little way south. You will see two people fishing. Nearby you will see a barbed wire fence. You'll find that a hole has been cut in the wire." It was the border.

In the early hours of the morning, at the safe house in Hong Kong, Zhao Hongliang wolfed down a slab of watermelon. Then he smoked a whole pack of cigarettes, one after another, without stopping. Afterward, he lay down in his clothes and fell into the sleep of the dead for two days straight.

By the time Bai Hua and Zhao Hongliang escaped to Hong Kong, the time of greatest anxiety had passed for the Chinese government. Martial law was lifted on January 11, 1990. "A good sign," said U.S. President George Bush. "A very sound step." The inhabitants of Beijing had been bludgeoned into silence, and the worst offenders in the conspiracy had been arrested. Painstakingly, the criminal justice system began to assemble its case against Wang Juntao and Chen Ziming. The case against them was reassuringly airtight, the Party felt, especially given that the two men's record of anti-Party activity stretched back so far.

Each faction of the Party had its own reasons for singling out Wang and Chen for punishment, but the conservatives, and above all Li Peng himself, led the charge. Li was not a towering intellect, but he was smart enough to grasp that he was forever stigmatized in the eyes of the Chinese for his role in the June 4 massacre. The Premier had been stung by the manifest hatred of him displayed on the streets after martial law, by the cartoons that depicted him as Goebbels, by the repeated demands for his overthrow. Who had been directing the protests during that crucial period of late May? Wang Juntao and Chen Ziming, his security people told him.

Li found a ready audience among the Party hierarchy when he argued that the democrats' real crime had been to ally themselves with Zhao Ziyang as he set about creating "two headquarters." To level this charge at Wang Juntao and Chen Ziming was absurd. Their experiences of the Cultural Revolution ingrained in them an abiding fear of Party leaders who took their factional struggles to the streets. As Chen had written in his final essay for *Economics Weekly*, "The more the Party's internal divisions are mixed up in mass movements, the more chaos there will be." But evidence like this, which tended to undermine the black hands theory, was simply disregarded.

The older leaders, including Deng Xiaoping himself, had deep-rooted reasons of their own for identifying Wang and Chen as the black hands. The Party's earlier lenience toward the two young scholars, who always presented themselves as moderates, as loyalists, as the most reluctant of conspirators, had backfired. In the Party's eyes, Chen and Wang had repaid the Party's indulgence by persisting in their activities and refusing to acknowledge the error of their ways. To punish them was also, in a certain sense, a way to destroy the institutional memory of the democracy movement. The leaders of earlier outbursts, like Wei Jingsheng, had been locked away and silenced. But the security services had been amassing their files on Wang Juntao and Chen Ziming for more than a decade now; these two alone provided the clear thread that linked Tiananmen Square 1976 and Tiananmen Square 1989. The time had come to erase that whole thirteen-year history.

All factions of the leadership were united in their opposition to anyone who challenged the Communist Party's monopoly of politics and power. *Zheng ke,* agents of politics, had always been a dirty word in China, under both the Nationalists and the Communists. And Chen and Wang were the epitome of *zheng ke.* Their desire for a thriving civic culture and their talk of pluralism as the symbol of society's necessary "ecological balance" was simply intolerable, and it had led the Party to the brink of disaster in Tiananmen Square. April Fifth, Democracy Wall, *Beijing Spring,* the China Institute of Political and Administrative Sciences, SERI, the Capital Joint Liaison Group—each of these had been a building block in the careers of China's first professional politicians. The Party, when it considered the matter carefully, was quite prepared to accept what Li Peng said: Chen Ziming and Wang Juntao were indeed *heishou de heishou*—the black hands behind the black hands.[9]

18

Crime and Punishment

Red Queen: Now, are you ready for your sentence?
Alice: Sentence? But there must be a verdict first.
Red Queen: Sentence first, verdict afterwards.
—Lewis Carroll, *Alice in Wonderland*

In 1942, in one of his countless speeches at the Communist stronghold of Yan'an, Mao Zedong took up the difficult question of how the Party should reform the thought of those who held undesirable or "unorthodox" opinions during the struggle between the Old and New Societies. "Two principles must be observed," Mao felt. "The first is, 'punish the past to warn the future,' and the second, 'save men by curing their ills.' Past errors must be exposed with no thought of personal feelings or face."

China's "thought reform" program, wrote Robert Jay Lifton almost twenty years later, "consists of two basic elements: *confession,* the exposure and renunciation of past and present evil; and *reeducation,* the remaking of a man in the Communist image."[1] The doctrine drew its nourishment from both the Soviet Marxist and the Chinese Confucian traditions. Both held that a person could be remolded and made submissive to authority. Through the arduous rituals of "ideological struggle"—criticism, self-criticism, and confession—the Communist Party, in China as elsewhere, believed that miscreants would acknowledge the error of their ways and bow to the higher will of the Party. Confucianism, meanwhile, stressed filial duty, obedience, and loyalty to the well-regulated kingdom. "Let the ruler be ruler, the minister be minister," Confucius had said. "Let the father be father, the son, son." The two schools of thought converged in their demand for "sincerity." The penitent, whether in school, barracks, or prison, must learn to blur the distinction between his or her real identity and assumed role. "One first learns the more or less formal requirements for thought and behavior," Lifton observed, "and only much later becomes in his essence the thing aspired to. This is called achieving complete 'sincerity.' "

Mao's 1942 Yan'an speech served for almost a half century as the formal basis for the Party's efforts to reform the views of dissenters. But the old guard had argued for years that these efforts had flagged under Deng Xiaoping. Each successive campaign against bourgeois liberalization and spiritual pollution had foundered because of a failure of political will at the top. After Tiananmen, however, the conservatives were once more in the driver's seat, with their worst adversaries—Hu Yaobang, Zhao Ziyang, and their ilk—out of the way. Some Maoist fundamentals were once more in order. In his June 9, 1989, speech to the martial law commanders, Deng returned energetically to the field of "ideological struggle."[2] His Four Cardinal Principles were not the issue, Deng told the PLA. The problem lay "in wavering in upholding these principles and in the very poor work done to persist in political work and education."

The rituals of confession and reeducation were to be revived, in other words, for the benefit of the Tiananmen prisoners. There were a number of problems with this plan, however, for the 1950s were long gone. In the early days of the revolution, Mao's penal philosophy was at least consistent with absolute principles. There was a clear struggle between the old and the new; the enemy, whether Guomindang agent, abusive landlord, or foreign spy, wanted to recover his lost power; Marxist ideology was ascendant, carried along on a tide of mass enthusiasm. The Party devoted special attention to reforming the thought of the intelligentsia, and in the campaigns of the 1950s, 1960s, and 1970s, tens of thousands of intellectuals engaged in elaborate and theatrical acts of public self-abasement to show their repentance.

But by 1990, history had begun to repeat itself as farce. Now the fight was no longer between old and new, but between the Four Cardinal Principles and bourgeois liberalization—and no one could say with any certainty what those grand abstractions meant. Indeed, it seemed apparent to many people that bourgeois liberalization was little more than the natural consequence of Deng's policies of reform and opening to the outside world. The Party was now instructing the penal system to punish the results of its own actions. The prison authorities were happy enough to go through the tried-and-true motions of exacting confessions and self-criticisms, but the sense of a higher guiding purpose was lacking. Worse, the prisoners proved oddly unwilling to cooperate.

There were exceptions, of course. Sometimes the brutal routines of Chinese prison life still appeared to pay dividends. Interrogators knew that the ritual of confession was designed to exploit—not to offer solace for—such human weaknesses as the tendency to feel guilt and shame. The state, in both its Marxist and Confucian modes, had long played on a prisoner's feelings of guilt for the dereliction of filial duty. That no longer worked. But other weaknesses remained to be probed, like raw nerves by the dentist's drill. One such weakness was the authorities' knowledge that many of the student leaders were plagued by remorse over what had happened at Tiananmen and recognized that the catastrophe might have been averted if they had acted differently.

The interrogators and propagandists concentrated their efforts on those who had been closest to Wang Juntao and Chen Ziming. The serious and introspective student leader Wang Dan was a prime candidate for this kind of treatment. Wang had been "co-operative" since his arrest on July 2, 1989, the authorities announced with satisfaction. According to an official publication, the young history student had made this statement: "I keenly regret and feel compunctions [sic] for the consequences arising from the turmoil and rebellion and I am willing to accept the legal responsibility for my actions." The tough-minded Liu Gang, on the other hand, refused to confess; indeed, in his early months in jail, he dared to lead other prisoners in stirring verses of the *Internationale*. He acquired a nickname: "the iron man of Qincheng." For that, he was rewarded with solitary confinement. And he could expect no mercy at his trial, the authorities took pains to point out, in keeping with the dictum that guides the Chinese legal system: "To those who confess, leniency; to those who resist, harshness."

Perhaps the saddest case was that of Bao Zunxin, the nervous middle-aged historian who had fled Beijing in the company of

Wang Juntao and Wang Dan. Arrested just five days after Wang Dan, Bao's health deteriorated rapidly as he was shuttled back and forth between the notorious Qincheng jail, solitary confinement in Beijing Prison Number 2, and an army hospital. Prisoners saw him scrunched up in a wheelchair, tiny and frail, looking as if he weighed no more than seventy pounds. He was on daily medication for heart disease and high blood pressure. He attempted suicide several times after discovering that the statements he made under interrogation were used to arrest others, and he displayed signs of mental illness. By the spring of 1991, Bao was racked by stomach pains. One morning he noticed blood in his stool. He broke out in the cold sweat of fear. He was sure he was dying, surer still that the prison authorities would ignore his condition. But he misunderstood their methods.

Bao's ailment turned out to be a minor one, merely a polyp that was removed in a simple surgical procedure. But the operation gave the authorities the leverage over Bao that they required. His health restored, Bao was sent back to his cell. The official press carried fulsome news of his reaction. "During the fifty days in the hospital," Bao was reported to have said, "I received medical treatment as well as a profound education. I feel grateful as well as ashamed for the intensive care received in the hospital. I feel grateful because I have gotten a new life, but ashamed because I stood on the opposite side of the Party during the turmoil, and opposed the April 26 *People's Daily* editorial and martial law. I violated the criminal law, totally betrayed the Party, and became a sinner of the republic." Bao vowed to serve out his sentence, conduct a serious self-examination, and transform himself. It was a piece of confessional theater such as the interrogators of the Maoist era would have relished.

It is doubtful that anyone who participated in the 1989 democracy movement set much store by these accounts. The Party's credibility, and above all its ability to instill fear, had been fatally punctured, and most prisoners knew it. The rituals of prison life remained outwardly similar to those of the past, with the endlessly repeated cycles of interrogation, each culminating in the same cry of "Confess your crimes!" and the same paper and pen thrust forward for signature. But the ambitious goal of remaking the prisoner's personality degenerated into a mundane regimen of petty abuse at the hands of bullying guards. Indeed, Chen Ziming must have wondered, as he thought back to the beatings and "struggle sessions" he endured in the cowpen during the final days of the Gang of Four, had the motivation ever really been anything else?

Han Dongfang began to ask himself the same question. And as the prison authorities observed the behavior of their prize catch, they began to wonder what kind of person they were dealing with. The guards at the Ministry of Public Security had been delighted in June 1989 when Han turned himself in. They sat him down; they poured him tea. "So," they said, "you want to confess your crimes."

"No," Han answered patiently. "You don't understand. I haven't come to admit anything. I'm not a criminal. I've just come here to set the record straight."

They drove Han to a "shelter and investigation" center of the sort he had once guarded as a young recruit in the *Gong An Bing.* At first glance, Paoju Lane seemed like any other *hutong,* but as the jeep pulled up outside Number 21, Han noticed the high walls of red and black brick. The State Security guards pushed him in through the doorway and threw him into a cell. It was bare, except for a porcelain washbasin in one corner. The cell already held two other men—*ermu,* Han soon realized, "eyes and ears" placed there to watch his every move. The interrogation sessions began almost immediately.

The chief interrogator smiled. "We know all about you," he began. "We really admire you and respect your ideas, you know. And since you have acknowledged your guilt by turning yourself in, I hope we will be able to show you leniency."

"Wait a minute," Han interrupted. "I did not turn myself in. I merely *reported* to you to inform you of the facts in my case."

The man slammed his fist on the table in rage. "Don't try any clever arguments or your family will suffer," he yelled. "We've already executed plenty of other hooligan workers, and we won't hesitate to give you the same treatment, especially since your crimes are much more serious."

And so it continued for ten days, round-the-clock sessions that lasted until two or three o'clock in the morning. What seemed to interest the interrogators most was the joint worker-student declaration that Han and Li Jinjin had written on the first day of martial law.[3] But Han told them nothing. Back in the cell, the *ermu* sat motionless, watching him. He hardly slept. He feared that he would crack under the interrogators' pressure. He feared for his sanity. He calculated the distance to the far wall, wondering if he could generate enough force to kill himself by ramming his head against the porcelain washbasin.

Han guessed the *ermu* had read his thoughts, because after ten days he was moved into solitary confinement in a padded cell— walls, floor, ceilings all of dark blue rubber. It was Paoju Lane's version of the *xiao hao,* the small punishment cell that exists in every Chinese prison. A tiny aperture in the steel door is the only source of light. "The *xiao hao* is certainly no guest house," says one Chinese account published in 1986. "It is an operating table for felons. Loneliness is the scalpel, used for performing surgery upon the souls of those overly fond of fun and excitement.

"Day 1: They lock [the prisoner] up in the *xiao hao* for a period of forced introspection. Day 2: He's still lying on the bed, feeling quite happy . . . Day 3: He feels a little lonely . . . Day 4: He starts to feel rather afraid. The ray of light piercing the little aperture has been mercilessly halved in size by a steel bar. The room is like some dim cave. Day 5: He is plunged into terror. The ghostly shadows of loneliness play over the four walls around, seeming to grin hideously at him. He involuntarily breaks out in a cold shiver. He screams insanely and bangs on the door. He jumps up and down on the bed, and then starts rolling around underneath it. *Over the next few days, he begins to repent.*"

But Han did not repent, and after a week they threw him back in his old cell. He remained there for two months. The interrogation sessions stopped. They seemed to have forgotten all about him. But one day in early September, the guards hauled him out and told him it was time for him to have some company. Slowly he took in his new surroundings; two dozen people were crammed into a room twelve feet square. There were normally fewer, someone said, but the numbers had risen since June 4.

Paoju Lane held a thousand prisoners, half of them *zhengzhi fan,* politicals, and the rest common criminals. The mix in Han's new cell was no accident; the Beijing prison authorities routinely instructed the common criminals to beat up recalcitrant politicals as a spur to confession. The overcrowded cell was equipped with a single washbasin and a urinal. Hygiene was nonexistent; the room stank of sweat, urine, and diarrhea. Anyone who got up to use the toilet lost his floor space. Nighttime was a torment. The floor was always wet, and the prisoners slept, jammed in on their sides like sardines, on damp bedrolls. A single low-wattage bulb suspended from the ceiling burned day and night. Giant cockroaches swarmed over Han's face. All night there was the incessant sound of coughing and scratching. Lice were everywhere—in socks, shirts, and bedding, in the cracks of the floor. One after another, the prisoners all came down with scabies.

Daylight, which filtered in through a small window high up on one wall, brought little relief. From reveille at 6:30 A.M. until bedtime at 9:30 P.M., the prisoners sat on the floor in four rows of six without moving or talking. The only respite was lunch at 10:00 A.M. and dinner at 4:30 P.M.. The meals never varied, and they comprised a starvation diet: a small bowl of thin vegetable soup and two half-cooked *wotou*, steamed cornmeal buns. A warder would often withhold the *wotou* as punishment for a "bad attitude." Hungry prisoners who tried to claim extra portions were beaten and handcuffed. One prisoner who attempted to hoard food was shackled for more than a week. Han watched in dismay as the pounds fell away from his own slim frame.

Occasionally, as a great privilege, a copy of *People's Daily* appeared, to be passed around several cells and hundreds of hands. No books were allowed, no paper, no pens, no visitors, no mail. Han heard no news of his wife. He had almost no opportunity for exercise, reading, or communication with the outside world. Every couple of weeks the prisoners were allowed to run around a small yard for twenty minutes or so, accompanied by a police officer. Han went out once, but it was hard to run on legs that were stiff and swollen from weeks of sitting cramped in the hellish room. He leaned against the wall of the exercise yard, grimacing with pain. The wall was covered with prisoners' graffiti, and one inscription caught his eye. All it said was "Beida Doctor—LJJ," but Han knew instantly what it meant. Li Jinjin was here, too! Underneath, he scrawled "HDF VVV"—the victory sign, three times.

The prison authorities had little patience when Han began to complain of stomach problems, the result of the bad food and poor hygiene. Your problem, the guards told him, is that you have a bad attitude. They told him the stomach pains were all in his imagination. Han sank into a deep gloom, but the other prisoners interceded on his behalf. This man really is sick, they told the guards. Eventually, the guards relented and took him to the infirmary. His cellmates heard him yelling down the corridor: "How pitiful we Chinese are! We don't even respect our own kind. I wouldn't want to be a Chinese again in my next life."

The warden of Paoju Lane took personal charge of the case of the obstinate young railway worker. "So," the official said, "stomach problems, eh? You obviously need an acupuncturist."

The warden summoned the doctor. The man selected a huge needle. "Spread your hand," he ordered, plunging the needle deep into the fleshy base of the thumb and continuing to push until it emerged under Han's little finger. Han writhed in pain. But the acupuncturist only increased the pressure, dragging the needle back and forth in the wound to increase the agony. There was no pretense that any of this was designed to help Han's stomach ailment.

The warden put him back in his original cell, with the "eyes and ears," but far from repenting, Han declared that he intended to go on a hunger strike until the prison authorities agreed to give him proper medical care. In response to Han's ultimatum, the warden arrived at his cell with a group of prisoners, common criminals. They pinned him to his bed while an orderly rammed a rubber feeding tube up his nose. As the tube slid in, Han saw that the man's fingernails were thickly encrusted with dirt. Although at least a foot of the feeding tube had disappeared, Han could feel that it was not going down his throat as it should. A terrible feeling of congestion told him that the tube had kinked and jammed somewhere inside his nasal passages. But still the orderly kept forcing it in deeper. The pain was excruciating. "Ahhh! You beasts," Han tried to scream. But his cries were stifled by a sudden squelching jet of liquid food from the pump. There seemed to be an explosion deep inside his skull; he choked and then, mercifully, passed out.

For several hours, Han drifted between unconsciousness and delirium. When he finally came to, the warden was standing over him. "So," the man inquired. "Ready to give up this nonsense about a hunger strike?"

Han stared back at him grimly. "Never," he replied.

There was a pause. "Very well," said the warden. "We'll take you to a doctor in a week."

It was Han's first small victory, a triumph for his obstinacy and willpower. But it was short-lived. The doctor saw him as promised, but told him he could find nothing physically wrong. Again, the prison guards told Han he was faking the whole thing, even though by now he was too weak to stand. The warden seemed to take special pleasure in tormenting Han. One day another group of prisoners arrived at his cell and dragged him, semiconscious, into the corridor. "Prop him up against the wall," the warden ordered. The prisoners did as they were told and held Han there in a crucifixion position. "Now let go."

"But he's too weak," one man dared to object.

"Just do it," the warden snapped.

For a long moment, Han swayed and rocked. Then he toppled forward full-length, unable to break his fall with his hands as the floor rushed up to smash his face. The warden stood over him with a sneer and told him, "This is what happens to people like you."

In January 1990, a guard brought news that Han was to be moved again. "You're afraid of illness, huh?" the man said. "Well, that's what we're going to give you." Han was taken to his new quarters, an overcrowded cell with sixteen or seventeen prisoners suffering from contagious diseases. He could hardly hear himself think for the noise of constant coughing. More than half of his new cellmates had tuberculosis.

The warden kept Han there for two months. By winter's end, he had been in and out of the prison clinic six times, on and off intravenous drips, his illness never diagnosed. But the first mild days of spring 1990 brought an important piece of news. Han was to be transferred to Banbuqiao, the notorious pretrial detention center that had housed famous prisoners like Wei Jingsheng, Xu Wenli, and Liu Qing after the crackdown on Democracy Wall.[4] The reason for his transfer was that the interrogators from State Security had wrapped up their investigation.

For the transfer to Banbuqiao, Han was briefly reunited with two other prisoners: Li Jinjin and Zhou Yongjun, the student who had worked closely with the BWAF. It should have been an emotional reunion, but the guards prevented the men from speaking to each other. Han and Zhou were put in one PSB van, Li in another. Upon arrival at Banbuqiao, they were separated again.

Han felt that he was entering the gates of hell. Guards looked down from their watchtowers atop the high, electrified walls. The tall buildings of Banbuqiao's infamous K-block rose before him like tombstones. Next to death row was the women's block, where prisoners would lean out of the windows to sing to the men as they were taken out to be executed.

Han's interrogators were harsher than those at Paoju Lane, but they made no greater progress. They informed him that he was to be charged with "counterrevolutionary propaganda and incitement," but before they could say anything else, Han interrupted. "Let me make two things clear before we start," he said in his usual measured way. "First, forget all the talk about lenience for those who repent. I'm not here to look for lenience. I'm here to clarify the facts for you, nothing else. Second, if you ask me a question and I say 'I don't know,' then please drop that subject. You will never get a different answer. If you already have evidence, go ahead and use it. Please don't bother me with it."

The interrogator exploded. "Where do you think you are, prisoner Han!" he screamed. "This is the Public Security Bureau. Are you trying to stage a political demonstration? Don't you realize this is an organ of the Dictatorship of the Proletariat?"

"I apologize," Han said mildly. "I am only trying to help you do your job more efficiently."

The same charges of "counterrevolutionary propaganda and incitement" were brought against virtually all the leading figures of the 1989 democracy movement. From the investigators' point of view, they had only two practical alternatives: to hand the accused over to the police for "administrative" sentencing and a short spell of "reeducation through labor," or to acquit. In the case of someone like Han Dongfang, the choice was a foregone conclusion.

On the afternoon of June 4, within hours of the Beijing massacre, the Supreme People's Court had issued its opinion that the Tiananmen protests had been "counterrevolutionary" in character, thus foreclosing any real possibility that the lower courts could rule otherwise on those involved. Article 90 of the 1980 Criminal Law would apply in these cases: "All acts endangering the People's Republic of China committed with the goal of overthrowing the political power of the dictatorship of the proletariat and the socialist system are crimes of counterrevolution."

The law, in China, is an instrument of the Party line; there is no separation of powers.[5] China's politico-legal system, in defiance of both the letter and the spirit of the Universal Declaration of

Human Rights, explicitly rejects the idea that a detainee should be presumed innocent until proven guilty. To presume innocence would prejudge the issue, so the argument goes, and would deter the Chinese police from ever making an arrest. China claims not to presume guilt, but the first thing detainees see upon entering a police station is the large sign on the wall that promises lenience to those who confess, severity to those who resist. The show of penitence is indispensable; protestations of innocence are taken as evidence of a bad attitude, further proof of guilt, and grounds for a harsher sentence. Acquittal or release are rare, because they would suggest that the original arrest was a mistake, and this, for the authorities, would mean an unacceptable loss of face.

During the period of pretrial custody and interrogation, access to a lawyer is denied; no one is on hand to advise detainees of their rights—they have virtually none—or to monitor ill-treatment, beatings, or torture. A prisoner may seek legal counsel only after an indictment has been issued and the case is ready to go to court. This usually leaves no more than a week before the trial, insufficient time for a lawyer to prepare a proper defense. Powerful incentives discourage a lawyer from defying the will of the court. A defense lawyer who enters a "not guilty" plea in a sensitive case cannot expect his or her career to prosper. Some local justice departments even require a not-guilty plea to be cleared in advance with the local Party organization. Even assuming the lawyer clears these hurdles, the judges' verdict has usually been determined by either the Party's politics and law committee or the court's own "adjudication committee" before anyone sets foot in the courtroom. The role of the panel of judges is merely to transmit formally what has already been agreed.

In the brave days before Tiananmen, many Chinese legal scholars had begun to challenge these practices. The Shanghai journal *Minzhu Yu Fazhi* (*Democracy and Law*), for example, wrote in 1988:

> "Verdict first, trial second" is tantamount to walking along a road on the top of one's head; it violates the law of proper procedure. . . . "Brilliant luminaries," who have not carried out any investigations or even read the case dossier, but have instead merely listened to an oral report on the case, are allowed to make the ruling in advance. Even if they reach an erroneous verdict, the panel of judges must submit to it completely and unconditionally; there is no room

allowed for debate or disagreement. . . . [This] gives the green light to those who seek to put their own word before the law.

A large body of legal opinion had begun to crystallize around the idea that the concept of counterrevolution should be excised from the criminal statutes altogether. A January 1989 article in the official *Faxue Pinglun* (*Law Review*) summed up this new thinking as follows:

The twin categories of revolution and counterrevolution exist as a formal expression of the class struggle. The term "counterrevolution" carries heavy connotations of political struggle. In terms of both form and content, it is constantly and unpredictably changing, in line with changes that occur from time to time in the political situation. During periods of alternation between old and new systems, and during the changeover from one to the other, both the tasks and the targets of the revolution change accordingly. As a result, the meaning and content of the term "counterrevolution" has to be revised and supplemented. The term "crime of counterrevolution" is thus, strictly speaking, not a legal concept at all. It is a political concept, broad and general in nature.

This was just what Chen Ziming and Wang Juntao had argued for years. The rule of law was nonexistent in China. Nothing offered citizens formal protection from the wild mood swings of an arbitrary state. "Revolution" and "counterrevolution" had become Alice-in-Wonderland terms. As the Red Queen said, "When I use a word, it means whatever I choose it to mean." Labeling the Tiananmen protests counterrevolutionary dispensed with all the new, enlightened legal scholarship with one rhetorical stroke. The rule of law, at least for dissidents, turned out to have no greater meaning under Deng than it had under Mao or the Gang of Four.

———

For the system to release a detainee without charge was unusual, but it did happen occasionally. On April 22, 1990, it happened to Hou Xiaotian, who had been detained at the Paoju Lane center for more than five months. Even though she was married to Wang Juntao, and had worked with him at SERI, the prosecutors could find no specific reason for bringing her to trial.

After the police picked her up at the end of October, Hou received no news of her husband. She knew only that he had been captured, but she had no idea where he was being held. In February, at Spring Festival time, she went to the prison authorities to demand some news, any news of Wang. "He's doing better than you are," they told her. "Why don't you think about your own situation before you worry about him?"

The authorities underestimated Hou. The surveillance reports from the PSB told them that the marriage was rocky, that Hou and Wang had seen each other only three times during the entire seven-week course of the 1989 protests, that the dashing Wang was known to have an eye for other women. Hou did not appear to them to be a threatening figure. A small, pretty woman of twenty-seven with a ready smile that lit up her whole face, Hou had a careful, precise manner, a neat way of dressing, a demure quality of the sort that is common to many Chinese women. When she asked after her husband's welfare, the prison guards teased her with lewd jokes and guffaws. But they failed to detect the reservoirs of will that lay beneath Hou's placid exterior.

The authorities thought, in fact, that five months in prison, sleeping on a bare concrete floor, had broken her. By mid-April 1990, still getting no response to her request for news of Wang, Hou seemed deep in depression; her usual self-confidence appeared to have ebbed. On April 16, a Monday, her depression reached its nadir. This can't go on, she told herself, and she called for a guard.

"I want to see my husband," she announced.

"You know that's impossible," the guard replied.

"Then go to your superiors," she snapped, "and tell them that unless they give me some news of him, I intend to begin a hunger strike on Friday. They have until Thursday afternoon to get back to me with an answer."

Urging her not to do anything as rash as a hunger strike, the authorities stalled until the weekend. Then, on Sunday, a cadre from the Public Security Bureau appeared unexpectedly to inform Hou that the investigation of her activities was concluded. The case was closed. No charges would be brought; she was free to go.

From the moment she stepped out of the jail, there was a new determination about Hou Xiaotian. She was now a political activist in her own right, and in the process she had redefined her marriage. Before Tiananmen, friends had warned her that she was too independent-minded to marry someone like Wang Juntao. He was too much the traditional Chinese male, the kind who expected his wife to devote herself to his interests. Now, with her husband in jail, Hou exercised her independence in ways that no traditional Chinese wife would dream of. And yet in the process she was dedicating herself to her husband totally. She was too intelligent a woman not to appreciate the ironies in her new role.

Time after time, week after week, during the spring and early summer months of 1990, Hou made her way to the Public Security Bureau. Her two demands never varied: Show me the "shelter and investigation order" that provides the legal basis for my husband's detention; and let me see him. The first request was reasonable, the PSB replied amiably, but unfortunately the document in question had been mislaid. The second request could not be granted. "I'll go to the gate of Qincheng prison myself and stand there until they let me in," she told them. They merely shrugged. On July 11, Wang's thirty-second birthday, Hou decided to make good on her threat.

Qincheng, or Q1—"a twentieth-century Bastille," Wei Jingsheng called it in a celebrated manuscript written in 1979—is the maximum-security prison for China's top political offenders and appears on no maps. It lies in Changping County, due north of Beijing, amid picturesque countryside in a region of hot springs. The Empress Dowager Cixi was fond of coming here to take the waters.

A lonely but well-maintained asphalt road runs north from the spa. At the roadside, a large sign states in several languages, "Foreigners prohibited." The road leads to a nondescript gate house. A building several stories high rises behind the screen wall, hidden from view. This building is entered through an archway, flanked by two sentry boxes and with a rusty iron gate in its center. Former inmates jokingly call this "the Atheists' Gate to Hell." Beyond the gateway is the prison proper, enclosed by a ten-foot-high wall topped with electrified barbed wire. At the foot of a hill, to the east, are a number of cell blocks built during the Cultural Revolution to house the sudden influx of high-ranking prisoners. President Yang Shangkun was incarcerated here; so was Wang Guangmei, the brilliant widow of another president, Liu Shaoqi, and despised rival of Mao's wife, Jiang Qing. After her husband was tortured to death in 1969, Wang endured ten years in Qincheng before emerging as a white-haired skeleton.[6]

Wang Juntao and Chen Ziming, along with most of the leading prisoners from the 1989 movement, had been held in Qincheng since their arrest nine months earlier. Conditions had improved somewhat since Mao's day, and Chen put his early captivity to good use. In just four months, writing in longhand and working entirely from memory, without notes or reference sources, he completed a 250,000-character manuscript that he called *Looking Back on the Reform Decade*. Even then, Chen seemed to cling to his hope of influencing those in power. His only request was that his manuscript be sent straight to the new General Secretary, Jiang Zemin, and to Li Ruihuan, the member of the Politburo Standing Committee responsible for propaganda.

The midsummer heat was paralyzing as Hou rode the bus out to Changping County accompanied by Wang Juntao's mother. In her bag Hou carried a birthday card, some food, books, and family photographs. There was also a copy of a fifteen-page appeal she had delivered the day before to Chinese officials as well as to a foreign reporter living in Beijing. The document was one of the first open displays of dissent that anyone had risked in China since June 4. "My husband is a patriot," Hou wrote. "He always had a glorious hope: that the students and the government could solve their problems through reason and compromise. He never supported turmoil and never took part in any conspiracy." However, the letter went on, "Since they have characterized it as counterrevolution, they need counterrevolutionaries." Wang "is the pillar of my life," she ended. "Were he not there, my life would have no meaning. I give no thought to my personal safety. . . . I will use all of my strength to appeal on behalf of his rights."

After the bus dropped the two women off, it took them a long time to find Qincheng. The local peasants pretend not to know of its existence and refuse even to speak of the place with outsiders. When they finally reached the prison gate, they were hot and exhausted. The guards at the front gate sent Hou to a side entrance; from there she was sent to a security checkpoint. Hou could feel her temper rising. The weeks since her release from detention had been difficult for her. She was still tormented by insomnia; often, when she finally fell asleep, it was only to wake up again in an uncontrollable crying fit. Now she was in no mood to tolerate the guards' obstructiveness. In the end, she was told brusquely that her timing was "not convenient." "What do you mean, not convenient?" she screamed. "Don't push me too far, or you'll regret it." A superior was summoned. He made inquiries. Eventually, he told Hou to report the next morning to the nearby Banbuqiao detention center.

When Hou arrived at Banbuqiao, a PSB cadre handed her a letter from Wang Juntao. Now at least she knew that her husband was alive. The cadre promised that the couple would be allowed to exchange letters once a month. Four days later, Wang's parents were finally given a copy of his shelter and investigation order.

But the events of July were less a breakthrough than just the first stage in a bitter and protracted struggle. Although Hou wrote to Wang faithfully each month, no letters arrived in reply. Meanwhile, the threats and pressures against her mounted. As many as eight secret police agents tailed Hou conspicuously wherever she went. Her work unit at the Ministry of Personnel's job-training center evicted her from her apartment to punish her for her activities. She also wound up in a Beijing hospital in November with a series of physical ailments she had contracted while in jail, compounded by her state of nervous exhaustion. From her hospital bed, she scribbled a fearful appeal to a foreign reporter friend, Jeffrey Parker of United Press International. "I feel tiny and weak," Hou wrote, "as insignificant as a droplet of water in the sea. When I call out on behalf of my husband, I hear not a sound in response." But the letter only earned her a renewed series of threats; did she not realize that it was a crime to "rely on foreign forces to put pressure on the motherland?" The Ministry of Personnel threatened to fire her; her work unit organized a rally to alert Party members to her aberrational behavior. Finally, on a bitter day in January 1991, the PSB pulled her in for questioning; was it true, they wanted to know, that she was planning to hold a press conference to discuss her husband's impending trial? The Party had taken almost fifteen months to prepare its case, but now it was ready to bring the conspirators to court.

19

To Those Who Resist, Severity

Totalitarian regimes have many quirks, none odder perhaps than their penchant for earnest and lengthy debate about the legal basis of their actions and their fondness for setting loose posses of scribes and bureaucrats to construct labyrinthine legal codes, regulations, and safeguards—which are then blithely set aside the moment they prove inconvenient. Whenever cornered by a foreign reporter or diplomat, the Chinese authorities took pains to stress that the proceedings against Wang Juntao and Chen Ziming were in strict accordance with Chinese law. Even on its own terms the claim was ludicrous.

In one clause after another, China's 1980 Criminal Law stipulates the limits of lawful pretrial detention: properly made out detention warrants; due notification of the prisoner's family and *danwei;* first interrogation within twenty-four hours; a seven-day period during which the procurator's office must grant permission for a formal arrest; production of an arrest warrant; the family's right to demand release if these terms are abused; provisions for an extension by approval of the Standing Committee of the National People's Congress; formal timetables for the matter to be brought to court.

Add all these provisions together, stretch each to the limit, and bind them together with red tape; what emerges is that the maximum period a prisoner can lawfully be held before trial is five and a half months. Even *shoureng shencha,* shelter and investigation—a convenience that allows the police to evade many of the restraints of the Criminal Law—expires after three months. Yet the black hands of the 1989 movement had been in pretrial detention from thirteen to nineteen months. As Chinese officials eventually admitted to a number of visiting human rights delegations in 1991, the limits of *shoureng shencha* were considered too restrictive, so they were set aside altogether in the wake of the June 4 massacre. The NPC, which can extend "investigative custody," received instructions from the highest levels of the Party to stay out of the matter of the June 4 dissidents. The reason, it was told without a hint of irony, was that parliament should not compromise the independence of the judiciary.

The entire business of the trials, in fact, was handled at the highest levels. In sifting through the evidence, the Party made a crude division of the protesters into three main groups. First, there were the workers, large numbers of whom had been executed in the early months of the crackdown with great public fanfare; together with special treatment for the troublesome Han Dongfang, the Party thought the action already taken sufficient to prevent any further problems with workers. Second, there were the students. It was a galling loss of face for the security services to have allowed Chai Ling and Wu'er Kaixi to slip through their fingers. But no matter; Wang Dan was still in custody, and a finely tuned sentence for him—stern, but not excessive—should be enough to keep the campuses quiet. Other students had already buckled under the pressure of prison and could safely be shown lenience. Third, there were the intellectuals, who could further be divided into two subgroups, the Party thought. First, there were those who had done no more than sign petitions. The Party decided on indulgence for them, even if they were still infected with bourgeois liberalism. But the second, hard-core group, the few who had worked behind the scenes to shape the tactics of the movement, were to be singled out for the harshest punishment. Within a few months, the Party had whittled the list of black hands down to about a dozen names, and those of Wang Juntao and Chen Ziming were surfacing in internal Party documents as the "chief criminal agitators."

Not that the Party saw Wang and Chen as inseparable. There were different reasons for making an example of each of them. Chen embodied the long-term political challenge to the regime, the cancer that had grown quietly under the Party's nose during the years of the Deng reforms. Wang was the activist, the magnetic political leader, the "organizer and commander of the counterrevolutionary rebellion." At a special session of the Politburo called to discuss the disposition of the Tiananmen caseload, Li Peng's face contorted with anger when the conversation turned to Wang Juntao. "This man must be severely punished," the Premier squawked. "He must be shown no mercy; he must not be allowed to make a political comeback. He is a veteran of four movements [1976, 1979–1980, 1986, and 1989]. To show him leniency would be like letting the tiger back into the mountains after it has been caught."[1]

Normally, Deng Xiaoping did not automatically support his Premier, but on this occasion he nodded his assent. In late November 1990, the families of Chen and Wang were notified that the two men had been charged with "plotting to subvert the government." A short time later, the same charges of sedition were lodged against two of their closest collaborators, Chen Xiaoping and Liu Gang. Chen Xiaoping, the legal scholar, recalled clearly how the relevant article of the Criminal Law was worded: "Whoever plots to subvert the government or dismember the state is to be sentenced to . . . not less than ten years of fixed-term imprisonment . . . [and] may be sentenced to death when the harm to the state and the people is especially serious and the circumstances are odious."

The Communist Party needed now only to agree on the precise sentences and the timing of the trials. There had been a number of complications and delays of a political nature. Worst of all, the Politburo had reached a stalemate over the thorny question of Zhao Ziyang and his aide, Bao Tong. Was Zhao himself to be brought to trial? Expelled from the Party? Publicly disgraced? Would Bao Tong, the alleged leaker of state secrets, be fingered as the principal black hand? The conservatives wanted the heads of Zhao and Bao on a platter. The remaining reformists, perhaps even Deng himself, preferred to leave the door open to their eventual rehabilitation. Was the official verdict to be that Wang Juntao and Chen Ziming had actively conspired with Premier Zhao and his top aide? Even the intelligence services seemed unsure of how far the connection had reached.

In some respects the timing of the trials was propitious. A three-month window should be enough to wrap up the trials before the

1991 Spring Festival. The country was quiet; its overheated economy was back on course. The Asian Games in October, which had
brought the foreign media flooding into Beijing, had proceeded
without a hitch. Most Western sanctions had been lifted, and the
Western media, with their limited attention span, were safely absorbed in a new drama in the Persian Gulf. The irritating Amer-
icans were distracted by this unexpected political turmoil in the
Middle East. The Iraqi dictator, Saddam Hussein, had invaded
Kuwait, and the United States was now busy lining up a United
Nations–backed coalition to dislodge him. China's vote in the Security Council would be crucial. On November 26, the authorities
announced that the trials of Wang Juntao and Chen Ziming would
be held in the near future; three days later, in New York, Foreign
Minister Qian Qichen promised that China would not oppose the
use of force against Iraq.

The trials were held, in a carefully orchestrated sequence, at the
Beijing People's Intermediate Court. The first proceedings began
in November 1990, but the drama began to climax on January 5,
1991, with the trials of a cluster of students from the Most Wanted
list. These students were small fry, chosen as if to test the waters
of international opinion: Zheng Xuguang (number 9 on the list of
21); Ma Shaofang (number 10); Wang Youcai (number 15); and
Zhang Ming (number 19). The sentences, ranging from two to four
years, were fairly lenient, the foreign diplomats agreed.

Bao Zunxin, still feeble from his long illness, was hustled into
court on January 15, as the first Allied bombers prepared to take
off for Baghdad. He was sentenced to five years in prison for counterrevolutionary propaganda and incitement.

Eleven days later came the rulings on the biggest batch of prisoners to date. In a half dozen separate courtrooms, judges handed
down a confusing and contradictory set of sentences. Guo Haifeng,
a middle-ranking student leader, was sentenced to four years for
"sabotage." Three men were given sentences of three to five years
each for aiding Wu'er Kaixi in his successful escape. But most of
the attention that day focused on Wang Dan, number one on the
list of Most Wanted students. Wang's parents learned of the trial
only that morning and were given no opportunity to hire their own
defense lawyer. Even so, after a perfunctory three-hour hearing,

the sentence handed down was muted: four years in jail with two more years of "deprivation of political rights." Just down the hall, another judge read out the sentence on Ren Wanding, the veteran campaigner who had organized the China Human Rights League during the Democracy Wall period. There were gasps when the sentence was announced: seven years. Ren had played no direct part in the 1989 protests and belonged to no organization; he had delivered only a couple of speeches, and those had been interrupted by jeers and catcalls from students who had no idea who this old-timer was.[2]

As if deliberately trying to send mixed signals, the authorities also chose to announce a number of releases on January 26. Liu Suli of SERI went free, as did Liu Xiaobo, one of the four hunger strikers who had finally persuaded the students to evacuate the square in the early hours of June 4. The sentences depended upon attitude, explained the spin doctors from the Xinhua News Agency. Wang Dan had cooperated with his captors, whereas Ren Wanding had "shown no repentance." Liu Xiaobo had "committed serious crimes but has acknowledged them, showed repentance, and performed major meritorious services." Just as the PLA commissar in Tiananmen Square had hinted to the hunger strikers, the fiery young literary critic, Liu, had been rewarded for helping to persuade the students to leave—for succeeding, in other words, where Wang Juntao had failed.[3]

A fresh pair of trial notices flapped in the cold winter wind outside the People's Intermediate Court on the morning of February 6, although a cordon of dozens of police kept inquisitive onlookers at bay, especially if they were foreigners. The first names to appear were those of Liu Gang and Chen Xiaoping. Both men faced the charge of sedition. Chen had told his family that he expected to receive five years, and he appeared unconcerned about lessening that sentence by his behavior in the courtroom, telling the judges at one point that he would have liked to overthrow the "corrupt government." Liu Gang's bad attitude was already quite apparent to his captors, and the former physics student had spent long periods of his detention in leg irons for one breach of prison discipline after another.

The proceedings against Liu were perfunctory, lasting barely three and a half hours. The state prosecutor argued that Liu had been the driving force behind the establishment of the Beijing Students Autonomous Federation; soon afterward, he had "urged Chen Ziming and Wang Juntao to form an illegal organization 'to influence the students by social forces' in order to intensify the disturbances." He had then attended their meetings at the Jimen Hotel, joined Wang in "spying" on the martial law forces, and called for Beijing residents to stage mass demonstrations against the troops every third day.

Liu spoke for an hour in his own defense. He denied vehemently that he had conspired to overthrow the government. He swore that his prison "confession" had been extracted only under threat of death. "What I said before doesn't count," he declared. "What does count is what I say this morning." Liu's defense attorneys also weighed in with bolder arguments than Chinese legal custom called for. The prosecution evidence was paper-thin, they asserted, and relied too heavily on statements by other students that implicated their client. But the court was unimpressed with these arguments and handed down its predetermined sentence— six years in jail.

The lawyers' performance was, in fact, one of the few uplifting notes in the whole affair. As the Tiananmen trials approached, the government formed its own special group of defense lawyers to represent the black hands; the remainder of the Beijing legal community was warned by the Justice Ministry to steer clear of these cases. But as the date of their husbands' trials approached, Hou Xiaotian and Wang Zhihong—Wang only recently out on bail herself—persisted in their efforts to hire independent counsel. The two women were followed, threatened with reprisals, and had their telephones bugged. But in the end, the courts yielded. It was their sole concession. Only two members of the prisoners' immediate family would be allowed to attend the trials; otherwise, the court would admit only "relevant personages" of its own choosing; there would be no outside observers.

At eight-thirty on the morning of Monday, February 11, 1991, the clerk rose to intone the rules of the court in the matter of the People's Republic of China against Chen Ziming, male, thirty-nine, former head of the Beijing Social and Economic Sciences Research Institute. There were to be no photographs, no tape recordings, no talking in the public gallery. As Chen scanned the courtroom, he could not find Wang Zhihong, who had been barred from attending. But there was his mother, and next to her, Zihua, the younger sister of whom he was so fond. Everyone else present seemed to be either an officer of the court or a member of the security services.

The fifteen months in Qincheng had taken their toll. Chen was also showing the effects of the hunger strike he had begun the week before. His lawyers had been given an absurdly short time to prepare their case; by fasting and refusing to wear prison clothes since the preceding Thursday, Chen had tried vainly to force a two-week postponement of the trial.

As the clerk of the court droned on, the room seemed to sway slightly before Chen's eyes, and he found his mind ranging back over the events that had brought him here. One conversation in particular drifted back to him. It was back in 1980, at the time of the Beijing election campaign. A certain reform-minded official, a later ally of Zhao Ziyang, came to him to offer advice. "Remember," the man said, "in times of complex political struggle, you are pawns to be sacrificed. This is an unavoidable fact, but history will remember your dedication and your sacrifice."

The public prosecutor rose to make his opening address. "From April through June 1989," he began, "the defendant Chen Ziming and his colleague Wang Juntao, together and in concert with Liu Gang and Chen Xiaoping, did carry out a series of organized, planned, and premeditated activities aimed at subverting China's government." The state's case was built almost entirely on the recorded proceedings of a series of meetings. "On April 23," the prosecutor continued, "Chen Ziming convened a meeting at SERI on the topic: 'Evaluation of the Past Ten Years and Assessment of the Current Situation.' At the meeting, Chen Ziming, Wang Juntao, and Chen Xiaoping spoke in concert and molded the counterrevolutionary opinion to intensify the turmoil in an organized way." The prosecutor read into the record a number of inflammatory remarks that Chen allegedly made on that occasion.[4]

Next, the prosecutor cited the May 15 symposium on "Political Structural Reform and the Labor Unions," sponsored by the editorial board of *China's Labor Movement*. "There, Chen Ziming acted further to mold public opinion, conspiring to subvert the government." Then came the meetings at the Jimen Hotel; the plans "to form an illegal organization that would unite all the various circles"; the drafting, at Chen Ziming's suggestion, of the May 19 "Letter to the People"—though the prosecutor mentioned only its first, unamended draft, the one that called for "an immediate general strike [and a] nationwide class and market boycott."

One by one, the meetings, the faces, passed across Chen's memory. Everything had been infiltrated, every room bugged, every word secretly recorded. All the security precautions SERI had taken seemed, with hindsight, so amateurish, so ineffective. How they had underestimated their opponents! Again, Chen felt the room swimming. Several times he asked the judge for a brief pause in the proceedings; he felt so tired.

The judge invited Chen's lawyers to respond. In essence, their defense was a simple one. They attacked the quality of the evidence. The prosecution had taken the transcripts of the April 23 and May 15 meetings, pulled nine separate sentences out of context, and stitched them together to give the misleading impression of a conspiracy. The previous weekend, while listening to the secret tapes of his speeches, Chen found at least five cases of blatant doctoring. His attorneys submitted that these tapes were of questionable legality and should therefore be withdrawn as evidence.

"Request denied," snapped the presiding judge.

The lawyers next requested the right to cross-examine the seventeen witnesses whose depositions had been presented as evidence for the prosecution.

"Denied."

"We also have here a number of additional statements from witnesses on behalf of the accused; we would welcome the opportunity to read these into the record."

Again, "Denied."

The judges listened impassively as Chen's lawyers soldiered on. The charges of conspiracy were without foundation, they argued. What did it matter if the accused had called for "organizing intellectuals?" The Chinese Constitution granted him that right. And what if he had spoken out in favor of political reform? This was only to be expected; the man was a political scientist, after all. Chen Ziming's writings on political matters are voluminous, they pointed out. Nowhere in them would the court find a single word that advocates the armed overthrow of the government. On the contrary, all of them support the socialist system.

Suddenly a commotion broke out in the public gallery. A security guard had discovered that Chen's mother and sister were tape-recording the proceedings. The presiding judge angrily expelled them from the court and called for an adjournment.

"Chen Ziming, do you have any statement to make in your own defense?" the judge asked when the session resumed.

"Yes, I do."

"You may proceed."

After the recess, Chen was strong enough to speak for forty minutes. He tried to combine a political critique of his trial with a specific rebuttal of the evidence.[5] "The people who attribute my actions to counterrevolutionary motives," he began, "are the few who stick to extreme leftist viewpoints. In order to label me as a 'counterrevolutionary,' they have tampered with the evidence, altered tape recordings, and extorted confessions, disregarding any higher principles.

"Wang Juntao and I believed in political order and stability," he continued. "We opposed chaos and rebellion. We opposed the new attitudes of 'the kid who sells his father's fields without a qualm,' the prattling about 'without destruction there can be no construction,' the desire to start everything from scratch, the yearning for the foreign. . . . Instead, we promoted the idea, 'Do not destroy things before you have exploited their full potential; do not start building something new until you have tested your efficiency. . . .'

"I will regret for the rest of my life that we were not able in time to exert sufficient influence over the impetuous, emotional young students. . . . In my opinion, the 1989 student movement was an emotionally sincere, well-intentioned, pigheaded, mismanaged historical incident with a tragic ending and far-reaching implications for the future; its entire atmosphere, entire process, and entire consequences were all infused with a tragic color, and its solemn sense of beauty will always merit the people's admiration, since it greatly enriched the spiritual civilization of the Chinese people. . . .

"What really made the movement into a tragedy were all kinds of psychological factors similar to those in *Romeo and Juliet;* all kinds of determining habits of thought which fixed the behavior of the government and the students, and which are shared by society at large; all kinds of beliefs which have been commonly accepted for a long time, but have no basis in reality." Much of the blame for this, Chen said, lies with "the phony Marxism created by Soviet hack writers, starting in the 1930s. We seem unable to shake off this counterfeit notion that 'all political struggle is class struggle,' and that all political action is aimed at seizing power. . . .

"It is a good thing that Wang Juntao and I have been singled out as the principal defendants, since we are the most prepared in our thinking for the wrong that has been done. In order to save the students from the tiger's jaws, from the start we considered the possibility that their good intentions would meet with a bad response, and we did not hesitate to sacrifice ourselves. . . . From start to finish we emphasized a sober, rational, and compromising approach. With all our energy we sought to achieve understanding and mutual trust between the government and the students. . . ."

Chen ran briefly through the meetings that had been singled out by the prosecution. His remarks to the April 23 conference, he explained, were intended to persuade China's intellectuals to rise above the heated emotions of the moment and to act rationally. His comments at the May 15 trade union meeting discouraged workers from joining the protests. The conversations at the Jimen Hotel aimed to persuade the students to evacuate the square peacefully: "After May 18 I did all kinds of things to find a compromise. . . .

"The crucial problem is this," Chen concluded. "Do those in power really want to reform or to return to the past? The verdict on me can be decided by reform standards, based on the spirit of the rule of law, or by the standards of the Cultural Revolution in which leaders decide everything and speech is a crime. Each will have its own political consequences. If Cultural Revolution standards are reaffirmed in my case, this will cause even more disunity between the intellectuals and young students on one hand and the government on the other. It will make the broad masses of the people even more despondent and depressed. It will mean that the cadres who have supported the path of reform will worry about their own political futures. And it will send an ominous signal to the world. The choice is yours."

His strength exhausted, Chen sat down. The presiding judge banged his gavel. The court would reconvene the next morning for the verdict to be read and the sentence to be passed.

Throughout the six hours of the hearing, Chen Ziming had kept his usual calm, sober demeanor. He was not a man given to bitterness. As the guards led him away, was there still a trace of irony in some private corner of his thoughts? He knew the trial was a charade, that prosecutors, defenders, and judges were playing familiar, scripted roles. The outcome was preordained. Yet one goes through the motions anyway, because conscience demands it.

Almost ten months after her own release from jail, Hou Xiaotian was finally allowed into Qincheng prison on February 9, 1991, for a single visit with Wang Juntao. Two PSB guards stood close beside her for the whole hour. Wang was shocked to learn that she had been jailed, too. "They didn't even spare you," he exclaimed, "even though you did nothing at all!" He had been sick for some weeks, he told her. He was familiar with the symptoms—the deep pain under the ribs, the aching muscles, the nausea. He did not need a doctor to tell him that prison had brought on a renewed bout of the hepatitis that had felled him during his student days at Beida.

Over the weekend, Hou scurried back and forth between the prison, the Public Security Bureau, and the Justice Ministry, imploring one official after another to allow her husband a fair and open trial. She petitioned for adequate time for Wang to consult with his lawyers and prepare the case for his defense. The PSB had required eighteen months to assemble its case, Hou pointed out, on the grounds that it was "too complicated." How could the defense possibly muster its arguments in less than a week? She pleaded for family members to be granted unrestricted access to the courtroom; for timely public notification of the trial; for the presence of Chinese and foreign reporters; for the right to subpoena defense witnesses. But her pleas were in vain. The trials had been too thoroughly orchestrated.

On the morning of February 12, as Chen Ziming was being led back into court for sentencing, Wang Juntao rose unsteadily to his feet in a cramped courtroom upstairs on the third floor. The room was only half full, but again only two family members were allowed in: Hou and Wang's younger brother. Dressed in a blue Mao suit that he had picked up during his four months on the run, Wang appeared pale and haggard. He sweated profusely. He felt faint and dizzy and complained that he had difficulty keeping up with the proceedings. There was a ringing in his ears that grew worse as the morning wore on.

It took the state prosecutor just two and a half hours to present his evidence. Much of it read the same, word for word, as the charges against Chen, and the same conspiratorial sequence unfolded. But the charge sheet against Wang had a number of additional details, suggesting that the government saw his counterrevolutionary path as an even longer one than Chen's. Wang was accused of "hatching a plot" at the May 25 meeting of the Capital Joint Liaison Group "to instigate the masses to erect barricades, obstruct army vehicles, and take to the streets in public demonstrations." The prosecutor cited the ten-point statement of May 27, with its demand to extend the occupation of the square for another three weeks, the very idea that Wang had disputed. The state's chronology of Wang's seditious activities led right up to the eve of the massacre. He had used the Capital Joint Liaison Group, the prosecutor claimed, to appoint "People's Spokespersons" and initiate a so-called Campus Democracy Movement. He had "supported Liu Xiaobo and three others in their hunger strike in Tiananmen Square and other subversive activities."

Wang's lawyers, Sun Yachen and Zhang Sizhi, rose to respond to the charges. Zhang practiced law in Beijing; Sun worked in Luoyang, a city in Wang Juntao's home province of Henan. It took considerable courage for the two men to appear in court at all. They had disregarded the usual injunctions for defense lawyers to present their evidence "in the context of a guilty plea." They had ignored specific threats from their superiors. Now, to their enormous credit, they had the courage to pick the government's case apart point by point.

They began with the April 23 SERI conference. "The prosecution claims that this was convened to coincide with the 'April disturbances.'" In fact, "According to the minutes of the meeting transcribed from tape recordings made by the PSB, which now appear as volume 18 of the files of the present case, Min Qi, who was in the chair, declared at the outset that 'preparations for this meeting have been under way for some twenty days and more. It can be said that it has nothing to do with the student demonstrations.'" Then there was the matter of what Wang had said. Like Chen's lawyers the day before, Sun and Zhang showed how the prosecution had cobbled together seditious statements from phrases and sentences taken out of context. It was implied that Wang had called for the removal of the present government. But what he had actually said was that "The political old man [Deng Xiaoping] . . . has set up a structure at the top, a structure in which all the forces are quite mature and stable. . . . With [Xiaoping] on the scene, that structure can be maintained. Once old Deng leaves the scene, a new round of power struggles will ensue." Wang went on to say, "This would be a time when there would be a surge in social thinking. Viewed from that angle, China now faces a threshold; there is also an opportunity, a moment filled with opportunities." The defense pointed out that these were no more than the considered opinions of a scholar; they had nothing to do with the charge of "conspiring to subvert the government."

The May 15 conference was an even more blatant example of trumped-up charges. The prosecution was not above tampering with grammar to prove its case, Wang's lawyers went on. In Chinese, they pointed out, "The deletion of a pronoun or the replacement of a conjunction" can be enough to transform the meaning of a remark. "If it's really a case of setting up a political party," Wang was accused of saying, "then behind-the-scenes manipulation is permissible." But the full text of Wang's remarks was quite different. "Even if a political party is in fact organized or manipulated from behind the scenes, it can (*ye keyi*), indeed should still be within the scope of the law (*zai ni zhege hefa fanwei zhi nei*)." The deliberate omission of this final phrase made the words *ye keyi* acquire the false meaning of "permissible."

None of the later evidence against Wang Juntao, the lawyers continued, moving toward the crux of their case, made any sense without an explanation of the political background. "The United Front Work Department of the Central Committee of the Chinese Communist Party and its leader, Yan Mingfu . . . invited Wang Juntao et al. to get involved immediately in the disturbance and to serve as a bridge between the students and the government. The goal was to persuade the students to leave the square so that the visiting Gorbachev could be properly welcomed, and then to go one step further to calm the disturbance down. . . . [I]t was precisely at the suggestion of high-ranking officials of the Party that Wang Juntao et al. changed their posture from noninvolvement in the past to involvement. They were 'pushed to center stage,' in the words of Chen Ziming."

The meetings at the Jimen Hotel between May 17 and May 19 had been no more than "a practical plan designed to fulfill the task assigned to them by the Party. Now all this is construed as a 'secret conspiracy' and so on and so forth. This flies in the face of historical reality." Wang had made it clear that the conversations at the Jimen were designed "to solve problems. That meant primarily reaching a compromise between the students and the government, and the key to that was for the students speedily to leave the square." Yes, admittedly others at those meetings had favored a more confrontational approach; in the end, tragically, their voices had prevailed with the revised version of the May 27 Declaration. But Wang had no hand in writing that statement. "It is necessary to point out emphatically here," the lawyers said as they prepared to close, "that the reason why Wang Juntao did not oppose the Ten-Point Statement was primarily because the eighth point originally contained a demand that the students leave the square within a time limit. It was due to factors beyond Wang Juntao's personal control that this demand was not included and the statement finally became a mere scrap of paper."

This was a skillful defense, for it went straight to the heart of the Party's weakness. It was impossible for the Party to rebut the facts about Yan Mingfu, the lawyers knew, without exposing its unresolved internal conflicts.[6] Yet, if the question of Yan Mingfu were avoided, then it was apparent that Wang and Chen were to be scapegoats.

Wang was allowed to speak briefly in his own defense. He remained in his seat, sweat streaming from his face. At first he had thought of contesting the accusations point by point. But when the time came he spoke, as so often, from the heart. "I got angry," he told his lawyers later, "when the public prosecutor accused me of being counterrevolutionary for opposing leaders. A defense should not be limited to saying 'I do not oppose leaders,' but should allow for the legitimate right of opposition." There was another consideration, too. Wang had been deeply shaken by much of the testimony that the prosecutor had presented. So many of the leaders of the democracy movement seemed to have refused to face the consequences of their actions. So many had bowed to the pressures of the interrogation chamber and had told the Party what it wanted to hear. How could their consciences be at peace? So Wang Juntao chose not to defend himself; instead, he offered a general defense of the movement, a defense even of those with whom he had often bitterly disagreed. Every two or three minutes, one of the judges would interrupt with a cry of "Stick to the point!" But Wang pressed on, even though he knew that his show of defiance must surely seal his fate.

The presiding judge ordered a recess. From the public gallery, Hou Xiaotian passed her husband a paper bag with the lunch she had prepared for him. He picked at the food in thoughtful silence. Then, abruptly, the three judges returned to the courtroom and announced that they were ready to deliver their ruling.

Thirteen years had been required to develop the case against Wang Juntao; fifteen months to document it; four days to prepare a defense; five hours to hear it; and less than an hour to consider the verdict. The court made no pretense that it had even listened to the arguments for the defense. The presiding judge read from a prepared text, several pages long, that would have taken more than an hour just to type. The wording was almost identical to the verdict against Chen Ziming read earlier that day in another courtroom.

"In order to uphold the political authority of the People's democratic dictatorship and the socialist system, and to crush the destructive activities of counterrevolutionary elements, this court renders, on the basis of the facts of the defendant Wang Juntao's criminal acts, the nature and circumstances of his crimes, and the degree of harm caused thereby to society, and in accordance with Article 92, Article 102, Article 52, and Article 64 of the Criminal Law of the People's Republic of China, the following judgment:

"For the crime of conspiring to subvert the government, the defendant Wang Juntao is sentenced to a fixed-term period of thirteen years imprisonment, with four years subsequent deprivation of political rights."

Wang, standing now, smiled faintly as the sentence was read. He may even have wondered what horse-trading had gone on inside the Politburo to arrive at the figure of thirteen years. It was, after all, less than the fifteen years given to Wei Jingsheng and Xu Wenli after Democracy Wall. And the charges against him carried the death penalty, at least theoretically. Could a thirteen-year term even be construed as a modest victory for the Party's reform faction? Such speculation, Wang knew, was ultimately futile, for the inner deliberations of the Party were forever shrouded from view.

Whatever arguments may have gone on within Zhongnanhai, it was clear that the sentences were as carefully calibrated as the trials themselves. For Wang and Chen, thirteen years. For Liu Gang, only six. Although Liu was found guilty on all charges, the Party stressed that he had been "in a secondary position," and he had confessed. Chen Xiaoping, the fourth member of SERI to be charged with sedition, was found guilty but released. The reason, so the Xinhua News Agency reported, was "for voluntarily giving himself up to police and showing willingness to repent." Some were stunned by the contrasting sentences, but those who understood the Chinese system saw their logic. Chen Xiaoping's release drove home the arbitrary and fearsome nature of the Party's power and delivered an object lesson in the old line about resistance and harshness, confession and leniency.

But in China, absolution is not the same as freedom, and it remained for Chen Xiaoping to be punished in other, perhaps equally cruel ways. Within three months of his trial, he was fired from his job at Politics and Law University, stripped of his Party membership, deprived of his Beijing residence permit, and forced to return to his family home in Hunan Province. What was a constitutional lawyer to do in the depths of the countryside? Besides, there would always be lingering doubts about the reasons for his release: Had he perhaps turned state's evidence and betrayed his friends? Whether or not there was any basis to that suspicion, Chen would not easily regain the confidence of his fellow democrats, and that in itself constituted a victory for the Party.

The loose ends were tied up in the provincial courts. Wu Litang and the others who sheltered Wang Juntao in Wuhan were given from eighteen months to three years in jail. Li Longqing and Li Peicheng, the two Hong Kong couriers for the underground railroad, got four years and five years, respectively. Businessman Luo Haixing, who had set up the contact with Chen Ziming, fared no better.

"Mimi," he wrote to his wife from a Guangdong jail, "I was sentenced to five years in prison, and they described that as 'a light sentence in view of the circumstances.' . . . My sentence is even one year longer than that meted out to Wang Dan. I really don't understand it at all. . . . I shall meet with my attorney tomorrow or the day after to consider whether I should appeal. To be sure, it is only a formality. The dish had long ago been prepared for me to swallow."

All of the lesser actors were jailed, but no charges were ever brought against Fei Yuan, the principal organizer of the escapes of both Wang Juntao and Chen Ziming. The suspicion that his role had been a sinister one only tended to grow when the members of the Wuhan escape network were brought to trial, since the PSB took great pains to conceal his identity, and the judges mentioned him in their April 19 verdict only as "Fei X."

To finalize the trial proceedings, the Party turned its attention to the lawyers who had the temerity to defend Wang and Chen. It was bad enough that the defense attorneys had ignored the Party's earlier warnings, but worse that they now seemed intent on appealing the cases.

As soon as Chen's lawyers, Ji Suwan and Gao Xiaofen, agreed to argue his case before a higher court, they were told that their licenses were being withdrawn for "reregistration." Wang Juntao's lawyers were also pressured. Hou Xiaotian told friends that when she tried to reach Zhang Sizhi at his office, she was curtly informed that he had left Beijing to avoid "unnecessary troubles." His partner, Sun Yachen, had been given a furious reception when he returned to his hometown of Luoyang after the trial. No sooner was he off the train than he was summoned to see the cadre in charge of the local Justice Ministry. Why had he ignored the warnings of higher authorities? the cadre demanded to know. Why had he refused to submit the contents of his defense in advance, as the ministry required? His trip to Beijing had been "erroneous," and things would go badly for him if he breathed a word of the case to anyone. Sun was not a man easily cowed. He retorted that he fully intended to represent Wang on appeal and would agree to keep the case confidential only if the Party promised to take no reprisals against him. This impertinence went too far, and the ministry's Party committee informed Sun that he was forbidden to travel to Beijing again. It also told him that his right to state housing was being withdrawn, a much-favored weapon in a country where apartments are in short supply.

Hou Xiaotian declared that she would pursue the case herself, even though she knew little of the law.[7] But it was a futile gesture.

On March 18, the Beijing People's High Court ruled that it found no reason not to "uphold the original sentences" against Wang and Chen.

Back in their prison cells in Qincheng, both Chen Ziming and Wang Juntao did what came most naturally to them: they wrote. Chen composed an eloquent forty-thousand-character essay summarizing the arguments he had used in the courtroom. Echoing Confucius, he wrote, "He who wins the people's hearts, wins all under heaven. But he who wishes to win the people's hearts must first win the hearts of the scholars. This is a clear lesson from ancient times. . . ."

But there was no bitterness. "Regardless of how much I am misunderstood, wronged, or subjected to injustice, I will maintain love in the face of hate, return anger with love, and consistently treat those in power as comrades and friends. . . .

"If I were asked to choose between personal freedom and truth, I would, without any hesitation, choose the latter. I love my wife, parents, sisters and brothers, and my friends deeply, and I hope to be reunited with them all soon. But I will not sacrifice truth or abandon my moral integrity, treating them as a mere means of exchange. . . .

"I will always keep my self-confident smile, my oceans-wide good intentions, my backbone as erect as a pine tree, and I will continue to believe firmly that the strength and heat of love can melt even the hardest and most frozen of hearts.

"I firmly believe that it is no crime to discuss the affairs of the nation, to participate in politics, to uphold the Constitution and to support reform; the real crimes are those of fabricating information, making false charges against loyal people and scheming to turn the clock back. In the final analysis, the people will give the fullest verdict on who it was who committed the crime against history.

"The 1989 student movement was a moment in Chinese history that will be the subject of songs and tears.

"The tide of reform and modernization cannot be halted."

Wang Juntao, meanwhile, wrote a letter to thank his lawyers for their "outstanding" work. Like Chen, he displayed more sorrow than bitterness. "I feel sad," he began, "when I see that so many leaders and sponsors of the movement, when facing the consequences, dare not shoulder their responsibility.[8] They will certainly suffer less themselves as a result. But what about the dead?

"The dead are unable to defend themselves. Many of them intended to fight for China and her people, for truth and justice. I decided to take my chances to defend some of their points, even if I did not agree with all of them all the time. I know that my penalty was more serious because of this action. But only by doing so can the dead rest in peace. . . . The trial has brought me a sort of relief and consolation. I once again have a clear conscience. . . .

"Yet what I am most concerned about is the loss of spirit and morality of our nation. I was surprised by much of the testimony that was given. I do not want to get into the superiority or inferiority of particular individuals. What I value is whether a human spirit has nobility—a noble and pure soul.

"In China, even intellectuals lack it. As soon as political pressure comes, the entire professional stratum of people freezes, their professionalism paralyzed. This is intolerable, especially when dealing with the law, a most sacred and solemn profession. See, after such an enormous disturbance in 1989, how few people face trial and how even fewer are speaking their conscience.[9]

"At this point I am afraid that our generation is not as good as the one that came before it. . . . I respect our elder generation very much, and it is ironic today that I should have faced sentencing at their hands. They had more devotion and determination in their time than we have in ours. They also have less tolerance and kindness.

"I will not yet come to any conclusions about old Deng or Li Peng. If there is something to be sad or upset about today, it is the troubled spirit of our generation. . . .

"I have one more request. Please help me console Xiaotian. Help her calm down and not make unnecessary trouble, to say nothing of violating the law. She should remain in control of herself. I have been trying to act conscientiously and calmly, suppressing personal feelings. She should do the same. Dear sirs, I have no one else to write to and trust. Please excuse me for making such demands of you. I am very sorry.

"Thank you once again. I wish you a happy Spring Festival!"

20

Petitioners

Mycobacterium tuberculosis acts slowly. The onset of the disease can take as long as two years after first exposure to airborne droplets from the cough of someone who is infected. But the symptoms eventually began, just as Han Dongfang had feared they would after the warden at Paoju Lane had thrown him into the contagious diseases unit, where he had spent four miserable months. First came the fever, the drenching night sweats, the malaise, and the weight loss. Then there was the sudden, frightening feeling of air starvation, the racking pain in the chest wall, and the foul, discolored sputum that doctors call "green oysters."

Han was in Qincheng prison by the time the symptoms began in earnest. This was his third place of internment. In March 1990, when he was formally charged as a counterrevolutionary, the Public Security Bureau transferred Han from Paoju Lane to the harsh Banbuqiao detention center. In November 1990, they moved him to Qincheng to await trial. His illness was an irritating complication for the authorities. Han was an uncooperative prisoner at the best of times, but now he threatened to derail their plans for bringing him to trial. By February 1991, when the prosecution case against him was ready, Han's health had gone rapidly downhill. He had trouble walking, his heartbeat raced, and speech came only with great difficulty. For long hours each day he lay on his cot in leg irons, semiconscious and shaking with a 104-degree fever. To make matters worse, the doctors in Qincheng showed no interest in finding out what was wrong with him. With his sickness undiagnosed and untreated, Han slipped deeper into fever and delirium.

As the weeks dragged on, the PSB grew seriously alarmed. One of their most celebrated political prisoners appeared to be dying on the eve of his trial. The black hands trials of January and February had provoked a flurry of diplomatic criticism, and although Han Dongfang was still an unknown name to most Chinese, his case was attracting some notoriety abroad. In Washington, a fresh round of debate was imminent on renewing China's Most Favored Nation (MFN) trade status, and there was much talk of attaching human rights conditions.

On April 10, a pretrial investigator from Qincheng arrived unexpectedly at Han's home in Xibiaobei *hutong*. "Your husband is gravely ill," he told Chen Jingyun. "He wants you to come and visit him. It's a matter of some urgency. We can leave right away." This was the first time since his arrest that the authorities had allowed any contact between Han and his family.

A divisional chief of State Security was waiting in the car. A female procurator went along as well. The chief seemed worried. Did the prisoner have a history of chronic illness? he wanted to know. Had his condition perhaps been brought on by the hunger strikes in Tiananmen Square? Chen Jingyun bristled at the insinuation that her husband was responsible for his own disease. The chief warned her that she should say nothing to anyone about Han Dongfang's case.

After driving for less than an hour, the car drew up outside a building near Shahezhen, northwest of Beijing. A sign identified it as Military Hospital Number 261. A guard led her to an isolation ward off a small courtyard. Two soldiers wearing face masks stood guard at the door. Inside the room was an anxious-looking warden who had accompanied Han from Qincheng. Han himself lay motionless on the bed, an intravenous drip attached to his arm. He was emaciated and weak but mentally alert and able to speak in a whisper.

Han explained haltingly that they had moved him here two weeks earlier. Number 261 was not the first facility they had tried; several public security hospitals had refused to admit him for fear of contagion. He was getting three meals a day, he went on, rice gruel for breakfast, rice with meat and vegetables for lunch, steamed *wotou* with more meat and vegetables for dinner. But most of the food was inedible. At first they had put him on frequent supplies of oxygen; now he was only on the IV and a low-grade antibiotic called *hongmeisu,* erythromycin. It did not appear to be helping.

Since no doctor was on hand, there was no way for Han's wife to glean any information about what was actually wrong with him. And since the man from State Security, the procurator, the Qincheng warden, and a guard remained clustered warily around Han's bed the whole time, it was also impossible for Chen to ask him anything that might appear sensitive. At one point, however, Han whispered to his wife that none of her letters had gotten through. And he managed to add, "You know I have a bad temper. I often used to lose my temper at home. Well, I'm still the same. I haven't changed." Chen realized what he was trying to tell her and smiled inwardly at the thought of the prison authorities being on the receiving end of her husband's stubborn defiance as they pressed futilely for him to repent of his crimes. After an hour, the man from State Security motioned that it was time to leave. Leaving Han two hundred *yuan* ($35) and some fresh fruit, Chen promised him that she would be back.

A few days later, Chen Jingyun was called back to State Security. "We have a diagnosis," they informed her. On the basis of a single X ray, the doctors at Hospital Number 261 had concluded that Han was suffering from Legionnaires' disease, and they proceeded to treat him accordingly.

On April 24, Chen was called to the hospital again. She found the patient a little brighter this time and the security less obtrusive. A different military guard was on duty, and he stood off at a distance. "What's going on?" she asked her husband.

"The guy who was on guard last time you came is sick," he smiled. "They think he's got Legionnaires' too. This new guard is terrified of coming near me."

In the more relaxed atmosphere they were able to talk more freely. Chen told her husband to keep his spirits up. There was a lot of international pressure concerning his case. In fact, former U.S. President Jimmy Carter had been in Beijing the week before and had called for Han's release in a speech to a class of future Chinese diplomats. This was understood to be another salvo in the dispute over MFN.

"Don't worry about me," Han replied. "There's nothing wrong with my spirits." In fact, he said, during the lucid spells when he was not laid low with fever, he even took a grim pleasure in the war of nerves with his captors, telling them that the prison doctors were incompetent and that he refused to undergo the treatment they prescribed. "I told them, I won't kill myself, but if you don't treat me properly I will die, and then we'll see what happens to you." Interrogators from the Beijing prosecutor's office showed up at the military hospital after his admission, he continued. "I was on oxygen when they got here," Han said, "and I couldn't talk. So I asked them for a piece of paper and just wrote on it, 'I refuse to cooperate.'"

Han's high-risk tactics paid off. Fearful that he really would die in jail, the authorities backed down. On April 28, Han's family received a call to say that they could collect him and take him home. This was not a release, the PSB pointed out; it was a temporary discharge on medical grounds.[1] None of the charges had been dropped. In fact, to add insult to injury, the prisoner would not be handed over until his wife agreed to sign a pledge to pay all his medical expenses.

Han's family took him to a private physician at Beijing's Capital Hospital, which had been known in Mao's time as the Anti-Imperialist Hospital. It was one of the city's best. They showed the doctor the X ray, which the Ministry of State Security had finally agreed to hand over after considerable delay and difficulty. The doctor held it up to the light screen; the upper lobe of the right lung was ravaged with infection. "But they told you it was Legionnaires' disease?" the doctor asked scornfully. "There's no way you can pin that down from just an X ray. We'll have to do additional tests." He prescribed an initial course of antibiotics. The bill came to five hundred *yuan* ($87), or four months' salary.

But the drugs seemed to make little difference. Back in his own bed, Han drifted in and out of a restless sleep. His fever still raged, and his body was convulsed by uncontrollable bouts of coughing. Each day he seemed to grow a little weaker. After two anxious weeks, his family decided that they had to risk seeking outside assistance. Through personal contacts in Hong Kong, they secured an offer of help from an American physician, Dr. David S. Fedson of the University of Virginia.

Dr. Fedson arrived in Beijing on May 19. A cautious and discreet man, he spent the evening reviewing his options. Meet the patient directly either at his home or in a safe house? Unwise, the doctor thought; the family had been warned unambiguously about contact with foreigners, and the patient himself was still bound to be under police surveillance. In any case, it would be hard to arrive at a diagnosis without access to the medical records. Make a direct approach to the physician at Capital Hospital? Not a good idea either; the man would be sure to regard this as an unprofessional intrusion. The only option that remained was to arrange for the patient to be seen by another doctor. This seemed altogether the best plan; it would not jeopardize anything that had already been achieved, and it would give the benefit of a second opinion.

The next morning Dr. Fedson went to the Beijing Union Medical College, whose doctors had run the emergency tents on Tiananmen Square during the 1989 protests. Mutual friends had given him the name of a helpful professor there. But one of the man's colleagues explained that he was out of town for a week. Could someone else be of assistance, perhaps? The situation was a little delicate, Dr. Fedson explained. "I have a friend who has a friend who is seriously ill, and he needs to see a senior physician as soon as possible, within the next day or two." The Chinese doctor was guarded. "Why doesn't your 'friend' come to the emergency room and see a resident?" he asked. Dr. Fedson insisted quietly that a more senior consultant would be advisable in this case. The Chinese doctor hesitated and studied his visitor carefully. Then suddenly, he broke into a broad grin.

"Yale Medical School?" he asked.

"Excuse me?"

"Your tie," he pointed. "I was there too."

The problem, it appeared, was solved. The professor left the room and returned after a few minutes, smiling. "It's all arranged," he said. "The Deputy Chairman of the Medical Department will see your 'friend' at three-thirty. Why don't we talk this evening, and I'll let you know what he thinks."

At about eight that night the professor called Dr. Fedson at his hotel. "We have the sputum test results from Capital Hospital," he announced. "It's TB; couldn't be clearer."

As Han began his slow recovery with proper medication, news of the outside world began to trickle in, initially from his wife and sister, and then from the first cautious visitors, old friends of Han's from the Beijing Railways Bureau. They told him about the dozens of workers publicly executed for their roles in the 1989 protests. The government had singled out two intellectuals, Chen Ziming and Wang Juntao, as the black hands of the movement. Han took the news grimly, remembering the two men from the meeting of the Capital Joint Liaison Group that he had attended.

He asked for news of his colleagues from the BWAF, but there was not much to tell. He Lili was free. Liu Qiang was in jail.[2] Did he remember Zhao Hongliang, the former bus conductor, and Lü Jinghua, the determined young woman who had run the BWAF's broadcasting station? Both of them had fled the country. Li Jinjin had been seen with his wife in Wuhan, although the authorities had never officially announced his release. Most of the other members of the old standing committee had simply vanished. Somebody told him that Solidarity had won the national elections in Poland. Who could have imagined such a thing? When was that? Han asked. On June 4, 1989, he was told—the very day that the Chinese democracy movement was being crushed.

Solidarity's victory at the ballot box had done nothing to diminish Deng Xiaoping's unease. The birth of the Polish union, he continued to stress in internal Party speeches, had been the single most important factor behind the dissent in Eastern Europe. The paramount leader felt that the balance sheet from the 1989 events showed the need for vigilance rather than panic. The events in Tiananmen Square showed how quickly things could get out of hand. There were two main lessons to be drawn from the affair, Deng thought. The ACFTU had proven itself to be less than reliable under stress, and the Party now needed to devote renewed attention to official union matters. At the same time, the security services needed to crack down hard on any new signs of working-class dissent the moment they appeared.

For the third time in his career, the cautious liberal Zhu Houze, who had donated ACFTU funds to the student hunger strikers but stepped back from the idea of a general strike, was purged from his post. A hard-line ideologue from Shandong Province, Yang Xingfu, took over effective control of the union's affairs. On his appointment as ACFTU vice-president in December 1989, Yang immediately announced that only "trustworthy Marxists" would be allowed to rise to senior positions, and he stepped up efforts to weed out "disloyal" cadres. At the same time, the Communist Party beefed up its own organizing, propaganda, and intelligence activities at the shop-floor level.

The intelligence services appeared to disagree among themselves on the extent of the threat they faced. Toward the end of 1990, obedient to Deng Xiaoping's instructions, both the Public Security Bureau and the Ministry of State Security handed the Politburo their assessments of the mood in China's factories. The PSB was cautiously optimistic. Although the working class harbored a number of bad elements who should be dealt with, the overall situation appeared to be stable. The economy was back on track. Inflation, which had triggered so much of the unrest in 1989, was under control. There would be no repeat of what had happened in Eastern Europe. The MSS, China's equivalent of the KGB, was less sanguine. "We cannot afford to underestimate the impact and effects of the international situation on our country's working class," State Security reported. Besides, "hostile forces inside and outside the country have switched their focus of activities from university students to the working masses." The MSS had evidence of underground workers' groups in at least a half dozen provinces, and its report cited thousands of instances of assassinations, sabotage, mysterious explosions, and "reactionary slogans."

State Security's gloomy assessment may have been closer to the mark. In December 1991, the Chinese security services and leaders of the judicial system held a joint conference to discuss the status of domestic unrest. The bland reports of the meeting from the official Xinhua News Agency betrayed a lingering anxiety. General Secretary Jiang Zemin called on the security forces to "keep a clear head" and "maintain sharp vigilance" against the forces of "peaceful evolution." Premier Li Peng went further, asking for "resolute measures" to quell "the sabotage activities of hostile elements."

In fact, dissident workers' groups had been responsible for a number of strikes during 1981, including one in a factory with one thousand workers that had been called off only after the personal intercession of Beijing Mayor Chen Xitong. The secret police had seized a number of illegal pamphlets and magazines that these groups had published, and many of the "hostile elements" had been "uprooted." However, silencing them altogether was not proving to be easy.[3] Many of the new organizations had learned the bitter lessons of 1989 and were operating deep underground in the strictest secrecy, like the Communist Party cells of old. Some took the form of discussion groups or salons, meeting discreetly in the homes of individual members.

The Communist Party was particularly alarmed by the underground organizations it detected in Beijing itself—a dozen or more, State Security estimated, each of them with anywhere from twenty to three hundred members. At least two were modeled explicitly on Polish Solidarity, and one even had the audacity to use the same name. The secretive new groups did not call for the overthrow of the government; they said their aim was to build a new worker-based political party, one that would champion "real democracy." In January 1992, in one of the boldest acts of dissent since the Beijing massacre, a group calling itself the Preparatory Committee of the Free China Union sent an outspoken manifesto to hundreds of workplaces controlled by the official ACFTU.

"Free trade unions are emerging everywhere from the soil of China like bamboo shoots after a spring rain," the document declared. "What does it matter if the authorities refuse to recognize and authorize our own union? . . . Didn't Polish Solidarity get banned and suppressed ten years ago? What were the results? Solidarity won, and their oppressor fell." The document urged caution, however: "Do not try to look for a free trade union to join. Do not be discovered by the secret police in the course of expanding our network. Do not treat the free trade union as a forum for idle talk."

Han Dongfang was savvy enough to keep his distance from these new underground labor activists, although some of them sent out discreet feelers to him. He realized that any kind of contact would only be asking for trouble. The police had already visited Han at home several times. On the third occasion, he snapped at them to go away and stay away: "Every time I see a police uniform," he told them, "it makes me feel sick." Surprisingly enough, the PSB kept its distance after that, although it made no secret of its continued routine surveillance.

As the winter gave way to the first mild days of spring in 1992, Han began to feel better. One lung was badly damaged, and he tired easily. He rarely got a good night's sleep, and sometimes the raging fevers returned. But he felt strong enough to resume his lonely battle with the Communist Party. Having studied China's new, post-Tiananmen Law on Assemblies, Parades, and Demonstrations, Han decided to test its limits. In the middle of March, he made an unusual request to the police. He wanted to ride his bicycle in a one-man protest from his home in Xibiaobei *hutong* to the Fengtai Railyard, his old workplace, and then back north, in a circle around Tiananmen Square, before ending up outside the Great Hall of the People, where the National People's Congress was in session. He intended to hand out leaflets with two demands. First, he wished to condemn China's new draft labor law, which represented no real advance on the old legislation of 1950, and to petition the NPC to allow workers to join trade unions of their own choice.[4] Second, he wished to request that the Beijing Railway Bureau guarantee proper health benefits to its workers, including notably the two thousand *yuan* ($350) for his own medical expenses. In deference to the Party's sensibilities, he promised, he would refrain from shouting any slogans.

As he had during the Tiananmen Square protests, Han continued to behave as if pure principle were all that mattered. "Speak truth to power" might have been his motto, even if the power had subjected him to a two-year ordeal that had almost killed him. Not that Han was a reckless naïf. When the police refused his request, as he knew they would, and resumed their threatening visits to his home, he sought protection by granting his first well-timed, high-profile interviews with the Western press. "If the law allows me to do something, I'll do it," he told one reporter. "If it doesn't allow me to do it, then I'll press for a new law." On April 16, 1992, the skinny boy from the dirt-poor peasant village in Shanxi Province even made the front page of the *New York Times*.

When Han Dongfang was admitted to Military Hospital Number 261, wasted by his untreated TB, he had no idea that he was in the very emergency room that Wang Juntao had occupied just a few weeks earlier after coming down with hepatitis B. In the weeks following his trial and sentencing in February 1991, Wang's health showed no improvement.

On April 2, seven weeks after their trials, both Wang and Chen Ziming were told that a bus was waiting to transfer them from Qincheng to Beijing Prison Number 2. To the untrained eye, the building resembles a factory, set amid open fields southeast of the capital. But the conditions at Number 2 made Qincheng seem as luxurious as the Great Wall Sheraton Hotel.

Guards led Wang and Chen down a long corridor to two identical *xiao hao,* small punishment cells. Chinese law is studiedly murky on the matter of solitary confinement. It usually lasts for seven to ten days; fifteen days is the maximum period allowed by law. But Wang and Chen were to spend several months in their *xiao hao.* Bao Zunxin and Wang Dan were held in similar quarters down the hallway.

And what quarters they were. These were prison cells contrived to break the psyche and crush the spirit of rebellion. The very proportions were grotesque; each cell was no more than seven feet square but with an inordinately high ceiling. It was like being enclosed in an oversized, upended coffin. A single naked 40-watt bulb hung about fifteen feet above the bed and burned only when the guards decided to turn it on, which was a matter of whim. Otherwise, the only light came from a tiny window on one wall, high above an iron door that opened to a small exercise yard.

The window slit was also the only ventilation, and it did almost nothing to ward off the suffocating stench from the open sewer that served as a toilet. The unheated cell contained nothing but a wooden bed platform and a cold water tap. In the winter, when Wang and Chen arrived, an icy wind howled down the corridor; the guards wore two overcoats against the chill. Then, as spring turned to summer, the cell became an oven. If it rained, the ventilation slit leaked and the encrusted grime on the floor turned to black slime. The bare wooden platform that served as a bed was mushy and pitted with rot. It was also home to every kind of crawling insect—mites, ticks, fleas, bedbugs, lice, cockroaches—and the two men's bodies were soon a mass of bites that turned into infected open sores. Chen was tormented by a scaling rash that covered his head and neck with crusted, reddish-yellow eruptions. But neither man was allowed a change of clothing. Wang requested a washbasin and soap, but the guards refused.

Beginning in mid-May of 1991, Hou Xiaotian was allowed a single monthly visit of half an hour to Beijing Number 2. She spent the time stiffly in the company of Wang's parents, who had never approved of their son's political activities or his marriage choice. The family brought food for Wang, but it was usually confiscated. They asked for brighter lighting, a desk, and a chair so that Wang could study. No need for that, the prison authorities said briskly. He'll soon be put to work in the fields; no time for reading then. When Hou complained about her husband's solitary confinement, they told her that it had been imposed for his own good: So incensed were the other prisoners by his counterrevolutionary plotting that he had to be kept in isolation for his own safety. When she protested that Wang was being denied the medical treatment he required, they blandly told her that the prison files showed no record of any illness. The authorities at Qincheng had made no mention of Wang's hepatitis in approving his transfer to Number 2.

Wang himself complained incessantly, but the more he did, the more his jailers were convinced of his bad attitude. He wrote dozens of letters to high officials, including the Party security boss, Qiao Shi, but they were never answered. He begged the guards to pass on word to their superiors, but they never brought any reply. In his despair, he pounded on the iron door of his cell and screamed into the silence of the corridor until he was hoarse and breathless. The guards responded by handcuffing him. But he did finally achieve two small concessions. The guards allowed him to receive a little of the food that his mother brought to supplement the prison rations. And the warden consented to a blood test, which confirmed what he already knew, that he had hepatitis. It was now June 30, and he had languished for three months without treatment. Two weeks later, Hou Xiaotian was told that she could bring him medicine if she wished. But what good is that, she demanded, if there is no doctor to supervise the treatment? Hou was in despair when she saw Wang, weak and emaciated, during this, her third monthly visit. "Death would be better than this kind of life," she wept.

Despite his enfeebled condition, Wang told his wife and parents that he saw no other way to press his demands but through a hunger strike. His parents threw up their hands in horror and said it would surely kill him. In deference to them he agreed to hold off for a month. But when August 13 came around, the date of the next visit, both Hou Xiaotian and Wang Zhihong learned that their visiting rights had been withdrawn. "You have told foreign correspondents and other people made-up stories about the situation in the prison," the two women were informed. "You have violated the administrative law of prisons; no one is allowed to invent stories about prison life." Hou could regain her privileges, she was told, if she would agree to write a signed corrective account in the official *People's Daily*. She refused. A self-criticism, then, the authorities insisted. Hou offered only a limited one. She acknowledged her contacts with the foreign press but denied that there was anything wrong in this. The episode took its toll on Hou's health, however, and for the second time since her own release from jail she was hospitalized, this time for a week, suffering from erratic heart rhythms.

On August 14, the day after the scheduled family visit, Wang Juntao refused further food until he was given proper medical care. Down the hall, the news reached Chen Ziming via the prison grapevine and he, too, declared a hunger strike in sympathy with his old friend. Their actions were in many ways less remarkable than the response of the Chinese government.

Deng Xiaoping's policy of opening China up to the outside world had brought all sorts of effects, many of them unintended and undesirable. For all the official fulminations about "hostile foreign forces," this was no longer the closed, impenetrable China of Mao's time. "Things foreign should serve China," Mao had said, but neither he nor Deng had ever resolved the dilemma of how to separate the "good" foreign influences from the "bad." How was China to secure Western technology without bourgeois liberalization, or trade without peaceful evolution?

International pressure could not simply be wished away. Deng's program of economic reform, which had never wavered from its course, despite Tiananmen, depended on China's being accepted as a trading partner and a member in good standing of polite international society. For most of Deng's decade in power, he enjoyed a love affair with the West. The United States, with the full force of its missionary innocence, embraced this little man who had buried the legacy of Maoism. The curious concept of "human rights," thanks to President Jimmy Carter, had hovered at the edges of U.S. foreign policy during Deng's early years, but it was never used as a weapon against China. As Deng liked to say, we imprisoned Wei Jingsheng and the West stood mute.

But with Tiananmen, and with the crumbling of the Soviet empire, the world had changed. Insincere though it often was, the language of human rights was now embedded in the policy-making machinery of most Western nations. Those changes were, in essence, what Tiananmen Square had been all about: rights that were based on the sanctity of the individual citizen rather than the collective rights promised by Mao and Deng. Chen Ziming and Wang Juntao had now become something of a cause célèbre beyond China's borders, even though they had never been out of the country themselves. International human rights groups campaigned for their release. Editorials about their plight appeared in the *New York Times*. The *Wall Street Journal* championed them, if with dubious logic, as heralds of Western capitalism in China.[5] Delegations of parliamentarians visiting China invariably inquired about them. Foreign Ministry officials were forced into the unfamiliar and distasteful position of having to comment on the conditions of their confinement.

The question of how to deal with the outcry over Chen and Wang's hunger strike fell to Li Ruihuan, the Politburo member responsible for propaganda. Li was one of the new crop of younger Communist leaders, the "Third Echelon" promoted to the Party hierarchy by Deng in 1985. He and these younger leaders were the kind of figures that Chen Ziming and Wang Juntao had looked to as the eventual successor generation to Deng and the old guard.

Li issued instructions for selected Chinese media to rebut the Western charges that Wang and Chen were being ill treated. In mid-September of 1991, the Beijing bureaus of the Cable News Network and the British Broadcasting Corporation received a surprising offer from Central China Television. Might they be interested in some exclusive footage of the famous counterrevolutionaries Chen Ziming and Wang Juntao in their comfortable prison quarters?

The video clips, broadcast across the world, showed Chen Ziming, in a white shirt and shorts, sitting in a chair. He was thin but otherwise did not appear unwell. Wang Juntao was filmed in a hospital setting. Dressed in a blue-and-white striped pajama top and blue sweatpants with white piping, he got up from his seat with an amiable smile to be weighed on a doctor's scales. Still photographs followed: Chen Ziming, dressed in a blue-and-white knitted cardigan over a blue sweater, a white open-necked shirt, and pale blue T-shirt, standing, with his characteristic half smile, in front of a shelf stacked high with books; Wang Juntao, looking puffy and overweight in a heavy down coat, seated among a large group of young men in dark blue prison uniforms; most of them are laughing, while Wang smiles a little, as if at a private joke.

The foreign-language services of the Xinhua News Agency produced a series of earnest dispatches on the virtues of the Chinese prison system. One story explained that Wang and Chen had been placed in isolation cells "so that they can familiarize themselves with the prison regulations and reflect on their crimes for further remolding." The recently constructed Beijing Number 2 was a benign place, said the North American edition of the *Beijing Review*. "The buildings are neatly designed and constructed, and the rooms are tidy and clean. Without the electrified barbed wire on the walls, it could be mistaken for a newly built residential quarter." Another report argued that it was inconceivable that the prisoners could be in poor health, since "China's prisons deal with matters strictly in accordance with the law and stick to revolutionary humanitarianism." Each man was receiving 19,000 grams of food per month and 250 grams of edible oil, the same as ordinary Beijing residents.

Medical bulletins were also issued, offering excruciating detail, based on interviews with Dr. Mo Yishen of the Central Hospital of the Beijing Reform-Through-Labor Administration. Yes, Dr. Mo confirmed, both Wang Juntao and Chen Ziming had been given a number of checkups since being admitted to Number 2 Prison. Chen's most recent physical examination had resulted in a diagnosis of seborrheic dermatitis, for which ointment had been prescribed. "The report by some overseas media organs that Chen is suffering from a disease that has been festering from his back to his head and endangering his internal organs is absolutely an alarmist talk." As for Wang, a checkup on July 24 "showed that [his] heart, stomach, spleen, and kidneys were functioning normally. His liver functions were normal except for the SGPT [a liver enzyme], which was slightly elevated. His urine, excrement, and blood were also normal." Because Wang had continued to complain of liver pains, he was given another checkup on August 22, Dr. Mo went on. "The result showed that, of all the thirty indexes of Wang's liver functions, seven including the GPT were higher than normal, while the rest, such as HBSAG [Hepatitis B Surface Antigen], were normal. The examination showed there were signs of a relapse of hepatitis." But Dr. Mo's clinical opinion was "that this might stem from Wang's irregular eating in the recent time." Deputy director Li Jinghai of Number 2 Prison added that Wang would soon be moved to "a better hospital for further examination and necessary treatment."

For Hou Xiaotian, the blackest period was over. Official harassment eased. The cruel whispers that she was trying to be "China's Winnie Mandela" stopped. Her bitter estrangement from Wang's parents ended as they saw the results of her efforts. Although the authorities still complained about Chen Ziming's "bad attitude," they moved him out of solitary confinement to share a cell with three other inmates. Wang Juntao was transferred to a prison hospital at Yanqing, in the hills northwest of Beijing, where the video footage was almost certainly shot. He was given an entire floor to himself and allowed plenty of fresh air. He began to eat better. The authorities even allowed him to have a television in his room. His guards listened for hours to his reminiscences of fifteen years in the democracy movement. At Spring Festival 1992, Wang sent cards to each of his guards and interrogators. He wrote, "I bear you no grudge; I feel no animosity. I think of us as friends, not enemies."

"China abides by its own laws to administer prisoners," a Justice Ministry official told the *Beijing Review*. "This is China's internal affair." But there was a strong element of wishful thinking in the official's defiance. Whether the Communist Party liked it or not, the fates of its most celebrated political prisoners were now woven into the fabric of China's difficult relationship with the world beyond its borders.

Even after the bloodletting of June 4, many refused to surrender to the Party's authority. The effort to silence them went on relentlessly, although concealed—to the best of the Party's ability—from the prying eyes of a hostile outside world. The domestic propaganda machine, likewise, had little interest in publicizing the continued cycle of arrests and trials, since these only reminded people that dissident activity still continued. The official line demanded that the book be closed on the 1989 movement with the trials that took place a year and a half later. After that, it was time for the broad masses to go home, eat the rich foods of Spring Festival, and forget about the whole troubling episode.

But in one case after another, evidence filtered out of China to confirm that the official line was fiction. Clandestine pro-democracy journals, mimeographed in tiny numbers, were passed from hand to hand. Cautious support groups of former political prisoners, sometimes legally registered as *getihu,* formed to exchange information and organize material support for those left jobless and indigent. Countless instances of passive resistance occurred, of *danwei* closing ranks to shield dissident members from the scrutiny of the security forces. And as the security chief Qiao Shi divulged, there were outbursts of working-class protest on all sides.

It was inevitable that such outbursts would continue, for they were bred in the bone of Deng Xiaoping's China. Social scientists struggled to find a term that would adequately describe the bizarre hybrid system that Deng had created. Officially, the system was called "socialism with Chinese characteristics," but as Zhao Ziyang had remarked, no one could say quite what that meant. Others called it "market Stalinism." As Chen Ziming had grasped, the tragedy of the Deng years was that the old man refused to accept that he could not smash the "iron rice bowl" in the name of economic growth without allowing channels for the anger that the loss of old securities would provoke. Deng's economic reforms had created a new China, one that had moved beyond the sterile doctrines of class struggle. Whether the patriarch liked it or not, China was on the way to becoming a modern, plural society; yet every effort to embrace that pluralism was uprooted as ruthlessly as Mao had uprooted the "poisonous weeds" of "ideological deviation." Chen and Wang believed that China could grow and prosper, and become truly modern, only if its leaders would learn how to listen to the divergent opinions of independent thinkers. But as Chen had written from his prison cell, "A small number of shortsighted people in power cannot see the importance of the intellectual stratum for political and social development. They think that as long as you hold the gun-stock, you can hold dominion over the rivers and the mountains."

Although the government opened up entire areas of the economy to the untrammeled play of market forces, it still responded in only one way to the flickerings of dissent: by destroying them the instant they appeared. One tiny clandestine group after another was uprooted: A Committee to Protect Human Rights in China, founded the day after the Beijing massacre, was smashed in its infancy. The short-lived Study Group on Human Rights Issues, based in Shanghai, was also broken, and its leaders were arrested and held incommunicado. A young student at People's University was secretly arrested for trying to publish a dissident magazine on campus; another group of students in the ancient capital of Xi'an was arrested for sending a telegram of congratulations to Mikhail Gorbachev after the failure of the August 1991 coup in the Soviet Union.

Sometimes the punishment was even more savage than it had been for the leaders of the 1989 movement. Persistence, in China, only compounded the crime of dissidence. In early 1990, two former Beijing students, Chen Yanbin and Zhang Yafei, formed a group they called the Chinese Revolutionary Democratic Front. They mimeographed four hundred copies of a journal named *Tieliu* (*Iron Current*), which condemned the Communist Party as "an authoritarian tyranny" and described forty years of Marxism as "China's pitfall and calamity." But Chen and Zhang eluded the police for only a few months. They had set forth "a reactionary political program with the abolition of the Four Cardinal Principles as its central content," the Beijing Intermediate People's Court ruled. They had "put forward a reactionary organizational principle" and were guilty of "organizing and leading a counterrevolutionary clique." The court concluded that "The crimes are serious, their nature sinister, the offense grave." For Chen Yanbin, the sentence was sixteen years in jail; for Zhang Yafei, eleven. But not even these draconian punishments could silence dissent.

All these activities, though apparently unconnected, were joined to a set of common concerns and ideals. If the ideal could be summed up in a single word, it was the idea of *gongmin,* the citizen. The ideal first emerged, in a raw and formless fashion, among the petitioners who thronged Beijing in the early days of Deng Xiaoping's rule, demanding redress for the arbitrary injustices of the Cultural Revolution. But it crystallized for the first time in China's history during the 1989 protests in Tiananmen Square. The *gongmin* had certain inalienable rights; the *gongmin* did not kowtow to emperors. The legal scholars at the forefront of the 1989 movement, men like Chen Xiaoping and Li Jinjin, used their classrooms at Politics and Law University as platforms to argue that the individual civil rights of the *gongmin* could only be safeguarded through the rule of law.

The civil lawsuit—the tort case, in Western legal parlance—became the latest and most novel form of challenge to arbitrary state power in the years after Tiananmen. The most celebrated action was brought by China's former Culture Minister, Wang Meng, who announced in September 1991 that he was suing a literary paper for printing a reader's letter that denounced his short story, "Thin Porridge," as an example of bourgeois liberalization. From his personal experience (exiled to Xinjiang for twenty years by Mao as a rightist), Wang knew that obscure literary feuds of this sort often heralded ruinous political campaigns. At about the same time, Zhang Weiguo, former Beijing correspondent for the liberal *World Economic Herald* of Shanghai, declared that he intended to sue the Public Security Bureau for endangering his livelihood by subjecting him to improper surveillance and threats. "I must protect my basic human rights," Zhang told a friend.[6]

Han Dongfang also continued to be stirred by the desire for individual rights. Soon after his unsuccessful attempt to stage a one-man bicycle protest outside the Great Hall of the People, Han found an eviction notice nailed to the door of his tumbledown courtyard house. When he arrived at the local People's Court for a hearing on the case, he was attacked by security guards, beaten, kicked, shocked with an electric cattle prod, and thrown into a holding cell. Han ended up in the hospital once more, seriously ill, but he still summoned the will to file a demand that the procurator's office investigate the court officials for alleged assault and battery and illegal detention.

For Hou Xiaotian, too, life had become a series of skirmishes in an unending guerrilla war. But her spirits did not flag. Although she had lost her government job, friends found ways of channeling funds that allowed her to go on campaigning. Hou seemed to lead a charmed existence as the only person in Beijing willing to speak to the foreign press about human rights issues. On one of her monthly visits to the Yanqing prison hospital in early 1992, she requested an extension of her visiting hours so that she and Wang

Juntao might consult on some legal matters. Although they knew that it was absurd to expect any Chinese court to grant them a hearing, they explored a number of possible cases: an appeal to the Supreme Court to recover the money and personal effects confiscated from Wang on his arrest in Changsha; separate libel suits against the Public Security Bureau and the Xinhua News Agency for false and defamatory comments.

Hou was still tormented by the thought that Wang might die in jail and petitioned the authorities continually for his release on medical grounds. Perhaps if he develops liver cancer or cirrhosis, was the flippant response from Justice Minister Cai Cheng; Hou knew that both diseases were a distinct possibility if the hepatitis went unchecked. She accused Wang's new doctors of prescribing "bogus" drugs that merely suppressed his symptoms. But above all, she blamed the authorities at Qincheng for allowing Wang to suffer a recurrence of hepatitis in the first place. She and Wang discussed suing the maximum-security prison for illegal detention and medical neglect. Hou even filed protests with the warden at Yanqing for denying her the right to a conjugal visit that might allow her to conceive the child that she would never otherwise bear.

Yet it was Wang Zhihong, the quieter, more self-effacing of the two women, whose petitions really went to the heart of the matter. In the late spring of 1992, as the third anniversary of the Beijing massacre drew near, she wrote a letter to the deputies of the National People's Congress. Wang began by reviewing once again the procedural failings in her husband's trial: the summary nature of his conviction, the court's refusal to grant the defense access to key evidence, the deliberate distortions in the prosecution case. "This breach of law in trying a case," Wang went on, "is a betrayal of the legal system that has been taking shape for more than ten years now. It is a kind of retrogression."

Was it not time, she asked, for the Party to reverse its verdict on Tiananmen Square? "It has been three years since the June 4 incident," she wrote. "Our society has remained stable; the three-year economic adjustment has ended; and our human rights status has received much attention around the world. . . . For the sake of the country's development and prolonged stability, for strengthening the unity and confidence of people in different social circles, there is a need to follow the pulse of history for a gradual and phased settlement of the June 4 issue."

It might have been Chen Ziming himself speaking. Yes, a kind of stability had been achieved in the three years since June 4, but it was a stability built on dubious foundations. Too many of the present Party leaders shuffled forward with the slow, leaden steps of old men. As long as the likes of Peng Zhen, Chen Yun, and Bo Yibo survived, the Party would remain what it had been for the sixteen years since Mao's death—an unwieldy coalition of contending factions, conservatives and reformers in rough balance, tugging first one way and then the other, with Deng himself holding the whole rickety structure together.

In his cell at Number 2 Prison, Chen tried to read between the lines of the copy of *Beijing Daily* that the guard brought him each morning. Once again, he saw, in one last attempt to secure his legacy as a reformer, Deng had gathered his strength for a fresh economic reform drive, berating leftist tendencies as the greatest danger to the Party. The economy was booming again; it seemed that Deng's goal was to secure the dreams of Lenin and Mao by turning all of China into a laboratory for capitalism in its rawest form.

The Fourteenth Party Congress in October 1992, though keenly anticipated, resolved nothing. Deng's economic reforms once more received the green light, but the eighty-seven-year-old patriarch still held the line against any talk of opening up the political system. On the matter of Zhao Ziyang, the Congress was silent. The former Premier remained in limbo, neither vilified nor rehabilitated. This came as no surprise to Chen, given the ambiguous verdict that the courts had delivered three months earlier on Zhao's chief aide, Bao Tong, in the last of the black hands trials. Bao was sentenced to seven years on charges of divulging "state secrets" that were never specified—enough to placate the still-powerful conservatives, but not enough to intimidate the liberals or cause an international scandal.

The forgotten Zhao Ziyang would have been happy to endorse the economic proposals of the Fourteenth Congress. Indeed, many of the new plans were identical to those Bao Tong had drawn up years earlier. Figures no less liberal than Zhao and Bao remained in positions of power, as long as they had kept quiet at the time of Tiananmen. What determined one's fate in China, Chen Ziming had learned from bitter experience, was not so much what you believed in as when you believed in it—or rather, where you positioned yourself in relation to the current Party line.

In the greatest irony of all, Chen found that his own skills were once again in demand. The survivors of SERI, the institute he had labored so hard to build, had regrouped and were conducting a number of new research projects for the Ministry of Labor and Personnel. Chen Ziming, with the full knowledge of the authorities, even began to direct some of his colleagues' work from his prison cell.

It was still impossible to foresee the future of China after Deng Xiaoping. But the octogenarians were beginning to pass from the scene. Li Xiannian, Deng Yingchao, Hu Qiaomu: All died this year. Like 1976, 1992 was a year of deaths—and 1976 had also brought a rebirth. Chen's thoughts went back to the day when he heard that Deng Xiaoping had reversed the Party's verdict on the Tiananmen Incident of 1976. That news changed Chen's own life, and it changed China. He realized that his wife's appeal for his early release was an impossible dream. His sentence could never be shortened, nor could that of his old friend Wang Juntao, until the Party reversed its verdict on the 1989 democracy movement. And that would not happen as long as the present leadership endured. But it would not endure forever.

Chen had a certain tranquility these days. His conscience was clear. Even if he served his full thirteen-year sentence, he would be only fifty-two, a young man still, when they let him out. Since the hunger strike, his quarters at Beijing Number 2 had been improved a little. The warden allowed Wang Zhihong to bring him the books he craved, and he read them all avidly—works on Chinese politics, economics, history, the classics of philosophy that he had relished as a teenager in the yurt in Inner Mongolia. He even went back and reread Karl Marx.

Chen does not intend to spend his days in idleness. Indeed, he has told his wife, he plans to write three books of his own. His plans are nothing if not ambitious. The first will be a history of Chinese civilization. Next, a volume on modern Chinese history. And finally, if time allows, a survey of all the world's great ideologies. He cannot promise that they will be masterpieces; after all, his prison bookshelf is no substitute for a good library. But, if nothing else, they will help pass the time as Chen Ziming waits, like the rest of China, for old Deng to die.

CAST OF CHARACTERS

THE "BLACK HANDS BEHIND THE BLACK HANDS"

CHEN ZIMING

Born 1952 in Zhejiang Province, near Shanghai, the son of middle-ranking Party cadres. Chen's political career spans every important stage of the Chinese democracy movement. Arrested and imprisoned toward the end of the Cultural Revolution, he played a leading role in the Tiananmen Incident of April 5, 1976, and was a member of the editorial board of the independent journal *Beijing Spring* during the Democracy Wall movement of 1978–79. In 1981, he married Wang Zhihong (qv).

From 1984 to 1989, Chen created and ran China's most influential private network of think tanks and publishing agencies, but he was repeatedly unsuccessful in his efforts to bring his research to the attention of the official reformers around Zhao Ziyang. After May 13, 1989, Chen's Beijing Social and Economic Sciences Research Institute (SERI) tried unsuccessfully to mediate the conflict between student protesters in Tiananmen Square and the Communist Party. After the imposition of martial law a week later, Chen and Wang Juntao organized the Joint Liaison Group of All Circles in the Capital to Protect and Uphold the Constitution as a representative body of intellectuals, students, workers, and ordinary citizens. It was this, above all, that led to Chen and Wang being identified as the principal conspirators behind the 1989 protests.

In February 1991, Chen Ziming was jailed for thirteen years on charges of sedition. He is currently (November 1992) serving his sentence in Beijing's Number 2 Prison.

WANG JUNTAO

Born 1959 in Henan Province, the son of a high-ranking officer in the People's Liberation Army. As a teenager, Wang was involved in the Tiananmen Incident of 1976 and spent seven months in jail as a result. He was deputy editor of *Beijing Spring,* and thereafter his career closely mirrored that of Chen Ziming. After several years in Wuhan during the mid-1980s, Wang returned to Beijing in September 1986 to join Chen in the creation of his new think tank, the China Political and Administrative Sciences Research Institute, which was superseded the following year by SERI. In December 1986, he married Hou Xiaotian (q.v.). Wang continued to organize meetings of the Capital Joint Liaison Group right up to the eve of the Beijing massacre of June 4, 1989.

In February 1991, Wang Juntao received the same sentence as Chen Ziming, and on the same charges—thirteen years for sedition. He is currently serving his sentence at a prison near Beijing officially known as the Yanqing Brick and Tile Factory, which also houses a number of psychiatric patients.

CHEN AND WANG'S NETWORK

BAI HUA

Born 1955, the daughter of a low-ranking PLA officer. After taking degrees in communications and journalism at People's University, she became a consultant for the official think tank, RIRES, and in 1988 was made head of SERI's Opinion Research Center of China. Bai Hua—no relation to the writer of the same name persecuted in 1980—escaped from China in 1990 and now lives in the United States.

CHEN XIAOPING

Born 1962, grew up in a poor family in a small town in South China. Professor of constitutional law at Beijing's Politics and Law University; active in student demonstrations of 1986–87; a leading force behind the creation of the Beijing Residents Autonomous Federation during the 1989 protests. Found guilty on charges of sedition in February 1991, Chen was "exempted from punishment" because of his alleged cooperation with authorities. He was subsequently stripped of his Party membership.

FEI YUAN

Born c. 1954 in the industrial city of Zhenjiang, near Nanjing. Friend of Chen Ziming and Wang Juntao since 1980 Beijing University election campaign and appointed by Chen as director of SERI in 1987. Accused in prosecution indictments of being the mastermind of Chen and Wang's attempted escapes but never faced charges. Now believed to be at liberty in China.

Hou Xiaotian

Born 1960, daughter of a Party cadre. Married Wang Juntao in 1986 and two years later obtained a master's degree from Beijing College of Economics. Employed as a government personnel worker and occasional collaborator with SERI. Jailed for more than five months in 1989–90 and detained by the police several times since. Despite promises by the Chinese government that she would be allowed to travel to the United States, she had not been able to do so by the end of 1992.

Liu Gang

Born c. 1962, a native of Liaoyang, Jilin Province, and the son of a Public Security Bureau official. A one-time physics student and factory worker, he became a close collaborator with SERI and was the driving force, with Wang Dan, behind the 1988–89 democracy salons at Beijing University. During the Tiananmen protests, he was head of logistics for the Capital Joint Liaison Group. Liu was sentenced to six years' imprisonment in early 1991 on charges of sedition. He is reliably reported to have been badly beaten and tortured in jail.

Min Qi

Born c. 1952. A former Red Guard and veteran of the Democracy Wall movement. General secretary of SERI and editor of *Zhongguo She Hui Ke Xue* (*Social Sciences in China*). May have been detained after the 1989 crackdown but was never formally charged.

Wang Zhihong

Born c. 1957 in Shanghai. Married Chen Ziming in 1981. Over the next decade collaborated closely in building her husband's network of think tanks, and in 1987 became deputy director of the Human Resources Testing and Evaluation Center, a division of SERI. Jailed for a year without charges after being arrested in October 1989. Now lives in Beijing.

ZHANG LUN

Born 1962 in Shenyang, the son of intellectuals who fell victim to Mao's Anti-Rightist Movement. A Beida graduate student in sociology and part-time collaborator with SERI who was placed in charge of all pickets in Tiananmen Square after May 23, 1989. Escaped the crackdown and now lives in Europe.

ZHOU DUO

Born c. 1948, an economist with the Stone Corporation, a successful Beijing computer company, and head of its Strategic Planning and Public Relations department. Frequently attended meetings of the Capital Joint Liaison Group and drafted the May 19 "Letter to the People," warning of the imminent imposition of martial law. A member of the four-man hunger strike that began in Tiananmen Square on June 2, 1989, and a negotiator with the martial law troops on the peaceful evacuation of protesters from the square. Jailed for ten months without charges after the massacre.

BEIJING WORKERS AUTONOMOUS FEDERATION

HAN DONGFANG

Born 1963 in Shanxi Province, the son of a poor peasant and a construction worker, but largely brought up in Beijing. Spent three years as a guard in a labor camp and six months as an assistant librarian before joining the Chinese National Railways in 1984 as a refrigeration engineer. Made numerous speeches at Tiananmen Square beginning in mid-April 1989, and after the imposition of martial law on May 19 became convenor of the Beijing Workers Autonomous Federation (BWAF), the first independent labor organization in China since 1949. Han was jailed for almost two years after June 1989, but after an international campaign he was eventually released on medical grounds and allowed to travel to the United States for treatment in September 1992.

LI JINJIN

Born c. 1955, a friend of Wang Juntao's from Wuhan and a doctoral student in constitutional law at Beida. Legal adviser to the BWAF. Jailed for two years after June 1989.

LIU QIANG

Born c. 1963, a Beijing printing worker, member of the Standing Committee of the BWAF, and featured on the government's Most Wanted list of workers. Arrested after June 1989, his present whereabouts are unknown.

LÜ JINGHUA

Born 1962 in Beijing. Her mother was a Party cadre in a bookbinding factory. Lü was a garment worker and the operator of the BWAF broadcasting station in Tiananmen Square. One of four women out of forty people on the government's Most Wanted list, she escaped from China after the June 4 crackdown and now lives in New York City.

ZHAO HONGLIANG

Born 1965, worked as a Beijing bus conductor and department store clerk. In charge of logistics for the BWAF. Escaped from China after June 4 and now lives in Canada.

THE STUDENT LEADERS

CHAI LING

Graduate student in psychology at Beijing Normal University. Initiator and principal symbol of the May 13 hunger strike and, after martial law, commander in chief of the Tiananmen Square Command Headquarters. Chai Ling escaped the crackdown; she now lives in the United States.

LI LU

Student at Nanjing University and Communist Party member who became Chai Ling's deputy commander in chief. Escaped from China after the June 1989 massacre and now lives in the United States.

WANG DAN

History undergraduate at Beijing University, organizer of campus democracy salons, and editor of the journal *New May Fourth*. Organizer of the Beijing Students Autonomous Federation (BSAF) and frequent participant in meetings of the Capital Joint Liaison Group. Captured in July 1989 and imprisoned for four years, but released in February 1993.

WU'ER KAIXI (UERKESH DAOLET)

Leader of the Beijing Students Autonomous Federation. A member of the Uighur ethnic minority from Xinjiang Province. Fled China after the crackdown and now lives in the United States.

COMMUNIST PARTY LEADERS

DENG XIAOPING

Born 1904. Paramount leader of the Chinese Communist Party since his return to favor after the Cultural Revolution, despite being formally semiretired since 1987. Reshaped the country after Mao's death and the defeat of the Gang of Four with his pragmatic policy of "reform and opening up" of the economy but is fiercely opposed to any political reform that might challenge the Communist Party's monopoly of power. The Party's Fourteenth Congress in October 1992 is regarded as having secured Deng's legacy of continued economic reform.

HU YAOBANG

Born 1915. A longtime ally of Deng Xiaoping, but a more outspoken and erratic figure who repeatedly antagonized Party conservatives after his appointment as the Party's General Secretary in 1980. Removed from his post in January 1987 after that winter's student protests; accused of having turned a blind eye to "bourgeois liberalization." His death from a heart attack on April 15, 1989, was the immediate trigger for the protests in Tiananmen Square.

LI PENG

Born 1928. A Soviet-educated technocrat who became Premier after the downfall of Hu Yaobang; later named General Secretary after the removal of Zhao Ziyang in May 1989. Long regarded as a moderate conservative but publicly identified as the main instigator of martial law and the June 4 massacre. Li's position was rumored to have been in danger in the lead-up to the Fourteenth Party Congress, but he apparently withstood the challenge.

Zhao Ziyang

Born 1919. As a regional Party secretary in the 1970s, Zhao pioneered economic reform of the Chinese countryside. Appointed Premier in 1980, he sponsored the creation of a network of reform-minded official think tanks during the 1980s. Became General Secretary after the downfall of Hu Yaobang in 1987, but lost power to ascendant Li Peng amid the economic crisis of 1988, for which his policies were blamed. Zhao was stripped of all his posts and placed under house arrest on May 26, 1989, for his actions during the Tiananmen protests.

OTHER IMPORTANT PARTY FIGURES

Bao Tong

Born 1933 in Shanghai. An early member of the Party underground in that city. Purged as a "capitalist roader" during the Cultural Revolution but later Zhao Ziyang's top aide and an advocate of far-reaching political reform. Bao Tong was director of the Research Institute for the Reform of the Political Structure (RIRPS), political secretary to the Standing Committee of the Politburo, and a member of the Central Committee. He was arrested in May 1989 and sentenced in July 1992 to seven years' imprisonment on charges of "leaking state secrets."

Chen Xitong

The hard-line mayor of Beijing responsible for delivering the Communist Party's official verdict on the events of spring 1989.

Chen Yizi

Liberal economist, adviser to Zhao Ziyang, and director of the Research Institute for the Reform of the Economic Structure (RIRES), an elite official think tank. Escaped from China in 1989 and now lives in the United States.

Yan Mingfu

Head of the Central Committee's United Front Work Department. Party liberal and ally of Zhao Ziyang; launched a failed mediation attempt with the student protesters in May 1989. Removed from his post after the crackdown.

ZHU HOUZE

A leading liberal reformer and former protégé of Hu Yaobang. Acting head of the official All China Federation of Trade Unions (ACFTU) at the time of the Tiananmen protests. Purged after the crackdown.

NOTES

CHAPTER 1

1. The word "intellectuals" is more broadly applied in China than in the West; in China it is used to indicate most of the educated, white-collar professions. On occasion, in the interests of precision, we have preferred the term "intelligentsia." Of nineteenth-century origin, this term referred originally to those who were neither members of the nobility nor landed gentry nor peasants and shopkeepers. It covered, in other words, civil servants, teachers, clerks, and others who did not work with their hands. In Poland, China, and other Communist countries, the term persisted as a designation of social class. At the time of martial law in Poland in 1981, for instance, the indictments of many political prisoners named "the intelligentsia" as the social class from which they were descended. The authors are indebted to Aryeh Neier for this point.

2. The precise distinction between a "big-character" poster (*dazibao*) and a "small-character poster" (*xiaozibao*) is elusive. A *xiaozibao* is usually letter-size or smaller; the size of the characters used in each kind of poster is less well defined, however, and a *dazibao* may in fact contain characters that are small.

3. The most dramatic bloodletting of the Cultural Revolution took place during the so-called Wuhan Incident of the summer of 1967, when Lin Biao sent his troops in to quell the forces of the regional military commander, Chen Caidao, who had captured the representatives of the Beijing Central Cultural Revolution Group.

4. The *li* is the standard Chinese measurement of distance, equivalent to approximately one-third of a mile, or 0.52 kilometer.

5. The *Banner* system reflects the traditional administrative divisions of the Manchu emperors. The higher administrative district is known as a *League*.

6. The three "major and unjust cases" are detailed in an internal document of the Communist Party Central Committee known as Document Number 28, dated August 5, 1981. The Party blamed the slaughter on Lin Biao and the Gang of Four. See *News from Asia Watch,* "Crackdown in Inner Mongolia," July 28, 1991.

7. Thomas Heberer, *China and Its National Minorities: Autonomy or Assimilation?* (Armonk, NY: M. E. Sharpe, 1984).

8. The description of Beijing in the mid-1970s relies heavily on the fascinating book by the British diplomat Roger Garside, *Coming Alive: China After Mao* (London: André Deutsch, 1981).

9. The eight works of "model theater" approved by Jiang Qing consisted of four operas: *The Red Lantern, Shachiapang* (originally called *Fire Among the Reeds*), *Taking Tiger Mountain by Strategy,* and *Raid on White Tiger Regiment;* two ballets: *The Red Detachment of Women* and *White-Haired Girl;* one piece of music, the *Yellow River* Piano Concerto; and a series of sculptural tableaus, *The Rent Collection Courtyard.*

10. Jiang Qing was, in fact, born in Shandong Province but first entered radical political circles when she was a B-movie actress in pre–World War II Shanghai.

11. Yao Wenyuan was the author of a celebrated article published on November 10, 1965, in the Shanghai paper *Wenhuibao.* The article was, on the surface, a literary review entitled "Comments on the New Historical Play 'Hai Rui Dismissed from Office.'" Hai Rui was a minister during the Ming dynasty who was dismissed for criticizing the emperor Jiaqing. Hai Rui was widely understood to represent Peng Dehuai, who lost favor with Mao Zedong (the counterpart of the play's villainous emperor) after the 1959 Lushan conference, when he condemned the folly of Mao's Great Leap Forward with the comment, "Putting politics in command is no substitute for economic principles."

12. The Long March was the epic six-thousand-mile retreat made by Mao's Red Army in 1934–35, as the troops of the Guomindang put intolerable pressure on their Jiangxi headquarters. It took them to the mountain hideaway of Yan'an, which served as the Communists' new base of operations until 1946.

13. Mao's catastrophic crash program of industrial modernization, launched in 1958, aimed to propel China to the same level of development as Great Britain by the mid-1970s.

14. Lin Biao had perished in 1971 in a mysterious plane crash in Mongolia, supposedly while fleeing to the Soviet Union in the wake of a failed attempt to overthrow Mao.

15. "Reform through labor," a criminal sanction applied by the courts, is different from "reeducation through labor," a lighter administrative sanction imposed by the Public Security Bureau. Involving no

trial, reeducation through labor allows the police to dispose of troublesome elements with a minimum of fuss.

CHAPTER 2

1. The Four Modernizations refer to industry, agriculture, science and technology, and national defense. They were first mentioned by Liu Shaoqi at the Eighth Party Congress in 1956 but were closely identified with Zhou Enlai and, later, Deng Xiaoping.

2. The Communist Party had always understood its history as a dialectical process of "Two-Line Struggles." One of those who saw this poster was a *People's Daily* reporter loyal to the Gang of Four. He immediately reported its contents to the Gang, entitling his summary "An Extremely Important Development." It was, of course, a daring and prescient act by the poster writer, since the Party had still not officially launched the "Eleventh Two-Line Struggle."

3. The word used by Chen was *yexinjiamen,* a term applied to the Gang of Four after their downfall.

4. The word used by Chen was *huoshou,* source of calamity, another buzzword later employed as an epithet for the Gang of Four.

5. The comparison is made by the British diplomat Roger Garside in his book, *Coming Alive.*

6. Many Chinese subsequently came to believe that scores, if not hundreds, of people were killed in the clearing of Tiananmen Square on April 5, 1976. But an exhaustive study of the event by Yan Jiaqi, a scholar of the Cultural Revolution and an important figure in the 1989 democracy movement, demonstrated conclusively that no one had died, though many were beaten and wounded. On the implications of this debate, see Chapter 13.

7. There are several other claimants to the glorious title of "crewcut shorty," notably one Liu Di, who was another leading figure in the 1976 protests. Given the above-mentioned reference by the Party to "a few bad elements, sporting crewcuts," they may all be correct. Of the various "crewcut shorties," Chen himself was more closely characterized by the authorities as being "the one with the dark glasses" (*dai hei yanjingde*).

8. The arrest of the Gang of Four is described in lively detail in Harrison Salisbury, *The New Emperors: China in the Era of Mao and Deng* (Boston: Little, Brown and Company, 1991).

9. The Chinese embalmers botched the job, and in the end Mao's corpse was entrusted to a team of Vietnamese experts who had preserved the body of Ho Chi Minh seven years earlier.

CHAPTER 3

1. The entry of the 1977 class was postponed until January 1978; the 1978 class began as usual in September. For this reason, both are sometimes referred to together as the entry class of 1978.

2. A less savory achievement of the Liu-Deng army was its occupation of Tibet in 1951.

3. This is how Chen classifies the factions in a manuscript, subsequently published as *Chen Ziming Reflects on the Ten-Year Reforms* (*Chen Ziming Fansi Shinian Gaige*) (Hong Kong: Dang Dai Monthly Press, June 1992), that he wrote in Qincheng prison after his arrest in 1989.

4. It is more customary to refer to the Dengists as the "practice" faction.

5. This mirrors exactly the assessment that Mao once made of Deng—as well as the assessment that he made, at an earlier date, of Stalin. In all three cases, however, use of the Chinese phrase *"san qi kai"*—literally, "to make a three–seven division"—served a dual purpose: It conveyed a generous measure of criticism but at the same time upheld the overall reputation of the person being criticized.

6. This phrase is inescapably associated with Deng, who used it in an article he wrote for the Higher Party School, of which Hu Yaobang was vice-president. Actually, he had borrowed it from Hu Fuming, a professor at Nanjing University.

7. The technical limitations of mimeographing restricted most issues to about five hundred copies. But the experience of typesetting was not to be repeated. The Foreign Languages Press workers were sharply reprimanded and forced to write several self-criticisms. This, and other fascinating details about *Beijing Spring,* is contained in Claude Widor, ed., "Documents sur le mouvement démocratique chinois, 1978–1980," vol. 2 (Paris: Éditions de l'École des Hautes Études en Sciences Sociales, 1984).

8. Having said that, a word of caution is necessary about using the term "worker" too freely. Many of these people were forced to take factory and manual jobs because of the punitive policies of the Cultural Revolution and would otherwise surely have ended up at university. They were usually well read and self-educated. "Worker-intellectual" might describe them more accurately.

9. A series of angry rallies in Shanghai culminated on February 5, 1979, with an overnight sit-in on the tracks of the city's railway station, delaying hundreds of trains and tens of thousands of passengers. The "Restorationists" in the Party began to warn that this behavior raised the specter of the Cultural Revolution all over again.

10. In theory, certain police stations functioned as reception centers for the petitioners, but they were invariably sent packing or, if they were

persistent, tossed into a prison called Virtue Forest, known before Liberation as Beijing Prison Number 2. Virtue Forest continues to function to this day, and petitioners for justice are still treated much as they were in 1979.

11. *Beijing Spring* described a typical case in its first issue. "At 7:00 P.M. on December 27, 1978, a man set fire to himself in Tiananmen Square. Discovered by the soldier on duty, he was promptly rescued and taken to the collecting post. Upon investigation, it was found that the man's name was Wang Guohui, a worker at the Dalian Oil and Fat Chemical Plant. Because of the wrong classification of his family, he sought an audience with the authorities but got nowhere, and he was even detained. Desperate, he tried to commit suicide by setting fire to himself."

12. The petitioners' leader was Fu Yuehua, a construction worker in her late twenties. The specific grievance that brought her to Beijing was that she had been raped by a local Party secretary in 1973. Nine months after her arrest, she was brought to trial. The judge told her that since she had marched at the head of the petitioners' January 8 demonstration, she was obviously its leader. In tones that were not exactly familiar in a Chinese courtroom, she shot back: "If I had been in the rear, you would be saying that I controlled it from behind the scenes, and if I had been in the middle you would be saying that I was in the mainstream." Turning her original complaint against her, the judge sent her to a labor camp, accusing her of sexual promiscuity.

13. The poster was typed and photocopied—a rarity in China, where few people had access to a photocopier. This fact gave rise to rumors at the time that the document had been produced in the Soviet Union.

14. In case Deng had not received its message of loyalty, *Beijing Spring* even went so far as to condemn Alexander Dubček's 1968 "Prague Spring" for slipping into the "restoration of capitalism."

15. Ren Wanding, prosecuted separately, got four years. Wei was charged under Mao's 1952 Regulations on the Suppression of Counter-revolutionaries. His trial took place just a few weeks before the introduction of the Criminal Procedure Law in January 1980, which, at least in theory, might have offered him more protection. The charge of divulging state secrets alleged that Wei had passed on to a Reuters correspondent details of Chinese troop strength and military command structure in the war with Vietnam, information that was available to anyone watching the news on Central China Television (CCTV).

Wei's trial was supervised by Peng Zhen, the Maoist traditionalist who had been so fulsomely praised by *Beijing Spring*. It was ostensibly public, but when another democracy activist, the worker-intellectual Liu Qing of *April Fifth Forum,* tried to circulate copies of the transcript, he too was arrested. Liu had scant regard for the rituals of guilt, confession, and repentance demanded by the Chinese judicial system. When his interrogator accused him of carrying out propaganda on behalf of a convicted counterrevolutionary, Liu answered with a laugh, "What I sold was the taped record of the actual proceedings of the trial of Wei Jingsheng in court. I did not add any of my own personal opinion. If you think this content is doing propaganda work for the counterrevolution, are you not saying that the court proceedings were also propaganda activities for the counterrevolution?" Liu got three years of reeducation through labor in a provincial prison called Lianhuasi, "Lotus Flower Temple." Later, he was sentenced to an additional seven years.

CHAPTER 4

1. The comment was made by investigative reporter Liu Binyan, who also complained that Hu Yaobang had been inconsistent in his support for freedom of expression. Liu had in mind especially a notorious 1985 speech in which Hu instructed journalists to report "80 percent good and 20 percent bad" news. See Liu Binyan, *Another Kind of Loyalty* (New York: Pantheon Books, 1990), pp. 237–48.

2. Not since 1912 had such an open vote been permitted in China. The Party endorsed independent candidates for the first time, and any individual with the signatures of three sponsors could run.

3. The first pilot election was held in April at Fudan University in Shanghai. The authorities were generally supportive, publishing the results without comment in *Shanghai Youth News*. But in October it was the turn of Hunan Teachers College, in the provincial capital of Changsha. There bureaucratic interference with the vote provoked a student hunger strike and class boycott, and the authorities responded by annulling the vote.

4. Another who contested the 1980 elections was Zhong Yueqiu, a twenty-three-year-old worker in a South China smelting plant who edited two unofficial journals, *Voice of the Commoner* and *North River*.

5. Among Fu's writings for the journal was a moving account of the execution in 1977 of a close friend whose only crime was to have written a letter to his girl friend complaining that Mao Zedong Thought had been turned into a rigid and unchallengeable dogma. Fu Shenqi was among those arrested after the crackdown on the 1989 democracy movement.

6. The phrase is associated particularly with the activities of the Red Guards as they spread out across China to "make revolution."

7. Chen Ziming and Wang Juntao's *Beijing Spring* group also seems to have played no part in the new national journal *Zeren* (*Responsibility*), which produced at least nine issues under the editorship first of He Qiu

and later Fu Shenqi. Other Beida election activists were involved, however, in an individual capacity. Fang Zhiyuan, who placed just behind Wang Juntao in the election, was one of the architects of a new draft publications law that was issued in December 1980 and distributed through the informal nationwide network of the democracy movement.

8. The letter read, "To our dear brothers, the workers of Poland! Your strike actions and general struggle have secured a great victory, one which has become the focus of world attention. This victory has demonstrated the tremendous power of the new class awakening generated by working-class solidarity . . . and shows clearly that proletarian-democratic revolution is an inevitable trend in historical development. It has broken through national boundaries and is of far-reaching significance. We of the young generation of the working class in China congratulate you and express to you our deepest respects. We wish you continuous progress toward the goal of democratic socialism!"

9. The horse-trading at the December "work meeting" was actually quite complex. Deng had finally managed to dump Hua Guofeng, and the trial of the Gang of Four in December wrapped up the last of the loose ends of the Maoist period. But some bones still needed to be thrown to the Left, and especially to the security apparatus that Hua Guofeng had once headed. The obvious sacrificial lamb was the troublesome democracy movement.

10. Other sentences handed down at this time were almost as harsh. Fu Shenqi got seven years. Chen Erjin, a coal-mine statistician from Yunnan Province, was given ten. His essay "On Proletarian-Democratic Revolution" was first published in *April Fifth Forum* and later translated as *Crossroads Socialism* (London: Verso Books, 1984, with an introduction by Robin Munro). Liu Qing, who had already been sentenced to three years for trying to distribute the transcript of Wei Jingsheng's trial, was given an additional seven years for smuggling out a frank account of his experiences in Banbuqiao prison.

11. All through the spring and summer of 1980 the campaign against "bourgeois liberalization" raged, with the PLA playing a central role. In April, the army's *PLA Daily* ran a scathing attack on the writer Bai Hua and his screenplay, *Bitter Love*. Bai Hua's film was an exposé of the Cultural Revolution through the eyes of a patriotic young writer. It ended with the protagonist on a beach, drawing a question mark in the sand and musing, "I love my country, but does my country love me?" The real target of the campaign was not Bai Hua himself, but Hu Yaobang, who had overall charge of cultural affairs and made no secret of his distaste for this latest witch-hunt.

12. This was only the second of such "Resolutions." The first was issued in 1945, and it summarized the course of all the Party's "Two-Line Struggles" since its foundation in 1921.

CHAPTER 5

1. The *yuan* at this time was worth approximately $2.93 (U.S.). Its value declined slowly until 1989, when there was a steady series of sharp devaluations. All dollar equivalents in the text reflect the "National Swap Rate" for the month in question, according to figures supplied to the authors by the U.S.-China Business Council.

2. Much of the conservative counterattack was conducted on the streets. Police squads grabbed kids off the streets for an instant "short-back-and-sides" haircut; a campaign against "smuggling" in early 1983 clamped down on get-rich-quick schemes, such as the sale of Chinese antiquities to foreigners, and tried to stem the illicit flow of consumer goods, including electronic equipment and pornographic videotapes, across the sievelike border with Hong Kong.

The crackdown on common crime, also begun in 1983, was perhaps the most chilling development. Over the next several years, millions of people were arrested and disappeared into the vast network of prisons and labor camps in China's remote frontier regions. Their urban residence permits were often revoked, which obliged them to stay in the borderlands after the completion of their sentences. Perhaps ten thousand were executed. The trials were rudimentary, and the death sentence might be imposed for something as trivial as the theft of a wristwatch. One of the Communist Party's most closely guarded secrets, however, was that political dissidents, too, were a primary target of the campaign. A secret Central Committee directive, dated August 25, 1983, listed "seven types of criminal elements" who "should all be dealt resolute blows and given severe and prompt punishment." It went on, "Those requiring severe punishment must be sentenced heavily, and those who deserve to die must be executed." In all the official reports of the crackdown, only six groups of offenders were ever mentioned. Category Number 7, never spoken of outside the secret directive, was "active counterrevolutionary elements who write counterrevolutionary slogans, flyers, liaison messages, and anonymous letters."

3. Looking back at this period from his trial in 1991, Chen named Sun Yat-sen and Chen Duxiu as "examples of independent intellectuals who did not cooperate" and Kang Youwei and Hu Shi as "examples of intellectuals who cooperated but lacked independence." Sun Yat-sen was the founder of the Chinese Republic; Chen Duxiu was one of China's first Marxists and a founder of the Communist Party; Kang Youwei was a scholar-official who tried to reform the imperial system at the end of the nineteenth century; and Hu Shi was an intellectual prominent in the 1920s and 1930s who favored U.S.-style constitutional democracy.

4. The idea of establishing stock markets was still an extremely dangerous one in 1983. On Hainan Island, for instance, one of the most

freewheeling centers of economic reform, a fifteen-year jail term was handed down to a person named Zheng Qiuwu for forming a group that proposed setting up a stock market. The man's mistake—and Chen Ziming's, in a sense—was to have espoused an idea whose political time had not quite come.

5. China's *getihu* swelled from less than six million in 1983 to almost twelve million two years later. Some grew into veritable economic empires, like Chen's network of publishing agencies and think tanks.

6. There is a detailed study of the effects of the urban reforms on industrial Wuhan in Leung Wing-yue, *Smashing the Iron Rice-Pot: Workers and Unions in China's Market Socialism* (Hong Kong: Asia Monitor Resource Center, 1988), especially pp. 43–122.

7. *Youth Forum* came under fierce attack from the leftist propaganda commissar Deng Liqun in March 1987, after the fall of Hu Deping's father, Hu Yaobang. But Hubei propaganda officials stalled. They agreed merely to "suspend the publication and reorganize its management," not close it down entirely, as Deng Liqun had wished.

CHAPTER 6

1. Chen Ziming, as usual, took care to do everything in accordance with the law. He registered his schools, as the law required, as *gua kao danwei*—affiliates of state work units. Many state units were quite happy to provide this kind of service, since it automatically brought them 5 to 10 percent of the affiliate's profits in the form of a "management fee."

2. Bezoar is a hard intestinal mass, traditionally used in China as a purgative. There is considerable detail on Zhu Houze and other leading personalities in the political battles of this period in Willy Wo-Lap Lam's *The Era of Zhao Ziyang: Power Struggle in China, 1986–1988* (Hong Kong: A. B. Books and Stationery, 1989).

3. The institute actually emerged from the Research Group on the Developmental Problems of Rural China, which was set up by pro–Deng Xiaoping economists in 1978. In late 1984, the RGDPRC split into RIRES and the Research Institute for Rural Development.

4. RIRES also drew on the support of about one hundred fifty young social scientists, the cream of the Beijing intelligentsia. In 1985, it spawned the Beijing Young Economists Association. The name, however, was misleading: The association was open to young scholars from other disciplines, and Wang Juntao eventually became a member. Bao Tong was the president of the association, and Chen Yizi vice-president.

5. He rose to become secretary to An Ziwen, who was accused by Mao in 1966 of being a spy and a member of the "Group of 61 Traitors."

6. In 1982, at the same time China's new Constitution was enacted, a civil procedure law authorized courts for the first time to hear challenges to the Public Security Bureau and other government agencies. But a greater breakthrough came in 1986, with the passage of the General Principles of Civil Law, which instituted, in rudimentary fashion, the concept of tort. An interesting summary of cases brought before the courts is Richard Dicker, "China's Long March to Full Legal Rights," *Legal Times,* August 24, 1992, pp. 20–21.

CHAPTER 7

1. The proximate cause of the Hefei protests was in fact the Communist Party's insistence on designating official candidates for the December elections to the county-level People's Congress. Fang Lizhi's wife, Li Shuxian, contested the election and was elected overwhelmingly. The episode is described well in Orville Schell's *Discos and Democracy: China in the Throes of Reform* (New York: Pantheon, 1988), pp. 211–18.

2. He was still luckier than Deng Xiaoping's brother, Deng Shiping, who committed suicide during the Cultural Revolution. Pufang's ordeal is fully described in Harrison Salisbury, *The New Emperors,* pp. 320–21.

3. Li Shengping went on to found a think tank of his own, the China Technology Development Institute. He also worked as a researcher at the Marxism-Leninism Institute of the Chinese Academy of Social Sciences. After 1988, Li and Chen resumed their former amicable relationship, and Li, too, played an active part in trying to resolve the impasse in Tiananmen Square in 1989. He was one of those who accompanied Yan Mingfu, head of the Party's United Front Work Department, on his visit to the students in the square on May 16. After June 4, Li Shengping was arrested and detained for more than a year without charges before eventually being released.

4. Modern China's sufferings at the hands of Japanese militarism are legendary. The 1985 protests were held to mark the fifty-fourth anniversary of the Japanese occupation of Manchuria, but they also drew attention to a string of other dates: the six-month war of 1894–95, when the newly modernized Japanese army humiliated China; May 4, 1919, when patriotic students protested the Allies' decision at the Versailles Peace Conference to hand over to Japan the former German concessions in the Chinese city of Qingdao and the province of Shandong; the joint Communist-Guomindang rallies against Japanese imperialism in 1926; and, worst of all, the rape of Nanjing in December 1937, when three hundred thousand Chinese citizens were slaughtered in ten days.

The protests had a second level, too, since Japanese consumer goods were a clever, indirect way of drawing attention to the growing phenomenon of corruption in the Communist Party. All those Sonys, Panasonics, and Toyotas tended to find their way most rapidly into the hands of venal cadres.

5. In the northern industrial province of Liaoning, to give only one example, there were 276 reported incidents of factory managers being attacked and beaten by angry workers during the first six months of 1988.

6. These were only the ACFTU's figures, and, like most official statistics, they were highly suspect. Other sources said there had been more than one hundred stoppages that year in the Special Economic Zone of Shenzhen alone.

7. The Party admitted officially to a figure of 18.5 percent, but it was common knowledge that the real rate was much higher—and higher still in the cities.

CHAPTER 8

1. Their talk echoed the despondency of earlier intellectuals such as Liang Qichao, who wrote at the turn of the century of the "slavish mentality" of the Chinese. On Liang, see Jonathan Spence's masterly book, *The Gate of Heavenly Peace: The Chinese and Their Revolution, 1895–1980* (New York: Viking Penguin, 1981), passim.

2. There is a remarkably complete listing of SERI's output over this period in *China Spring,* November 1989.

3. Min Qi, *China's Political Culture: Socio-Psychological Factors Behind the Delayed Birth of a Democratic Politics (Zhongguo Zhengzhi Wenhua: Minzhu Zhengzhi Nanchan de Shehui Xinli Yinsu)* (Beijing: Yunnan Publishing House, no date).

4. There was already one celebrated book on the Cultural Revolution, by the social scientist Yan Jiaqi, director of the Political Science Institute of CASS. This book had been published in Hong Kong, but the Party banned it from seeing the light of day in China. Yan was severely reprimanded when a Japanese translation appeared.

5. China's Ministry of State Security was set up in 1983; its original mandate was to prevent espionage, detect counterrevolutionary cases, and conduct counterintelligence work. Today it also carries out espionage overseas, as does the intelligence division of the People's Liberation Army. (In practice, the Public Security Bureau also continues to deal with a large number of activities considered counterrevolutionary.)

6. "It became clear to me in retrospect," Soros later wrote, "that I had made a mistake in setting up the foundation in China. China was not ready for it because there was no independent or dissident intelligentsia. The people on whom I based the foundation were members of a Party faction. They could not be totally open and honest with me

because their primary obligation was to their faction. The foundation could not become an institution of civil society because civil society did not really exist. It would have been much better to make an outright grant to Chen Yizi's institute, which deserved support." The episode is recounted in George Soros, *Opening the Soviet System* (London: Weidenfeld and Nicolson, 1990).

7. The full flavor of the pun, of course, is impossible to render in English. Chen's arguments are summarized in a valuable article by Xie Xiaoqing, former head of SERI's Human Resources Testing and Evaluation Center, "The Viewpoints and Opinions of Chen Ziming and Wang Juntao," (*Baixing,* Hong Kong, June 16, 1990). According to their former colleague, Chen and Wang were trying to look beyond the Zhao Ziyang–Li Peng fight to identify the next generation of leaders from the "third echelon." As possible Premiers, they identified Li Tieying, head of the State Education Commission; Zou Jiahua, head of the State Planning Commission; Li Ruihuan, former mayor of Tianjian; and Zhu Rongji, sometimes referred to as China's Gorbachev. They were optimistic that a relative liberal might end up as General Secretary—someone like security chief Qiao Shi, Hu Qili, or even Zhu Houze.

8. Wang sometimes cited the case of the Pahlevi regime in Iran to illustrate the dangers of a modernizing regime that failed to respect its country's cultural traditions. In the case of China, Wang believed that both Confucianism and Marxism were vital ingredients of the political culture. His writings on New Authoritarianism are included in *Guoqing Yanjiu (China Studies)*, Beijing, no. 3, 1989.

9. Chen Ziming and a SERI delegation had a fruitful first meeting with Li Tieying, head of the State Education Commission, on April 28, 1989. A meeting with Zhao Ziyang was provisionally scheduled for May, but it was superseded by the events in Tiananmen Square.

10. The reporter was Jane Macartney of Reuters' Beijing bureau. Macartney's highly colored views on how the students in Tiananmen Square were used by people like Wang Juntao were published as "The Students: Heroes, Pawns or Power-Brokers," in Geremie Barmé and John Minford, eds., *The Broken Mirror: Chinese Voices of Conscience* (New York: Hill and Wang, 1988), pp. 3–23.

CHAPTER 9

1. Liu Gang was active in a campaign to get Li Shuxian, wife of the dissident astrophysicist Fang Lizhi, on a ballot for election to the National People's Congress. After Liu was sentenced to six years in jail, Li Shuxian published a portrait of her young supporter, entitled "The 'Crimes' of Liu Gang" (*Washington Post,* March 29, 1991).

2. On May 4, 1919, thousands of students congregated at the Gate of Heavenly Peace to condemn the humiliating concessions that China had made at the Versailles Peace Conference. The May Fourth movement spoke of China's urgent need for "Mr. Democracy and Mr. Science"— thus the monument at Beida. The phrase, coined by Chen Duxiu, Dean of Students at Beijing National University, expressed a yearning for modern Western ideas. Chen later became the first General Secretary of the Chinese Communist Party on its founding in Shanghai in 1921. Although the Party appropriated the meaning of May Fourth as a vital thread in the linear march of the Communist revolution, May Fourth remained a shining symbol for all later stages of the Chinese democracy movement.

3. Shen Tong's Olympic Institute started as a group of seven people. According to Shen's colorful autobiography, they held their initial meetings at a restaurant off campus. "We argued and exchanged ideas about everything from Karl Popper to Heisenberg's uncertainty principle. . . . We also decided to keep the group small and focus on academic matters, in an effort to stay out of political trouble. Our motto was 'Use rational means to approach all things' " (Shen Tong, *Almost a Revolution* [Boston: Houghton Mifflin, 1990], p. 148)

4. Fang Lizhi's writings and speeches are collected as *Bringing Down the Great Wall* (New York, Knopf: 1990). His letter to Deng Xiaoping is also reprinted in Han Minzhu, ed., *Cries for Democracy: Writings and Speeches from the Chinese Democracy Movement* (Princeton, NJ: Princeton University Press, 1990), pp. 24–25.

5. The conflicting accounts of the exact sum involved indicate Chen's desire to maintain a confidential monopoly over the financial affairs of the Institute, a habit for which he was often criticized by colleagues. After the June 4 massacre, large sums of cash belonging to SERI were confiscated during a police raid.

6. From "Verdict in the Case of Chen Ziming: Criminal Verdict of the Beijing People's Intermediate Court (1991) Intermediate/Criminal/No. 294." This and other court documents were obtained by Asia Watch from confidential Chinese sources and published as "Guilt by Association: More Documents from the Chinese Trials" (*News from Asia Watch*, June 1991).

CHAPTER 10

1. After June 4, Xiao was placed on a secret Most Wanted list. In an attempt to avoid arrest, he mutilated his own face and badly disfigured himself. He was caught, nonetheless, and later sentenced to three years' hard labor.

2. After June 4, Zhao was placed on the same wanted list as Xiao Delong (Lu Jinghua's was the third name on the list), but he was never caught. In the winter of 1992, after three and a half years on the run, Zhao escaped to Hong Kong. He now lives in the United States.

3. The accusations about Deng Pufang and corruption may in fact have been unfair, although Ge Yang, former editor of the banned *New Observer,* has implicated him in the duty-free import of thirty thousand television sets. There is no doubt, however, that corruption flourished in Kangua Enterprises, the giant trading company that Deng headed. Much more notorious cases of corruption among the *taizi dang*—the Party of princes—involved the children of Hu Yaobang, Peng Zhen, and Zhao Ziyang. There is considerable detail on these and other cases in the Fund for Free Expression report, "Off Limits: Censorship and Corruption" (New York, July 1991), pp. 14–24.

4. Walder speaks of the Party's "divided sovereignty" in his interesting essay, "The Political Sociology of the Beijing Upheaval of 1989," *Problems of Communism,* Sept.–Oct. 1989, pp. 30–40.

5. Zhao's son, Zhao Dajun, was involved extensively in business dealings in the Special Economic Zone of Shenzhen, across the border from Hong Kong.

6. This was not the first time that Deng had acted in this manner. He had done essentially the same thing, in fact, in January 1987, when Hu Yaobang was dismissed as General Secretary. According to the Party rule book, Hu's dismissal should have been a decision of the full eighteen-member Politburo. But when the Politburo balked at taking the action the elders demanded, it was joined for a new vote by seventeen members of the Central Advisory Commission, which included a number of the semiretired "veteran proletarian revolutionaries."

CHAPTER 11

1. China does not technically consider itself a one-party state. A number of tiny "democratic" parties have been allowed to function within strict limits since 1949, and the Chinese Communist Party's relations with them are handled by the United Front Work Department of the Central Committee. The department is also responsible for liaison with overseas Chinese.

2. The students' demands changed continually during the course of the demonstrations. They first presented formal demands as early as April 17, after their memorial wreaths to Hu Yaobang were removed from the Monument to the People's Heroes—a further echo of the events of April 5, 1976. On April 17, a crowd of three thousand Beijing students demanded: a reevaluation of Hu Yaobang's life and work; repudiation of

the 1987 Campaign Against Bourgeois Liberalization; freedom of the press; an increase in the education budget; freedom to protest and demonstrate; publication of the financial holdings of senior government officials; and abolition of the Beijing municipal regulations governing the holding of demonstrations.

3. Twelve prominent members of the Beijing intelligentsia visited the square to try to persuade the students to leave. The group was headed by Dai Qing, a reporter for *Guangming Daily*. It also included Yu Haocheng, the editor in chief of *Faxue Zazhi* (*Legal Studies Journal*); Li Honglin, president of the Fujian Academy of Social Sciences; Yan Jiaqi, former director of the Political Science Institute at the Chinese Academy of Social Sciences (CASS) and author of a renowned (and officially banned) history of the Cultural Revolution; Su Xiaokang, the principal author of *River Elegy;* Bao Zunxin, former editor of the *Walk Toward the Future* book series; Wen Yuankai, professor of chemistry at China Science and Technology University; Li Zehou, a philosopher at CASS; Zhou Duo, an economist at the Stone Corporation; and Ma Tianshu, whose identity we have been unable to establish. The group's appeals were ignored by the students.

4. A second poll on the same subject was conducted at about the same time by Beijing Normal College. This poll, however, involved interviews with people on the streets, not in their homes, and was therefore likely to be biased in favor of the students. Not surprisingly, perhaps, it found that more than 90 percent of those surveyed supported the student movement.

5. This rumor is reported in Roger Garside's book, *Coming Alive,* although Garside himself implies that the accusation against Ni Zhifu was without foundation.

6. Yan Mingfu was accompanied on this occasion by none other than Li Shengping, Chen Ziming's old friend and one-time professional rival. Li had been associated with the Marxism-Leninism–Mao Zedong Thought Institute of the Chinese Academy of Social Sciences, a liberal stronghold, and was again in close touch with Chen Ziming by the end of 1988.

7. This was a "blunder" only in the sense that it roused the conservatives further against Zhao. It can also be seen, however, as a shrewd act of self-protection, designed to stress to Gorbachev, and to the wider public, that Zhao Ziyang himself was not to be held responsible for the government's inflexible stance toward the student movement. The same can be said of Zhao's final, tearful visit to the square on the eve of martial law—this being not just an admission of defeat but an act that would enhance Zhao's liberal image in the event of some future comeback, of the sort Deng Xiaoping had twice made in the 1970s.

CHAPTER 12

1. Yet Bao Tong also rejected Western-style parliamentary democracy as "irrelevant" to China's needs, according to a report in the *Asian Wall Street Journal* (December 26, 1988).

2. According to Chen Yizi and one of his senior associates, Zhang Gang, RIRES met again the next day, May 20, and issued four additional documents, some of which were rapidly withdrawn and never received wide public circulation. The titles of these documents were: An Urgent Appeal to Fellow Countrymen; A Basis for the Right to Call a Special Session of the Standing Committee of the National People's Congress; An Urgent Call to the NPC to Impeach Li Peng; Li Peng the Person. Zhang Gang, who was present at the May 20 RIRES meeting, argues that it was these four documents that gave details of the proceedings of the May 17 meeting of the Standing Committee of the Politburo. From this, Zhang surmises that the "Letter to the People," written at the Jimen Hotel by Zhou Duo and dated May 19, in fact was composed on May 20 on the basis of information contained in the four RIRES documents and then for some reason backdated—an appealing but implausible theory, and one contradicted by the testimony of Zhou Duo himself.

3. One should not take this to mean that either man held consistent positions on any single issue. Like everyone else attempting to navigate the crisis, they were capable of changing their views from one day to the next, and indeed of holding two contradictory opinions simultaneously. In addition, as Chai Ling has suggested in an interview with the authors, it was apparent that Wang Juntao's private opinions were not necessarily always in agreement with the views he felt constrained to express as chair of the meetings of the Capital Joint Liaison Group—which was, as he repeatedly reminded those present, merely a consultative body.

4. The "Letter to the People" reported that Zhao had set forth six proposals, all of which had been overruled by his colleagues. These were: (1) That the April 26 *People's Daily* editorial be repudiated; (2) That Zhao himself take personal responsibility for the editorial; (3) That the National People's Congress set up a special body to investigate profiteering by the sons and daughters of high officials, including his own children; (4) That the official résumés and personal backgrounds of officials with the rank of deputy minister and above be made public; (5) That the income and benefits of senior officials be made public; and (6) That the special privileges of high-ranking cadres be abolished.

The complete text of the "Letter to the People" is reproduced in Han Minzhu, ed., *Cries for Democracy,* pp. 248–50. A variant text with some important differences, notably the omission of the call for a general strike, was published as a *samizdat*-style supplement to *People's Daily* and is reproduced in "Recent Political Trials in China" (*News from Asia Watch,* March 1992).

5. Wu Xuecan, the journalist who produced the *People's Daily* supplement, was later sentenced to four years in prison.

6. It remains distinctly possible that not even the Public Security Bureau or the Communist Party ever established the authorship of the various versions of the document. The remaining mysteries about the May 19 "Letter to the People" may perhaps be resolved in Zhou Duo's own forthcoming book, *Bloodstained Dawn.*

7. The foreigner in this dialogue is Robin Munro. This account was first printed, with some minor differences, in Human Rights in China, *Children of the Dragon: The Story of Tiananmen Square* (New York: Collier MacMillan, 1990), pp. 95–102.

8. This important document was unsigned. It was, however, expertly typeset by computer. Only a limited number of institutions in Beijing would have had the technology to produce such a document, although the list would include, at a minimum, SERI, RIRES, and the Stone Corporation.

CHAPTER 13

1. There may have been sound reasons for self-protection in the tone and language of this document. Elsewhere in a "Letter to all Chinese Compatriots," dated May 17, the BWAF wrote, "We have carefully considered the exploitation of the workers. Marx's *Capital* provides a method for us to understand the character of our oppression." Like the student movement, but unlike the movement of a decade earlier, the BWAF was not distinguished by very sophisticated theoretical statements or analyses.

2. Guo had also added his signature to the joint student-worker appeal drafted by Han Dongfang and Li Jinjin. At 2:00 A.M. on June 4, Guo was seized by troops in front of the entrance to the Zhongnanhai leadership compound. According to an official report on Beijing Radio, he was apprehended while "he and a gang of ruffians were trying to set fire to an army unit's armored vehicle." He was held in prison for more than a year and a half before being brought to trial on January 26, 1991, when the Beijing Intermediate People's Court sentenced him to four years in prison, with one year's additional deprivation of political rights, on charges of counterrevolutionary sabotage.

3. The incident of the five helicopters only contributed additional fuel to the rumor mill. While some students believed their appearance meant paratroopers were about to be dropped into Tiananmen Square, others maintained that the pilots were defectors from the PLA, and that their overflight was intended as a show of support for the democracy

movement. In any event, their appearance was greeted with loud cheers and applause—some sincere, some sarcastic.

4. These documents are included in a two-volume anthology of source materials issued by the Hong Kong magazine *October Review.*

5. There was one notable case in which the students exercised these powers of arrest. The very next day, May 23, three young men from Hunan Province defaced the giant portrait of Mao Zedong that hangs over Tiananmen Gate by hurling ink- and paint-filled eggshells at it. The three were seized by Beijing students. After some deliberation, the students decided to hand them over to the Public Security Bureau. In September 1989, the three were convicted by the Beijing People's Intermediate Court of "counterrevolutionary sabotage" and "counterrevolutionary incitement and propaganda" and sentenced to terms that ranged from sixteen years to life in prison. See Asia Watch, *Anthems of Defeat: Crackdown in Hunan Province,* May 1992, pp. 27–29.

6. The principal function of each of these sections was quite strictly defined as being the defense of the Command Headquarters of Tiananmen Square.

7. The text of the "Final Showdown" also sheds interesting light on the tactical situation that the Capital Joint Liaison Group believed it was facing. "We no longer have any path of retreat," the document stated. "If we allow the tiny minority [in the Party] to persist in their retrograde, anti-people plans, they will inevitably carry out a 'settling of accounts after the autumn harvest.' They will resort to their so-called campaigns of 'eradicating spiritual pollution' and 'opposing bourgeois liberalization,' and the fruits of ten years of reform and opening will be squandered. If that happens . . . our republic will be transformed into a world of white terror."

8. Zhou Yongjun, it should be said in fairness to the other student leaders, seems to have acted unilaterally and without due regard for the federation's (embryonic) democratic procedures. A document was issued declaring that the federation had "decided to cancel the April 27 rally," but it carried only the signature of Zhou Yongjun. Shen Tong writes (in *Almost a Revolution,* p. 202) that "We all suspected that Zhou Yongjun had made it by himself, because no other signatures were on the message, and we didn't think the federation could have had a meeting in the past couple of hours."

9. For a fuller sense of Chai Ling's personality, it is worth reading the interview that she gave to an American graduate student, Philip Cunningham, on May 28. This is reprinted in Human Rights in China, *Children of the Dragon,* pp. 107–115.

10. "Authority" may not be the best word. Later comments by her peers in the student movement suggest that Chai Ling's power was in

some ways more symbolic than real. Li Lu, for example, in an interview with the authors, remembers that one reason she was often sent as the student representative to the meetings of the Capital Joint Liaison Group was that "she needed a rest"—implying that these meetings, which Li Lu regarded as largely ineffectual, were a good place to get it.

11. Wu'er Kaixi's recollections of the student movement, unfortunately, never became available. Soon after June 4, there was some discussion in the United States of his publishing a personal memoir, but this never materialized. Instead, Wu'er Kaixi's exile became an unhappy affair filled with tales of scandalous personal conduct and the misuse of democracy movement funds, many of which are recounted in Joseph F. Kahn, "Better Fed Than Red" (*Esquire,* September 1990, pp. 186–97). Almost the only detailed memoirs of the movement available in English are Shen Tong's *Almost a Revolution,* whose value is limited by the essentially peripheral role played by Shen during the denouement of the crisis, and Li Lu's *Moving the Mountain: My Life in China from the Cultural Revolution to Tiananmen Square* (London: Pan Books, 1990).

12. Beijing was gripped at this point by rumors of a major split between the 27th and 38th Armies, which were widely reported in the Western press. General Xu Qinxian, commanding officer of the 38th Army, was placed under arrest, and later court-martialed, for refusing to obey the martial law decree.

CHAPTER 14

1. The strike was to have begun at noon on May 21, a Sunday, and it was somehow to have excluded essential workers, such as those involved in electricity, gas, and water supplies and mail and telecommunications services. It was unclear how the BWAF intended to achieve any of this, and the call appears to have gone unheeded.

2. The Capital Joint Liaison Group's investigation of the case appears to have been prompted by testimony from Yi Jingyao's sister and based on reports in the leftist *Beijing Daily.* The paper reported on May 22 that Yi had "tried to pass himself off as a college student, rushed to a certain factory and spread rumors." The following day, *Beijing Daily* ran a follow-up article that said Yi had "incited the workers to go on strike, shouted indiscreet slogans, and disrupted social order." (See "Guilt by Association," *News from Asia Watch,* June 1991, pp. 18–19.) The Yi Jingyao case was not the only independent investigation carried out by Wang Juntao and the Capital Joint Liaison Group. Wang also attempted, without success it appears, to assemble evidence on the reported death of one of the student hunger strikers during the week preceding martial

law. Student leaders told him that the young man's death was not a consequence of his fast, but rather of a preexisting medical condition.

3. The *China Daily* report, entitled "Steel Factories' Output Normal," said that officials of the Beijing municipal government had visited a number of important factories in a bid to "help restore normal production." Among the many "rumors" that they tried to dispel was the interesting one that "troops had entered the corporation's premises to impose 'military control.'" (Foreign Broadcast Information Service, FBIS China Daily Report, May 26, 1989.)

4. The classic English-language account of the events of 1966–67 in Shanghai is Neale Hunter's sympathetic *Shanghai Journal: An Eyewitness Account of the Cultural Revolution* (Boston: Beacon Press, 1969).

5. The three arrested workers were released later that same day without charges. In the evening, a student demonstration went ahead as scheduled outside the Ministry of Public Security. The protesters interpreted this course of events, quite wrongly, as an encouraging sign of the government's lack of resolve.

6. The remaining two members of the hunger strike were the Stone Corporation economist Zhou Duo, author of the May 19 "Letter to the People," and Gao Xin, a Communist Party member and former editor of the *Normal University Weekly*. Their June 2 manifesto contained a number of arguments that were strikingly similar to those advanced by Chen Ziming and Wang Juntao. "In the face of the irrational, high-handed military violence of the Li Peng government, Chinese intellectuals must dispose of their age-old disease, passed down over centuries, of being spineless, of merely speaking and not acting." In essence, the four hunger strikers recognized that the students would only listen to their moderating arguments if they were willing, like the students, to put their lives on the line. Their manifesto was also highly critical of the students for maneuvering themselves into a corner. "The students' mistakes," the hunger strikers wrote, "are mainly manifested in the internal chaos of their organizations and the lack of efficient and democratic procedures. Although their goal is democracy, their means and procedures for achieving democracy are not democratic. Their theories call for democracy, but their handling of specific situations is not democratic." For the complete text of the manifesto, see Han Minzhu, ed., *Cries for Democracy*, pp. 358–64.

7. Han was interviewed by the Dutch reporter Heleen Paalvast. Elsewhere in the interview, he commented, "I support the Communist Party wholeheartedly. But I think that the workers should have the right to point out and correct the Party's mistakes. We are prepared to enter into a dialogue with the authorities."

CHAPTER 15

1. The most comprehensive analysis of the performance of the foreign media (though extremely guarded in its criticisms) is a study of eight U.S. news organizations conducted by the Joan Shorenstein Barone Center on the Press, Politics and Public Policy at the John F. Kennedy School of Government at Harvard University. The center's report, entitled "Turmoil at Tiananmen: A Study of U.S. Press Coverage of the Beijing Spring of 1989," analyzes the television news reporting of the American Broadcasting Company (ABC), the Columbia Broadcasting System (CBS), and Cable News Network (CNN); and the print coverage of the *Los Angeles Times,* the *New York Times,* the *Washington Post,* the Associated Press, and *Time* magazine.

2. This comment was made by the scholar Ross Terrill of Harvard University during an interview on a June 29, 1989, ABC-TV special by Ted Koppel. Koppel, to his credit, noted that the bulk of the killing had not taken place within the physical confines of Tiananmen Square, but he downplayed the distinction as a "loophole" that could be exploited by the Chinese government.

3. In one of the lesser but more startling images of the Beijing Spring, the city's growing contingent of thieves and pickpockets declared a temporary halt to their activities after the imposition of martial law.

4. A technically incorrect answer, in fact. Some counterrevolutionary offenses are punishable by longer sentences, even by death.

5. Once more, it was the hard-line *Beijing Daily* that served as the spearhead of the official conservative campaign. According to the paper, "The Beijing Municipal Trade Union Council issued a statement on June 1, strongly requesting that prompt steps be taken to ban an illegal organization called the Workers' Autonomous Federation. . . . They have fabricated rumors, distributed leaflets, advocated the overthrow of the People's government, instigated workers to go on strike, and stormed public security organs. . . . This is an illegal act attempting to divide the ranks of the working class and openly disrupt the normal order being restored in the capital." ("Illegal Beijing Worker Association to Be Banned," Beijing Domestic Service in Mandarin, FBIS China Daily Report, June 2, 1989.)

6. Li Lu, in an interview with the authors three years after the massacre, was in fact critical of Wang Juntao and Chen Ziming for withdrawing from the fray during the final days of the occupation of the square. According to his account, by May 26 or May 27, the Capital Joint Liaison Group had gone so far as to set up a tent at one corner of the Monument to the People's Heroes. After the first day, however, members of the group were hardly ever seen there.

7. The account that follows is drawn largely from the personal observations and recollections of Robin Munro, who remained in Tiananmen Square during the entire night of June 3–4, leaving with the final departing columns of students at dawn. His memories are supplemented in places by the free-lance journalist Richard Nations. Munro's complete account, "Who Died in Beijing, and Why," was published in *The Nation,* June 11, 1990, pp. 811–22.

8. Hou Dejian eventually published an extensive account of the final hours in the square that was published in a number of overseas Chinese newspapers. Extracts also appeared in *People's Daily,* since Hou's account tended to give credence to the government's narrow contention that there had been no killing *in Tiananmen Square itself.* The complete text of Hou's account, entitled "Blame Me If You Want!" is included in Yi Mu and Mark V. Thompson, *Crisis at Tiananmen: Reform and Reality in Modern China* (San Francisco: China Books, 1989), pp. 239–49.

9. On a visit to Beijing in July 1991, the authors were able to verify that only the upper portion of the Monument—namely, the bare central column and not the ornamented lower levels that were occupied by the students—is visible from the top-floor balcony of the Beijing Hotel.

10. Claudia Rosett of the *Asian Wall Street Journal* and John Pomfret of the Associated Press were also present at the Monument at this time.

CHAPTER 16

1. Most notably, Chen discussed this in relation to the Democracy Wall movement of 1978–79 in a symposium on democracy that was published in *Beijing Spring* (see p. 51).

2. The rumor was that Deng was dead, or dying, of prostate cancer. An additional rumor at this time held that Li Peng had been wounded in the leg by a gunshot, in a failed assassination attempt by a security guard.

3. Some of these names disappeared from later elaborations of the black hands theory—particularly Hong Kong Chinese, overseas Chinese, or those supposed to be in the pay of hostile foreign powers. The references to "peaceful evolution" and the assertions of a CIA role in the 1989 protests were an important element of leftist rhetoric in the period leading up to the trials of early 1991; however, they seemingly were dropped thereafter, as Deng pressed ahead once more, with renewed vigor, with his program of economic reform.

4. It in fact is true that the Alliance receives a substantial portion of its funding from Taiwanese sources.

5. The delicate matter of the CIA was passed over in Mayor Chen Xitong's speech, as was the fate of a man named He Weiling—Beida

chemistry professor, member of RIRES, sometime Public Security agent, and friend of Bao Tong—who had also been arrested at the time of imposition of martial law. He Weiling was suspected of espionage but never charged; he died in an automobile accident under suspicious circumstances several months later, allegedly while driving the wrong way down a one-way street.

6. The term *liumang* is difficult to translate; it has overtones of such words as loafer, bum, hoodlum, and punk. As conventionally used by the Chinese Communist Party, it refers to street rowdies. In wider parlance, however, it can also describe China's emergent alternative street culture. One of the more interesting articles to appear in Wang Juntao and Chen Ziming's *Economics Weekly* was Yi Shuihan's "The *Liumang* Society." This bold essay depicted the phenomenon as something much wider, a corruption of moral standards that permeated the whole of Chinese society from the top down. "During the political campaigns after 1949," Yi wrote, "again it was such people who formed the vanguard of 'heroic elements'. . . . This social stratum is adventurous, vengeful, opportunistic, and destructive. This *liumang* mentality has already insinuated itself into some Party and state organs, companies, and industries." See Geremie Barmé and Linda Jaivin, eds., *New Ghosts, Old Dreams: Chinese Rebel Voices* (New York: Times Books, 1992), pp. 248–54.

7. This anecdote was recounted to the authors by Zhang Boli, a deputy commander of the Tiananmen Square headquarters, after his escape to the United States in the summer of 1991.

CHAPTER 17

1. The proclamation also banned three other groups: the Beijing Residents Autonomous Federation (*Beijing Shimin Zizhi Lianhehui*); the Capital Intellectuals Federation (*Beijing Zhishijie Lianhehui*); and the Autonomous Federation of Students from Outside Beijing (*Waidi Fu Jing Gaoxiao Zizhi Lianhehui*).

2. Among the other names on this blacklist of authors were Yan Jiaqi, Bao Zunxin, and Su Xiaokang.

3. Hong Kong press accounts of this sort must be treated with a certain amount of caution. According to other versions, this comment was made not by Li Peng, but by Li Ximing, the hard-line Beijing Party secretary.

4. These details are taken from the lively documentary by the British correspondent Gavin Hewitt for the television program *Panorama*. Some of Hewitt's details are inaccurate, however. There is no evidence, for example, that the Hong Kong escape network was ever officially known as "Operation Yellow Bird."

5. The account of Wang's sojourn in Wuhan is reconstructed in part from two legal documents concerning those who harbored him in the city. These documents, obtained from confidential Chinese sources, are the "Criminal Indictment of the Wuhan City People's Procuracy against Defendants Wu Litang, Liu Hanyi, Liu Danhong, Tong Chongwu, and Jiang Guolian," dated February 16, 1990, and the "Criminal Verdict of the Wuhan City Intermediate People's Court against Wu Litang, Liu Hanyi, Tong Chongwu, and Jiang Guolian," dated April 19, 1991.

6. SERI's Human Resources Testing and Evaluation Center dealt with personnel and employment issues. Its director was another of Wang Juntao's Wuhan circle, Xie Xiaoqing. The center's deputy director was Chen Ziming's wife, Wang Zhihong.

7. Much of the account of Chen Ziming's attempted escape and capture is reconstructed from legal documents concerning the case against Luo Haixing and his associates. See the various appendices to "Guilt by Association: More Documents from the Chinese Trials" (*News from Asia Watch,* June 1991).

8. In a final twist to the story of the failed operation, Wang Juntao, Chen Ziming, and Wang Zhihong all later asserted that they had never, in fact, had any plan or intention of trying to escape from China.

9. The source for Li Peng's *heishou de heishou* remark is the Hong Kong weekly magazine *Tangtai (Contemporary)*. Again, one must acknowledge problems with accuracy in the Hong Kong press, but in this case the source seems quite reliable. *Tangtai* is reputed for the quality of its Chinese sources and for its knowledge of the inner workings of the Chinese Communist elite. Its account of Li Peng's arguments against Wang Juntao and Chen Ziming was widely reported in Hong Kong's English-language media, such as the *South China Morning Post* and the *Hongkong Standard* (December 1, 1990).

CHAPTER 18

1. This section draws heavily on Robert Jay Lifton, *Thought Reform and the Psychology of Totalism: A Study of "Brainwashing" in China* (New York: Norton, 1961).

2. Deng went on to defend the basic correctness of his policy of "reforms and opening up." "Naturally, in reform and in adopting the open policy," Deng said, "we run the risk of importing evil influences from the West and we have never underestimated such influences. . . . In political reforms, we can affirm one point: We have to adhere to the system of the National People's Congress, and not the American system of the separation of three powers. . . . What do we do from now on? I would say that we should continue, persist in implementing our set basic line,

principles, and policies. Except where there is a need to alter a word or a phrase here and there, there should be no change in the basic line or the basic policy." These remarks should be required reading for those who persist in seeing Deng as a moderate besieged by hard-liners, as a closet Maoist uninterested in economic reform, or as a man who shifts mercurially from one extreme to another. His speech to army commanders, delivered just five days after June 4, makes it clear that economic reform and political repression are part of a single, comprehensive vision.

3. This hand-written document, the *Joint Declaration of All Workers and Students in the Capital,* later formed the main basis of the charges of counterrevolution that were eventually brought against Han Dongfang and Li Jinjin, who had co-authored it. During their imprisonment, however, the two men thought the text of the document had been lost; their police interrogators never revealed to them that they in fact had a copy.

The *Joint Declaration* was one of the most radical and uncompromising documents of the entire 1989 prodemocracy movement. It called for a special court to be set up to try Li Peng and other "enemies of the people" within the leadership, and it urged "all officials in the Chinese People's Liberation Army to turn their guns on the oppressors." It threatened that the workers would "use all peaceful means, including strikes" to achieve their goals, and added: "With our blood, we will reconstruct the walls of the Paris Commune."

4. Banbuqiao is administered by Department 7 of the PSB and is reserved for the most serious criminal cases. One of the prisoners in the women's block at the time of Han Dongfang's arrival was Chen Ziming's wife, Wang Zhihong. In late 1991, K-block was demolished, to be replaced by new facilities, and the inmates, including Han, were temporarily transferred to Qincheng Prison. Executions at Banbuqiao were often timed to coincide with the demand for organ transplants at Beijing hospitals, and doctors stood by in a closed van nearby to remove the organs immediately after execution.

5. For a fuller discussion of the operation of the Chinese legal system, see the Asia Watch report *Punishment Season: Human Rights in China After Martial Law* (New York, March 1990).

6. There is extensive and fascinating discussion of the sufferings of Wang Guangmei, Liu Shaoqi, and other members of their family at various points in Harrison Salisbury's *The New Emperors.*

CHAPTER 19

1. Even in Li Peng's own terms, the charge is preposterous. Wang Juntao's involvement in the 1976 Tiananmen Incident was of a sort to

which no current Party leader, not even one as conservative as the Premier, could take exception. Furthermore, there is no evidence that Wang took any part in the campus upheavals of December 1986 and January 1987.

2. Ren Wanding's speeches in Tiananmen Square may have been additionally irritating to the authorities because of the veteran campaigner's insistence on the pivotal role of the working class. In a speech on April 21, Ren argued that the democracy movement should organize its own independent political parties, and called for workers to break with the monolithic unity of the official unions. "Students should join with the workers," he said, "who in their turn should fight for independent trade unions. Only when several million production workers understand that their democratic rights are not handed down to them, but are something that must be fought for, and take command of the situation, will democracy be realized." See Ren Wanding, "Why Did the Rally in Memory of Hu Yaobang Turn into a Democracy Movement?" and "Reflections on the Historical Character of the Democracy Movement," in Mok Chiu Yu and J. Frank Harrison, eds., *Voices from Tiananmen Square: The Beijing Spring and the Democracy Movement* (Montreal and New York: Black Rose Books, 1990), pp. 42–53.

3. Of all the court verdicts on the 1989 democracy movement, this was perhaps the most surprising. It was widely expected among overseas Chinese that Liu Xiaobo would be charged with the grave crime of sedition, and some campaigns were even organized around the possibility of his being given the death penalty.

4. According to the prosecutor, Chen's remarks included the following: "China's independent intelligentsia has risen in history. Its next step toward maturity obviously requires a process of organizing, and [it must] move forward from a politically conscious to an organizationally powerful force. . . . The epochal duty of the intelligentsia, of the advanced elements of the intelligentsia in particular, is rapidly to complete the process of organizing the intelligentsia," in order to "form a new source of leadership for the common people." See "Verdict in the Case of Chen Ziming: Criminal Verdict of the Beijing Intermediate People's Court (1991) Intermediate/Criminal/No. 294," in "Guilt by Association" (*News from Asia Watch,* June 1991).

5. The authors have reconstructed Chen Ziming's arguments in the courtroom from a forty-thousand-character document he wrote in prison after his conviction. Chen entitled his document "Who Has Committed the Real Crime Against History? A Brief Statement in My Defense." Smuggled out of China, this was published in an abridged form in the Hong Kong magazine *Ming Pao.* It was subsequently published in English

as "Defense Statement of Chen Ziming" (*News from Asia Watch,* June 1992). English translation by Sophia Woodman.

6. Yan Mingfu, who was disgraced after the June 4 massacre, did manage to make a partial comeback but was eventually dropped from the Central Committee at the Fourteenth Party Congress in October 1992. A number of high-profile Party reformers—including labor leader Zhu Houze—were quietly restored to positions of influence in the complex process of horse-trading that took place between 1989 and the Fourteenth Party Congress.

7. The above account of the lawyers' travails is substantially the version given by Hou Xiaotian herself. Others close to Wang Juntao suggest that his wife may have deliberately chosen to pursue the appeals process herself. Robin Munro, Interview with Zhou Duo, Beijing, August 1992.

8. Wang is referring here, obliquely, to the sworn statements of Wang Dan, Bao Zunxin, and others that were used by the prosecution at his trial.

9. Wang's remark about "how few people face trial" was true only in respect of the top leadership of the Tiananmen protests, a number of whom received considerable leniency from the authorities despite the severe sentences given to Wang, Chen, and others. Across the country as a whole, however, it emphatically did not apply. Thousands of workers, students, and intellectuals active in the 1989 movement were subsequently arrested and brought to trial, on either political or common criminal charges, and handed down sentences ranging from several years to life imprisonment.

CHAPTER 20

1. The formal document issued to Han by the Beijing Procuracy did not even concede this much but merely stated that he had been "released on bail awaiting trial."

2. Liu Qiang was subsequently released. In general, the heaviest sentences were applied to the least known of the worker-activists, those whose cases attracted little international attention and pressure. In Hunan Province, for example, the average sentence handed down to workers was more than eight years. Leaders of the BWAF, by contrast, got off remarkably lightly, despite the authorities' fury at their activities.

3. The Chinese leaders' comments are cited by the pro-Beijing Hong Kong paper *Kuang Chiao Ching,* December 16, 1991. MSS fears of union activity are reported in Willy Lam, "Beijing Cracks Down on Illegal Unions," *South China Morning Post,* December 13, 1991.

4. The amendments to the Trade Union Law of 1950 were revealed in March 1992. The new law describes trade unions as "the working class's

mass organizations, formed by staff and workers on a voluntary basis." All trade unions must be approved by "trade unions at the next higher level"—meaning the official ACFTU, since no other exists. In some respects, the new amendments may even be seen as a retreat from the provisions of the 1950 law. That law stipulated that if an employing institution wanted to dismiss a worker, it had to present the worker's name and its reasons in writing to the trade union, which then had seven days to challenge the decision. The amended law says only that "where an enterprise encroaches upon any staff or workers' rights and interests relating to work, the trade union may put forward its opinions." See "Unionist Speaks Out Against Labour Law," *South China Morning Post,* March 29, 1992.

5. "Jailing a Wang Juntao," the *Wall Street Journal* declared in its editorial, "Verdict on China" (March 26, 1991), "amounts to sabotaging strategic resources more precious than the oil wells of Kuwait."

6. Zhang Weiguo in the end did not pursue his lawsuit, although he continued to be a thorn in the government's side.

A NOTE FROM
THE AUTHORS

A word is in order here about our methodology and division of labor. We began our collaboration due to the encouragement of Aryeh Neier, Executive Director of Human Rights Watch, and his colleague Hamilton Fish, who found themselves in possession of raw material about the Tiananmen protests that begged to be turned into a story. With this in mind, they introduced us to each other, and we most gratefully acknowledge their assistance and support. George was at that time foreign editor of *The Nation* magazine. Robin was working in Hong Kong as a research associate of Asia Watch, part of Human Rights Watch. He had followed the development of the Chinese democracy movement since the late 1970s, when he went to China as part of the first generation of exchange students after the end of the Cultural Revolution. He was an intimate observer of the Democracy Wall movement of 1978–79 and knew many of its leaders. A decade later, he was one of the handful of foreigners who remained in Tiananmen Square right through the night of June 3–4, 1989. His eyewitness account of that night contradicted much of the received wisdom about the Beijing massacre. This first collaborative effort resulted in a special issue of *The Nation* devoted to Tiananmen, which was nominated for a 1991 National Magazine Award. Robin's research on the post-Tiananmen crackdown continued throughout 1991, and was published in the form of periodic newsletters—*News from Asia Watch*—that had an enormous impact on the debate about human rights and U.S. policy toward China.

It was Robert L. Bernstein, chairman of Human Rights Watch, who grasped the potential for this material to reach a broader audience, and he encouraged us to write the book. Bob has a long and distinguished history of bringing the leaders of the underground dissident movement in the Soviet Union to the attention of Western readers, and he understood that sympathy for China's democrats in the West had long been hampered by their facelessness. China had no Sakharov and no Bonner, no Orlov, no Scharansky. He has our enduring appreciation for his support of this book and his wise counsel at every stage of the project.

Once the Black-Munro partnership was renewed, it benefited immeasurably from the warm personal and collegial support of Sidney Jones, executive director of Asia Watch. Nicole Haberland and Lydia Lobenthal provided helpful assistance in the early stages of this project. Marianne Spiegel, in addition to sharing her encyclopedic knowledge of China's prisons and their inmates, was endlessly supportive. Jeannine Guthrie was marvelously tolerant of our demands and what may politely be termed our idiosyncrasies. While many other members of the staff of Human Rights Watch have earned our gratitude, we must make special mention of Susan Osnos, Lemuel Thomas, and Jennifer VanDale.

Xiao Qiang and his colleagues at Human Rights in China; Allison Liu Jernow of the Committee to Protect Journalists; and Richard Dicker of the Committee to End the Chinese Gulag were all good friends to this book. Above all, we are indebted to our exemplary research assistant, Sophia Woodman of Human Rights in China, for her skills as an interviewer, translator, and archival researcher. Without Sophia, there would have been no book.

Some additional explanation about our collaboration and research methods is in order. Robin provided the initial core of raw materials. We then conducted additional research together in Hong Kong and Beijing, and George and Sophia Woodman conducted extensive interviews with Chinese exiles in the United States and Canada. George then wrote the entire manuscript and subsequently revised it to incorporate a final round of interviews by Robin in Beijing in the summer of 1992.

Almost by definition, this book posed enormous problems of documentation. We have had few written sources to rely on beyond the ephemera of the democracy movement itself—the pamphlets, independent journals, and small- and big-character posters that have been its primary means of expression. But the heart of the matter was the interview, and we conducted scores of them. These, too, posed special difficulties. Two of the three principal characters remained in jail and inaccessible to us. The third—Han Dongfang—was in jail for part of the time, sick and under close surveillance in Beijing for much of the remainder, but finally available to us for exhaustive interviews in August and September of 1992.

The quality of an interview rests largely on the powers of recall and intellectual clarity of the subject, and in this sense we are fundamentally indebted to Bai Hua. A series of interviews with this remarkable woman over the course of more than two years provided us with the core of the story of Chen Ziming's "independent kingdom." Her account of the Beijing Social and Economic Sciences Research Institute (SERI) was supplemented by those of Shi Tianjian, Wang Wei, and Zhang Lun (who joked that his marathon, week-long session of interviews with us was more grueling than his interrogation by the Public Security Bureau). To flesh out other details of Chen Ziming and Wang Juntao's early political history, we relied heavily on the testimonies of Fang Zhiyuan, Gong Xiaoxia, Hu Ping, Qian Jianjun, Yang Zi, Zhang Gang, and Zhang Xiaogang. On the activities of Chen and Wang's Capital Joint Liaison Group (JLGACC) during the Tiananmen protests, Zheng Di and Zhou Duo added important revelations. On the relationship between the JLGACC and the student movement, we benefited from interviews with Chai Ling, commander in chief of the Tiananmen Square Command Headquarters, with Li Lu and Zhang Boli, two of her deputy commanders, and with Wang Chaohua of the Beijing Students Autonomous Federation. Hou Xiaotian and Wang Zhihong, whose imprisoned husbands are the main subjects of our story, graciously acceded to our requests for interviews and provided additional personal material. Like every other Chinese acknowledged here, their courage in agreeing to speak to us openly and for attribution cannot be overstated.

The story of the independent workers' movement presented even greater problems of documentation. Chinese workers labor in anonymity, deprived of foreign contacts and subject to the harshest of penalties for speaking out. Han Dongfang himself, convenor of the Beijing Workers Autonomous Federation, was unstintingly generous of his time both in Beijing and, eventually, in New York. His sister, Han Dongmei, bravely relayed information to the outside world on her brother's situation throughout his imprisonment and later provided us with many additional details. When we had heard the full story of Han's life, we were almost led to sympathize with the interrogators who were given the thankless task of trying to break the spirit of this indomitable young man. Special thanks are due to Gabriella Bianci and Daniel Alberman, who kept open a vital channel of information from Beijing for over two and a half often tense and difficult years. Han's own account of the BWAF was supplemented by detailed interviews with Li Jinjin, Lü Jinghua, and Zhao Hongliang. Yue Wu, Li Lin, and Li Zhi gave us first-hand accounts of their participation in the workers' movement, while Wang Shaoguang and Qi Haibin added valuable scholarly perspectives on the BWAF.

There were, of course, other notable "black hands" behind the 1989 democracy movement apart from the few key figures we have chosen to focus upon here; in particular, the name of Zheng Yi, a writer and polemicist now in exile in the United States after three years on the run inside China, springs to mind. But we could not have access to all of them. Some were—or still are—in prison, others were in anonymous exile overseas. We offer a blanket apology, therefore, to all those in China who have been conspiring and plotting for years to bring greater political freedom and choice to the Chinese nation, but who remain unacknowledged in these pages.

Among the many unsung heroes of this book, perhaps none are more worthy of mention than the still-imprisoned veterans of the Democracy Wall movement of the late 1970s. Xu Wenli—a self-professed "electrician who puts out fires"—was, like Chen Ziming and Wang Juntao, a politically moderate activist who supported Deng Xiaoping. He edited a *samizdat* journal called *April 5th Forum* during the Democracy Wall period, and in 1982 he received—like his better-known contemporary, Wei Jingsheng—a fifteen-year prison sentence for "counterrevolution." Both Xu and Wei have remained in solitary-confinement cells ever since, subjected to untold mental torment by the authorities simply because they refused to confess. It is our earnest hope that this book may contribute in some small way towards ensuring that Chen Ziming, Wang Juntao, and other imprisoned leaders of the 1989 democracy movement will not also have to serve out, to the last bitter and lonely day, the full terms of their sentences.

Among the many others who helped make this book possible, we must especially thank Bao Pu, Cheng Yu, Yu Dahai, and Joy Chen. In Hong Kong, Trini Leung may have grasped the significance of the independent workers' movement in Tiananmen Square earlier than anyone, and the incomparable Willy Lam of the *South China Morning Post* was a mine of insider knowledge and advice. Of all those on the Hong Kong scene who, through their ceaseless efforts on behalf of prodemocracy activists on the mainland over the years, have contributed in an indirect but nonetheless crucial way to this book, our warmest thanks go to Reverend Chu Yiu Ming, council member of the Hong Kong Alliance; his colleague in the Alliance leadership, independent labor leader and elected member of the Legislative Council, Lau Chin Shek; and Lau Kin Chi, co-founder and organizer (among her many other roles) of the Hong Kong branch of the Tiananmen University of Democracy.

Among scholars and China-watchers, we are grateful to Merle Goldman, Harrison Salisbury, Orville Schell, James D. Seymour, and Carolyn Wakeman for their sympathetic interest and valuable practical support. In addition, Munro owes a special debt of gratitude to Professor Stuart Schram for patiently trying to teach him the value of academic rigor and fresh ideas in the study of Chinese politics, and for encouraging him to pursue what often seemed, in the early 1980s, the somewhat unfruitful topic of Chinese human rights and democracy.

Bob Bernstein persuaded his colleagues at John Wiley & Sons of the merits of this book. Roger Scholl shepherded the manuscript through its early incarnations before passing it on to the capable hands of Emily Loose and Scott Renschler. Thank you all.

The road to hell is paved with the acknowledgments of male authors to the spouses who typed, provisioned, and otherwise fulfilled their appointed roles. Our debt is not of that sort. Both Anne Nelson and Huang Paolien are accomplished writers. Paolien's delightfully unsentimental fictional accounts of the human condition, together with her almost complete lack of interest in the minutiae of Chinese politics, provided her partner with the perfect antidote to the threatened pomposities of our narrative, and she brought him joy and renewal when it was most needed. Anne's collaboration with Human Rights Watch on the life story of the Cuban political prisoner Jorge Valls was the seed from which this project first grew, and if circumstances had been a little different, her name might well have appeared on the cover of this book instead of George Black's. Its completion has caused her to make extraordinary sacrifices, and that debt will be repaid.

Robin Munro has known China intimately for fifteen years; if his co-author remains deficient in that regard, it is in part because he shaved each research trip to the minimum in order to spend as much time as possible with David and Julia in their passage from infancy to childhood. They brightened every one of their father's days as he wrote what David called "papa's story about those bad men in China and the good men who got put in jail."

INDEX